INTERNATIONAL CONFLICT AND SECURITY LAW

Hilaire McCoubrey wrote extensively in the area of armed conflict law (governing the use of force in international relations, and the conduct of hostilities), and on the issues of collective security law and the law relating to arms control. Although he died at the early age of forty-six in 2000 he had contributed significantly to the separate study of these areas, but also to the idea of studying the issues as a whole subject. The collection covers difficult and controversial issues in the area of conflict and security law. Within a coherent framework provided by extracts from Hilaire's own work, the contributors, drawn both from academe and practice, provide expert analysis of many aspects of the law governing armed conflict and collective security. These include the application of international humanitarian law in the operational context; the duty to educate in humanitarian law; superior orders; command responsibility; the protective emblem; the relevance of international humanitarian law to terrorism; and legitimate military targets. The book then moves from a consideration of the laws of war to the law of peace with a consideration of the application of human rights law in international armed conflict law. An essay on democracy as an aspect of peace and security widens the human rights debate out further and takes us into regional security regimes. The essays then move on to discuss aspects of collective security law. As well as providing a fitting tribute to the main aspects of Hilaire's contribution to knowledge, the volume provides a coherent reconsideration and development of key aspects of conflict and security law at a time when that law is being applied, breached, debated or reformed on almost a daily basis.

RICHARD BURCHILL is Director of the McCoubrey Centre for International Law. His research concerns the development of democracy in international law. He is author of *The European Union and the Promotion and Protection of Democracy in International Law* (2005).

NIGEL D. WHITE is Professor of International Organisations at the University of Nottingham. He is the editor of *Collective Security Law* (2002), and co-editor of the *Journal of Conflict and Security Law*.

JUSTIN MORRIS is Senior Lecturer in International Politics at the University of Hull. He is co-author (with the late Professor Hilaire McCoubrey) of *Regional Peacekeeping in the Post-Cold War Era* (2000).

INTERNATIONAL CONFLICT AND SECURITY LAW

Essays in Memory of Hilaire McCoubrey

Edited by

RICHARD BURCHILL, NIGEL D. WHITE AND JUSTIN MORRIS

Published in association with the McCoubrey Centre for International Law

CAMBRIDGE
UNIVERSITY PRESS

CAMBRIDGE UNIVERSITY PRESS
Cambridge, New York, Melbourne, Madrid, Cape Town, Singapore, São Paulo

CAMBRIDGE UNIVERSITY PRESS
The Edinburgh Building, Cambridge CB2 2RU, UK

Published in the United States of America by Cambridge University Press, New York

www.cambridge.org
Information on this title: www.cambridge.org/9780521845311

First published 2005

Printed in the United Kingdom at the University Press, Cambridge

A catalog record for this book is available from the British Library

ISBN-13 978-0-521-84531-1 hardback
ISBN-10 0-521-84531-9 hardback

CONTENTS

BIOGRAPHY

The Reverend Professor Hilaire McCoubrey 1953–2000

Hilaire was educated at Hymers College, Hull (1962–8) and Portsmouth Grammar School (1968–72). He studied for a law degree at Trinity College Cambridge (1972–5), and qualified as a solicitor in 1978 after serving his articles with the Greater London Council. He was appointed by Professor Sir John Smith to a lectureship in the Law Department at the University of Nottingham in 1978, and was promoted to a Senior Lectureship in 1991. He taught mainly Public International Law, Legal Theory and Planning Law while at Nottingham and wrote extensively in these areas, as shown by the bibliography of his work. His specialization in conflict and security law, evidenced by his seminal book *International Humanitarian Law* published in 1990, led him to establish the Centre for International Defence Law Studies in 1991. Its chief publication – *The International Law and Armed Conflict Commentary* – became the *Journal of Armed Conflict Law* in 1996 published by Nottingham University Press, and then the *Journal of Conflict and Security Law* published by Oxford University Press from 2000. While at Nottingham he completed a Ph.D in 1990, the thesis being published as *The Obligation to Obey in Legal Theory*. Between 1992 and 1995 Hilaire studied part-time for a Diploma of Theological and Pastoral Studies and was ordained as a deacon in the Church of England in 1995. He became a non-stipendiary minister in the Parish of Rowley and Skidby after moving to Beverley, Yorkshire. This was after his appointment to a Chair at the University of Hull in 1995 where he also became Director of Postgraduate Studies in the Law School. He relocated the Centre for International Defence Law Studies to Hull and continued to produce numerous books and articles on humanitarian law and more widely on collective security issues, as well as significantly expanding the postgraduate curriculum in Public International Law at Hull. He was a member of numerous bodies and organizations, playing an active role in the British Red Cross, the

International Committee of the Red Cross, the British Institute for International and Comparative Law, the International Law Association, the Political Studies Association, the San Remo Institute of International Humanitarian Law and the International Society for Military Law; and was invited to give lectures and papers around the globe. It was on a lecturing visit to Pakistan in April 2000 that he died at the age of forty-six.

McCoubrey Centre for International Law

Following Hilaire's death the University of Hull Law School felt it would be appropriate to create a Centre that would carry on his work in international law and relations. The Centre was instituted in 2001 with the goal of promoting the study and research of international law and relations. The Centre hosts a number of guest speakers through its International Law Seminar Series and the Hilaire McCoubrey Memorial Lecture. Further information about the Centre and its activities may be found at www.hull.ac.uk/law/research/intlaw.html

CONTRIBUTORS

Dr Richard Barnes is currently the Sir Q. W. Lee and Dr Peter Thompson Lecturer in Maritime Law at the University of Hull, where he taught Public International Law and Law of the Sea with Hilaire McCoubrey. He is currently researching in the areas of shipping and security and maritime resource use and his publications include 'Refugee Law at Sea', (2004) 53(1) *International and Comparative Law Quarterly* 47 and 'Barecon 2001: The Barecon 89 Bareboat Charter Revised', (2002) 4 *Lloyds Maritime and Commercial Law Quarterly* 528.

Dr Neil Boister is Senior Lecturer at the School of Law, University of Canterbury, New Zealand. He is the editor of two volumes of the *South African Yearbook of Human Rights* and author of *Penal Aspects of the UN Drug Conventions* (Kluwer Law International, 2001). He has delivered numerous papers on aspects of criminal, international and transnational criminal law and is the author of numerous articles in refereed journals including most recently 'Transnational Criminal Law?', (2003) 14(5) *European Journal of International Law* 953 and 'The Trend to "Universal Extradition" over Subsidiary Universal Jurisdiction in the Suppression of Transnational Crime', [2003] *Acta Juridica* 287. He has been a Contributing Editor to the *South African Journal of Criminal Justice* (Jutas, CTO), and is a member of the founding editorial team of the *New Zealand Yearbook of International Law.*

Dr Richard Burchill is Director of the McCoubrey Centre of International Law, University of Hull. His research focuses on the role of international organizations in the promotion and protection of democracy in international law. His publications include *The European Union, International Law and the Promotion and Protection of Democracy* (Hart Publishing, 2005); 'The European Union and European Democracy: Social Democracy or Democracy with a Social Dimension?', (2004) 17(1) *Canadian Journal of Law and Jurisprudence* 185; 'The Role of Democracy in the Protection of Human Rights: Lessons from the European and Inter-American Human Rights

Systems', in David Forsythe and Patrice McMahaon (eds.), *Human Rights and Diversity: Area Studies Revisited* (University of Nebraska Press, 2003), pp. 137–56.

Dr Robert Cryer is Lecturer in Law at the University of Nottingham, where he teaches criminal law and international law, including international legal theory, international criminal law and the law of collective security. He has published mainly in the area of international law, in particular international criminal law, the law of armed conflict and international legal theory. His publications include *Prosecuting International Crimes* (Cambridge University Press, 2005); 'General Principles of Liability in International Criminal Law', in Dominic McGoldrick, Peter Rowe and Eric Donnelly (eds.), *The International Criminal Court: Legal and Policy Issues* (Hart Publishing, 2004), pp. 233–86; 'Implementation of the International Criminal Court Statute in England and Wales', (2002) 51 *International and Comparative Law* 733; and 'The Fine Art of Friendship: *Jus in Bello* in Afghanistan', (2002) 7 *Journal of Conflict and Security Law* 37.

Scott Davidson is Professor of International Law, Pro Vice Chancellor and Dean of the Law School at the University of Canterbury, New Zealand. He has been an occasional consultant to the New Zealand Ministry of Foreign Affairs and Trade and a number of law firms. He represents New Zealand on the Maritime Cooperation Working Group of the Council for Security and Cooperation in Asia Pacific and is a member of the editorial and advisory boards of the *International Journal of Marine and Coastal Law*, the *New Zealand Yearbook of International Law* and the *New Zealand Journal of Public and International Law*. Publications include *Contemporary Issues in International Law: A Collection of the Josephine Onoh Memorial Lectures* edited with David Freestone and Surya Subedi (Kluwer, 2002); *New Zealand Handbook on International Human Rights* (Ministry of Foreign Affairs and Trade, 1998).

Gary J. Edles is a Visiting Professor at the University of Hull Law School and a Fellow in Administrative Law and Adjunct Professor of Law at American University Washington College of Law, Washington, DC. A retired career civil servant, he is co-author of *Federal Regulatory Process: Agency Practices and Procedures* (Prentice Hall, 1987, revised 1997).

Colonel Charles Garraway, CBE, retired in 2003 after thirty years in Army Legal Services. He is now a Senior Research Fellow at the British Institute of International and Comparative Law and a Visiting Professor in

Law at King's College, London. He is due to take up the Stockton Chair in International Law at the United States Naval War College in August 2004. His publications include contributions to Roy Lee (ed.), *The International Criminal Court: Elements of Crimes and Rules of Procedure and Evidence* (Kluwer Law International, 1999), as well as a number of articles on international criminal law and the law of armed conflict.

Michael Meyer is the Head of the International Law Department at the British Red Cross. He is a member of the Council of the International Institute of Humanitarian Law in San Remo, Italy, and a member of the UK Group of the International Society for Military Law and the Law of War. His publications include *Reflections on Law and Armed Conflicts*, co-edited with Hilaire McCoubrey (Kluwer, 1998); 'The Relationship between the Red Cross and the Armed Forces: A Partnership for Humanitarian Purposes', in Liesbeth Lijnzaad *et al.* (eds.), *Making the Voice of Humanity Heard* (Martinus Nijhoff, 2004), and 'The Role of the International Red Cross and Red Crescent Movement: Problems Encountered', in Peter Rowe (ed.), *The Gulf War 1990–91 in International and English Law* (Routledge, 1993).

Justin Morris is Senior Lecturer in International Politics and Deputy Dean in the Faculty of Arts and Social Sciences at the Department of Politics and International Studies, University of Hull. From 1997 to 2003 he was Secretary of the British International Studies Association. He was co-author (with Hilaire McCoubrey) of *Regional Peacekeeping in the Post-Cold War Era* (Kluwer, 2000), and has written articles and book chapters on Security Council reform, humanitarian intervention and the role of international law in international relations. He is currently working on a book on Security Council reform.

Gordon Risius is a circuit judge, currently on temporary secondment to the Immigration Appeal Tribunal as a Vice President. A solicitor by training, he was commissioned into the Army as a legal officer in 1973 and served for thirty years, the last six as Director of Army Legal Services in the rank of major general. Until his retirement from the Army in January 2003 he was a Vice President of the International Society for Military Law and the Law of War as well as an instructor at the International Institute of Humanitarian Law in San Remo, Italy. His publications include 'Prisoners of War in the United Kingdom', in Peter Rowe (ed.), *The Gulf War 1990–91 in International and English Law* (Routledge, 1993), pp. 289–303 and 'The Protection of Prisoners of War Against Insults and Public Curiosity', (1993) 295 *International Review of the Red Cross* 298, with Michael Meyer.

Peter Rowe is Professor of Law and Head of the Law School, Lancaster University. He has published widely on international humanitarian law and military law. He is the editor with Dominic McGoldrick and Eric Donnelly of *The International Criminal Court: Legal and Policy Issues* (Hart Publishing, 2004); *International Humanitarian Law: A Guide to Action* (British Red Cross and Foreign and Commonwealth Office, 2003) with Michael Meyer and *The Gulf War 1990–91 in International and English Law* (Routledge, 1993), and his publications include 'Responses to Terror: The New "War", (2002) 3 *Melbourne Journal of International Law* 301 and 'A New Court to Protect Human Rights in the Armed Forces of the UK: The Summary Appeal Court', (2003) 8 *Journal of Conflict and Security Law* 201.

Dr Lindsay Moir is a Senior Lecturer in Law at the University of Hull, and a member of the McCoubrey Centre for International Law. He is the author of *The Law of Internal Armed Conflict* (Cambridge University Press, 2002) along with several articles on humanitarian law and human rights, including 'Law and the Inter-American Human Rights System', (2003) 25 *Human Rights Quarterly* 182 and 'The Implementation and Enforcement of the Laws of Non-International Armed Conflict', (1998) 3(2) *Journal of Armed Conflict Law* 163.

A. P. V. Rogers is Yorke Distinguished Visiting Fellow of the Faculty of Law and Fellow of the Lauterpacht Research Centre for International Law, University of Cambridge; formerly Director of Army Legal Services; author of the prize-winning book, *Law on the Battlefield* (2nd edn, Manchester University Press, 2004).

Dr Nigel White is Professor of International Organisations in the School of Law at the University of Nottingham. His publications include *Keeping the Peace: The United Nations and the Maintenance of International Peace and Security* (Manchester University Press, 1997); *The UN System: Toward International Justice* (Lynne Rienner, 2002) and *The Law of International Organisations* (Manchester University Press, 1996). He edited a collection of essays on *Collective Security Law* (Ashgate, 2003). He was co-author of three books on international law with Hilaire McCoubrey: *International Law and the Use of Force* (Dartmouth, 1992), *International Organizations and Civil Wars* (Dartmouth, 1995) and *The Blue Helmets: The Legal Regulation of United Nations Military Operations* (Dartmouth, 1996). He has written numerous articles and essays including a contribution to the American Society of International Law project on *Democratic Accountability and the Use of Force in International Law*, co-edited by Charlotte Ku and

Harold Jacobson (Cambridge University Press, 2002). He is co-editor with Eric Myjer (Utrecht) of the *Journal of Conflict and Security Law* published tri-annually by Oxford University Press. The *Journal* covers the areas of arms control law, humanitarian law and collective security law, and endeavours to explore the interfaces between them.

FOREWORD: THERE ARE MEN TOO GENTLE TO LIVE AMONG WOLVES

GARY EDLES

Hilaire McCoubrey was an expert on the law of armed conflict or the law of war. Those terms themselves appear to be an oxymoron, and his relationship to them seems incongruous for such a gentle man. But if you give the subject its current, more fashionable name – 'humanitarian law' – Hilaire's association with the subject is thoroughly understandable. His purpose, after all, was to inject humanitarian principles into a hostile environment. That was both his professional calling and an essential element of his character. During the brief period of our association, before his untimely death, I came to admire and respect him as a colleague and genuinely value him as a friend.

Hilaire had exceptional academic achievements and encouraged others to think and write about the subjects with which he was concerned. Other commentators in this compendium are better equipped than I to address these matters. But Hilaire's character and spirit were equally, if not more, impressive. He was a full-time academic and an ordained Anglican priest. He pursued both callings simultaneously with equal devotion. At his death, he was assistant curate of St Mary's Church in Beverley.

Hilaire came relatively late to his clerical calling. He studied for the priesthood after having first established himself as a legal scholar and teacher at the School of Law at the University of Nottingham and as a qualified solicitor. His capability as a clergyman was tested almost immediately upon his ordination. Virtually his first pastoral activity, which coincided with his appointment to the Law School at Hull in 1995, was to preside over the funeral of Raymond Smith, a distinguished member of staff and former Dean of the Law School. Despite his being quite a novice clergyman, Hilaire performed with characteristic kindliness and sensitivity that everyone appreciated.

His first ecclesiastical post, which he held for three years, was as the assistant curate at Rowley Parish Church. He was once again quickly tested, and again carried out his duties superbly. When the full-time vicar left the community, Hilaire took over his responsibility for Rowley and the neighbouring churches of Skidby and Bentley. Not only did Hilaire drive from village to village every Sunday morning to take the service at the various churches, he served fully as spiritual leader of the communities. He performed marriage services, presided at funerals and provided pastoral counselling that occupied a considerable portion of his time. On numerous occasions, despite a long day in the classroom or otherwise coping with his considerable Law School responsibilities, he would be awakened during the night because a member of one of his parishes had died and he was needed to oversee arrangements. He did so unflinchingly and was always available to his parishioners. It was a full-time job on top of his full-time job. At all times he served the Church without remuneration. That was thoroughly in keeping with his personality. Service to his God and his community required no financial reward.

Hilaire's unassuming manner camouflaged his eclectic interests and sophisticated tastes. He played both the piano and organ and was a member of the Malt Whiskey Society. We both lived in Beverley and on several occasions I would drive him to the local fish and chip shop so he could pick up a take-away evening meal. But, when my wife and I were dinner guests at his home, we had the opportunity to sample his considerable culinary talents. He had a special interest in maritime matters. On the evening of our visit, we discussed turn-of-the-century shipping lines and I made a passing reference to the vessel that took my grandparents from Europe to America nearly a century ago. Hilaire took the time to search his personal archives to find information about, and a picture of, the ship that transported them. His intellectual interests ranged far beyond the law and he was both resourceful and unfailingly helpful.

His cluttered desk belied an extraordinarily sharp mind. I never attended any of his lectures. But I once attended a service at St Mary's at which Hilaire was the officiant. He delivered a thoroughly integrated and rather poignant thirty-minute homily entirely without notes. As the Reverend David Hoskin, Vicar of St Mary's, noted in his eulogy, one of Hilaire's great strengths was an ability to render complex or technical issues understandable to those less familiar with the subject.

Hilaire had a wry and ironic sense of humour. David Hoskin tells a story about the period when Hilaire was both teaching at Nottingham and studying for the priesthood. While a student in the ordination course, Hilaire led an 'organised truancy from a boring lecture' to go to the pictures and for an Indian meal. Totally in character, this event was re-enacted annually thereafter as a reunion for his year group on the course, according to Revd Hoskin.

James Kavanaugh, the American author and poet, himself a former priest, penned a poem whose thoughts may capture some of Hilaire's special qualities. Kavanaugh wrote:

> There are men too gentle to live among wolves
> Who prey upon them with IBM eyes
> And sell their hearts and guts for martinis at noon.
> There are men too gentle for a savage world
>
> Who dream instead of snow and children and Halloween
> And wonder if the leaves will change their color soon . . .
>
> There are men too gentle for a corporate world
> Who dream instead of candied apples and ferris wheels
> And pause to hear the distant whistle of a train . . .
>
> There are men too gentle for an accountant's world
> Who dream instead of Easter eggs and fragrant grass
> And search for beauty in the mystery of the sky . . .
>
> James Kavanaugh,
> *There are Men too Gentle to Live Among Wolves*
> (Nash Publishing, 1970)

Hilaire McCoubrey was a gentle man whose compassion for the victims of injustice was not purely academic. He was a Council Member of the International Red Cross, where he put his compassion into practice. He now rests in the graveyard outside the church at Rowley, alongside his father. It is a tranquil and dignified setting that befits this kindly human being. He was truly a man too gentle to live among wolves. So he devoted his ample intellect and energy to civilizing the wolves.

ABBREVIATIONS

ALS	Army Legal Services
CSCAP	Council for Security Cooperation in Asia Pacific
ECHR	European Convention on Human Rights
ECOWAS	Economic Community of West African States
ECtHR	European Court of Human Rights
EEZ	exclusive economic zone
FRY	Federal Republic of Yugoslavia
HCNM	High Commission on National Minorities (OSCE)
HQ ARRC	Allied Command Europe Rapid Reaction Corps
HRA 1998	Human Rights Act 1998
ICC	International Criminal Court
ICRC	International Committee of the Red Cross
ICTR	International Criminal Tribunal for Rwanda
ICTY	International Criminal Tribunal for the former Yugoslavia
IHL	international humanitarian law
ILC	International Law Commission
IMB	International Maritime Bureau
IMO	International Maritime Organisation
IMT	International Military Tribunal
LOAC	law of armed conflict
MDA	Magen David Adom
MPC	Model Penal Code
NIMA	US National Imagery and Mapping Agency
OAS	Organization of American States
OSCE	Organization for Security and Cooperation in Europe
POW	prisoner of war
ROE	rules of engagement
SLOC	sea lines of communication
SOFA	status of forces agreement
SUA	Convention for the Suppression of Unlawful Acts Against the Safety of Navigation 1988

SUAPROT	Protocol for the Suppression of Unlawful Acts Against the Safety of Fixed Platforms Located on the Continental Shelf 1988
UNCLOS	UN Convention on the Law of the Sea
UNMOVIC	UN Monitoring, Verification and Inspection Commission
UNPROFOR	UN Protection Force (Croatia)
UPD	Unit for the Promotion of Democracy
WMD	weapons of mass destruction

1

Hilaire McCoubrey and international conflict and security law

NIGEL D. WHITE

Introduction

Hilaire was a prolific writer. Although he died at the early age of forty-six while on a lecturing visit to Pakistan in April 2000, he had written or co-written ten books in the areas of international humanitarian law,[1] collective security law,[2] legal theory[3] and even planning law.[4] His output in terms of journal publications was similarly impressive with, for example, seminal articles in the *International and Comparative Law Quarterly*,[5] *La Revue de Droit Militaire et de Droit de la Guerre*,[6] the *International Review of the Red Cross*,[7] *International Relations*,[8]

[1] H. McCoubrey, *International Humanitarian Law: The Regulation of Armed Conflicts* (1st edn, Dartmouth, 1990); M. A. Meyer and H. McCoubrey (eds.), *Reflections on Law and Armed Conflicts: Selected Works on the Laws of War by the Late Professor Colonel G. I. A. D Draper, OBE* (Kluwer, 1998).

[2] H. McCoubrey and N. D. White, *International Organizations and Civil Wars* (Dartmouth, 1995); H. McCoubrey and N. D. White, *The Blue Helmets: Legal Regulation of United Nations Military Operations* (Dartmouth, 1996); H. McCoubrey and J. Morris, *Regional Peacekeeping in the Post Cold-War Era* (Kluwer, 2000).

[3] H. McCoubrey, *The Development of Naturalist Legal Theory* (Croom Helm, 1987); H. McCoubrey and N. D. White, *Textbook on Jurisprudence* (3rd edn, Blackstone Press, 1999); *The Obligation to Obey in Legal Theory* (Dartmouth, 1997).

[4] H. McCoubrey, *Effective Planning Appeals* (BSP Professional, 1988).

[5] H. McCoubrey, 'From Nuremberg to Rome: Restoring the Defence of Superior Orders', (2001) 50 *International and Comparative Law Quarterly* 386.

[6] H. McCoubrey, 'The Nature of the Modern Doctrine of Military Necessity', (1991) 30 *La Revue de Droit Militaire et de Droit de la Guerre* 217; H. McCoubrey, 'Medical Ethics, Negligence and the Battlefield', (1995) 34 *La Revue de Droit Militaire et de Droit de la Guerre* 103.

[7] H. McCoubrey, 'Before "Geneva" Law: A British Surgeon in the Crimean War', (1995) 304 *International Review of the Red Cross* 69.

[8] N. D. White and H. McCoubrey, 'International Law and the Use of Force in the Gulf', (1991) 10 *International Relations* 347; H. McCoubrey, 'The Armed Conflict in Bosnia

International Peacekeeping,[9] the *Journal of Armed Conflict Law* and its successor the *Journal of Conflict and Security Law*.[10] Quite often his calling as a minister in the Church of England was reflected in his work.[11] This, by no means complete, catalogue of Hilaire's writings is sufficient to show that he covered the whole spectrum of international law relating to armed conflict from the pre-conflict stage when the issues include those of arms control,[12] disarmament and conflict prevention, through the outbreak of armed conflict and discussion of the legality of resort to force (the *jus ad bellum*), to the coverage of the conduct of military operations and the protection of non-combatants by international humanitarian law (the *jus in bello*). He also covered collective security mechanisms that are applicable throughout these different stages.

The *jus ad bellum* and the *jus in bello* are terms still deployed by international lawyers, concerning the law governing the use of force in international relations and the law governing the conduct of hostilities. Hilaire's work covered both areas as well as the wider aspects of collective security and arms control, though he is probably best known for his work in the *jus in bello*, or to use its more modern term, international humanitarian law, with the publication of his leading text *International Humanitarian Law* in 1990.[13] In her review of the book, Susan Marks noted that it should serve the essential function of being a 'companion volume to the humanitarian treaties', and thus should secure an 'appreciative readership'.[14] It certainly achieved both of these aims. Hilaire's ethical, but at the same time practical, approach to the subject was reflected in the Preface to the second edition of this book:

and Proposed War Crimes Trials', (1993) 11 *International Relations* 411; H. McCoubrey, 'International Law and National Contingents in UN Forces', (1994) 12 *International Relations* 39; H. McCoubrey, 'Kosovo, NATO and International Law', (1999) 14 *International Relations* 29.

9 J. Morris and H. McCoubrey, 'Regional Peacekeeping in the Post Cold-War Era', (1999) 6 *International Peacekeeping* 129.

10 H. McCoubrey, 'The Concept and Treatment of War Crimes', (1996) 1 *Journal of Armed Conflict Law* 121; H. McCoubrey and J. Morris, 'International Law, International Relations and the Development of European Collective Security', (1999) 4 *Journal of Armed Conflict Law* 195; H. McCoubrey, 'The Protection of Creed and Opinion in the Laws of Armed Conflict', (2000) 5 *Journal of Conflict and Security Law* 135.

11 *Ibid.*

12 For example, F. Hampson and H. McCoubrey, 'Giving Legal Evidence in Proliferation Cases', in J. Dahlitz (ed.), *Future Legal Restraints on Arms Proliferation: Arms Control and Disarmament Law* (United Nations, 1996), p. 25.

13 McCoubrey, *International Humanitarian Law*, (1st edn).

14 S. Marks, (1990) 49 *Cambridge Law Journal* 525 at p. 526.

> This book seeks to emphasise that international humanitarian law is no Utopian aspiration – there is nothing 'Utopian' about any aspect of war – but a severely practical prescription which is entirely workable in the harsh exigencies of warfare. Obedience to it does not impede legitimate military efficacy, nor does violation gain any real advantage, but merely gains the perpetrator a deserved reputation for barbarism, to the detriment of its relations with other states.[15]

Considering the continued prevalence of warfare since the inception of the United Nations in 1945, it is remarkable that international humanitarian law was, until the advent of the international criminal tribunals in Yugoslavia and Rwanda in the mid-1990s, treated by mainstream international lawyers as a bit of a backwater. This is reflected in Susan Marks' review of the first edition of *International Humanitarian Law* when she wrote that 'if it was ever thought to be an esoteric subject of little contemporary relevance, recent events show that this is unfortunately not so'.[16] Hilaire's approach to the subject was to focus on the rules and principles of international humanitarian law and on the education of those involved in warfare, whether soldiers or politicians, in the law and its importance. He did not believe for an instant that there was a contradiction in espousing the necessity of rules embodying basic principles of humanity in a context where the normal peacetime rules against killing and destruction are basically suspended. The point Hilaire never tired of making is that war did not signify that any amount of death and destruction was permitted; it should and could be regulated. This was the issue he grappled with in his inaugural lecture to mark his appointment to a Chair at the University of Hull in 1996.[17]

Furthermore, Hilaire always saw the *jus ad bellum* and the *jus in bello* as two halves of a whole subject underpinned by a coherent philosophical framework. In 1992, while colleagues together at Nottingham University, we published a co-authored work *International Law and Armed Conflict*[18] which was intended as a textbook to cover the whole area. Although the work was divided evenly, Hilaire was almost exclusively the inspiration behind, and the writer of, the introductory chapter that still provides a most insightful explanation of the coherence of the

15 H. McCoubrey, *International Humanitarian Law* (2nd edn, Dartmouth, 1998), p. vii.
16 S. Marks, (1990) 49 *Cambridge Law Journal* 525.
17 H. McCoubrey, *International Laws of Armed Conflict: Practical Prescription or Dangerous Utopia?* (Hull University Press, 1997).
18 H. McCoubrey and N.D. White, *International Law and Armed Conflict* (Dartmouth, 1992).

whole subject area, while maintaining a firm distinction between the *in bello* and *ad bellum* limbs. The chapter is largely reproduced in the following section as part of an introductory chapter to this work, in which the contributors take a number of the difficult and controversial topics raised in that introductory work a great deal further. It seems fitting that Hilaire's approach to the subject matter should form the framework of enquiry for the current collection of essays in his memory.

Law and war: the theory of constraint[19]

War or armed conflict, the technically preferable general term, represents a major breakdown of the 'normal' conduct of international relations. It is also, tragically, a recurrent feature of the modern world and provision is accordingly made for its potential occurrence in public international law. This provision comprises principally the *jus ad bellum*, relating to resort to armed force in the conduct of international relations, and the *jus in bello*, relating to constraints upon the actual conduct of hostilities, and forms the subject matter of this book. It is appropriate before considering the substance of the law to examine as a preliminary issue its theoretical bases. In the particular case of the laws of armed conflict this is especially important since its very existence involves an apparent paradox.

The post-1945 world legal order enshrined in the Charter of the United Nations proscribes, by Article 2(4) of the Charter, the threat or use of force against the territorial integrity of a state, building upon and strengthening earlier principles and provisions which failed at the onset of the Second World War. The Charter does however, by Article 51, admit resort to armed force in the exercise of an 'inherent right of individual or collective self-defence' in the event of an 'armed attack', pending 'measures' being taken by the UN Security Council. Under Chapter VII of the Charter, the Security Council itself may authorize forceful measures to restore peace and security. These principles involve in application a complex canon of interpretation, but the broad conceptual base is clear enough. Discounting bizarre and unlikely circumstances of error, armed conflict will generally result from *prima facie* unlawful acts by one or more of the states involved and may to that

[19] This is drawn from McCoubrey and White, *International Law and Armed Conflict*, ch. 1, with kind permission of Ashgate Publishers. Some footnotes and text have been omitted.

extent be considered an unlawful condition of international relations. In this context the making of regulatory provision, beyond a simple ban, in anticipation of such a situation has a strongly paradoxical appearance and requires explanation. Beyond this, there must too be considered the practical viability of such regulation, a matter which is perhaps most problematic in the context of the *jus in bello.*

The logic of formal limitations upon armed force

The great Prussian military theorist Karl von Clausewitz stated in his classic work *Vom Kriege* that '[w]ar . . . is an act of violence intended to compel our opponent to fulfil our will',[20] adding the elaboration that:

> War is . . . a real political instrument, a continuation of political commerce, a carrying out of the same by other means. All beyond this which is strictly peculiar to War relates merely to the peculiar nature of the means which it uses.[21]

These statements may of course be greatly elaborated, but the essential depiction of armed conflict as a pursuit of policy objectives, including national self-defence, by means of military force leading to actual hostilities may surely be accepted as accurate. Once armed conflict has actually commenced its limitation presents difficulties. Clausewitz makes the point succinctly in the following comment:

> [H]e who uses force unsparingly, without reference to the bloodshed involved, must obtain a superiority if his adversary uses less vigour in its application . . . [F]rom the social condition both of States in themselves and in their relations to each other . . . War arises, and by it War is . . . controlled and modified. But these things do not belong to War itself, they are only given conditions; and to introduce into the philosophy of War itself a principle of moderation would be an absurdity.[22]

This seemingly brutal passage must be read carefully and upon examination can be seen not only to state a problem but to resolve it. Whether or not armed conflict could upon an absolute level be made subject to 'a principle of moderation', such conflicts do in practice take place in the political society of the community of nations. That 'society' embodies certain

[20] Karl von Clausewitz, *Vom Kriege* (Berlin, 1832); F. N. Maude (ed.) (J.J. Graham (trans.), Routledge, 1982), p. 101.
[21] *Ibid.*, p. 119. [22] *Ibid.*, p. 102.

expectations which are in part enshrined in public international law and these expectations determine the 'given conditions' even under the ultimate stress of armed conflict. Expectations are not, of course, necessarily fulfilled and it would be foolish to pretend that legal moderation of hostilities is invariably successful. Nonetheless, the pressures for compliance with communal expectation are by no means negligible for any person, or in this case state, which aspires to be a fully participant member of the society concerned. An analogy is sometimes sought to be drawn between the community of nations and 'primitive', meaning non-technological, human societies. Such an analogy must be treated with great caution, but in the sense of the relative weakness of central institutions vis-à-vis the periphery and the importance of customary norms and the role of 'self-help' in the performance of 'legal' tasks it is not without value. In the context of legal anthropology Simon Roberts has written:

> Some degree of order and regularity must be assured if social life in any community is to be sustained. This state need not be one of quiet harmony, and indeed societies differ widely as to the amount of friction and disorder which their members seem able to tolerate; but conditions must be such that ... an element of order [can] ... endure over time within the group.[23]

The analogy with violent resort in the international community may here be considered of some value in so far as the point is made that communal expectations do not terminate at the point of resort to violence but reach even into it.

If law may be accepted as having a role even in the collapse of international relations, the question then becomes one of the nature of the limiting 'given conditions' implicit in the expectations of the international community. Although Clausewitz directed his observations largely to what is now termed the *jus in bello*, the same general issue arises in the context of the *jus ad bellum*. The 'given conditions' derive ultimately from perceptions of armed conflict and here a broad spectrum of thought exists.

Philosophies and wars

There are those who in various ages have considered armed conflict a positive benefit. Before the First World War, Fieldmarshal von Mackenson

[23] S. Roberts, *Order and Dispute* (Penguin, 1979), p. 30.

was reported to hold the view that each generation should have a war to toughen it. The more general opinion, across a range of times and cultures, has been that hostilities may on occasion be 'necessary' to avert a yet worse evil but are not in themselves desirable. Warfare was far from being condemned in either ancient Greece or Rome, but in the *Nichomachaean Ethics* Aristotle wrote, in a discussion of the relation of happiness and leisure:

> [W]e make war in order that we may live at peace ... [N]obody chooses to make war or provokes it for the sake of making war; a man would be regarded as a bloodthirsty monster if he made [friendly states] ... into enemies in order to bring about battles and slaughter.[24]

This is certainly reflected by political rhetoric in cases of armed conflict and those who, like Adolf Hitler, transparently did manoeuvre in order to engender war have indeed emerged with the reputation of 'bloodthirsty monsters'. On the other side of the planet, classical Chinese thought was more overtly 'pacific', including both the 'official' Confucianism adopted as the Imperial ideology by the Han and later dynasties and Taoism which on many other issues diverged sharply from Confucian orthodoxy. The second great Confucian thinker, Mencius (Meng K'e), wrote:

> Confucius rejected those who enriched [evil] rulers ... How much more would he reject those who do their best to wage war on their behalf. In wars to gain land, the dead fill the plains; in wars to gain cities, the dead fill the cities ... Death is too light a punishment for such men.[25]

The Taoist classic *Tao-Te Ching*, attributed to Lao Tzu, states more concretely that:

> One who assists the ruler of men by means of the way does not intimidate the empire by a show of arms ... [A good commander] aims only at bringing his campaign to a conclusion ... but only when there is no choice; bring it to a conclusion but do not intimidate.[26]

These views involve, variously, both *jus ad bellum* and *jus in bello* concerns, but clearly treat warfare as, at most, an evil necessity. Against this background, military endeavour in classical China was, at least until

[24] Aristotle, *Nichomachaean Ethics*, 1177b; H. Tredennick (ed.) (J. A. K. Thomson (trans.), revised edn, Penguin, 1976), p. 329.

[25] *The Mencius*, IVA: 13, (D. C. Lau (trans.), Penguin, 1970).

[26] Lau Tzu, *Tao-Te Ching*, xxx, 69, 69b (D. C. Lau (trans.), Penguin, 1970).

the Ch'ing (Manchu) conquest in 1644, in theory accorded lower status than civil activity. In practice, however, this by no means necessarily inhibited military initiatives.

Judaeo-Christian thought has contributed a rather different strand of theory which, notwithstanding the vision of Christ as 'Prince of Peace', includes a somewhat misunderstood concept of 'Holy War'. Islamic thought includes the parallel concept of *jihad* or war of duty. From the same general sources comes an idea of 'just warfare' which requires comment in the immediate context. Ideas of *bellum justum* or just war have acquired an evil reputation summarized by Jean Pictet in his description of:

> the well known and malignant doctrine of the 'just war' . . . [which] did nothing less than provide believers with a justification for war and all its infamy . . . [E]very effort has been made on every occasion to justify aggression . . . [and] to justify the cruelties which abounded in [a] . . . sanguinary age.[27]

This was undoubtedly the effect of abuse of the doctrine in its various forms, but in its origin it was an attempt to limit resort to armed force to justified causes. This became necessary when Christianity was adopted by Constantine the Great as the official religion of the Roman Empire and the Church was obliged to develop a conceptual framework for its relations with the secular life of the Empire. The true intent can be seen in the, much later, thirteenth century criteria for a just war set out by St Thomas Aquinas, who, in summary, wrote that war is in principle a sin because punishment is ordained only for sin and Scripture tells us that all who draw the sword shall die by it.[28] War may, however, be just where it is used to remedy wrongdoing by those intending to advance virtue and avert evil.

The currency of this particular form of just war theory may be considered to have ended with the 1648 Treaty of Westphalia which concluded the Thirty Years War. In the succeeding era, less emphasis was placed upon the justification of causes, in law if not in practice. The incident of the Ems telegram used by Bismark to elevate a heated dispute over the Hohenzollern candidature for the throne of Spain into the 1870 Franco-Prussian War may serve as an illustration of the continuing

[27] J. Pictet, *Development and Principles of International Humanitarian Law* (Nijhoff, 1985), pp. 13–14.

[28] St Thomas Aquinas, *Summa Theologica*, 2a2ae. 40, 1.

practical importance of 'causes'. The *jus ad bellum* as it has developed since the First and Second World Wars has to some extent returned to a concern with causes. Not to 'just war' concepts *stricto sensu* but at least to formalized concepts of 'justifiable' exceptions to a *prima facie* general proscription of resort to armed force in the conduct of international relations. Modern concepts of 'self-defence' and 'national liberation', the latter owing some of its modern shape to post-1917 developments in 'socialist' thought, fit this mould. Such ideas, like the earlier *bellum justum* theories, are of course open to abuse. In the earlier part of the modern era, the use by Hitler of the *auslanddeutsch* population in post-1918 Czechoslovakia as a cover for aggression provides a clear illustration, even granted that self-determination was at the time more a 'political' than a juridical concept.

In both its essential aims and its attendant problems the basic doctrines of the modern *jus ad bellum* may perhaps be considered to represent a revised and strict form of a well established view of armed conflict as an evil occasionally 'necessary' for the aversion of some yet greater peril. Such a view conflicts, of course, with any idea of a human right to peace, advanced by a number of writers in the field of the laws of armed conflict.[29] An unqualified right to peace raises serious and extra-legal questions as to whether warfare is the worst conceivable evil in international society or whether some consequences of non-resistance might exceed it, the spectre of the Third Reich and other atrocious regimes being obviously an important element in such vexed debates. Whatever view of that issue may for the time being be taken, the focus of continuing contention in the modern *jus ad bellum* rests, and it is here suggested rests properly, upon the particular nature of the 'necessities' for military action which are to be recognized and their vulnerability to abuse.

The viability of constraints upon the conduct of hostilities

Whatever view is taken of resort to armed force in the conduct of international relations, it is an inescapable fact of the modern world that armed conflicts continue to occur. The legal constraints imposed upon their conduct by the *jus in bello* are clearly subject to the serious

[29] See G. Herczeg, *Development of International Humanitarian Law*, trans. (Sandas Simon and Lajos Czante (trans.), Akademiai Kiado, 1984).

practical difficulties outlined more than a century and a half ago by von Clausewitz. Geoffrey Best has written:

> The passionate and chancy business of war has never been and can never be helpful to the practice of that coolness and self-control which respect for any sort of law ideally requires.[30]

One may agree that moderation in the use of armed force can never be prescribed with perfect effect and much may depend upon the extent of a particular conflict, for example whether or not continued national existence depends upon the outcome. A much more extreme viewpoint was expressed by the novelist Leo Tolstoy in his account of Napoleon's 1812 campaign against Russia. In a brief discussion of the relevance of 'rules' of warfare, published interestingly at about the time of the negotiation of the highly significant 1868 Declaration of St Petersburg, Tolstoy wrote in relation to the resistance 'guerilla' warfare that followed the occupation of Moscow:

> From the time [Napoleon] ... took up the correct fencing attitude in Moscow and instead of his opponent's rapier saw a cudgel raised above his head, he did not cease to complain to Kutuzov and to the Emperor Alexander that the war was being carried on contrary to all the rules, as if there were any rules for killing people.[31]

This rather crude statement of the primacy of force, which goes very far beyond anything which Clausewitz argued, was made by a proponent of broad pacifism. As to the rules of warfare in the early nineteenth century, the ideas of 'guerilla' warfare – the phrase derives from the Napoleonic occupation of Spain – and the *levée en masse* received little or no recognition but were in practice not unknown. The evidence suggests that the Russian army as such in the 1812 campaign was not markedly different in formal 'rectitude' from that of France, a point implicitly conceded by Tolstoy in criticism of the restraint counselled by members of the Imperial General Staff. Tolstoy's analysis suggests a

[30] G. Best, 'Preface' to M. A. Meyer (ed.), *Armed Conflict and the New Law*, vol. I, *Aspects of the 1977 Geneva Protocols and the 1981 Weapons Convention* (British Institute of International and Comparative Law, 1989), p. v.

[31] L. Tolstoy, *War and Peace* (Moscow, 1868–9; L. and A. Maude (trans.), Macmillan, 1943), Book XIV, ch. 1, p. 1139. The Kutuzov referred to was Fieldmarshal Prince Gollenitschev-Kutuzov, appointed to command by Tsar Alexander I and generally praised for his cautious and successful conduct of the campaign, which relied heavily upon the harshness of the Russian winter.

Utopian division between 'war' and 'not war' so far as civilized conduct is concerned which, whatever its theoretical justifications might be, is a cruel prescription indeed in the realities of international conduct. In the real world it may perhaps be agreed that as Georg Schwarzenberger states, '[i]t is the function of the rules of warfare to impose some limits, however ineffective, to a complete reversion to anarchy by the establishment of minimum standards on the conduct of war'.[32]

The practicality of moderation in the conduct of actual armed conflicts rests upon the balance which may be drawn between the inherent ferocity of warfare and the expectations of humanity. The point was made by implication in the Preamble to 1907 Hague Convention IV Respecting the Laws and Customs of War on Land, which states that '[i]t is . . . necessary to bear in mind the case where appeal to arms has been brought about . . . [and] to serve, even in this extreme case, the interests of humanity and the ever progressive needs of civilization'.

The viability of the moderating norms prescribed by the *jus in bello* in the extreme circumstances of armed conflict may be seen as posing in an especially problematic form the nature and extent of the obligatory characteristic of law. This has from time to time occupied a prominent, if arguably somewhat misunderstood, place in general jurisprudential debate. The nineteenth-century positivism of Jeremy Bentham and John Austin located, with slightly different emphases, the obligatory characteristic of positive law in the combination of 'sovereign' commands with, primarily, coercive sanctions for non-compliance.[33] The revised and modernized positivism of H. L. A. Hart emphasizes rather the formal authority of law derived from the combination within a legal system of primary, duty-imposing, rules with secondary, power-conferring, rules.[34] In contrast with such analyses, the ancient and multifaceted tradition of classical naturalism, with its modern development in work such as that of Finnis, emphasizes the importance of the moral quality of positive prescription in the obligation which it imposes.[35] Such a brief description is, of course, a gross over-simplification and leaves out of account many subtle shadings of debate and indeed strands of theory.

[32] G. Schwarzenberger, *International Law*, vol. II, *Armed Conflict* (Stevens, 1968), p. 10.

[33] Bentham admitted sanctions of reward, whereas Austin adhered more strictly to a logic of coercion. See J. Bentham, *Of Laws in General* (H. L. A. Hart (ed.), Athlone, 1970); J. Austin, *The Province of Jurisprudence Determined* (1832; Weidenfeld and Nicholson, 1954), lecture I.

[34] H. L. A. Hart, *The Concept of Law* (Clarendon, 1961).

[35] J. Finnis, *Natural Law and Natural Rights* (Clarendon, 1980).

The three elements here emphasized – coercive, formal and moral sources of 'obligation' – may, however, reasonably be accepted as basic to the analysis of the obligatory characteristic of positive law. Varying combinations of these elements may be found associated with particular provisions or principles and an argument may be constructed that, far from there being any inherent conflict between them, the absolute quality of the obligation associated with any given part of positive law may rest upon the degree of their convergence. In the case of the *jus in bello*, the moral claim of moderating prescription for the conduct of warfare may surely be accepted as generally obvious. The formal claim, notwithstanding the relative institutional weakness of public international law, may be seen in the embodiment of accepted norms in customary law and in multilateral treaties. It is in the pragmatic incentives for compliance, taken as a crude analogy with the 'sanctions' of classical positivism, that the most obvious difficulties arise in the present context.

Leaving aside transnational criminal processes in respect of 'war crimes', which have in practice arisen only in very unusual circumstances, there may be argued to be a number of pragmatic incentives for compliance with the *jus in bello* which are more effective than might, *prima facie*, be thought. Some of these have been cogently stated by Lt Col. Klaus Kuhn as follows: 'the quickest way of achieving and maintaining a lasting peace is to conduct hostilities humanely . . . [I]t is evident that humanitarian considerations cannot be dissociated from the strategic concept of military leaders.'[36]

Lt Col. Kuhn's statement was made in a specifically 'Geneva' context, being indeed derived from the view of General Dufour, one of the founding fathers of the International Red Cross movement, but it may readily be applied to the broad spectrum of the *jus in bello*. An enemy made desperate by belief, well-founded or otherwise, in the ruthlessness of their adversary may themselves be driven by fear to extremities which might otherwise be avoided and may also prolong a struggle which has become militarily hopeless, potentially to the great loss of all parties to it. Further, a state which is seen blatantly to ignore the demands of the *jus in bello* in its efforts to secure a superiority, or even to escalate hostilities beyond a level seen as reasonably necessary in the particular context,

[36] Lt Col. K. Kuhn, *Responsibility for Military Conduct and Respect for International Humanitarian Law, Dissemination* (International Committee of the Red Cross, August 1987), p. 1.

runs the risk of suffering detriment in its general international relations which may devalue or even nullify a victory so gained. Such considerations may not perhaps be equated with classical positivist 'sanctions', but may nonetheless be argued to supply significant incentives for compliance. It may be added that violations of the *jus ad bellum* may attract various international responses, including ultimately the use of force under United Nations authority, as in the case of the Iraqi invasion of Kuwait in August 1990. The pressure for such measures may be exacerbated where a conflict in progress is marred by serious violations of the *jus in bello*.

To the pragmatic arguments for compliance with the *jus in bello* there may be added the consideration of post-conflict relations between the adversaries. Assuming that both, or all, the states involved in an armed conflict remain in existence thereafter, as generally they will, at some point a return to a semblance of 'normal' relations will be necessary. Even after a 'limited' conflict such as that in the Falklands in 1982, relations between Britain and Argentina remained severely strained for the best part of a decade and in the case of (even) more traumatic conflicts the subsequent strains may well, of course, endure far longer. In assessing this factor, the degree of ideological divergence between the former adversaries must naturally also be taken into account.

Such pragmatic, or rather 'political', counsels for compliance supply a powerful counter to contentions that the *jus in bello* is a dangerously Utopian prescription, in the opposite direction from Tolstoy's, fettering a compliant state in conflict with a more ruthless enemy. The law could not realistically seek to restrain effective action within the legitimate dictates of military necessity, but in setting limiting norms bound to civilized expectations, it defines barriers which are crossed only at potentially damaging cost.

It has so far been assumed that the moderation of armed conflict is, in so far as it can be achieved, beneficial. There is, however, a counter argument that such moderation in fact engenders war by conferring upon it a spurious cloak of 'acceptability'. This view, of which elements may be seen in Tolstoy's argument considered above, might have a superficial plausibility but is in practice readily countered. No laws of armed conflict are going to render warfare anything other than sanguinary and if the sheer horror of warfare were going to abolish it, it could hardly be believed that the phenomenon should have survived the Somme campaign. In fact, of course, it did. One is drawn back to Schwarzenberger's argument of 'minimum standards' and the desire to mitigate an inherently appalling condition, which is not by any means to argue that endeavours to ensure peace are or should be thereby compromised.

Transgressions of the laws of armed conflict

It would be idle to pretend that the laws of armed conflict are entirely effective, whether in relation to resorts to armed force or to the conduct of hostilities in being. States all too evidently do resort to aggressive armed force and do subsequently wage warfare in manners contravening the *jus in bello*. A legal prescription which is wholly ineffective could reasonably be dismissed as inutile, representing a real if not formal manifestation of desuetude. On the other hand no law, whether municipal or international, is completely effective and the question of a minimum threshold criterion of effectiveness in the operation of law perhaps opens the gate to needless and sterile statistical assertion. In practice it may be argued that the conduct of sufficient numbers of states in relation to resort to and operational use of armed force is modified for the prescription to be considered to play a useful, albeit imperfect, role. The question of transgression does, however, raise a number of important theoretical issues.

One derives from the fundamental paradox involved in the legal regulation of a *prima facie* unlawful condition of international relations, to which reference has been made above. The relationship between the *jus ad bellum* and the *jus in bello* is open to some debate. In principle, the two prescriptions are distinct, not least for the avoidance of the development of the extreme abuses associated with 'just war' concepts in which it might be assumed that the party 'in the right' is subject to no restraint. Thus, the origins of a conflict do not as such affect the application of the norms of the *jus in bello* as such. It is, however, possible to argue that a continuing norm of non-escalation of conflicts confers upon the *jus ad bellum* a limited impact in the actual conduct of the hostilities. Any such restraints would, however, again apply to both, or all, parties to an armed conflict. In this sense the impartiality of the constraints upon the conduct of warfare may be considered to be upheld.

A more serious practical question arises where a state in conflict clearly resorts to unequivocally unlawful means of waging warfare. This involves in particular the sensitive question of the reciprocity of obligation as regards the *jus in bello* in particular. The *jus ad bellum* clearly involves an element of reciprocity in so far as a state which unlawfully resorts to the aggressive use of armed force lays itself open to legitimate counter-action by the victim state or by the international community which, in the absence of the prior aggression, would itself have been *prima facie* unlawful. So far as the *jus in bello* is concerned more complex issues arise. The multilateral treaties which underlie the *jus in bello* are subject to the same principles in their application as other treaties, that is to say that they bind states party to them in their mutual relations except in so far as they are sufficiently widely ratified to achieve the status of customary law binding upon all states, or have become 'peremptory norms' as *jus cogens* from which no derogation is permitted. Common Article 2 of the four 1949 Geneva Conventions, the basic provisions of 'Geneva' law, provides:

> Although one of the Powers in conflict may not be a party to the present Convention, the Powers who are parties thereto shall remain bound by it in their mutual relations. They shall furthermore be bound by the Convention in relation to the said Power, if the latter accepts and applies the provisions thereof.

This is clearly founded upon reciprocity of obligation but Jean Pictet remarks of the general *jus in bello*:

> In view of their impartial character and the higher values for which they stand ... and their extension throughout the world, we may ... assert that the Geneva and Hague Conventions, to a great extent are no longer merely reciprocal treaties ... but have become absolute and universal commitments.[37]

In so far as a claim is made for a special obligation deriving from moral force, at least in the formal legal context, this must be regarded as rhetorical. In so far, however, as the claim is founded upon the very large proportion of states which are party to the basic treaties it is clearly true to say that much of their provision has entered into customary law. Further, as Pictet points out,[38] the 1969 Vienna Convention on the Law of Treaties provides by Article 53 for the recognition as *jus cogens* of peremptory norms, 'accepted and recognized by the international community of States as a whole as a norm from which no derogation is permitted'.

[37] Pictet, *Development and Principles*, p. 89.
[38] *Ibid.*, pp. 87–8.

In particular, therefore, a subsequent treaty which violates a current norm of *jus cogens* will be void. There is some reason to argue that the basic principles of 'Geneva' law might be considered *jus cogens* and certainly the bulk of the general *jus in bello* is comprised within customary law and is therefore binding upon all states, irrespective of whether or not they are parties to the treaties concerned. To this extent the question of reciprocity loses much of its importance in practice. This is not, of course, the case in respect of some of the more controversial modern provisions such as 1977 Protocol I Additional to the 1949 Geneva Conventions. Rather more difficult questions may arise in the context of breaches and reprisals. Belligerent reprisals are defined by Frits Kalshoven as:

> a deliberate violation of a rule of the law of armed conflict . . . the idea being that this violation finds justification in . . . earlier wrongful conduct on the part of the adversary and [is intended] . . . to bring about a change of the policy pursued by the adversary.[39]

In reference to the termination of treaty obligations as a consequence of breach, Article 60(5) of the Convention then excepts 'provisions relating to the protection of the human person contained in treaties of a humanitarian character, in particular to provisions prohibiting any form of reprisals against persons protected by such treaties'. Upon this basis reprisals against, for example, the sick and wounded, prisoners of war or civilians (as rather variously protected) may reasonably be contended to be unlawful. It may be added upon a purely pragmatic level that any such distasteful action would not be likely to be very effective in any event. A state sufficiently ruthless to have perpetrated relevant breaches in the first place is highly unlikely to be much affected by equivalent counter-measures and will on the contrary be more likely to treat them as an internal and external propaganda bonus. The more effective, and entirely lawful, response is surely to ensure that any of those responsible for the original outrages who fall into the hands of their enemies will be held accountable therefore. From the viewpoint of civilization as well as law this is certainly to be preferred to a descent into tit-for-tat barbarities against the helpless. 'War crimes' trials themselves, of course, present a variety of jurisprudential and practical complications.

[39] F. Kalshoven, *The Law of Warfare: A Summary of its Recent History and Trends in Development* (Sijthoff, 1973), p. 111.

If reprisals in relation to the direct concerns of 'Geneva' law may be considered *prima facie* unlawful, the same is not necessarily true of the generality of 'Hague' law. Where a state in conflict is using unlawful means or methods of warfare to secure victory it might be considered unreal to prohibit an effective response. Here, the problems lie less in the admissibility of reprisals as such than in the questions of the relation of the counter-action to the original outrage and its proportionality.

Laws of armed conflict and human rights

The formal proximity of the laws of armed conflict in their various divisions to provision for 'human rights' is open to considerable debate. The 'Geneva' division of the *jus in bello*, termed 'international humanitarian law' seems perhaps most closely related to ideas of human rights. However, in so far as the broad endeavour of both the *jus ad bellum* and the whole *jus in bello* is to mitigate, where it cannot be avoided, the impact and extent of hostilities, the general laws of armed conflict may be thought to serve a cause analogous to 'human rights' in peculiarly extreme circumstances. Against this there must be set the contention of those who, like Geza Herczeg,[40] argue that armed conflict is itself a violation of human rights and that a discourse of 'human rights' in such a context is a contradiction in terms. On the other hand, Igor P. Blishchenko argues that 'the essential problem in all situations of armed conflict is the international protection of human rights; in other words, the fundamental objective of what is known as the laws of war is the protection of human rights'.[41] However, Blishchenko also considers that 'Hague' law should be excluded from this model in view of the unlawfulness of resort to aggressive force.[42] This view seems ill-founded. 'Rights' of any sort are *ex hypothesi* most in need of conservation where most obviously under threat, in general terms armed conflict by definition represents a major threat to human life and conditions and its exclusion in this context would seem at best illogical.

It has elsewhere been suggested that '[i]t seems reasonable to conclude that ... the laws of armed conflict are best regarded as a specialist

40 Herczeg, *Development.*

41 I. P. Blishchenko, 'Humanitarian Norms and Human Rights', in M. Bedjaoui (ed.), *Modern Wars: A Report for the Independent Commission on International Humanitarian Issues* (Zed Books, 1986), p. 145.

42 *Ibid.*

application of human rights principles in peculiarly extreme circumstances'.[43] This statement was made in the specific context of 'Geneva' law but in so far as the laws of armed conflict are intended to mitigate the effects, and incidence, of warfare it may reasonably be extended to the whole spectrum. It should, however, be conceded to the proponents of distinction that the circumstances are in fact so extreme that the categoric differentiation from what may be termed the 'civil' jurisprudence is entirely appropriate. The suggestion here advanced is essentially one of consanguinity rather than identity in detail.

Theory and reality

'Practical' lawyers are frequently somewhat dismissive of theory, preferring the detail of provision and the exigencies of application. That the latter represents the reality of the substance of law is obvious, and for that reason is the subject of the remainder of this book. A law which existed only in the area of theory would be at best a somewhat sterile study. Equally, a substantive law which has no, or an inadequate, conceptual base has at its core a severely damaging weakness which may ultimately destroy its practical credibility. This is perhaps especially the case in an area of law which seeks to impose regulation in, arguably, the most difficult of all circumstances. The purpose of the arguments of theory here advanced is to show that the law to be considered hereafter has, in spite of some 'realist' critics, a strong conceptual base and a claim to perform an important task within the framework of the 'legal' structure of international relations.

Conclusion

Within the coherent framework provided by Hilaire in the above section the contributors, drawn both from academe and practice, provide expert analysis of many aspects of the law governing armed conflict and collective security law. They develop many of the themes and issues raised above to provide a stimulating and coherent collection of essays. In chapter 2 Gordon Risius looks at the application of international humanitarian law in the operational context. It provides an excellent overview of the significance of international humanitarian law, as well as

[43] McCoubrey, *International Humanitarian Law* (1st edn), p. 5.

a tribute to Hilaire as an educator in the subject. Neil Boister continues the theme of education in chapter 3 by looking at the duty to educate in humanitarian law in relation to the absence of a defence of mistake of law in the Rome Statute establishing the International Criminal Court. In so doing, it looks at a problematic interface between international humanitarian law and international criminal law. Chapter 4 by Robert Cryer on superior orders and the International Criminal Court and chapter 5 by Charles Garraway on command responsibility develop difficult areas of humanitarian law and follow logically from chapter 3 as detailed analyses of related topics. The debate on rationale of international humanitarian law is returned to in chapters 6 and 7 as the discussion is broadened out to discuss the hugely symbolic issue of the new neutral protective emblem by Michael Meyer and the issue of the unification of international humanitarian law by Lindsay Moir. Though a subject that can be traced back to antiquity, all the essays on humanitarian law contained in chapters 2–7 show how the subject is constantly evolving as it adapts to changing means of waging warfare and also to changing structures of international law and international relations. This is further illustrated by Richard Barnes' essential exploration of the relevance of international humanitarian law to terrorism in chapter 8, and again by Tony Rogers' illuminating discussion in chapter 9 of a controversial aspect of the Hague law, the issue of legitimate military targets. Chapter 10 marks a change in the book from the laws of war in both their Hague and Geneva forms to the law of peace, with Peter Rowe's consideration of the application of human rights law in international armed conflict law. This helps to shed light on a specific aspect of the difficult relationship between international humanitarian law, normally considered to apply in wartime, and human rights law, usually applicable in peacetime. Richard Burchill's consideration in chapter 11 of democracy as an aspect of peace and security widens the human rights debate out further and takes us into regional security regimes. Collective security and the rules governing the use of force are reconsidered by myself in chapter 12 in the light of the Iraq conflict of 2003, providing an assessment of the *jus ad bellum* in the light of the incredible pressures being placed upon the law in the early twenty-first century. Scott Davidson shows in chapter 13 that security issues cut across many areas of international law with his groundbreaking consideration of maritime violence. Finally, Justin Morris considers the complex interplay between law and politics, assessing the prospects for international law in a world characterized by an acute imbalance of power.

Overall the book moves from education on international humanitarian law, through specific and general matters of humanitarian law and laws of war, to human rights and then use of force and security matters. As well as providing a fitting tribute to the main aspects of Hilaire's contribution to knowledge – as educator, as academic on the laws of war as well as on the laws of peace – the volume provides a coherent reconsideration and development of key aspects of conflict and security law at a time when that law is being either applied, breached, debated or reformed on almost a daily basis.

2

The development of operational law within Army Legal Services

GORDON RISIUS

Introduction

The latter part of Hilaire McCoubrey's career as a leading academic in the field of international humanitarian law (IHL) coincided with the period when the British Army gradually came to recognize IHL as a subject to be taken seriously when planning and conducting military operations. Through his publications,[1] the courses he arranged for military lawyers at Nottingham and Hull,[2] and latterly as Chairman of the UK Group of the International Society for Military Law and the Law of War, Hilaire played an important role in this development. The purpose of this contribution, written from the perspective of a military lawyer, is to outline the increasing involvement of legal officers in the British Army in military operations over the last half century. Save to the extent that British military lawyers were actively involved between 1945–9 in investigating the conduct of German and Japanese operations during the Second World War and in prosecuting German and Japanese war criminals before British military tribunals, for much of this time IHL was regarded as a matter of purely academic interest. Today, it is an integral aspect of operational planning. The extent of the transformation was brought home to the author in 1999, when a young Army Legal Services (ALS) officer gave him an account of a British general's initial planning meeting on arrival at his HQ in the Balkans in the late 1990s. The general's opening words were, 'Where's my lawyer?' When the officer

[1] E.g. H. McCoubrey and N. D. White, *International Law and Armed Conflict* (Dartmouth, 1992).

[2] Nottingham University's first dedicated course for ALS lawyers in July 1996, which Hilaire organized in conjunction with Nigel White. It concluded with a mock war crimes trial over which Hilaire presided as the judge.

responded from the back row, the general told him that in future he was to be seated at his commander's side.

The Cold War period

A lawyer commissioned into ALS in the third quarter of the twentieth century could be forgiven for thinking he was unlikely to be called upon to play any part in the planning or execution of military operations, and that his role as a legal officer would be largely confined to matters of discipline and administration, military aid to the civil authorities, or helping soldiers and their families with legal problems. He was given little or no training in IHL, and the only publication issued to him on the subject was the *Manual of Military Law*, Part III, on 'The Law of War on Land', dating from 1958.[3] It was an impressive and authoritative work, but it was hardly if ever referred to in practice. Commanders had little interest in IHL, and even less in seeking advice on the subject. The same was true at Ministry of Defence level, to the extent that not a single Defence White Paper mentioned law of war issues for more than forty years after the end of the Second World War. Ten years after the Manual's publication it was 'almost unheard of for an ALS officer to become involved in anything operational', though '[o]ccasionally one was asked a question about guards and sentries'.[4] There were no doubt many reasons why it took so long for the United Kingdom to pass the legislation necessary to enable it to ratify the 1949 Geneva Conventions for the protection of victims of war,[5] but lack of interest was undoubtedly among them.

This is not to suggest that such issues were deliberately rejected by commanders, civil servants or politicians, but rather that the laws of war were in their view aimed more at certain other countries whose armies did not instinctively know, as British soldiers did, how to conduct themselves properly on the battlefield. Just as the European Convention on Human Rights (ECHR) signed in 1949 was, until relatively recently, regarded in the United Kingdom as intended primarily for European countries whose human rights standards were thought to fall somewhat short of our own, so the Geneva Conventions signed in the same year were for several decades thereafter looked on by the British

[3] *Manual of Military Law* (HMSO, 1958).

[4] Maj. Gen. D. H. D. Selwood, 'Scales of Justice: the First Fifty Years of Army Legal Services', (2002) *Military Law Journal* 78.

[5] Geneva Conventions Act 1957.

Army as legal niceties having little to do with the real business of defending Western Europe against attack from the Warsaw Pact.[6]

This author vividly recalls his first major divisional exercise in Germany in the early 1980s, during which he was looking forward to putting into practice the training he had recently been given at the Judge Advocate General's School, United States Army, at Charlottesville, Virginia, on how to conduct a legal review of a commander's plan of operations. However, on the very first day of the exercise he was quietly but firmly told that the divisional commander's operational plans were out of bounds to lawyers. Things were no better at desk level. About a hundred practical law of war problems (e.g. a message reporting the capture of an individual whose legal status was uncertain and seeking advice on how to deal with him) were fed into the exercise over the three weeks it lasted, yet not a single one was referred to the legal cell for advice. When asked afterwards for an explanation, the staff concerned responded that they had not appreciated that any of the problems involved legal issues and all had accordingly been dealt with on a common-sense basis.

At least military lawyers were present on that exercise, even if they were given nothing to do. For most of the preceding thirty years, the very idea that lawyers might have a role to play in training for war would have been regarded with amusement.

Falklands War

Although it must have been obvious that the Falklands campaign in 1982 was bound to raise numerous law of war issues, and indeed did so, no service lawyer accompanied the Task Force. It was eventually conceded that an Army lawyer should be deployed, but his departure, initially from the United Kingdom and later from the forward mounting base on Ascension Island, was repeatedly postponed in favour of higher priority personnel and stores. In the event he reached Port Stanley just too late to help draft the instrument of surrender, though thereafter he was kept busy, dealing primarily with prisoner of war handling issues.

[6] That was certainly the general view in HQ 4th Armoured Division in 1981, when the author was serving there, and it was echoed by the Commander-in-Chief, in discussion with the author at about that time.

1970–1980

An awareness that operations needed to be conducted in accordance with the law had been growing steadily within the Army for some years before 1982. For example, the United Kingdom's delegations to the Diplomatic Conference on the Reaffirmation and Development of International Humanitarian Law Applicable to Armed Conflicts held in Geneva between 1974 and 1977 included a senior ALS officer, as did the International Committee of the Red Cross' Conference of Government Experts on the Use of Certain Conventional Weapons, which met in Lucerne and Lugarno in 1974 and 1976. Interest in matters of international law did not yet extend to commanders, but ALS officers had been attached to HQ Northern Ireland to provide operational advice since the early 1970s, shortly after troops were first deployed to the province in substantial numbers. The idea of taking specialist legal advice in the course of operational planning was no longer new, even if the relevant law in that theatre was domestic rather than international. Whereas American military commanders came to accept military lawyers on their staffs as operational advisers as a result primarily of international armed conflict in Vietnam, in the United Kingdom the initial impetus came from internal security operations. However, when posts for ALS officers were established at divisional headquarters in Germany in the early 1980s, it was the firm intention of the then Director of Army Legal Services, Major General Sir David Hughes-Morgan Bt CB CBE, that their duties should include the provision of advice on the legal aspects of military operations.

At the suggestion of Peter Rowe, a number of military and international lawyers, academics and others met on 23 May 1988 at the Office of the Judge Advocate General and decided to form the UK Group of the International Society for Military Law and the Law of War. The Group has met with increasing frequency over the years, and a number of members have also contributed to the activities of the parent Society, based in Brussels. Hilaire was an active participant in the Group – delivering, for example, a paper on 'Medical Ethics, Negligence and Battlefield Practice' at a conference of the Group held on 3 December 1994 at the British Institute for International and Comparative Law[7] – and was Chairman at the time of his death. Other members, too, have made a

[7] The paper was later published in *International Law and Armed Conflict Commentary*, vol. I, Pt II (January 1994), p. 7.

notable contribution to the emergence of IHL as an important factor to be taken into account in military operations, including in particular Professor Christopher Greenwood CMG QC, Professor of International Law at the London School of Economics,[8] and Michael Meyer OBE, Head of International Law at the British Red Cross Society. Meyer's contribution has been extensive and varied, including assistance in the IHL training of ALS officers, the provision of practical advice and help on prisoner of war issues (e.g. during and after the Falklands and Gulf conflicts) and research into the enforceability of IHL under domestic law.

1990–1991 Gulf War

ALS established a post for an IHL specialist as early as 1977, with responsibility for IHL research, training and publications. The first incumbent was Lt Col. (later Maj. Gen.) Michael Clarke, who drafted the British Army's training pamphlet on the law of armed conflict, first published in 1979, designed for personnel of all ranks required to study or instruct in the subject.[9] In addition to the pamphlet, a pocket-sized Aide-Memoire on the Law of Armed Conflict (JSP 381), intended primarily for military personnel dealing with, or those with the potential to become, prisoners of war, was also produced. Despite these developments, there was still a general reluctance on the part of commanders and staff officers to acknowledge the importance of IHL in military planning. Following Iraq's invasion of Kuwait in 1990, a British military planning team went to Saudi Arabia to assess the size and make-up of the proposed HQ British Forces Middle East. Their initial 'shopping' list of specialist staff for the HQ was silent on the need for lawyers. On being asked why, they responded that the Foreign and Commonwealth Office Legal Advisers in London, and the British Embassy's local Arab legal advisers in Riyadh, ought between them to be able to provide an adequate service. When it was drawn to their attention that IHL is hardly bread and butter work for most lawyers in private practice, they quickly accepted that specialist military legal advice was indeed required, and in due course a number of ALS lawyers deployed to the Gulf. Others remained in the United Kingdom, but were actively involved in a supporting role, e.g. in providing deploying troops with refresher

[8] His 1992 paper, 'Command and the Laws of Armed Conflict', for example, made a very positive impact on British Army thinking.

[9] Army Code 71130.

training in IHL, helping to man the legal cell at the Primary Joint Headquarters at High Wycombe and providing legal advice to the staff at Rollestone Camp on Salisbury Plains where a number of Iraqi military personnel were detained as prisoners of war. Some were sent to the headquarters already mentioned, but the majority accompanied 7th Armoured Brigade and 1st (UK) Armoured Division.[10]

While British commanders would have been unlikely to echo the claim made shortly after the war by General Colin Powell, then Chairman of the US Joint Chiefs of Staff, that 'Decisions were impacted by legal considerations at every level. Lawyers proved invaluable in the decision-making process',[11] it appears that the military lawyers at HQ British Forces Middle East were heavily involved in military planning in conjunction with their American counterparts. Those accompanying 7th Armoured Brigade and 1st (UK) Armoured Division, however, were relegated to the Divisional Administrative Area and to peripheral, though not unimportant, duties such as prisoner of war handling. British military lawyers were not yet familiar faces round the commander's planning table.

However, the picture back in the Ministry of Defence in London was refreshingly different. Within days of the invasion of Kuwait and the capture and transfer to Baghdad of the British military members of the Kuwait Liaison Team, ALS staff were requested to prepare a paper for the Foreign and Commonwealth Office on the status of the detainees in international law. In due course the paper was used by the UN Secretary-General to help negotiate their release.[12] During the following weeks and months ALS advice on law of war issues was much in demand and was treated with unprecedented respect, almost as if it carried some form of divine authority. Ministers were anxious to maintain the greatest possible contrast between Iraq's disregard of, and the Coalition's compliance with, IHL, and were insistent that there should be no hint of justifiable criticism of British actions.[13]

[10] See P. Rowe (ed.), *The Gulf War 1990–91 in International and English Law* (Routledge, 1993), p. 57.

[11] A. Roberts, 'The Laws of War in the 1990–91 Gulf Conflict', (1993) 18 *International Security* 134.

[12] Maj. Gen. A. P. V. Rogers OBE in 'Scales of Justice', at p. 164.

[13] To the extent that on one occasion a MOD minister telephoned the author personally for confirmation of the United Kingdom's duty to notify Baghdad that Iraqi prisoners of war were being held in Rollestone Camp on Salisbury Plain.

The liberation of Kuwait and the successful conclusion to Operation Granby, as the Gulf War campaign was known in British military circles, did not mean that all British military lawyers could return home. One was required to stay on to advise on Operation Haven, the deployment designed to protect the Kurds in Northern Iraq from Iraqi attack. Just as deployed British military lawyers were heavily outnumbered by their American counterparts during the Gulf War, so too the sole ALS officer based in Incerlik in Turkey, responsible for advising 5,000 British troops, found himself surrounded by thirteen US Service lawyers looking after only a slightly larger contingent of American service personnel.[14]

The Balkans

The demise of the Warsaw Pact was largely responsible for the major reorganization of the British Army in the early 1990s which led, in turn, to the closing of the two senior military headquarters in Germany, HQ British Army of the Rhine based in Rheindahlen and HQ 1st British Corps located in Bielefeld. The former was subsumed within the new Land Command, with its headquarters in the United Kingdom, while the latter was transformed into HQ Allied Command Europe Rapid Reaction Corps (HQ ARRC), which moved to Rheindahlen in 1995. HQ ARRC is a multinational headquarters, with seventeen contributing NATO nations. Given that the United Kingdom was from the outset the designated Framework Nation of the new headquarters, it might have been expected that lawyers would be conspicuous by their absence, but by the time the HQ ARRC was established the tide had at last turned, and a Legal Branch was included as one of the Central Staff branches, with direct access to the Commander and his Chief of Staff. Its role has always been 'to advise, and to organise training, on ... the law of armed conflict, rules of engagement, status of forces, host nation legal issues and international agreements'.[15]

HQ ARRC deployed to Bosnia with its military lawyers in December 1995, following the Dayton Peace Accord, but they were not the first ALS officers in the Balkans since the disintegration of the former republic of Yugoslavia. Already in January of that year, one had accompanied HQ BRITFOR (HQ British Forces), which formed an element of the United Nations Protection Force (UNPROFOR), the UN operation set up to

[14] Maj. (later Lt Col.) G. A. R. Adams, 'Operation Haven 1991', [1995] *Military Law Journal* 3.
[15] ARRC pamphlet, amended July 2002, published by Media Ops, HQ ARRC.

oversee the withdrawal of Yugoslav troops from Croatia, and to police other areas where tensions were high. That officer[16] was concerned primarily with the status of forces agreement (SOFA) submitted by the United Nations to the governments of both Croatia and Bosnia Herzegovina. In the event Bosnia Herzegovina signed in May 1993, whereas in the case of Croatia the agreement was still unsigned more than two years after British troops deployed there, thus giving rise to numerous problems. Another officer[17] deployed in early December 1995, as Legal Adviser to the Joint Military Commissions, which were set up under the Dayton Agreement to assist in implementing its provisions. Yet others were sent to the Balkans at various times to assist in the transition from UN to NATO operations,[18] and one went to The Hague to assist in the prosecution of suspected war criminals before the International Criminal Tribunal for the former Yugoslavia.[19]

Planning for Operation Joint Endeavour, the name given to HQ ARRC's deployment under the Dayton Agreement, had been going on for more than two years before December 1995, and had kept both the headquarters' legal officers[20] busy, particularly in the autumn of that year. Their work had involved drafting rules of engagement (ROE) and SOFAs, together with various annexes dealing with such issues as customs, border crossings, vehicles, airport and seaport fees and the environment. Following deployment it fell to them to negotiate the final versions of the SOFA and its annexes with the lawyers representing the various governments concerned, in consultation with other NATO legal staffs, notably those from the American military.

In due course further operational legal issues occupied a number of ALS officers, e.g. the NATO approach to the arrest and detention of indicted war criminals[21] and the impact of the Dayton Agreement at the

[16] Maj. (now Lt Col.) N. F. Jones – see 'Bosnia, UNPROFOR and the SOFA', [1997] *Military Law Journal* 51.

[17] Maj. (now Lt Col.) R. J. Batty – see 'The Military Lawyer to the Joint Military Commissions', [1997] *Military Law Journal* 71.

[18] Maj. (now Lt Col.) E. K. Peters – see 'The Transition from UN to NATO Operations', [1997] *Military Law Journal* 59.

[19] Maj. A. T. Cayley (now a Senior Trial Attorney in the Office of the Prosecutor) – see 'The International Criminal Tribunal for the Former Yugoslavia: a Miscellany of Legal Issues', [1997] *Military Law Journal* 33.

[20] Lt Col. (now Brig.) A. S. Paphiti and his assistant from the Dutch Army, Maj. (now Lt Col.) W. Baron.

[21] See Lt Col. D. G. Reddin MBE, 'Persons Indicted by the International Criminal Tribunal for the Former Yugoslavia: the Role of International Peace Enforcement/Peace Keeping Forces', [1997] *Military Law Journal* 42.

level below HQ ARRC, notably HQ Multi-National Division South West, one of the three divisions supporting the ARRC Commander.[22]

The challenges facing military lawyers reached new levels during Operation Joint Guardian, the Kosovo campaign which once again involved HQ ARRC. During late 1998, when Richard Holbrooke of the US State Department was engaging in shuttle diplomacy with Belgrade, it became increasingly clear that HQ ARRC would be returning to the Balkans. In early 1999, following UN Security Council Resolution 1244 and the subsequent signing of the Military Technical Agreement, HQ ARRC deployed, initially to Macedonia and then, as KFOR, into Kosovo. During the headquarters' eight months in Macedonia and Kosovo, and in the preceding period of intense planning activity, the legal staff were presented with innumerable complex legal problems, frequently dominated by the inevitable doubts about the legal status of forces which were engaged not in conventional war fighting, but in the implementation of the new concept of humanitarian intervention.[23]

The present position

Whereas there was not a single ALS post dedicated to either operational or international law twenty-five years ago, the position today is dramatically different. Twenty-two officers now deal exclusively with the legal aspects of military training, planning, exercises and operations, in a variety of formations both at home and overseas, (e.g. at Supreme Headquarters Allied Powers Europe in Belgium; Primary Joint Headquarters at Northwood, HQ ARRC in Rheindahlen; HQ 1 (UK) Armoured Division in Germany; HQ 3 (UK) Division at Bulford). A further two concentrate on developments in IHL and conduct weaponry reviews. Most of them are in permanent, established posts, but others are undertaking short-term commitments (e.g. Operation Agricola (Kosovo); Operation Palatine (Bosnia); Operation Silkman (Sierra Leone); Operation Veritas (Afghanistan)). Together they account for about one-quarter of the overall strength of ALS of just over one hundred regular officers and twelve part-time reservists.

22 See Lt Col. G. A. R. Adams, 'The Divisional Legal Adviser', [1997] *Military Law Journal* 84.

23 See Lt Col. (now Col.) J. N. Stythe, 'Operation Joint Guardian', [2000] *Military Law Journal* 10 and Lt Col. D. G. Reddin MBE and Capt. (now Maj.) B. A. Gray, 'Restoring the Rule of Law in Kosovo', [2000] *Military Law Journal* 87.

An operational law branch

The demand for legal advice in the field of operational and international law has developed to such an extent that it now justifies a dedicated organization within ALS. An Operational Law Cell consisting of two junior officers was set up in the early 1990s, but operations in the Balkans meant that both individuals were more or less continuously deployed in former Yugoslavia with British Army formations having no legal advisers of their own. In consequence the Cell was usually unmanned and unable to function as a focal point for operational law. Although the twenty-four legal officers currently specializing in this area of military law have since 1997 come under ALS's Advisory Branch, pressure of other work in ALS Advisory has largely prevented it from acting as a true focal point for operational matters. In consequence the experience gained on operations has not always been passed on to those dealing with developments in IHL, while the lack of structure has meant that the international law specialists have had an uphill task disseminating those developments to officers in the field. A further major problem until recently has been the Army's reluctance to provide an adequate establishment for operational lawyers, preferring instead to borrow officers in prosecuting or non-operational advisory posts. More often than not the result has been delays in prosecuting and advisory casework, and officers being deployed at short notice and without adequate time for operational refresher training. On their return the priority has been to reduce the inevitable backlog of discipline and administrative casework, and all too often post-operation reports have not been completed and lessons learned have been inadequately disseminated.

An Operational Law Branch has accordingly been approved, consisting of a headquarters element and an adequate pool of trained, deployable officers. The intention is that permanent formations should always have legal officers on their establishments. However, experience has shown that a reserve of operational lawyers is required, not only to relieve individuals who have been deployed for long periods, but also to support ad hoc formations. It will act as a focal point for, and will provide professional legal supervision over, all the ALS officers serving elsewhere in operational and international law appointments, thus providing the necessary structure. It will thus be responsible for:

- leading on developments in IHL for the Army and, as appropriate, the MOD, drawing on experience gained on operations and in turn disseminating developments in IHL;

- carrying out legal reviews of weaponry, in accordance with international obligations;
- training ALS officers and the wider Army in operational law;
- supporting operations of all types with suitably trained legal officers from its own pool of deployable officers;
- coordinating, and exercising functional command over, ALS officers occupying operational appointments in independent formations;
- advising on doctrine, targeting, rules of engagement, memoranda of understanding, status of forces, military aid to government departments etc.;
- liaising with other ALS lawyers, the MOD Legal Advisers, the Foreign and Commonwealth Office Legal Advisers, academics, non-governmental organizations such as the British Red Cross Society, the International Committee of the Red Cross, the International Institute of Humanitarian Law and the International Society for Military Law and the Law of War, and also military counterparts overseas.

Conclusion

In *International Law and Armed Conflict,* Hilaire and Nigel White drew attention to the duty placed on commanders by 1977 Additional Protocol I 'to ensure adequate training programmes and otherwise to act for the suppression of breaches'. In relation to the need for legal training in the armed forces, they went on to emphasize that:

> Beyond ... various levels of requisite general knowledge, specialist legal advice will be necessary and this will normally be supplied by a corps of specialist career officers operating at national level and attached to major command centres.[24]

While much remains to be done, it can fairly be said that IHL considerations are now integral to British Army operational planning, that the standard of IHL training is continuing to improve, and that specialist legal advice is not only available at the appropriate level, but is also actively sought and taken into account.

[24] McCoubrey and White, *International Law and Armed Conflict*, p. 336.

3

Reflections on the relationship between the duty to educate in humanitarian law and the absence of a defence of mistake of law in the Rome Statute of the International Criminal Court

NEIL BOISTER

> [A]nd from the time [Napoleon] took up the correct fencing attitude in Moscow, and instead of his opponent's rapier saw a cudgel raised above his head, he did not cease to complain to Kutuzov and to the Emperor Alexander that the war was being carried on contrary to all the rules, as if there were rules for killing people.
>
> Tolstoy, *War and Peace*, Book 14, *Borodino* (Wordsworth, 1993), Ch. 1, p. 812

Introduction

Tolstoy's ignorance of the laws of war is probably feigned, rather than deliberate; his main thrust is at the irony of civilizing the barbaric practice of war, but more importantly for the purposes of this chapter, he also points to the possibility that many who enter combat are not aware of any legal restraint upon their actions. Today, education of potential combatants in the rules of international humanitarian law (IHL) is one of the principal duties of a state party to the Geneva Conventions. The availability and quality of this education remains, however, in doubt. Against this background the exclusion by the states parties to the Rome Statute of the International Criminal Court (ICC)[1] of all but a very narrow defence of ignorance or mistake of law in the Statute raises questions of adherence to the principle of legality. This chapter explores the relationship between this narrow defence and

[1] Rome Statute of the International Criminal Court, UN Doc. A/CONF. 183/9, (1998) 37 *International Legal Materials* 999.

the poor quality of education of combatants in IHL that currently pertains in many parts of the world. It concludes that international society, intent upon more effective prosecution of breaches of IHL through an international court, has been unwilling to fully embrace the logic of subjective fault. This cannot be reconciled with the acknowledged ineffectiveness of the dissemination of IHL, and the danger exists of convictions by the ICC of individuals who did not realize what they were doing was unlawful. The broader relevance is obvious: individual criminal responsibility for breaches of the rules of IHL presupposes an opportunity for knowing these rules. The unwillingness of international legislators to recognize that in certain situations no such opportunity may exist raises questions not about international humanitarian law, but about the validity of the system of international criminal law.

The duty to educate

Hilaire McCoubrey argued that the virtues of prospective implementation of IHL outweighed those of retrospective enforcement of this law through international criminal law. He noted that:

> criminal jurisprudence is, as even the coercively focused classical positivist Jeremy Bentham conceded, by definition a secondary office of law in general. It may readily be suggested that the primary endeavours of law in responding to socially destructive conduct are those of definition and aversion rather than ex post facto penalisation. The punishment of the war criminal is at best vicarious satisfaction to the victim of the war crime which has been perpetrated, better far that it should not be perpetrated at all.[2]

And further that:

> [t]he fundamental aim of international humanitarian law is to secure humane treatment for the victims of armed conflict and not the detection, trial and punishment of war criminals. Even a 'successful' war crimes trial is already a confession of failure, valuable as it might be as an example.[3]

[2] H. McCoubrey, 'War Crimes Jurisdiction and a Permanent International Criminal Court: Advantages and Difficulties', (1998) 3 *Journal of Armed Conflict Law* 9. Hilaire was an active member of the British Red Cross, particularly interested in the dissemination of IHL.

[3] H. McCoubrey, *International Humanitarian Law: Modern Developments in the Limitation of Warfare* (2nd edn, Dartmouth, 1998), p. 205.

Hilaire viewed the application of international criminal law as a failure to secure the effective implementation of international humanitarian law. While no amount of education will prevent the commission of some offences, securing effective implementation of IHL does require the adequate training of all potential combatants in IHL, and the political will to encourage application.

Effective prevention of violations of IHL requires that the primary agency for implementation must be the combatants themselves. Their instruction and education in the laws of war is a necessary condition for the establishment of a sense of legal obligation that will serve to prevent inhumane treatment and behaviour. How, for example, will a combatant recognize the illegality of an order to kill prisoners of war, if he has not been informed of the rule that prisoners are protected? And what if the rules are not widely disseminated? Reruns of 'The Great Escape' cannot be relied upon to get the information across. The dissemination of the laws of war is one of the most important tasks of IHL.[4] Hence we have provisions such as Article 83 of Additional Protocol I,[5] entitled 'Dissemination', which reads:

> 1. The High Contracting Parties undertake, in time of peace as in time of armed conflict, to disseminate the Conventions and this Protocol as widely as possible in their respective countries and, in particular, to include the study thereof in their programmes of military instruction and to encourage the study thereof by the civilian population, so that those instruments may become known to the armed forces and to the civilian population.

Common Article 47/48/127/144 of the Geneva Conventions[6] provides that parties undertake, in time of peace and time of war, to disseminate

[4] See McCoubrey, *International Humanitarian Law* (2nd edn); L. C. Green, 'The Man in the Field and the Maxim *Ignorantia Juris non Excusat*', in L. C. Green, *Essays on the Modern Law of War* (2nd edn, Transnational Publishers, 1999), p. 227.

[5] 1977 Geneva Protocol I Additional to the Geneva Conventions of 12 August 1949, and Relating to the Protection of Victims of International Armed Conflicts (1979) 1125 UNTS 3.

[6] Geneva Convention I for the Amelioration of the Condition of the Wounded and Sick in Armed Forces in the Field, Geneva, 12 August 1949 (1949) 75 UNTS 31; Geneva Convention II for the Amelioration of the Condition of Wounded, Sick and Shipwrecked Members of Armed Forces at Sea, Geneva, 12 August 1949 (1950) 75 UNTS 85; Geneva Convention III Relative to the Treatment of Prisoners of War, Geneva, 12 August 1949 (1950) 75 UNTS 135; Geneva Convention IV Relative to the Protection of Civilian Persons in Time of War, Geneva, 12 August 1949 (1950) 75 UNTS 287.

the texts of the Conventions and to include these texts in a programme of military and civil instruction, with the general purpose of educating the entire population, but in particular the military, medical personnel and chaplains. Article 19 of Protocol II[7] simply states that this Protocol shall be disseminated as widely as possible. The status of the duty to educate must now, given the almost universal adherence to the Conventions, be uncontroversial. Dissemination of IHL to combatants is usually achieved by the military educating ordinary soldiers in the basic rules and by providing them with easily accessible points of reference (e.g. the pocket cards used during the Gulf War), by providing commanders and staff officers with manuals written in a non-legal way, and by educating military legal advisers to, as stated in Article 82 of Protocol I, advise commanders on:

(a) the appropriate level of application of the Conventions and this Protocol; and
(b) the appropriate instruction to be given to armed forces on this subject.

The former function involves giving advice on the legality of a proposed action and particularly by briefing commanders about potential legal problems that others may not recognize.

All of this will take place in a fairly ideal situation. However, while states have shown their willingness formally to subscribe to the Conventions themselves – almost every state is party to the Geneva Conventions, while the Protocols are only slightly less popular – they are not as willing to implement them in practice. In addition to the efforts of the armed forces of the states parties, much effort is put into education by the International Committee of the Red Cross (ICRC), by national Red Cross and Red Crescent societies, by humanitarian organizations, through university courses, in civil awareness programmes, and so forth. But education is patchy. Sandoz notes that in respect of organized military structures:

> In recent years the ICRC has made considerable efforts to make international humanitarian law better known. The main objective of those efforts is naturally to spread knowledge of the law among those who are primarily required to comply with its provisions, namely members of the

[7] 1977 Geneva Protocol II Additional to the Geneva Conventions of 12 August 1949, and Relating to the Protection of Victims of Non-International Armed Conflicts (1979) 1125 UNTS 609.

> armed forces. Teaching of the law has often been neglected or taken lightly; if it is to be done efficiently, it must become an integral part of military instruction and be taken seriously by the military hierarchy from top to bottom.[8]

The problems associated with the knowledge of IHL become acute in conflicts where irregular groups participate, particularly non-international armed conflicts. Whatever the *de jure* position is in international law, a party to the conflict may not in fact undertake the task of dissemination of the existing rules. As Sandoz puts it:

> The humanitarian organizations will therefore have to go on dealing with conflicts of great diversity and complexity in which structured armed forces, be they governmental, opposition or international (particularly UN troops), will coexist with disorganized forces, which may be out of control or have no other objective than the immediate satisfaction of individual needs.[9]

In these more chaotic situations, where organizations that can be held responsible for education and chains of command that can make possible education are difficult to identify, to contact and to convert to humanitarian ways, education in IHL becomes difficult. Sandoz continues:

> [A] dialogue with parties other than the organized armed forces can usually take place only after the conflict has broken out, since it is in times of conflict that such irregular groups are formed. Nonetheless, it can still have a preventive function because many conflicts drag on and on. As mentioned earlier, however, the dialogue is extremely difficult, if not impossible, in some particularly chaotic contexts.[10]

The issue of implementation comes down to a question of the level of awareness of IHL among the members of armed forces involved in any particular armed conflict. The likelihood of combatants entering the field of combat unsure of the basic rules of IHL is high, and there are almost certainly going to be situations before the court where the defendants were unaware of the more technical rules.

[8] Y. Sandoz, 'Implementation of International Humanitarian Law: Challenges and New Approaches', paper given to the Third International Security Forum, Networking the Security Community in the Information Age, 19–21 October 1998, Zurich, Switzerland, available at www.icrc.org/Web/eng/siteeng0.nsf/iwpList113/FF34D2DCD0B9D025C1256B66005C3262 (visited 10 November 2004).

[9] *Ibid.* [10] *Ibid.*

Mistake of law in the Rome Statute

The states parties to the Rome Statute of the International Criminal Court have in terms of Article 30 embraced a subjective test for the mental element of criminal responsibility in respect of the material elements of the crimes to be prosecuted before the court. This implies that mistake of fact will be a good defence, and somewhat redundantly because such a mistake is a denial of intent or of knowledge or both in terms of Article 30,[11] it has by popular demand during the negotiation of the Rome Statute been made an explicit defence in terms of Article 32. Nevertheless, against the background of the likelihood that many combatants will enter armed conflicts with little or no knowledge of the rules of IHL, the states parties have also adopted in Article 32 the position that ignorance or mistake of law is no excuse.

The maxim *ignorantia lex non excusat*[12] (ignorance of the law is no excuse) has a long history, and according to Cassese its application to international crimes prior to the adoption of the Rome Statute seemed fairly settled.[13] This probably arises from the early dominance of the common law view that everyone is presumed to know of the prohibition of very serious offences. As Wharton says, '[t]he presumption of knowledge of the unlawfulness of crimes *mala in se* is not limited by state boundaries. The unlawfulness of such crime is assumed wherever civilization exists.'[14] Saland notes that one of the arguments made at the Rome Conference was that 'it was hard to conceive of a situation of mistake of law, given the nature of the crimes within the jurisdiction of the court'.[15]

[11] This appeared to be accepted by the Preparatory Committee, 'Draft Statute and Draft Final Act', p. 67, note 21, reproduced in M. C. Bassiouni (ed.), *The Statute of the International Criminal Court: A Documentary History* (Transnational Publishers, 1998), p. 145. See also R. Clark, 'The Mental Element in International Criminal Law: The Rome Statute of the International Criminal Court and the Elements of Offences', (2002) 12 *Criminal Law Forum* 291 at p. 308 (recording that he was among those who thought Article 32 unnecessary); A. Eser, 'Mental Elements: Mistake of Fact and Mistake of Law', in A. Cassese, P. Gaeta and J. R. W. D. Jones (eds.), *The Rome Statute of the International Criminal Court: A Commentary* (Oxford University Press, 2002), pp. 889–948 at p. 935 (pointing out that it would have been more useful if it had given details of when a mistake actually negated the mental element).

[12] Also know as *ignorantia iuris neminem excusat* or *error iuris nocet*.

[13] See A. Cassese, 'The Statute of the International Criminal Court: Some Preliminary Reflections', (1999) 10 *European Journal of International Law* 153 at p. 155.

[14] C. E. Torcia, *Wharton's Criminal Law* (15th edn, West, 1993), s. 25.

[15] P. Saland, 'International Criminal Law Principles', in R. S. Lee (ed.), *The International Criminal Court: The Making of the Rome Statute* (Kluwer, 1999), pp. 189–216 at p. 210.

But can it be fairly assumed that all those who may enter combat in 'civilized' states know all of the rules, and what about those in 'uncivilized' states, or states that have failed?

These questions appear not to have troubled many of the authors of the Rome Statute. The view that the serious crimes within the jurisdiction of the ICC are notorious appears to have dovetailed with a general reluctance to allow a defence of mistake of law. The Rome Statute's approach to mistake of law is broadly based on current common law practice.[16] It places in some difficulty the accused who kills a protected person:

(a) ignorant of the existence of a particular prohibition in international law or mistaken as to one or more of its elements/legal referents; or
(b) thinking in his evaluation that the person is not protected by international law when in fact he is; or
(c) thinking that he has a justification, such as military necessity, or an excuse, such as official capacity,[17] which does not exist in international law; or
(d) thinking that he has the factual basis for a justification such as self-defence, or an excuse, such as duress,[18] when he does not.[19]

These different types of mistake appear to be mistakes of a normative kind, mistakes of law, and are apparently not exculpatory under the Rome Statute. Article 32(2) reads:

> A mistake of law as to whether a particular type of conduct is a crime within the jurisdiction of the Court shall not be a ground for excluding criminal responsibility. A mistake of law may, however, be a ground for excluding criminal responsibility if it negates the mental element required by such a crime, or as provided for in Article 33.

[16] See A. Ashworth, *Principles of Criminal Law* (3rd edn, Oxford University Press, 1999), pp. 243–8.

[17] Official capacity does serve as a jurisdictional bar, but not as an excuse.

[18] Duress is only a partial excuse, see *Prosecutor* v. *Erdemović* (Case No. IT–96–22–T), 29 November 1996 (1998) 108 ILR 180.

[19] For a more complete list of evaluative mistakes see Eser, 'Mental Elements', pp. 936–7. For general discussion see G. Fletcher, *Rethinking Criminal Law* (Oxford University Press, 2000), pp. 684–5; and G. Fletcher, *Basic Concepts of Criminal Law* (Oxford University Press, 1998), pp. 155–67. It is worth noting in respect of (c) that official capacity does serve as a jurisdictional bar, while in respect of (d) that duress is only a partial excuse, see *Prosecutor* v. *Erdemović*.

Type (a) mistakes then, mistakes of law of the most simple kind, ignorance of or mistake in respect of the particular prohibition or its elements, are unacceptable. So too type (c) mistakes, simple errors as to the existence of justifications and excuses that do not exist. But Article 32(2) contains two exceptions where mistakes of law do exclude criminal responsibility.

The first is where they negate the mental element required for criminal liability. Clark submits that this does not refer to the aforementioned type (a) mistakes about the essential existence of a proscription – pure ignorance, for example, of the criminal prohibition against killing someone *hors de combat* is not such a mistake.[20] In this he must be correct, given Article 32(2)'s general exclusion. However, he goes further and argues that this exception is concerned with mistakes as to collateral legal issues that relate to the factual circumstances necessary to establish liability. In other words, the mistake is a type (b) mistake; it is normative or evaluative but it results in a factual error. Thus, an accused may make an exculpatory mistake of fact about the law, for example, as to a prisoner's POW status and force them to serve in hostile forces – a war crime.[21] The problem here is that the term 'may' implies that the ICC has discretion to acquit, and Clark recognizes that in his reading of the provisions 'may' will have to be read as 'must'. To recast mistakes of law as mistakes of fact in this orthodox common law way is difficult enough, but it is very difficult to take this analysis further and argue that it allows type (d) mistakes, defences of putative justification or excuse. This is mainly because the accused is not negating the mental element as set out in Article 30(1), which relates only to the material element of the offences and not to the absence of justification or excuse. Moreover, it does not square with the specific inclusion of a putative defence of superior orders in Articles 32(2) and 33.[22]

The second exception is where the individual accused has erroneously assessed the lawfulness of an order. Article 33 expands on this exception. It reads:

> 1. The fact that a crime within the jurisdiction of the Court has been committed by a person pursuant to an order of a Government or of a superior, whether military or civilian, shall not relieve that person of criminal responsibility unless:

[20] Clark, 'The Mental Element in International Criminal Law', p. 311.
[21] Article 89(2)(a)(v) of the Rome Statute.
[22] See Chapter 4 by Robert Cryer.

a. The person was under a legal obligation to obey orders of the Government or the superior in question;
b. The person did not know that the order was unlawful; and
c. The order was not manifestly unlawful.

2. For the purposes of this Article, orders to commit genocide or crimes against humanity are manifestly unlawful.

Article 33 is a difficult provision which has been subject to much criticism.[23] It is a compromise between the American position that superior orders is a substantive defence per se and the UK/New Zealand/German position that superior orders goes to the mental element of liability. Article 33 is only of interest here to the extent that it serves as an exception to Article 32(2)'s blanket adoption of the maxim that ignorance of the law does not excuse. It is a specific and restricted form of a type (d) defence. It does not provide an accused with an entirely subjective mistake of superior orders defence because objective factors such as the legal obligation and manifest illegality must also be established.[24] This serves to illustrate the reluctance of the delegates at the conference in Rome to embrace even a cut-down version of mistake of law.

Objections to and evasions of the existing position in respect of mistake of law under the Rome Statute

The central objection to Article 32(2) is that it is too narrow from the point of view of a subjective theory of criminal liability. Mistakes of types (a), (b) and (d), mistakes of an evaluative kind that do not result in a factual error negating intention or some other relevant form of advertence in respect of the elements of the offence, are not exculpatory. Efforts were made in the preparation of the Rome Statute to include even a conditional mistake of law defence of the kind contained in the Model Penal Code (MPC)[25] but they failed.[26] In s. 2.04(3) of the MPC, pure ignorance of the law was admitted as possibly exculpatory, providing it met certain conditions (the burden of persuasion was also reversed). It reads:

[23] See K. Ambos, 'General Principles of the Rome Statute', (1999) 10 *Criminal Law Forum* 1 at pp. 30–1.

[24] Unless the various parts are read disjunctively, as Clark suggests they should be. He recognizes that if this is so, Article 33(1)(b) may get close to providing a limited defence of mistake of law akin to s. 2.04(3) MPC for those acting under orders. Clark, 'The Mental Element in International Criminal Law', p. 333, notes 138 and 140.

[25] Adopted at the AGM of the American Law Institute, 1961.

[26] See Eser, 'Mental Elements', pp. 896–8.

> A belief that conduct does not legally constitute an offence is a defence to a prosecution based upon such conduct when:
>
> a. the statute or other enactment defining the offence is not known to the actor and has not been published or otherwise reasonably made available prior to the conduct alleged; or
>
> b. he acts on a reasonable reliance on an official statement of the law, afterward determined to be invalid or erroneous, contained in (i) a statute or other enactment; (ii) a judicial decision, opinion or judgment; (iii) an administrative body or grant of permission; or (iv) an official interpretation of the public officer or body charged with responsibility for the interpretation, administration or enforcement of the law defining the offence.

Ambos points to the comparative weakness of Article 32(2). He notes that:

> it does not cover all possible cases where, for considerations of justice, error ought to be taken into account as a defence. Article 33 is similar to § 2.04 Model Penal Code (MPC) in that it focuses on the mental element as the determining factor of the relevance or ignorance of mistake. It is however, narrower than the MPC's provision since it recognizes a mistaken belief in the legality of one's conduct only in the case of a superior order and not, as is the case in § 2.04(3) MPC, in the case of ignorance of statute law or of acting in reasonable reliance upon official statements of the law. Although the MPC follows a practical, non-principled approach, it recognizes at least that the reference to the mental element does not cover all possible cases. Nevertheless, both the MPC and the Rome Statute fall short, in that they do not contemplate all possible mistakes and thus do not allow the judges to find dogmatically correct and just solutions.[27]

Ambos takes the subjective test for culpability seriously, and is thus dissatisfied with the Rome Statute and the MPC; dogma demands that subjective mistakes of law should be exculpatory, and so does justice. Ambos gives as an example the position of the accused in *Erdemović*,[28] who attempted unsuccessfully to convince the Appeals Chamber of the International Criminal Tribunal for the former Yugoslavia (ICTY) that duress was a complete defence in international law. For Ambos, the court should have recognized duress as a complete defence in international law,[29] but more than that, if Erdemović had failed to establish his defence on objective grounds, the court should also have enquired as to whether he

[27] Ambos, 'General Principles of the Rome Statute', p. 29.
[28] *Prosecutor* v. *Erdemovic*, above n. 18.
[29] Ambos, 'General Principles of the Rome Statute', p. 28.

mistakenly believed he was acting under duress and if so, excused him.[30] Thus, Ambos supports a defence of putative duress, which in his view eliminates the blameworthiness or culpability of the conduct in question, as would putative self-defence, necessity, consent and so forth. By extension, he appears to support a general defence based on type (d) mistakes. For Ambos, the solution is for the ICC to have recourse to the general principles of national law in terms of Article 21(1)(c), in order to get around the fact that Article 32(2) does not recognize all possible cases of mistake of law.[31]

Triffterer appears to come to the same conclusion by close analysis of Article 32(2).[32] His argument is that the first sentence of Article 32(2) is clear. Where there is a mistake about the existence of a crime within the jurisdiction of the ICC (i.e. type (a) mistakes), it shall not be exculpatory. However, the second sentence implies some discretion through the use of the word 'may', and in the absence of guidance from the *travaux*[33] he suggests that this means that the ICC has the discretion to treat mistakes based on incorrect legal evaluations as exculpatory (he appears to mean both type (b) and (d) mistakes), provided they are unavoidable. Clark, who does not find this view compelling, notes that the notion of unavoidable mistakes was dropped during the drafting process, but that Triffterer's argument relies on the word 'may' to reintroduce it.[34]

Eser is of much the same view as Triffterer. He argues that 'may' refers to exclusion of criminal responsibility and not just negation of the mental element, and that while such exclusion is impossible in respect of the mistakes of law covered by the first sentence of Article 32(2), the 'admissibility of mistakes of law in terms of sentence (2) was intended perhaps to be limited, and therefore subjected to the discretionary non-exclusion of criminal responsibility by the Court'.[35] He further argues that the Rome Statute does not pay any attention to the unavoidability of mistake, contrary to the approach in provisions such as s. 2.04(3) of the MPC, and this absence of flexibility is made up for by the granting of discretion to the ICC with regard to the exclusion of criminal responsibility.

30 *Ibid.*, p. 30. 31 *Ibid.*, p. 30.

32 O. Triffterer, *Commentary on the Rome Statute of the International Criminal Court* (Nomos, 1999), pp. 561–71.

33 For the drafting history see W. Schabas, 'General Principles of Criminal Law', (1998) 4 *European Journal of Crime, Criminal Law and Criminal Justice* 84.

34 Clark, 'The Mental Element in International Criminal Law', p. 312.

35 Eser, 'Mental Elements', p. 942.

Clark believes that the ICC will have to resolve the problem. It seems fairly clear that Article 32(2) leaves room for judicial manoeuvre with respect to the normative implications of the material elements of the crimes within the court's jurisdiction (type (c) mistakes). Putative justifications or excuses (type (d) mistakes) are much more controversial,[36] and mistakes as to the existence of justifications and excuses which do not in fact exist (type (b) mistakes) and ignorance of the prohibition per se (type (a) mistakes) are definitely excluded, despite the fact that these kinds of mistake are considered by many national jurisdictions to be exculpatory in special circumstances.[37]

Mistakes of law under the Rome Statute in theoretical perspective

Eser, putting a positive gloss on Article 32(2), a gloss it may not bear, calls it a 'breakthrough to a more comprehensive understanding of culpability which doesn't fully equate to the psychological-mental elements of intent or knowledge but also requires some sort of normative blameworthiness'.[38] The break is from common law notions of the mental element of liability based on the psychological theory of an act. Yet he notes that Article 32(2) is inconsistent with a fully developed notion of responsibility in terms of Article 30(1), in that a mistake of law may not necessarily be exculpatory.[39] He records the disquiet of some states parties at the Rome Statute's adoption of the maxim that ignorance of the law does not excuse. Somewhat oddly, considering his earlier enthusiasm for Article 32(2), he notes that:

> by almost completely closing the door to mistake of law in requiring legal ignorance to nullify a mental element essentially focused on facts, the Rome Statute disregards growing sensitivity to the principle of culpability, particularly with regard to consciousness of unlawfulness (as distinct from and in addition to the fact-oriented intention).[40]

The arguments of Ambos, Triffterer and Eser reflect the scholarship of the advanced civilian legal systems, and in particular German criminal law. The once popular German *Vorsatztheorie* considered consciousness

[36] See *ibid.*, p. 944.
[37] Article 14 of the Spanish Codigo Penal; Articles 122–3 French Code Penal; s. 17 German Strafgesetzbuch. Section 9 of the Austrian Strafgesetzbuch is to much the same effect.
[38] Eser, 'Mental Elements', p. 891.
[39] *Ibid.*, p. 892. [40] *Ibid.*, p. 935.

of unlawfulness to be a part of intention. The more recent *Schuldtheorie* includes, within a separate element of culpability, a normative element; even in the presence of intention in respect of conduct, an accused may still not be considered culpable if he did not appreciate the unlawfulness of his action and such ignorance was unavoidable.[41] It is unnecessary to debate the relative merits of either theory here. All we are concerned with are two simple propositions: the concept of culpability entails avoidable ignorance of the law, and attribution based on culpability is impossible if such ignorance is unavoidable. As Artz points out, 'no plausible theory of criminal sanctions can explain why a person who does not know and cannot know that he is breaking the law should be punished'.[42]

In a Hartian sense, legal obligation flows from the concept that legal rules have an internal aspect rather than simply being Austinian commands.[43] It is the result of an internal appreciation by the individual subjects of laws that these laws are rules subject to significant social pressures and serving important social functions, even contrary to the wishes of the individual to whom they apply. This normative discourse requires an identifiable cognitive and volitional reality in the population engaged in it. In other words, the subjects of law must have the capacity to understand and choose to accept law. Without such capacity, law has no internal aspect and it loses its authority – its legal nature. What of the combatant who does not realize that his attack upon civilians is unlawful in international law? Can we safely assume that all rules of international humanitarian law have an internal aspect for all individuals? Hart's notion that in complex societies only officials need have a detailed understanding of rules is of no real use here. International society is, in Hart's terms, a primitive society and assumptions about the dissemination of rules, particularly to those quasi-subjects of international law, individuals, are unsafe. This is particularly so where there is no functional state or organ that has assumed responsibility for the dissemination of laws. In such situations it becomes unsafe to assume a link between law, obligation and punishment. As A. T. H. Smith puts it:

[41] *Ibid.*, pp. 904, 910, note 102.
[42] G. Artz, 'The Problem of Mistake of Law', in A. Eser and G. Fletcher (eds.), *Justification and Excuse: Comparative Perspectives* (Max Planck Institute, 1987), vol. II, p. 1025 at p. 1049.
[43] H. L. A. Hart, *The Concept of Law* (Clarendon Press, 1961), pp. 84–5.

> Persons who are subject to a legal regime must have both the capacity and the fair opportunity to make their behaviour conform to the law's demands, since they cannot logically otherwise behave in a culpable way. Where a person believes or assumes that his conduct was lawful, has no reason to suppose that what he was doing was against the law and no reason to know that there was a relevant applicable law, he does not have a fair opportunity.[44]

Ashworth makes the point that individual fairness demands the recognition of ignorance of or mistake of law as an excuse out of respect for individual autonomy.[45] He dismisses the counter-arguments based on social welfare.[46] The argument that allowing it as an excuse will undermine law enforcement by discouraging knowledge of the law merely establishes that ignorance of the law is harmful, not wrong, and is not borne out by experience in civilian states. The argument that judging accused on their view of the law contradicts the essential objectivity of the legal system is also dismissed by Ashworth, because the law remains unchanged by the effects of the accused's view. Ashworth does, however, justify a partial rejection of ignorance or mistake as an excuse on the basis of the duty of good citizenship, to place individuals in a society where it is reasonable to expect them to acquaint themselves with the law.[47] He would admit only reasonable mistakes; the uncertainty of the law, and the possibility that the state may have failed in its duty to make the offence known and knowable, mitigate against an absolute duty on citizens to acquaint themselves with the law.

Making presumptions about what good citizens should know about international law is more difficult in international society than within a state, given the weakness of international society and the uncertain place of individuals within that society, the uncertainty of IHL, and the failure of states and other belligerents to make it known to combatants. Nevertheless, Ashworth's approach does have the virtue of recognizing that there are situations where it is difficult for combatants to distinguish what is unlawful. Application of individual criminal responsibility under international law without recognition of the defence of mistake of law in principle and without pre-existing domestic instruction of the laws violated, especially to lower

[44] A. T. H. Smith, 'Error and Mistake of Law', in Eser and Fletcher, *Justification and Excuse*, vol. II, p. 1075 at p. 1122.

[45] Ashworth, *Principles of Criminal Law*, pp. 243–5.

[46] *Ibid.*, p. 244. [47] *Ibid.*, p. 245.

ranking individuals, ignores the dismal reality of the legal situation in many states.[48] Moreover, in other forms of international penal law, a stricter adherence to the principle of legality still holds sway. For example, mistake of law is implicit in international legal assistance in the requirement of double criminality. Gilbert notes that the fact that a fugitive is not a resident of the requesting state and does not know the particular law provides the only justification for double criminality.[49] In contrast, it appears that natural law thinking underpins international criminal law *stricto sensu*, because it applies a normative standard regardless of individual subjective comprehension. There is, as noted, a tendency to the view that these offences are so serious that it is difficult to accept that an accused may not have known that they were unlawful.

The civilian position has passed from theory into practice, and the recognition of this defence has not led to a breakdown of law and order in the countries in which it is recognized.[50] Nevertheless, it stands in marked contrast to the sterile common law position where, despite strong opposition from scholars,[51] it is still considered sound that ignorance of the law is no excuse, and marginal cases that produce irritating results are dealt with as mistakes of fact. The apparent reconciliation of irreconcilable common law and civilian views of culpability at the Rome Conference fails to disguise the fact that the common law view on ignorance or mistake of law predominates.[52] In result, international criminal law has, like the common law, become stuck in the initial phases of doctrinal development in the field of mistake of law.[53]

Conclusion

Article 32(2) may be simply a holding operation. Evasions of its exclusion of mistakes of law may be conjured from its confusing language.

[48] This point was made in respect of the German Federal Court's application of international standards in the International Covenant on Civil and Political Rights to the actions of East German border guards accused of homicide of individuals leaving the GDR, see M. Herdegen, 'Unjust Laws, Human Rights, and the German Constitution: Germany's Recent Confrontation with the Past', (1995) 32 *Columbia Journal of Transnational Law* 591 at p. 600.

[49] G. Gilbert, *Transnational Fugitive Offenders in International Law* (Kluwer, 1998), p. 105.

[50] Artz, 'The Problem of Mistake of Law', p. 1053.

[51] See Smith, 'Error and Mistake of Law', p. 1078 and authorities cited therein.

[52] Eser, 'Mental Elements', p. 892.

[53] See Artz, 'The Problem of Mistake of Law', p. 1028.

Moreover, Article 78(1) does, by implication, allow ignorance of the law to be taken into account in determining sentence. It seems, however, that eventually the court's own experience will consign *ignorantia lex non excusat* to history. Article 32(2) constrains the ability of the ICC to orient culpability to the perpetrator's capacity to realize the unlawfulness of his actions. As Eser notes:

> Even in recognizing the fact that international crimes, as in general of the gravest nature, are universally known as unlawful and highly reprehensible, there may be situations in which the perpetrator is without fault unaware of the criminal character of his conduct. The more the principle of culpability is recognized as an essential requirement of criminal responsibility, the less an international penal code can afford, particularly if it wishes to function as a model of enlightened criminal law, to completely ignore lack of culpability *by unavoidable mistake of prohibition.* As the recognition of such a ground for excluding criminal responsibility would function in favour of the perpetrator, it could be introduced and applied by the Court without violating the principle *nullem crimen sine lege* (Article 22 of the ICC Statute).[54]

There are those who will complain that such an approach will provide a further loophole in an already weak system of criminal responsibility. For the most part, however, conduct that is likely to draw a response from prosecuting authorities is obviously criminal and it will be very difficult for individuals to sustain a *bona fide* denial that they knew that conduct was unlawful. The normative judgment that must have been exercised would not be that of the trained lawyers; as Eser puts it, all that is required is a 'parallel evaluation in the layman's sphere'.[55] Moreover, not all breaches of IHL are criminal. General prohibitions are reasonably well-known because they are usually enforced through other systems of law such as constitutional rights and ordinary domestic criminal law, and it is the more formal technical rules which are (i) unlikely to be the subject of any training and (ii) have no criminal sanction for their breach.

At present, however, technical rules that do carry individual criminal responsibility find themselves in the borderland of incomprehension and penal responsibility, an unhealthy and 'primitive' mix. Currently in international criminal law, should does not imply could, what has to be

[54] Eser, 'Mental Elements', pp. 945–6 (emphasis in the original).
[55] *Ibid.*, p. 939.

done may not be possible, it is enough that there are laws to consult once one gets to the ICC. International criminal law can only serve to guide conduct if international society is capable of ensuring that people actually know what is required of them. This is not the case at present, which leads us back to McCoubrey's point that preventive action in this case in the form of education must remain the priority.

4

Superior orders and the International Criminal Court

ROBERT CRYER

Introduction

I would like to start by violating at least one rule of traditional legal writing. That rule is that, in such writing, personal matters should not be discussed. I will begin with my personal recollection of Hilaire McCoubrey. We were both at Cambridge University (his *alma mater*) in the summer of 1997, attending a British Red Cross course on international humanitarian law. I was a PhD student in Nottingham, he was teaching the course in Cambridge.[1] It was a beautiful evening, and we had finished for the day. Hilaire had been teaching the protection of the wounded, sick and shipwrecked.[2] Owing to the felicitous weather, he and a few others (myself included) repaired to a local pub overlooking the river Cam. There we watched the sun set, refreshed ourselves, and talked at length over one of Hilaire's favourite subjects, the Nuremberg and Tokyo International Military Tribunals (IMTs), a subject about which he had prodigious knowledge and understanding. The fond memory I have of that evening, although now tinged with sadness, is how I like to remember Hilaire.

Thanks are owed to Neil Boister for comments on an earlier draft. I have also benefited from discussions with Tony Rogers and Charles Garraway, who have patiently explained a number of issues to me. Of course, none of the above can be held responsible for errors in what follows.

[1] Hilaire McCoubrey was very active in the British Red Cross, and was a stalwart of their campaigns to disseminate international humanitarian law (IHL). As was clear in his writings, he believed strongly that prevention of violations of IHL was better than punishment, as then the harm was already done, see, for example, H. McCoubrey, 'War Crimes Jurisdiction and a Permanent International Criminal Court: Advantages and Difficulties', (1998) 3 *Journal of Armed Conflict Law* 9 at pp. 9–10.

[2] Hilaire's interest in naval matters was well known, although it was more a hobby than an academic pursuit for him. For occasional glimpses of this interest in his work, see McCoubrey, 'War Crimes', p. 11; H. McCoubrey, *International Humanitarian Law* (2nd edn, Dartmouth, 1998), pp. 113–32 and 223–6.

One of the issues raised at the Nuremberg IMT, superior orders, also provides the subject matter for my contribution to this volume. The defence of obedience to orders has been the subject of considerable attention by international lawyers.[3] Hilaire put in his 'two pennyworths' late in his life.[4] However, while some constitutional lawyers have discussed superior orders,[5] domestic criminal lawyers have not on the whole spent much time on the defence (though it should be mentioned that Dinstein's work is sophisticated from a criminal law point of view).[6] This may be because of its somewhat limited ambit in domestic criminal systems, particularly in peacetime. The same is not the case in trials of international crimes, where the plea of superior orders has been a frequent one throughout history. The plea of obedience to superior orders received an early airing in 1474, in the trial of Peter von Hagenbach which, although not international in the modern sense, 'was at least functionally transnational'.[7] Claims of superior orders were not novel then,[8] and they are a frequent aspect of trials of international crimes now. In this chapter I will attempt to cast a little light on this perennial plea not only from the point of view of international law, but also from that of criminal law and doctrine.

The history of the defence

As mentioned above, the defence has a considerable historical pedigree. For brevity's sake we will begin in the middle of the twentieth century, with the Nuremberg and Tokyo IMTs.[9] Despite the previous debates on

[3] See, for example, Y. Dinstein, *The Defence of 'Obedience to Superior Orders' in International Law* (Sijthoff, 1965); L. C. Green, *Superior Orders in National and International Law* (Sijthoff, 1976).

[4] H. McCoubrey, 'From Nuremberg to Rome: Restoring the Defence of Superior Orders', (2001) 50 *International and Comparative Law Quarterly* 386. The article was one of two articles Hilaire submitted to journals just before his death, and which were published posthumously. The other was H. McCoubrey, 'Protection of Creed and Opinion in the Laws of Armed Conflict', (2000) 5 *Journal of Conflict and Security Law* 135.

[5] See, for example, A. V. Dicey, *Introduction to the Law of the Constitution* (10th edn, Macmillan, 1959), p. 303.

[6] For examples see I. Brownlie, 'The Defence of Superior Orders: Time for a New Realism?', [1989] *Criminal Law Review* 396.

[7] H. McCoubrey, 'The Concept and Treatment of War Crimes', (1996) 1 *Journal of Armed Conflict Law* 121 at p. 123.

[8] In 1387, Honoré Bonet's *The Tree of Battles* (G. Coupland (trans.), Harvard University Press, 1949), contained a chapter entitled 'Does a Serf Who Commits Homicide at his Master's Command Merit Punishment?', pp. 169–70.

[9] For a pre-war history see Dinstein, *Superior Orders*, pp. 93–103.

the question of obedience to orders, the statutes of those two tribunals took a simple, strict line. Article 7 of the Nuremberg IMT Statute reads 'the fact that the defendant acted pursuant to an order of his government or of a superior shall not free him from responsibility, but may be considered in mitigation of punishment if the Tribunal determines that justice so requires'.[10] Thus, what previously was seen by many as a matter of law (a formal defence) was relegated to the realm of morality (in discretion relating to sentencing)[11] by the simple stroke of the drafters' pen.

The customary situation in the post-war period thus remained controversial.[12] It might be thought that the position was settled by the denial of the defence of superior orders in the Statutes of the International Criminal Tribunal for the former Yugoslavia (ICTY) and International Criminal Tribunal for Rwanda (ICTR).[13] If international law were that easy, it would not be so interesting. The drafters of the Rome Statute of the International Criminal Court took a different approach to that encapsulated in the statutes of the ad hoc tribunals on the applicability of a defence of superior orders. The defence was reinstated, in limited circumstances, in its own right. Article 33 of the Rome Statute deserves quotation in full:

> 1. The fact that a crime within the jurisdiction of the Court has been committed pursuant to an order of a government or of a superior, whether military or civilian, shall not relieve that person of criminal responsibility unless:

[10] Charter of the International Military Tribunal, annex to the London Agreement on the Prosecution and Punishment of the Major War Criminals of the European Axis and Establishing the Charter of the International Military Tribunal, (Annex) 8 August 1945, (1951) 82 UNTS 279, Article 8. Article 6 of the Tokyo IMT Charter is essentially the same, see Special Proclamation: Establishment of an International Military Tribunal for the Far East, 19 January 1946, TIAS no. 1589.

[11] For an interesting example of the relationship between a defence in law and moral reason for mitigation in sentence see *R* v. *Kingston* [1995] 2 AC 355.

[12] See, on the one hand, P. Gaeta, 'The Defence of Superior Orders: The Statute of the International Criminal Court Versus Customary International Law', (1999) 10 *European Journal of International Law* 172, and on the other, McCoubrey, 'From Nuremberg to Rome'; C. Garraway, 'Superior Orders and the International Criminal Court: Justice Delivered or Justice Denied?', (1999) 836 *International Review of the Red Cross* 785.

[13] See Statute of the ICTY, annex to Security Council Resolution 827, UN doc. S/RES/827, Article 7(4) and Statute of the ICTR, annex to Security Council Resolution 955, UN doc. S/RES/955, Article 6(4).

a. The person was under a legal obligation to obey orders of the government or the superior in question;
b. The person did not know that the order was unlawful; and
c. The order was not manifestly unlawful.

2. For the purposes of this Article, orders to commit genocide or crimes against humanity are manifestly unlawful.[14]

The customary status of this Article has been the subject of much debate.[15] The status of Article 33 in custom is important in both theory and practice. In states such as the United Kingdom, which incorporate customary law directly into their national legal systems, but have not expressly included the defence in implementing legislation, the applicability of the defence may turn on precisely this point.[16] Whatever its customary status, Article 33 is the provision with which many international criminal lawyers will now have to work. So perhaps we also need to approach its nature, scope and acceptability from a criminal law point of view. This approach, and controversy relating to Article 33, is something that was foreseen by the drafters of that provision. Per Saland, Chair of the Working Group in Rome that drafted Article 33, admitted that 'the article is very difficult to read and is bound to be debated'.[17]

What is the purpose of the superior orders defence?

It is impossible to appraise a defence without an understanding of the purpose that it is supposed to serve. One idea that has been mooted as a basis for the defence is dispensation.[18] This is the concept that the national legal order, by creating an obligation to obey orders, excludes the operation of international law to the extent that they diverge. The

[14] A/CONF. 183/9*, Article 33; see generally O. Triffterer, 'Article 33', in O. Triffterer (ed.), *Commentary on the Rome Statute of the International Criminal Court* (Nomos, 1999), p. 573.

[15] In addition to the articles referred to above at n. 12, see A. Cassese, 'The Rome Statute of the International Criminal Court: Some Preliminary Reflections', (1999) 10 *European Journal of International Law* 144 at p. 157.

[16] See R. Cryer, 'Implementation of the ICC Statute in England and Wales', (2002) 51 *International and Comparative Law Quarterly* 733 at pp. 740–2.

[17] P. Saland, 'International Criminal Law Principles', in R. S. Lee (ed.), *The International Criminal Court* (Kluwer, 1999), p. 189 at p. 212.

[18] It is possible that this is the justification given by the third edition of Oppenheim, see L. Oppenheim, (*International Law*, vol. II, *War and Neutrality* (3rd edn, L. Roxburgh ed.), Longmans, 1921), p. 343. See generally Dinstein, *Superior Orders*, pp. 41–3.

purpose is thus to avoid conflicts between national and international law. The idea that dispensation can form the basis of the superior orders defence can be quickly disposed of. As the Nuremberg IMT said, 'the very essence of the Charter [and now international criminal law] is that individuals have international duties which transcend the national obligations of obedience imposed by the individual State'.[19] As Antonio Cassese said back in 1984, referring to the general exclusion of the defence, the Nuremberg and Tokyo IMTs represented:

> one of the highest points ever reached by the new juridical conscience. Until that moment, individuals had to obey the imperatives of their own national laws ... when the international rules ... are in conflict with state laws ... every individual must transgress the state laws ... this was a veritable revolution both in the field of law and ethics.[20]

Although there has been a limited revival of the defence since the Nuremberg and Tokyo IMTs, this does not relate to a reassertion of the primacy of national law. As much can be seen from the *Einsatzguppen* case, where it was determined that if a person agreed with what he was being asked to do, the fact that he acted under orders could not be pleaded in defence.[21] Further, the manifest illegality test, as included, *inter alia*, in Article 33 of the Rome Statute, requires that the defendant not know, or not have been able to know, that the order was illegal, in addition to the issuance of the order. If dispensation was the basis, then it would not matter whether or not the person knew the order was illegal or agreed with it. The fact of the order being issued would suffice to oust international law here. As this is not the case, the reasons for the defence must lie elsewhere.

Perhaps the underlying idea of the defence is that the 'real criminal', when an offence is committed pursuant to orders, is the orderer, rather than the immediate perpetrator of the criminal act. Hence the rule that even when superior orders operates as a defence, the person ordering the offence remains liable. This would imply that the purpose of the defence is to reflect accurately the authorship of the act. This was the explanation of the *respondeat superior* rule. It was thought that there was no injustice flowing from the application of that rule because the appropriate question to be asked was where liability should fall, not if anyone could be held

[19] 'Nuremberg International Military Tribunal: Judgment and Sentences', (1947) 41 *American Journal of International Law* 171 at p. 221.

[20] A. Cassese, *Violence and Law in the Modern Age* (Polity Press, 1988), pp. 131–2.

[21] *United States* v. *Ohlendorf and others* ('*Einsatzgruppen*') IV TWC 411 at 471.

liable at all.[22] Those supporting the rule answered the former question by asserting that the most appropriate person to punish was the orderer. There is still responsibility for ordering offences, as has been affirmed in Article 25(2)(b) of the Rome Statute. The liability of those ordering offences also shows the excusatory nature of superior orders on conduct, rather than implying that orders act as a justification for the subordinate. Liability of others can only occur when conduct is excused. If the subordinate's actions were justified (for example by self-defence) then there could be no liability for other parties.[23] Equally, with the decline of the *respondeat superior* rule, and the rise of the manifest illegality test, this explanation can no longer be seen as a complete or satisfactory basis for the defence of superior orders.

The third possible explanation for the rule is the exigencies of combat, the purpose of the defence thus being to ensure military efficiency. Soldiers, for understandable reasons, are not generally supposed to question the orders they receive in battle. It is generally,[24] although not universally,[25] thought that military effectiveness relies on almost reflexive obedience to orders by subordinates. This may not be quite true, especially as the *Einsatzgruppen* case mentioned that 'the obedience of a soldier is not the obedience of an automaton'.[26] In practice, however, it cannot but be conceded that soldiers are generally unable to check the accuracy of facts upon which they are told to act, and will not have the time, resources or ability to weigh carefully the legality of orders given to them. As was said in the *Peleus* case, 'no sailor and no soldier can carry with him a library of international law, or have immediate access to a professor in that subject'.[27] This is why Article 33(b) requires that the defendant does not know that the order is illegal. The additional test, that the order is not manifestly illegal, is to exclude reliance on orders that are so

[22] L. Oppenheim, *International Law*, vol. II, *War and Neutrality* (Longmans, 1906), pp. 264–5.

[23] See A. Cassese, 'Justifications and Excuses in International Criminal Law', in A. Cassese, P. Gaeta and J. R. W. D. Jones (eds.), *The Rome Statute of the International Criminal Court: A Commentary* (Oxford University Press, 2002), pp. 951–2.

[24] See Dinstein, *Superior Orders*, pp. 5–6.

[25] See M. J. Osiel, *Obeying Orders: Atrocities, Military Discipline and the Law of War* (Transaction Publishers, 1999), p. 7: 'Efficacy in combat now depends more on tactical imagination and loyalty to combat buddies than on immediate, unreflective adherence to the letter of superiors' orders.'

[26] *Einsatzgruppen* case, above n. 21 at 470.

[27] *Peleus* case (1945) 13 ILR 248 at 249. See also chapter 3 by Neil Boister and L. C. Green, 'The Man in the Field and the Maxim *Ignorantia Juris non Excusat*', in L. C. Green, *Essays on the Modern Law of War* (2nd edn, Transnational Publishers, 1999), p. 227.

patently illegal that the failure to realize this is itself sufficiently reprehensible that the defence should not be allowed. The setting of the level at manifest illegality is to balance the requirements of military obedience (it would be too disruptive to allow subordinates to question every order) and the equal application of the law to all.[28] The underlying presumption is that a subordinate should normally be able to rely on orders by assuming the facts upon which they are based and their legality, and carry those orders out without delay. This also underlies the well-established link between the defence of obedience to orders and those of mistake of law and of fact, both of which are included in Article 32 of the Rome Statute.

The final basis suggested for the defence is that it respects the position of those who are placed on the horns of a dilemma, to obey or not to obey illegal orders, as eloquently expressed by Dicey:

> [t]he position of a soldier is in theory and may be in practice a difficult one. He may, as it has been well said, be liable to be shot by a court-martial if he disobeys an order, and to be hanged by a judge and jury if he obeys it.[29]

Understandable though this problem is, it only serves to fully justify the *respondeat superior* approach. It does not completely support the approach taken by the proponents of the manifest illegality approach such as that taken in the Rome Statute. This is because it presumes that the subordinate has (correctly) evaluated the order as illegal. If this occurs, then because the conditions in Article 33 are cumulative for the defence to be applicable, the defence could not be relied on in this instance, as Article 33(1)(b) will always serve to disapply the defence. It does, nonetheless, go to show the possible overlap with another defence, duress. This bolsters the case that superior orders amount to an excuse, not a justification of the conduct.

Superior orders and other defences

As the above should demonstrate, the plea of superior orders is frequently mixed with two other pleas, mistake and duress.[30] These are best shown by example. Consider an international armed conflict. In this

[28] See Dinstein, *Superior Orders*, pp. 6–8. We will return later to the question of whether or not this marks an appropriate balance.

[29] Dicey, *Introduction*, p. 303. See Dinstein, *Superior Orders*, pp. 49–51.

[30] See Cassese, *Violence and Law*, p. 131; Y. Dinstein, 'Defences', in G. K. McDonald and O. Swaak-Goldman (eds.), *Substantive and Procedural Aspects of International Criminal Law* (Kluwer, 2000), p. 367 at p. 379.

conflict a superior officer called David, who is driving a tank, orders his subordinate, a weapons operator called Sam, to aim at a 'military target' over the horizon, informing him it is an ammunition dump. David knows his statement is untrue, and that in fact, the 'ammunition dump' is a hospital, but he wants the hospital destroyed. If Sam knew the target was a hospital, his actions would clearly violate both the First Geneva Convention[31] and the Rome Statute (Article 8(2)(b)(ii)).

Here, if Sam does not know that it is a hospital but thinks he is attacking a legitimate military objective because he has been told so by David, the situation is different. In this instance, the order would work to form the basis of a defence of mistake of fact which would serve to undermine any suggestion that Sam had the necessary *mens rea*. The absence of *mens rea* because of a mistake of fact is a defence in Article 32 of the Rome Statute. In such a situation the order does not need to give rise to a superior orders defence per se, as it is the basis instead for an assertion that Sam had no intention to attack the hospital. Dinstein, for example, is of the view that it is not controversial that orders may 'contribute, together with the other facts of the case, to the formation of the undisputed defence of mistake of fact'.[32] It is difficult to disagree. There is no reason in law or in policy to exclude the defence of mistake of fact just because one of the causes of the error was an order.

The next possible overlap is with a defence of duress. As Dicey recognized in the statement quoted above, the choice of whether or not to obey orders is one fraught with danger for the subordinate soldier. Dinstein also noted this some time ago.[33] The relationship has also been brought to the fore more recently in the *Erdemović* case before the ICTY.[34] In this case, the defendant initially refused to obey an order to shoot Bosniak men who were *hors d'combat*, but then agreed to do so. When asked to plead at trial, he pleaded guilty, but also said:

> I had to do this, if I had refused, I would have been killed together with the victims. When I refused, they told me: 'if you are sorry for them stand up. Line up with them and we will kill you too'. I am not sorry for myself but for my family, my wife and son, and I could not refuse because then they would have killed me.[35]

[31] Article 18. [32] Dinstein, *Superior Orders*, pp. 83–4. [33] *Ibid.*, pp. 76–83.
[34] *Prosecutor* v. *Erdemović* (Case No. IT–96–22–A), judgment, 7 October 1997.
[35] *Prosecutor* v. *Erdemović* (Case No. IT–96–22–T), transcript, 31 May 1996 D. 241.

As the defence of superior orders is not applicable before the ICTY,[36] detailed discussion of the superior orders was not necessary to the case. Nevertheless, the Joint Opinion of Judges McDonald and Vohrah adopted a position akin to Dinstein's, that superior orders are not a defence but the fact of an order may give rise to a defence of duress or mistake of fact.[37]

The opinion of McDonald and Vohrah did not discuss the possibility of superior orders leading to a defence of duress in any depth. This was because they determined that on policy grounds the defence of duress should not be applicable when killings of innocents are involved.[38] President (as he then was) Cassese and Judge Stephen, in dissent, took the matter a little further, but the important thing to notice about the statement made by Erdemović is that he did not seek to rely on his order per se to found a defence, but on an express collateral threat of death.[39] This may not be the standard way in which the defence is raised, although Judge Cassese seemed to presume it would be in *Erdemović*:

> duress is commonly raised in conjunction with superior orders. However there is no necessary connection between the two. Superior orders may be issued without being accompanied by any threats to life or limb. In these circumstances, if the superior order is manifestly illegal under international law, the subordinate is under a duty to refuse to obey the order. If, following such a refusal, the order is reiterated under a threat to life or limb, then the defence of duress may be raised, and superior orders lose any legal relevance.[40]

The more traditional explanation of the defence of obedience to orders is that there are likely to be very serious penalties for refusing to obey orders. These penalties often include death sentences, imposed at least in the past after a field court martial which is unlikely to be

[36] See ICTY Statute, Article 7(4). [37] *Erdemović* Appeal, para. 34.

[38] *Erdemović* Appeal, para. 75. For critique, see R. Cryer, 'One Appeal, Two Philosophies, Four Opinions and a Remittal: The Erdemović Case at the ICTY Appeals Chamber', (1997) 2 *Journal of Armed Conflict Law* 195 at pp. 201–5; M. Shahabuddeen, 'Policy-Oriented Law in the International Criminal Tribunal for Former Yugoslavia', in L. C. Vohrah, F. Pocar, Y. Featherstone, O. Fourmy, C. Graham, J. Hocking and N. Robson, *Man's Inhumanity to Man: Essays on International Law in Honour of Antonio Cassese* (Kluwer, 2003), p. 889.

[39] This seems to have been noticed by Judge Li, see *Erdemović* Appeal, Separate and Dissenting Opinion of Judge Li, para. 1.

[40] *Erdemović* Appeal, Separate and Dissenting Opinion of Judge Cassese, para. 15. Note, however, that although orders lose their legal relevance, they retain an evidential one.

sympathetic to the defendant. So, where death sentences are a possibility, such a sentence could amount to the 'necessary connection' which Cassese denied existed. This can be supported by what was said in the judgment in the *Einsatzgruppen* case: 'even if the subordinate realises that the act he is called upon to perform is a crime, he may not refuse its execution without incurring serious consequences ... this therefore, constitutes duress.'[41]

However, it should be noted that the analogy drawn with duress is not exact. The defence of duress is traditionally limited to unlawful threats of death or serious injury from non-state actors. Here, we are dealing with what may amount to a lawfully imposed death sentence.[42] Nonetheless, where a person is put in Erdemović's position, of a direct collateral threat of death or serious injury for not obeying an order, there seems to be no reason to deny a separate defence of duress. It is worth noting at this point that Article 31(d) allows a defence of duress. In contrast to the decision of the majority of the Appeals Chamber in *Erdemović*, the defence of duress also applies to offences involving killing.

At least one further question about the relationship between superior orders and duress must arise. That question is whether or not the relationship/overlap with duress should be rethought, given the increasing trend towards abolition of the death penalty in many countries. Where a country does not have the death penalty for a refusal to obey orders, or where the national legal order only gives an obligation to obey legal orders, the usual orderee is not quite put in the position of a duressed person, even if it is accepted that the analogy between superior orders and duress is close in general.

Finally, we must move on to discuss the related defence of mistake of law. The text of the Rome Statute itself links the defence of superior orders to mistake of law. Article 32(2) reads:

> A mistake of law as to whether a particular type of conduct is a crime within the jurisdiction of the Court shall not be a ground for excluding criminal responsibility. A mistake of law may, however, be a ground for excluding criminal responsibility if it negates the mental element required by such a crime, *or as provided for in Article 33* (emphasis added).

[41] *Einsatzgruppen* case, above n. 21 at 480.

[42] There is a trend towards the abolition of the death penalty, but death sentences are not totally prohibited by customary international law. See generally W. A. Schabas, *The Abolition of the Death Penalty in International Law* (3rd edn, Cambridge University Press, 2002).

This links up with Article 33 to give the following position.[43] Normally, misunderstandings as to the law do not give rise to a defence except in the rare situation where the mistake serves to negate *mens rea*. However, when someone is ordered to do something, the fact that they believe the order to be legal will be a defence so long as that mistake is not utterly unreasonable, i.e. a belief in the lawfulness of an order that is manifestly unlawful. So, Article 33 is a specific, limited extension of the mistake of law defence. This conceptualization of the defence may be referable to the idea that soldiers cannot generally weigh the legality of orders too carefully in combat situations. Whether or not this justifies a relaxation of the conditions of the mistake of law defence is another question.

Article 33: a flawed formulation?

Leaving aside whether or not superior orders should ever be a separate defence, and accepting for the purpose of argument McCoubrey's view that it is,[44] let us examine the provision for superior orders in the Rome Statute. We need to see whether it represents a reasonable response to the problems it seeks to solve. Those problems are identified above.

To begin, a small defence of Article 33 from one of its critics. Dinstein criticizes Article 33 for only conceptualizing the defence as a mistake of law issue: '[w]hy deal with the fact of obedience of superior orders in combination with the defence of mistake of law while disregarding similar combinations between the fact and the defences of mistake of law and duress?'[45] The reason is this. No alteration was considered necessary for those defences to take into account the fact of superior orders, as they were enough by themselves. Yet as a compromise, it was thought necessary to tweak the defence of mistake of law to allow for some evaluative mistakes in relation to orders. Article 33 does not mean that orders are not relevant to the other defences, just that those defences

[43] I have derived much assistance on this point from chapter 3 by Neil Boister, along with R. S. Clark, 'The Mental Element in International Criminal Law: The Rome Statute of the International Criminal Court and the Elements of Offences', (2002) 12 *Criminal Law Forum* 291 and A. Eser, 'Mental Elements, Mistake of Fact, Mistake of Law', in Cassese *et al.*, *The Rome Statute*, p. 889.

[44] See McCoubrey, 'From Nuremberg to Rome'. I am a little more sceptical, but here is not the place for that discussion.

[45] Dinstein, 'Defences', p. 382.

have not been altered specifically to take orders into account as they were already broad enough to cover situations where they might be at issue.

Having defended Article 33 from Dinstein's charge, we should move to an evaluation of the text of that Article. Let us first take Article 33(1)(a), that 'the person was under a legal obligation to obey orders of the government or the superior in question'. This is interesting from the point of view of the supremacy of international law over national law. As discussed above, international law is clearly the superior system in the prosecution of international crimes. Yet, as Andreas Zimmermann has noted, the statute here 'refers back to the legal order within which both the superior ... and the offender were acting'.[46]

There are problems with this. It means that the defence will only be applicable to offenders from certain countries – those who are under legal obligations domestically to obey orders. This will be the case for soldiers in basically all countries, but civilians may be in a different position in different states. If, as argued above, the foundation of a separate defence of obedience to orders is based on the possibility of it being an unavoidable mistake of law in the exigencies of conflict, taking the defence closer to the civil law ideas of mistake of law,[47] then it should not matter whether or not there is an obligation to obey or not. The point is that there has been an inappropriate, but ostensibly accurate, statement of the law by a person in authority, which is not easily evaluated, not that there is an obligation to obey. The limitation on the defence is provided by the 'manifest illegality' aspect of the test rather than an obligation to obey orders. Dinstein makes a similar point, that whether or not a person is under an obligation, their *mens rea* is negated in this instance.[48] This position goes too far, as the defence is not based on a negation of the mental element, at least insofar as *mens rea* is formulated in Article 30 of the Rome Statute. This much is clear from Article 32 of the Rome Statute, which adds 'or as provided for in Article 33' to cases where the mental element is negated. Still, the basic point, that the obligation to obey does not really amount to a necessary aspect of the defence, stands.

Staying with the obligation to obey, the formulation in Article 33(1)(a) that a person is 'under a legal obligation to obey orders of the

[46] A. Zimmermann, 'Superior Orders', in Cassese *et al.*, *The Rome Statute*, p. 969; see also Triffterer, 'Article 33', p. 585.

[47] See chapter 3 by Neil Boister.

[48] Dinstein, 'Defences', p. 381.

Government or the superior in question' refers to a general obligation on the person to obey orders, rather than the obligation to obey the specific order.[49] Zimmermann takes a different view, reading Article 33(1)(a) as meaning '[t]he possibility of exempting an offender . . . only comes into play when that person was under a legal obligation to obey the said order'.[50] There is a clear reason to adopt the view that Article 33(1)(a) speaks of a general obligation to obey orders rather than the order in question. In certain military law contexts soldiers are only under an obligation to obey lawful orders.[51] In such situations, whenever an illegal order is issued, the obligation to obey the specific order disappears. Therefore, if a person who is subject only to an obligation to obey lawful orders inaccurately evaluates an unlawful, although not manifestly unlawful, order as being lawful, he will not know the obligation to obey has disappeared. However, if the obligation in Article 33(1)(a) referred to an obligation to obey the order in question, the defence of superior orders would fail as he had no legal obligation to obey that order.

The refusal of the defence of superior orders on this ground would not be on a ground related to the accused's culpability and should thus not be accepted. This was understood by the drafters of the Rome Statute, who framed the requirement as an obligation to 'obey orders', not 'the order'. Zimmermann believes that where a person believes an order to be binding when it is not so, Article 32 will apply, which would mitigate the impact of his approach.[52] However, this will only serve to exculpate the accused if the mistake serves to negate *mens rea*. The negation of *mens rea* is a high threshold, and is one which the drafters of the Rome Statute specifically sought to mitigate in the context of superior orders. Therefore, this refinement of Zimmermann's position is not a complete answer to the difficulty his interpretation involves.

In a related context, Article 33(1)(b) has been criticized as setting the test for excluding the defence too high, at manifest illegality.[53] Mark

[49] See Triffterer, 'Article 33', p. 585.

[50] Zimmermann, 'Superior Orders', p. 969. In the spirit of openness, I should confess to the same error, see Cryer, 'Implementation of the ICC Statute', p. 741.

[51] See Army Act 1958, s. 34 and P. Rowe, 'Murder and the Law of War', (1991) 42 *Northern Ireland Legal Quarterly* 217 at p. 227. A comparison of European approaches can be found in H. Kriege and G. Nolte, 'Comparison of European Military Law Systems', in G. Nolte (ed.), *European Military Law Systems* (de Gruyter, 2003), pp. 93–7.

[52] Zimmermann, 'Superior Orders', p. 969.

[53] See Osiel, *Obeying Orders*, pp. 357–66.

Osiel is of the view that this standard does not encourage soldiers to actively engage with their orders or help to create a culture of reflective practice in the military.[54] He would prefer a test of illegality that is at the level that the reasonable soldier could see that the order was illegal.[55] He may have a point. If we take the idea of mistake of law in its sophisticated civil law form, an unreasonable error of law could hardly be termed an unavoidable one, the latter being the concept used in many civil law jurisdictions to define mistake of law defences.[56]

On the other hand, the difference between the two tests may not be so large in practice. It all depends on the interpretation of the term 'manifest' and whether it is an objective or a subjective criterion. What is manifest to one person may not be to another. What is manifest should not depend only on the content of the order, but also, *inter alia*, on the length of time a person has to evaluate the order, their level of training, and their familiarity with the appraisal of orders. Some comments have appeared to set very high standards for manifest illegality, such as that:

> [t]he distinguishing mark of a 'manifestly unlawful order' should fly like a black flag above the order given . . . [n]ot formal unlawfulness, hidden or half-hidden, nor unlawfulness discernible only to the eyes of legal experts, but a flagrant and manifest breach of the law.[57]

Yet despite this, tribunals in practice have had little compunction in declaring orders to be manifestly unlawful, at least in cases involving non-nationals.[58] However, it should be noted that according to some, the manifest illegality test is an entirely objective one.[59] If this is the case, not only can the rule be criticized as over-indulgent, but Osiel's critique becomes more cogent. A purely objective standard may also be too harsh on those who, through lack of training or mental capacity, simply could not have correctly evaluated the order as unlawful.

In practice, where the requirement of manifest illegality may be thought unduly kind to defendants, certain factors may serve to mitigate

54 *Ibid.*, pp. 357–66.

55 *Ibid.*, pp. 357–66. It is notable that in the *Almelo* case ((1945) XII *Law Reports, Trials of War Criminals* 73–4) the standard set was that of the reasonable man.

56 See chapter 3 by Neil Boister.

57 *Attorney-General of Israel* v. *Eichmann* (1961) 36 ILR 275 at 277.

58 See Gaeta, 'Defence of Superior Orders', pp. 183–6; A. Cassese, *International Criminal Law* (Oxford University Press, 2003), pp. 234–9.

59 See Osiel, *Obeying Orders*, pp. 79–83; H. Arendt, *Eichmann in Jerusalem: A Report on the Banality of Evil* (Penguin, 1994), pp. 291–3.

the seemingly high standard set for excluding the defence. A bare statement by the defendant that he did not know that the order was illegal is unlikely to be accepted by a court trying such an offence where it would be unreasonable to reach such a conclusion. Although the distinction between the reasonableness of holding a belief and the fact of a person holding that belief is clear in the abstract, in practice the distinction is more fluid.[60] The reasonableness of a belief is usually taken as strong evidence of the honesty with which a belief is held.[61] As Zimmermann has mentioned, knowledge of legality may be proved by circumstantial evidence.[62] Early cases on superior orders, such as the *Llandovery Castle*,[63] used the manifest illegality test as a means to probe whether or not the accused was in fact aware of the illegality of the order.[64] It is clear that Article 33 goes beyond this, seemingly to presume against the accused that if the order was manifestly unlawful the defendant knew it to be so.

This takes us to Article 33(2). Article 33(2) provides that 'for the purposes of this article, orders to commit genocide or crimes against humanity are manifestly unlawful'. Although it is clear that Article 33(2) cuts the defence down,[65] it is riddled with ambiguity and inconsistency. At the outset, it should be mentioned that '[t]his distinction is not based in customary international law, nor does it exist in any domestic law'.[66] It was based on a compromise on the inclusion of superior orders in the Rome Statute.

It is exceptionally unlikely that an order to 'commit genocide' or an order to 'commit crimes against humanity' would ever be given, or indeed that the drafters intended that only those two orders be excluded. Thus, Article 33 cannot be read entirely literally as solely prohibiting orders repeating those phrases verbatim.[67] Even so, and contrary to an often expressed view,[68] the idea that the defence is per se inapplicable on a charge of genocide or crimes against humanity is difficult to reconcile

[60] For an example see *Einsatzgruppen* case, above n. 21 at 473–4.
[61] For example Sexual Offences (Amendment) Act 1976, s.1(2); J. C. Smith, *Smith and Hogan: Criminal Law* (10th edn, Butterworths, 2002), pp. 466–7.
[62] Zimmermann, 'Superior Orders', p. 970.
[63] *Llandovery Castle* case (1922) 16 *American Journal of International Law* 708.
[64] See also the discussion in Dinstein, *Superior Orders*, pp. 26–37.
[65] Zimmermann, 'Superior Orders', pp. 971–2. [66] *Ibid.*, p. 971.
[67] See Clark, 'Mental Element', p. 333.
[68] See, e.g. Zimmermann, 'Superior Orders', p. 971; T. Graditzky, 'War Crime Issues before the Rome Diplomatic Conference on the Establishment of an International Criminal Court', (1999) 5 *UC Davis Journal of International Law and Policy* 199 at p. 215.

with the wording of Article 33(2), which refers to 'orders to commit crimes against humanity or genocide'. The reference seems to be to the orders, and by implication the state of mind, of the orderer, rather than that of the person seeking to rely on the orders as a defence.

In the Rome Statute scheme, 'crimes against humanity – unlike war crimes – necessarily form part of either a systematic or widespread commission of similar acts and are therefore committed as part of a plan or policy',[69] to which may be added that genocide requires a specific intent.[70] Still, because the wording might not reflect what the drafters intended,[71] Article 33(2) is unclear on whether the relevant awareness of the context for crimes against humanity or specific intent for genocide is that of the superior or the subordinate.[72]

To explain this problem further, it may help to look at three situations: first, a situation where there are orders, the application of which would involve war crimes, such as killing civilians. The person so ordered carries them out, but with the relevant *mens rea* for crimes against humanity or genocide. In most, if not all, such cases, there is no problem with excluding reliance on the orders, as was said in the *Einsatzgruppen* case: 'if he accepts a criminal order and executes it with a malice of his own, he may not plead superior orders'.[73] To take an order and to carry it out with additional *mens rea*, as in our situation, may be covered by this. Oddly, though, the wording of Article 33(2) would appear not to be applicable. In this situation though, it may be difficult for the defendant to answer a prosecutorial assertion that the defendant knew the order was unlawful.

The next situation is where the orders were given by a superior aware of the context for crimes against humanity or the specific intention for genocide, where the additional mental element required is not known about by the orderee, who is charged with war crimes. The orders would appear to fall directly into Article 33(2) as 'orders to commit genocide or

69 Zimmermann, 'Superior Orders', p. 971.

70 See Rome Statute, Article 6; W. A. Schabas, *Genocide in International Law: The Crime of Crimes* (Cambridge University Press, 2000), ch. 5. See also A. K. A. Greenawalt, 'Rethinking Genocidal Intent: The Case for a Knowledge-Based Interpretation', (1999) 99 *Columbia Law Review* 2259.

71 Although when another defence (defence of property in Article 31(1)(c)) was intended solely to apply to war crimes a different form of words was used, perhaps not too much should be read into this, owing to the circumstances of the drafting of the Rome Statute.

72 See R. Cryer, 'The Boundaries of Liability in International Criminal Law, or 'Selectivity by Stealth', (2001) 6 *Journal of Conflict and Security Law* 3 at pp. 15–16.

73 *Einsatzgruppen* case, above n. 21 at 471.

crimes against humanity'. But in almost every instance, orders will be to engage in certain acts, not 'commit genocide' or 'commit crimes against humanity'. If the knowledge of the context, or specific intent, is that of the superior, we cannot simply presume that it is shared, known about, or even suspected by the subordinate. The darker recesses of the minds of others are not always immediately, if ever, open to others, particularly when the mind that is to be read is that of a military superior, who is unlikely to treat a subordinate as a confessor. It would be difficult to determine the applicability of the defence without either evidence from, or a trial of, the superior. Where the subordinate does not know of the intention of the superior, there is nothing related to the subordinate's culpability that requires the defence to be excluded on the grounds given in Article 33(2), but if the wording is taken seriously, that is what it may do.

The third situation is where the superior and subordinate share the intention, be it for crimes against humanity or genocide. In this instance, the outcome does not depend on whether Article 33(2) refers to the superior or subordinate, as they both have the relevant mental element.

Given the interpretative difficulties above, it may be more appropriate to adopt the position that the defence is excluded by Article 33(2) in cases where the defendant is charged with crimes against humanity or genocide. This could be supported by the idea that crimes against humanity and genocide are more serious than war crimes, therefore the defence should not apply to those charged with such serious crimes. Indeed, it has been plausibly contended that this is an implication of Article 33(2) itself.[74]

There are two objections to this. First, it is slightly disconcerting to see that fewer defences apply to a more serious charge than a less serious one. If the defence is accepted as serving a legitimate purpose, protecting reasonable mistakes of law in circumstances where the accused cannot be expected to know an order is unlawful, then if the defence is to be excluded, the reason that the purpose is no longer legitimate needs to be given. In cases of crimes against humanity and genocide, the mental elements for those crimes will make it extremely difficult to rely on the defence, in particular because of the requirements of manifest illegality and absence of knowledge of the illegality. But these conditions should be for the ICC to determine in individual cases, rather than the defence being *a priori*

[74] See M. Frulli, 'Are Crimes Against Humanity More Serious than War Crimes?', (2001) 12 *European Journal of International Law* 329 at pp. 339–40.

excluded by the Rome Statute. Again, a parallel with *Erdemović* may be apposite. In that case, the majority were unwilling, on policy grounds, to accept that a defence of duress should apply to offences involving killing innocents. Cassese responded, quite accurately, that a tightly-drawn defence responded adequately to their fears, and, unlike their position, did not risk injustice in the rare situations where a defence might be appropriate.[75]

There is another problem with interpreting Article 33(2) as excluding crimes against humanity and genocide altogether. Although seeing crimes against humanity as more serious than war crimes is contrary to the recent practice of the ICTY,[76] there are strong grounds for asserting that the characterization of an act as a crime against humanity or genocide is more serious than describing it as a war crime.[77] This does not mean that each act described as genocide or as a crime against humanity is more serious than any possible war crime. As was said by Judges McDonald and Vohrah in *Erdemović*, '*all things being equal*, a punishable offence, if charged and proved as a crime against humanity, is more serious . . . than if it were proceeded upon on the basis that it were a war crime'.[78]

It is possible to imagine an act properly considered genocide that may not be as serious as a particularly serious war crime. Consider, for example, a person who, owing to his hatred of a particular ethnic group, kills a member of that ethnic group, as his contribution to a 'manifest pattern' of similar acts with the intention to destroy a part of that ethnic group. Such a person certainly deserves a high level of censure and punishment. Next, though, imagine a general who, for personal sadistic reasons, decides to use a poison gas against a concentration of 10,000 foreign troops. In accordance with his wishes the gas leads to an appallingly slow and agonizing death for all of those troops. Françoise Hampson has said, in the context of reprisal action:

> [i]f, for example, it were agreed that a bombardment of a civilian target of 50,000 people with *x* weight of bombs were the equivalent to the use of *y* quantity of gas against 500 soldiers, the State taking the reprisal would know that it was acting within lawful limits and the offending State would

[75] Cassese, *Erdemović* Appeal, paras. 42–4.

[76] See *Prosecutor* v. *Tadić* (Case No. IT–94–1–A), sentencing judgment, 14 July 1997 and Case No. IT–94–1–A*bis*, 26 January 2000, para. 61.

[77] See M. Bohlander, '*Prosecutor v Tadić*: Waiting to Exhale', (2001) 12 *Criminal Law Forum* 217 at pp. 240–8; R. May and M. Wierda, 'Is there a Hierarchy of Crimes in International Law?', in Vohrah *et al.* (eds.), *Man's Inhumanity to Man*, p. 511.

[78] McDonald and Vohrah, *Erdemović* Appeal, para. 20, emphasis in original.

recognise the act as a reprisal rather than escalation. Such a scale does not, however, exist.[79]

A similar problem necessarily afflicts any reckoning here. But it is not clear, to this author at least, that despite the specific hate-based seriousness of the example given of genocide,[80] it is necessarily more serious than the example given of a war crime.[81] Both are very serious, but it does not diminish the seriousness of either to accept that specific examples of war crimes may be at times more serious even than specific examples of genocide.[82] The calculation of actual gravity exists in an unquantifiable relationship with the qualitative label used. Thus, if the Rome Statute presumes every war crime to be less serious than every example of a crime against humanity or genocide, and bases a refusal of a defence on that presumption, it is inappropriate. As can be seen, the interpretation of Article 33 is fraught with difficulty, and neither interpretation of Article 33(2) is particularly appealing.

Conclusion

Within the purview of a short work, it is difficult to give more than an introduction to the complex issues raised by superior orders. This is especially the case as it is difficult to explain the importance of any one defence without an equivalent investigation of the general principles of liability and the specific substantive crimes to which that defence applies. Such an investigation inevitably lies beyond the scope of this chapter. It is to be hoped that this chapter has shown that by an investigation of the underlying bases of a defence and by attempting to approach the subject from a criminal law, as well as an international law, angle, we may come to some conclusions about the appropriateness of individual provisions of the Rome Statute. It only remains to say that it is a matter of great regret that the person with whom I would most have liked to discuss the content of this chapter is the person whose untimely death has made this book an *in memoriam* volume rather than a *festschrift.*

[79] F. J. Hampson, 'Belligerent Reprisals and the 1977 Protocols to the Geneva Conventions of 1949', (1988) 37 *International and Comparative Law Quarterly* 818 at pp. 823–4.

[80] See A. M. Danner, 'Constructing a Hierarchy of Crimes in International Criminal Law Sentencing', (2001) 87 *Virginia Law Review* 415 at pp. 481–3.

[81] This would apply *a fortiori* to an example of a crime against humanity when compared to a war crime.

[82] See *accord*, Triffterer, 'Article 33', p. 587.

5

Command responsibility: victors' justice or just desserts?

COLONEL C. H. B. GARRAWAY

I first met Hilaire McCoubrey when I was a young Army officer just starting to show an interest in the law of armed conflict. His enthusiasm for the subject and his support, both to me and to many of my colleagues, encouraged me to delve deeper and has been a major factor both in my own career and in the increased knowledge of the subject throughout Army Legal Services. It is due to him that all junior officers now attend a one-week academic course to ensure that their foundation knowledge can support their operational work. His influence lives on!

The trials and tribulations of command

The philosophy that lies behind the modern day doctrine of command responsibility stretches back into the mists of time. Command by its very nature brings responsibility. It comes with the territory or in the famous words to be found on the desk of President Truman, 'The buck stops here.' Throughout history, commanders have taken responsibility for the success or failures of their subordinates, whether it was the Roman General parading down the Via Triumphalis into the Imperial Capital or Admiral Byng being shot on the quarterdeck of his own ship '*pour encourager les autres*'.[1] The philosophy is not unique to the military.

The author was a member of the UK delegation to the Diplomatic Conference in Rome that drafted the Statute of the International Criminal Court. The views expressed here are the veiws of the author and do not necessarily reflect those of the Ministry of Defence, the UK government or any other organization.

[1] The French writer Voltaire (1694–1778), writing in *Candide*, ch. 23 and referring to this case in which he had sought to intervene, said 'Dans ce pays-ci, il est bon de tuer de temps en temps un amiral pour encourager les autres.' (In this country, it is thought well to kill an admiral from time to time to encourage the others). The reference to Admiral Byng on

Traditionally, those in positions of responsibility have been held accountable for the successes or failings of their subordinates. Football managers are only too well aware of how their future rests on the ability of those whom they manage.

However, these are examples of 'command responsibility' in its most general sense. The idea of military command involving criminal responsibility is a comparatively new development. Although the 'laws of war' have existed in some form for millennia, the responsibility of commanders has been almost inextricably linked to success, as Admiral Byng discovered. Whilst Herodotus states that Xerxes recognized and submitted to the laws of war as then defined,[2] he would not have considered that such submission could end in criminal charges. However, it is worthy of note that one of the first examples of an 'international criminal tribunal', the trial of Peter von Hagenbach, in 1474, involved what would now be described as 'crimes against humanity', the vicious subjugation of the town of Breisach by way of murder, rape, pillage and wanton confiscation. It is unlikely that these crimes were carried out directly by von Hagenbach but, as Governor, he carried responsibility for the actions of those subordinate to him. That responsibility cost him his life.[3]

In the Hagenbach case, as in many of the cases that arose from the two World Wars in the last century, the commander was held responsible mainly as a principal. The acts had been committed on his orders or at least as part of a plan or policy that he had instigated.[4] But how far does the responsibility of a commander go where there is no evidence of direct involvemen't in the planning, initiation or carrying out of such a plan or policy? Can the commander be held responsible for omission, namely his failure to exercise his powers to stop illegal acts? As early as 1439, Charles VII of Orleans had published a law providing that captains would be held responsible for offences committed by their subordinates as if they had committed the acts themselves, if they failed to bring to

the National Maritime Museum website 'Frequently Asked Questions' (www.nmm.ac.uk/faqs) ends cryptically: 'It has not been necessary to shoot an admiral since then.'

2 See C. Phillipson, *The International Law and Custom of Ancient Greece and Rome* (1911), p. 59, cited in M. C. Bassiouni, *Crimes Against Humanity in International Criminal Law* (2nd edn, Martinus Nijhoff, 1999), p. 50.

3 See J. Deschines, 'Toward International Criminal Justice', in R. Clark and M. Sann (eds.), *The Prosecution of International Crimes: A Critical Study of the International Tribunal for the Former Yugoslavia* (Transaction Publishers, 1996), pp. 31–2.

4 See the Dostler Trial, 8–12 October 1945, where General Dostler was found guilty of having ordered personally the illegal shooting of fifteen prisoners of war. See (1949) United Nations War Crimes Commission, I Law Reports of the Trials of War Criminals, available at www.ess.uwe.ac.uk/WCC/dostler.htm

justice those deemed responsible.[5] Certainly this ordinance would have been taken into account at the Hagenbach trial though the facts were such that no real issue as to indirect responsibility arose.

The First World War: civil or criminal responsibility

However, it was not until the First World War that the issue was considered in detail. The recommendation of the Commission on the Responsibility of the Authors of War and on Enforcement of Penalties was that prosecutions should include those who 'ordered or with knowledge thereof and with the power to intervene, abstained from preventing or taking measures to prevent, putting an end to or repressing violations of the laws and customs of war'.[6]

However, the Japanese dissented from this and the limitation on numbers of those eventually prosecuted meant that there was no case where the broader definition of command responsibility became an issue. In the one case where it might have been relevant, the trial of Major Benno Crusius, he was found guilty of ordering the execution of wounded French prisoners of war and so was convicted as a principal.[7]

As a matter of treaty law, neither the 1907 Hague Regulations nor the 1929 Geneva Conventions dealt specifically with the issue of command responsibility, though the Fourth Hague Convention itself, to which the Regulations were attached, provided for state civil responsibility in the following terms: 'A belligerent party which violates the provisions of the said Regulations shall, if the case demands, be liable to pay compensation. It shall be responsible for all acts committed by persons forming part of its armed forces.'[8]

The 1929 Geneva Convention on the wounded and sick placed a responsibility on 'Commanders in Chief' to:

[5] See Charles VII's Ordinance, 'Ordonnances des Roi de France de la Troisiemme Race', cited in T. Meron, *Henry's Wars and Shakespeare's Laws: Perspectives on the Law of War in the later Middle Ages* (Clarendon Press, 1993), p. 149, note 40.

[6] See Commission on the Responsibility of the Authors of the War and on Enforcement of Penalties, Report Presented to the Preliminary Peace Conference, Versailles, 29 March 1919, reprinted in (1920) 14 *American Journal of International Law* 95 at p. 121.

[7] See W. H. Parks, 'Command Responsibility for War Crimes', (1973) 62 *Military Law Review* 12.

[8] 1907 Hague Convention IV Respecting the Laws and Customs of War on Land, The Hague, 18 October 1907, Article 3.

> arrange the details for carrying out the preceding articles as well as for cases not provided for in accordance with the instructions of their respective Governments and in conformity with the general provisions of the present Convention.[9]

There was also reference in Article 29, that proposals should be made to national legislatures to introduce 'the necessary measures for the repression in time of war of any act contrary to the provisions of the present Convention'. However, at that time, there was no direct link made between the responsibility of commanders and the requirement for criminal sanctions.

Yamashita: did he know?

The issue finally arose in the case of General Yamashita at the end of the Second World War. The Nuremberg Charter had provided that:

> Leaders, organisers, instigators and accomplices participating in the formulation or execution of a common plan or conspiracy to commit any of the [crimes listed in the Charter] are responsible for all acts performed by any persons in execution of such plan.[10]

This required some positive conduct by the accused and the vast paper trail left by the Nazi regime meant that, for the most part, positive conduct could be proved by means, particularly, of orders given. The situation was not so clear in the Tokyo trials. Although the wording governing the Tokyo proceedings was similar,[11] there was no equivalent paper trail and it became necessary to look also at omissions in the sense of failure to act. Did this amount to 'participation'? The question posed by Stone CJ in the *Yamashita* case itself, when it reached the US Supreme Court, was:

> whether the law of war imposes on an army commander a duty to take such appropriate measures as are within his power to control the troops

[9] Convention for the Amelioration of the Condition of the Wounded and Sick in Armies in the Field, Geneva, 27 July 1929, Article 26.

[10] Charter of the International Military Tribunal, annex to the London Agreement on the Prosecution and Punishment of the Major War Criminals of the European Axis and Establishing the Charter of the International Military Tribunal, (Annex) 8 August 1945, (1951) 82 UNTS 279, Article 6(a).

[11] See Charter of the International Military Tribunal for the Far East, Article 5, cited in *In re Hirota and others*, Case No. 118, (1948) Annual Digest and Reports of Public International Law Cases 357.

> under his command for the prevention of ... violations of the law of war ... and whether he may be charged with personal responsibility for his failure to take such measures when violations result.[12]

On 9 October 1944, General Yamashita took command of the Japanese 14th Area Army. His mission was to defend the Philippines against an anticipated American and British invasion. This duly occurred when, on 22 October 1944, American forces invaded Leyte. Yamashita remained as Commander of the Japanese Forces in the Philippines and as military governor until his surrender on 3 September 1945. The Philippines hostilities were intense and costly, with huge casualties on both sides.

During the time that General Yamashita was in command, his soldiers carried out a series of atrocities against the civilian population. The crimes were divided into three categories:

(1) starvation, execution or massacre without trial and maladministration generally of civilian internees and prisoners of war;
(2) torture, rape, murder and mass execution of very large numbers of residents of the Philippines, including women and children and members of religious orders, by starvation, beheading, bayoneting, clubbing, hanging, burning alive and destruction by explosives;
(3) burning and demolition without adequate military necessity of large numbers of homes, places of business, places of worship, hospitals, public buildings and educational institutions.[13]

General Yamashita was tried by a US Military Commission. He argued that, whilst he had command, the circumstances were such that he could have no control. Furthermore, he argued that he had no knowledge of the atrocities and therefore, on both grounds, he should be acquitted. The Tribunal ruled that he had both command and control but 'you failed to provide effective control of your troops as was required by the circumstances'.[14]

[12] See *Trial of General Tomoyuki Yamashita*, Case No. 21, US Supreme Court, 4 February 1946, United Nations War Crimes Commission, IV Law Reports of the Trials of War Criminals 43.

[13] *Ibid.*, at 4. For a fuller account of the facts on which the Yamashita indictment was based, see Parks, 'Command Responsibility for War Crimes', pp. 22–9.

[14] United Nations War Crimes Commission, IV Law Reports of the Trials of War Criminals 35.

The test therefore was whether he had 'effective control'. If he had such control but failed to exercise it, as the Tribunal found, then he must face the responsibility. However, the Tribunal were careful to point out that this was not an absolute liability. They stated:

> Clearly assignment to command military troops is accompanied by broad authority and heavy responsibility ... It is absurd, however, to consider a commander a murderer or rapist because one of his soldiers commits a murder or a rape. Nevertheless, where murder and rape and vicious, revengeful actions are widespread offences, and there is no effective attempt by a commander to discover and control the criminal acts, such a commander may be held responsible, even criminally liable, for the lawless acts of his troops, depending upon their nature and the circumstances surrounding them.[15]

The United Nations War Crimes Commission, in their commentary on this case, looked at the knowledge requirement and said:

> the crimes which were committed by Yamashita's troops were so widespread both in space and in time, that they could be regarded as providing either prima facie evidence that the accused knew of their perpetration, or evidence that he must have failed to fulfil a duty to discover the standard of conduct of his troops.[16]

We see here that the nature of the crimes themselves provided *prima facie* evidence of knowledge. However, the Commission also seemed to indicate that a commander had a duty to find out. This was explained somewhat in a later passage when the Commission commented that 'Courts dealing with cases such as those at present under discussion may in suitable instances have regarded means of knowledge as being the same as knowledge itself.'[17]

A full reading of the judgment leaves the clear impression that the Tribunal were satisfied that Yamashita had actual knowledge and his duty as a commander to 'discover the standard of conduct of his troops' and his means of knowledge were just further circumstantial evidence supporting that conclusion. The traditional interpretation of the test laid down in the *Yamashita* case is reflected in the text of the 1958 *British Manual of Military Law* which considers the commander responsible if 'he has actual knowledge or should have knowledge, through reports received by him or through other means'.[18]

[15] *Ibid.*, at 35. [16] *Ibid.*, at 94. [17] *Ibid.*, at 94.
[18] *The Manual of Military Law*, Part III, *The Law of War on Land* (HMSO, 1958), para. 631.

There is a degree of inconsistency in the later cases. In the *High Command* case,[19] the requirement for a 'personal dereliction' was stressed. The Tribunal stated:

> Criminality does not attach to every individual in this chain of command from that fact alone. There must be a personal dereliction. That can occur only where the act is directly traceable to him or where his failure properly to supervise his subordinates constitutes criminal negligence on his part. In the latter case it must be a personal act amounting to a wanton immoral disregard of the action of his subordinates amounting to acquiescence.[20]

In the case of *United States* v. *Oswald Pohl*,[21] however, the Tribunal said in relation to the accused Mummenthey: 'Mummenthey's assertions that he did not know what was happening in the labour camps and enterprises under his jurisdiction does not exonerate him. It was his duty to know.'[22] Again, in that case, it seems clear that the Tribunal simply did not accept the accused's protestations that he had no knowledge. The evidence was so overwhelming that it was not difficult for the Tribunal to find actual knowledge and no need for them to rely on any lesser standard.

Post 1945 developments

It is interesting to note, in this historical survey, the standard laid down in the *United States Manual* of 1956.[23] It reads:

> The commander is . . . responsible, if he has actual knowledge, *or should have knowledge*, through reports received by him or through other means, that troops or other persons subject to his control are about to commit or have committed a war crime and he fails to take the necessary steps to insure compliance with the law of war or to punish violators thereof.[24]

[19] The German High Command trial, *Trial of Wilhelm von Leeb and Thirteen others* (Case No. 72), United Nations War Crimes Commission, XII Law Reports of the Trials of War Criminals 1.

[20] *Ibid.* at 76.

[21] The *Pohl* case, *United States of America* v. *Oswald Pohl and others* (1950) V Trials of War Criminals before the Nuremberg Military Tribunals 195.

[22] *Ibid.* at 1055.

[23] US Department of the Army Field Manual, *The Law of Land Warfare* (1956, FM 27–10).

[24] *Ibid.*, para. 501 (emphasis added).

The principle of command responsibility, unlike that of superior orders, did manage to gain acceptance into Additional Protocol I to the Geneva Conventions when it was adopted in 1977. Article 86(2) reads:

> The fact that a breach of the Conventions or of this Protocol was committed by a subordinate does not absolve his superiors from penal or disciplinary responsibility, as the case may be, if they knew, or had information which should have enabled them to conclude in the circumstances at the time, that he was committing or was going to commit such a breach and if they did not take all feasible measures within their power to prevent or repress the breach.[25]

The test here again goes beyond actual knowledge. Similarly, in the Statute of the International Criminal Tribunal for the former Yugoslavia (ICTY), the text reads:

> The fact that [crimes were] committed by a subordinate does not relieve his superior of criminal responsibility if he knew or had reason to know that the subordinate was about to commit such acts or had done so and the superior failed to take the necessary and reasonable measures to prevent such acts or to punish the perpetrators thereof.[26]

The ICTY and its sister Tribunal for Rwanda (ICTR) have had to examine command responsibility in depth. Although in the earliest cases, such as *Tadic*[27] and *Erdemovic*,[28] the emphasis was more on the actions of subordinates, the increase in the number of high ranking defendants has made such a development inevitable. The issue arose at first instance in the *Celebici*,[29] *Aleksovski*,[30] *Blaskic*,[31] *Kunarac*[32] and

[25] 1977 Protocol I Additional to the Geneva Conventions of 12 August 1949, and Relating to the Protection of Victims of International Armed Conflicts (1979) 1125 UNTS 3, Article 86(2).

[26] Statute of the International Criminal Tribunal for the former Yugoslavia, UN doc. S/RES/827, Annex, Article 7(3).

[27] *Prosecutor* v. *Tadic* (Case No. IT–94–1), Trial Chamber, 7 May 1997 (Appeals Chamber, 15 July 1999).

[28] *Prosecutor* v. *Erdemovic* (Case No. IT–96–22), Trial Chamber, 29 November 1996 (Appeals Chamber, 7 October 1997).

[29] *Prosecutor* v. *Zejnil Delalic, Zdravco Mucic (also known as 'Pavo'), Hazim Delic, Esad Landzo (also known as 'Zenga')* (Case No. IT–96–21), Trial Chamber, 16 November 1998.

[30] *Prosecutor* v. *Zlatko Aleksovski* (Case No. IT–94–14/1), Trial Chamber, 25 June 1999 (Appeals Chamber, 24 March 2000).

[31] *Prosecutor* v. *Tihomir Blaskic* (Case No. IT–95–14), Trial Chamber, 3 March 2000.

[32] *Prosecutor* v. *Drogoljub Kunarac, Radomir Kovac and Zoran Vukovic* (Case No. IT–96–23/ IT–96–23/1), Trial Chamber, 22 February 2001 (Appeals Chamber, 12 June 2002).

Kordic and Cerkez[33] cases in the ICTY and in several cases at the ICTR, including *Kayishema.*[34] However, the most complete analysis is to be found in the judgment of the Appeals Chamber in the *Celebici* case.[35] The Chamber made a detailed analysis of the jurisprudence in order to interpret its own Statute and, in particular, examined the questions of the necessary relationship between the superior and the subordinates and what is the appropriate knowledge requirement for the superior.

Celebici

The *Celebici* case arose out of events in 1992 when forces consisting of Bosnian Muslims and Bosnian Croats took control of villages around the Konjic municipality in Central Bosnia. The villages contained predominantly Bosnian Serbs. Those people detained during these operations were held in a former Yugoslav Army facility in the village of Celebici. There, detainees were killed, tortured, sexually assaulted, beaten and otherwise subjected to cruel and inhuman treatment.[36]

The four accused, Zejnil Delalic, Zdravko Mucic, Hazim Delic and Esad Landzo, represented all levels of authority. Delalic was alleged to be the co-ordinator of the Bosnian Muslim forces in the area and later to have been the Commander of the First Tactical Group of the Bosnian Army. As such, it was alleged that he had authority over the Celebici Camp. Mucic was found to be the Commander of the Celebici Camp and Delic his Deputy Commander. Landzo was a guard at the Camp. The Trial Chamber – and later the Appeals Chamber – had to look at both personal responsibility for crimes under Article 7(1) of the Tribunal's Statute[37] and also command responsibility under Article 7(3).[38]

In examining the required relationship, the Chamber recognized the reality of modern conflicts. Conflicts now are much more fluid,

[33] *Prosecutor* v. *Dario Kordic and Mario Cerkez* (Case No. IT–95–14/2), Trial Chamber, 26 February 2001.

[34] *Prosecutor* v. *Clement Kayishema* (Case No. ICTR–95–1), Trial Chamber, 21 May 1999.

[35] *Prosecutor* v. *Zejnil Delalic and others*, above n. 29, Appeals Chamber, 20 February 2001, reported in (2001) 40 *International Legal Materials* 626.

[36] For a full account of the background facts, see the judgment of the Trial Chamber in *Prosecutor* v. *Zejnil Delalic and others*, above n. 29, paras. 120–57.

[37] Article 7(1) reads: 'A person who planned, instigated, ordered, committed or otherwise aided or abetted in the planning, preparation or execution of a crime referred to in articles 2 to 5 of the present Statute, shall be individually responsible for the crime.'

[38] Above n. 26 and text thereto.

involving a combination of regular and irregular forces. Formal command is difficult to ascertain and indeed in many cases will simply not exist. They said:

> concepts of subordination, hierarchy and chains of command ... need not be established in the sense of formal organisational structures so long as the fundamental requirement of an effective power to control the subordinate, in the sense of preventing or punishing criminal conduct, is satisfied.[39]

They went on to base responsibility on 'effective control' stating:

> The concept of effective control over a subordinate – in the sense of a material ability to prevent or punish criminal conduct, however that control is exercised – is the threshold to be reached in establishing a superior-subordinate relationship for the purpose of Article 7(3) of the Statute.[40]

However, the Chamber was not prepared to extend the meaning of control too far. The Prosecution sought to argue that 'substantial influence' was a sufficient measure of 'control' for the imposition of liability under Article 7(3). The Chamber stated:

> It is clear that substantial influence as a means of control in any sense which falls short of the possession of effective control over subordinates, which requires the possession of material abilities to prevent subordinate offences or to punish subordinate offenders, lacks sufficient support in State practice and judicial decisions. Nothing relied on by the Prosecution indicates that there is sufficient evidence of State practice or judicial authority to support a theory that substantial influence as a means of exerting command responsibility has the standing of a rule of customary law, particularly a rule by which criminal liability would be imposed.[41]

When looking at the thorny question of knowledge, the Chamber stated emphatically:

> as the element of knowledge has to be proved in this type of case, command responsibility is not a form of strict liability. A superior may only be held liable for the acts of his subordinates if he 'knew or had reason to know' about them.[42]

[39] (2001) 40 *International Legal Materials* 680. [40] *Ibid.*
[41] *Ibid.*, p. 683. [42] *Ibid.*, p. 677.

The Chamber then went on to expand on what was meant by the phrase 'knew or had reason to know'. The Trial Chamber had held that:

> [A superior] may possess the *mens rea* for command responsibility where: (1) he had actual knowledge, established through direct or circumstantial evidence, that his subordinates were committing or about to commit crimes . . . , or (2) where he had in his possession information of a nature, which at the least, would put him on notice of the risk of such offences by indicating the need for additional investigation in order to ascertain whether such crimes were committed or were about to be committed by his subordinates.[43]

After a detailed review of the jurisprudence, the Appeals Chamber upheld the decision of the Trials Chamber, stating:

> A superior will be criminally responsible through the principles of superior responsibility only if information was available to him which would have put him on notice of offences committed by subordinates. This information need not be such that it by itself was sufficient to compel the conclusion of the existence of such crimes. It is sufficient that the superior was put on further enquiry by the information, or, in other words, that it indicated the need for additional investigation in order to ascertain whether offences were being committed or about to be committed by his subordinates.[44]

However, this again did not go as far as the Prosecution would have liked. The Chamber distinguished the knowledge requirement from neglect of duty in terms stating:

> Article 7(3) of the Statute is concerned with superior liability arising from failure to act in spite of knowledge. Neglect of a duty to acquire such knowledge, however, does not feature in the provision as a separate offence, and a superior is not therefore liable under the provision for such failures but only for failing to take necessary and reasonable measures to prevent or punish. The Appeals Chamber takes it that the Prosecution seeks a finding that 'reason to know' exists on the part of a commander if the latter is seriously negligent in his duty to obtain the relevant information. The point here should not be that knowledge may be presumed if a person fails in his *duty* to obtain the relevant information of a crime, but it may be presumed if he had the *means* to obtain the knowledge but deliberately refrained from doing so. The Prosecution's argument that a breach of a duty of a superior to remain constantly

[43] *Ibid.*, p. 673. [44] *Ibid.*, p. 677.

> informed of his subordinates', actions will necessarily result in *criminal* liability comes close to the imposition of criminal liability on a strict or negligence basis. It is however noted that although a commander's failure to remain apprised of his subordinates' action, or to set up a monitoring system may constitute a neglect of duty which results in liability within the military disciplinary framework, it will not necessarily result in criminal liability.[45]

This is beginning to reflect some of the language to be found in the ICC Statute and is a tightening of the looser language contained in *Yamashita*.

With regard to civilian superiors, the Appeals Chamber held that it was not necessary for them to make a ruling but did say: 'Civilian superiors undoubtedly bear responsibility for subordinate offences under certain conditions, but whether their responsibility contains identical elements to that of military commanders is not clear in customary international law.'[46] It is interesting to note that, as a result of this detailed examination, the Appeals Chamber upheld the acquittal of Delalic by the Trial Chamber on the basis that he did not have sufficient command and control over the Celebici Camp and its guards to found his criminal responsibility as a superior for the crimes committed. Mucic was found guilty under the principles of superior responsibility for crimes committed by his subordinates, namely, murder, torture and inhuman treatment, as well as being found guilty on the basis of personal responsibility for the unlawful confinement of civilians. The guilty verdicts on Delic and Landzo were based on personal responsibility.

International Criminal Court

In July 1998, the Rome Statute of the International Criminal Court was adopted. The court itself came into existence on 1 July 2002 following the receipt of the sixtieth ratification. Article 28 of the Statute deals with command responsibility. It is one of the most complicated articles of the whole Statute and was the subject of extensive and detailed negotiation. Almost every word was fought over. As a result, it contains compromises and nuances, some of which are obvious and some less so. It differs from the wording used in the Statutes of the ICTY and ICTR but that does not necessarily mean that there is a risk that jurisprudence of the Tribunals

[45] *Ibid.*, p. 673. [46] *Ibid.*, p. 677.

and the ICC will develop in different directions. Indeed, the Appeals Chamber in the *Celebici* case seems to have made a deliberate attempt to develop the jurisprudence in a way that is consistent with the past case law and its own Statute but at the same time not inconsistent with the terms of Article 28. Article 28 reads as follows:

> In addition to other grounds of criminal responsibility under this Statute for crimes within the jurisdiction of the Court:
>
> (a) A military commander or person effectively acting as a military commander shall be criminally responsible for crimes within the jurisdiction of the Court committed by forces under his or her effective command or control, or effective authority and control as the case may be, as a result of his or her failure to exercise control properly over such forces, where:
>
> (i) That military commander or person either knew or, owing to the circumstances at the time, should have known that forces were committing or about to commit such crimes; and
>
> (ii) That military commander or person failed to take all necessary and reasonable measures within his or her power to prevent or repress their commission or to submit the matter to the competent authorities for investigation and prosecution.
>
> (b) With respect to superior and subordinate relationships not described in paragraph (a), a superior shall be criminally responsible for crimes within the jurisdiction of the Court committed by subordinates under his or her effective authority and control, as a result of his or her failure to exercise control properly over such subordinates, where:
>
> (i) The superior either knew or consciously disregarded information which clearly indicated, that the subordinates were committing or about to commit such crimes; and
>
> (ii) The crimes concerned activities that were within the effective responsibility and control of the superior; and
>
> (iii) The superior failed to take all necessary and reasonable measures within his or her power to prevent or repress their commission or to submit the matter to the competent authorities for investigation and prosecution.

The first area of difficulty here is in ascertaining to whom this provision is applicable. The text is divided into two parts and they are not all that they seem! The first part deals with military commanders and persons 'effectively acting as a military commander'. A distinction is thus drawn between military commanders and civilian superiors. This is based on the fact that military command brings with it both power and responsibility. Unlike a civilian superior, the military commander has powers of discipline over his troops and should be able to exercise a degree of control both on and off duty. The civilian superior has no such sanction. However, the first part is also designed to cover 'warlords' who may not have official military status but exercise the same degree of control.

Not all military commanders come under the first part. It will be noted that the crimes must be committed by *forces*. Thus, where crimes are committed by civilians under the authority of a military commander, this first provision does not apply. It is for that reason that the second part starts in such a cumbersome manner. Had it referred only to civilian superiors, there would have been a lacuna. As it is, although the text is primarily designed to cover civilian superiors, any superior/subordinate relationship not covered by the first part, falls within the second. There is thus no gap. All superior/subordinate relationships are covered.

The next area of difficulty is in the relationship itself and the text is not easy to follow here. The subordinates must be under 'effective command and control' or 'effective authority and control' and at the same time the crimes must be committed as a result of a failure to exercise control properly. The distinction between 'command' and 'authority' is to recognize the lack of a 'command' relationship outside military circles. Although the wording is difficult, the test is essentially one of control. It is perhaps unfortunate that the concept of 'command' or 'authority' has been retained though the relaxation of the definition of 'command' to be found in the *Celebici* jurisprudence is helpful.

The final key area is the knowledge requirement. Here again there is a split. Military commanders, and their equivalents, commanding forces must have known or 'owing to the circumstances at the time, should have known that the forces were committing or about to commit such crimes'.[47] For all other superior/subordinate relationships, the test is slightly different. The superior must have known or 'consciously disregarded information which clearly indicated that the subordinates were committing or about to commit such crimes'.

[47] This should be compared with the 'had reason to know' test to be found in Article 7(3) of the Statute of the International Criminal Tribunal for the former Yugoslavia, above n. 26 and text thereto.

If these knowledge requirements are met, then the superior is liable if he fails 'to take all necessary and reasonable measures within his or her power to prevent or repress their commission or to submit the matter to the competent authorities for investigation and prosecution'. It is thus his failure to act supported by the knowledge requirement that forms the *actus reus* of the crime.

Bringing the threads together

How does this text fit with the evolving jurisprudence? It seems clear that the Appeals Chamber in the *Celebici* case was at least influenced by the terms of the ICC Statute and took it into account in drafting their judgment.[48] There are passages which clearly reflect the language contained in the Statute[49] and, in other places, the court is careful not to contradict such language. Thus on civilian superiors, whilst the Tribunal held that it was not necessary for them to make a ruling on the facts of the *Celebici* case, they stated: 'Civilian superiors undoubtedly bear responsibility for subordinate offences under certain conditions, but whether their responsibility contains identical elements to that of military commanders is not clear in customary international law.'[50] This clearly acknowledged the fact that the ICC does indeed, controversially, provide for different elements to apply to civilian superiors.

The Chamber seems in some ways to be drawing the various different strands and wording together into a common thread. Whilst the jurisprudence in *Celebici* can stand alongside *Yamashita* with no difficulty, so can it stand also alongside Article 28 of the Rome Statute. There is nothing in the judgment that cannot be reflected in the ICC text. The declarations on the meaning of command and control are helpful and will assist the ICC in overcoming the problems implicit in the text as it stands. It was interesting that the Chamber rejected the prosecution argument that 'influence' could be enough to attract command responsibility in certain circumstances. Similarly, the tightened interpretation of the knowledge requirement will assist the court in interpreting the 'should have known' test in Article 28.

[48] In a different context, that of whether there is a strict separation between 'Hague' and 'Geneva' law, specific reference was made to the ICC Statute to provide confirmation of the Chamber's decision, see (2001) 40 *International Legal Materials* 656.

[49] Above n. 46 and the text thereto. [50] Above n. 47.

The *Yamashita* case has been criticized on the facts and also as 'victors' justice'. The language is in some areas loose and the principles outlined in it wide. However, the basic principle that commanders can be held responsible for the acts of their subordinates has not been challenged. The ICTY and ICTR have been able to build on that basic block, expanding and clarifying the *Yamashita* decision. Despite the differences in wording in the various legal texts that established the ICTY, ICTR and now the ICC, there is clearly a single thread of jurisprudence on which the ICC can build. Command responsibility is alive and well both as a concept and in practical reality.

The version of command responsibility articulated by the Appeals Chamber in the *Celebici* case is both realistic and in accord with both past jurisprudence and the ICC Statute. Commanders need have no fear if they conduct themselves in accordance with their duty. If they act in dereliction of duty and, as a result, crimes are committed with impunity, then the commander who finds himself in the dock will have no one to blame but himself.

6

The proposed new neutral protective emblem: a long-term solution to a long-standing problem

MICHAEL MEYER

Introduction

Hilaire McCoubrey wrote one of the first contemporary textbooks for university students on international humanitarian law; it is also one of the first to be called by that name.[1] One review of the book concluded 'in writing this book McCoubrey has made an outstanding contribution towards a better understanding of international humanitarian law'.[2] The term 'international humanitarian law' is now widely used and recognized by states internationally, and increasingly, at national level.[3] However, this was not always the case. The original term, 'laws of war' is still used[4] and the expression 'law of armed conflict', often abbreviated as 'LOAC', remains in use by the British military, and by the armed forces of other countries. As noted by Hilaire, '"international humanitarian law" as a term of art is of relatively recent date, having gained recognition largely through the work of Jean Pictet'.[5] It was indeed Dr Pictet, an influential lawyer and senior official of the International

The views expressed in this article are personal, and do not necessarily reflect those of any Red Cross or Red Crescent organization.

1 H. McCoubrey, *International Humanitarian Law: The Regulation of Armed Conflicts* (1st edn, Dartmouth, 1990).

2 (1991) 281 *International Review of the Red Cross* 240.

3 As examples, see the 1997 Ottawa Convention on the Prohibition of the Use, Stockpiling, Production and Transfer of Anti-Personnel Mines and on their Destruction, (1997) 36 *International Legal Materials* 1507, Preamble (final para.); numerous UN resolutions and documents, and the Belgian Law of 10 February 1999 Concerning the Punishment of Serious Violations of International Humanitarian Law, (1999) 38 *International Legal Materials* 918.

4 See, e.g., in the title of the premier collection of documents compiled and edited by A. Roberts and R. Guelff (eds.), *Documents on the Laws of War* (3rd edn, Oxford University Press, 2000).

5 McCoubrey, *International Humanitarian Law* (1st edn), p. 20, n. 1.

Committee of the Red Cross (ICRC), who did much to popularize the term. IHL emphasizes the humanitarian purpose of the international rules, established by treaties or custom, which protect the victims of armed conflict and regulate the conduct of hostilities.[6] The fact that Hilaire used 'International Humanitarian Law' as the title of his then innovative book contributed to establishing the respectability of the term among academics and others in the United Kingdom, and perhaps elsewhere in the English-speaking world.

I do not know whether the nomenclature international humanitarian law (IHL) helped to attract Hilaire to that particular area of international law and practice. I am certain, however, that the humanitarian character of the subject would have appealed to him, in part, because Hilaire was a genuinely humane individual. Like many of the most successful humanitarians, Hilaire was also a very sensible person, his compassion being informed by a strong sense of realism. This latter quality is very important in the study and application of IHL, which is underpinned by principles of humanity, military necessity and proportionality and the frequent need to balance the same. In making such assessments, one must always have in mind the realities of the battlefield and of air and sea operations, including developments in technology and strategy.

Hilaire also had a dry and very welcome sense of humour. In his book *International Humanitarian Law*, he writes succinctly and with authority on the topic of distinctive emblems (such as the red cross and red crescent), and their practical importance in identifying persons and establishments accorded protection by the Geneva Conventions.[7] He refers to the problem posed by having a multiplicity of emblems, arising from unacceptable associations of the cross, and the difficulty in finding a new emblem, devoid of non-neutral connotations. Hilaire wrote:

> As an illustration of this the author asked a class to suggest such an emblem: the answer finally determined upon was a red extended hand, palm outermost ... A hand presented in this way is a well known symbol of pacific intention (also of arrest) and therefore quite suitable. It is also,

[6] This is not the place to discuss the debates about the use of the term or its precise definition, see, for a brief discussion, G. Abi-Saab, 'The Specificities of Humanitarian Law', in C. Swinarski (ed.), *Studies and Essays on International Humanitarian Law and Red Cross Principles in Honour of Jean Pictet* (Martinus Nijhoff, 1984), p. 265.

[7] McCoubrey, *International Humanitarian Law* (1st edn), pp. 37–40.

when red on a white background, the heraldic emblem of Ulster (Northern Ireland) and therefore peculiarly unsuitable.[8]

Hilaire was very interested in this problem of the multiplicity or plurality of protective emblems, all intended to signify neutrality, including religious neutrality. For whatever reason – whether because of his own deep religious conviction, his sensitivity as a person, his liberal outlook, his knowledge of philosophy, keenly developed analytical skills, or a combination of these – he readily understood why, for example, countries whose population did not follow a Christian tradition, might find it difficult to accept the red cross emblem as a neutral protective sign. I believe that Hilaire would have been encouraged by, and fully supported, recent efforts to address this problem; for such reasons, I have selected this aspect of international humanitarian law as the subject of this chapter in his memory.

The emblem issue

Upon initial consideration, it may seem that the matter of protective emblems or signs under international humanitarian law is quite straightforward, and is hardly a topic of international concern. However, this would be too hasty a view since the matter of protective signs has different aspects, and in the case of the distinctive emblems prescribed under the 1949 Geneva Conventions for the Protection of War Victims, an important political component which may affect the future of one of the world's most respected humanitarian networks, the International Red Cross and Red Crescent Movement.[9]

Thus, this chapter will not address all of the protective signs established under IHL,[10] nor the challenges posed in using and protecting them, in peacetime as well as in armed conflict. Rather, it will focus on the distinctive emblems established by the 1949 Geneva Conventions (including relevant background elements, and noting the emblems' close connection with the International Red Cross and Red Crescent Movement); the current problems of protection and of achieving universality within the Movement, and the proposed solution of a new

[8] *Ibid.*, pp. 38–9.

[9] The International Red Cross and Red Crescent Movement consists of three components: the International Committee of the Red Cross (ICRC), the recognized National Red Cross and National Red Crescent Societies (currently, 181 in total), and the International Federation of Red Cross and Red Crescent Societies.

[10] For a collection of such signs, see P. Eberlin, *Protective Signs* (ICRC, 1983).

neutral protective emblem, established through the adoption of a Third Additional Protocol to the 1949 Geneva Conventions.

Selected background

Much has been written on the history and general background to the emblem issue, and it is not intended to provide an exhaustive examination here.[11] Still, the following points seem worth noting for an adequate understanding of the debate.

Identifying sign for protection

As indicated in the introductory section, distinctive emblems, such as the red cross and the red crescent, serve an important purpose as signs of neutrality and of protection. They are to be used only by officially authorized medical and religious personnel; they signify that these personnel and transports, establishments and objects marked with the same emblems, must not be attacked, and, as far as possible, these personnel must be assisted in performing their purely humanitarian functions. In simple terms, the red cross and red crescent emblems are intended to provide safety on the battlefield.

Long before the establishment of modern IHL, a flag of a single colour was sometimes used to mark hospitals and ambulances on the battlefield. However, this practice varied according to the battle or war, and the country.[12] From the beginning, those involved in founding the Red Cross Movement and modern IHL realized the importance of having a uniform international emblem, common to all, as the visible sign of the immunity and assistance to which medical personnel and the wounded should be entitled.[13] This immunity or protection from attack and

[11] Dr François Bugnion has written a number of very useful and authoritative texts: see, e.g., F. Bugnion, *The Emblem of the Red Cross: A Brief History* (ICRC, 1977); 'The Red Cross and Red Crescent Emblems', (1989) 272 *International Review of the Red Cross* 408; *Towards a Comprehensive Solution to the Question of the Emblem* (2nd rev. edn, ICRC, 2003). See also www. icrc. org

[12] J. S. Pictet (ed.), *Commentary to Geneva Convention I of 12 August 1949* (ICRC, 1952), p. 297. It is reported that at the 1863 Geneva International Conference (see above), 'delegates were aware that each country designated its field hospitals by a colour of its own choice: white for Austria, red for France, yellow for Spain and the United States', P. Boissier, *History of the International Committee of the Red Cross: From Solferino to Tsushima* (ICRC, 1985), p. 78.

[13] Pictet, *Commentary to Geneva Convention I*, p. 297.

capture was also called neutrality and the officially authorized medical personnel and the wounded were thus to be granted a special neutral status.[14] It needs to be borne in mind that it is not the emblems themselves that confer protection: this is granted to designated personnel, transports and objects under the 1949 Geneva Conventions and where applicable, their 1977 Additional Protocols, regardless of whether or not a distinctive emblem is displayed.[15] Thus, the red cross and red crescent are simply a useful tool, a practical means of seeking to ensure respect for a pre-existing international legal right of protection.

Close connection between the Geneva Conventions and the Red Cross and Red Crescent Movement

The founders of what became the International Red Cross and Red Crescent Movement were also instrumental in promoting the adoption of the original Geneva Convention in 1864, which is traditionally seen as being the first instrument of modern IHL. The Geneva Convention of 22 August 1864 was the first multilateral treaty concluded in peacetime providing for the treatment of the wounded on the battlefield, applicable to warfare generally. Before that, such arrangements, in the form of cartels or capitulations, were normally bilateral, being agreed between belligerents in specific wars or battles. The 1864 Convention is also notable in that it was open to all states, specifically, Article 9 provided for accession by states not represented at the diplomatic conference at which it was adopted. This close connection between the Red Cross and Red Crescent Movement, and subsequent updates and revisions of the Geneva Convention, and of IHL generally, continues to this day.

The 1864 Geneva Convention for the Amelioration of the Condition of the Wounded in Armies in the Field was based, in part, upon the resolutions and recommendations of an 1863 international conference, attended both by representatives of states and of private philanthropic organizations, held in Geneva the previous year. Subsequent international conferences have repeated this unique composition of having delegations from both states, i.e. those party to the 1949 Geneva

[14] See Boissier, *History of the International Committee of the Red Cross*, pp. 76–9, 115–17.

[15] Geneva Convention I for the Amelioration of the Condition of the Wounded and Sick in Armed Forces in the Field, Geneva, 12 August 1949, (1950) 75 UNTS 31, Articles 24–27; 38–43; Geneva Convention II for the Amelioration of the Condition of Wounded, Sick and Shipwrecked Members of Armed Forces at Sea, Geneva, 12 August 1949, (1950) 75 UNTS 85, Articles 36–37; 41–44. Additional articles and treaties could be cited.

Conventions (now 191 in total, which is nearly the entire international community), and private organizations, namely, the components of the Movement: the ICRC, the recognized National Red Cross and Red Crescent Societies, and the International Federation of these National Societies. Today, the International Conference of the Red Cross and Red Crescent meets, in principle, every four years.[16]

The 1863 international conference was the founding conference of the Red Cross Movement. It adopted a resolution that voluntary medical personnel, placed under military command, 'shall wear in all countries, as a uniform distinctive sign, a white armlet with a red cross'.[17] This conference, not being a diplomatic conference, did not have the authority to adopt a resolution selecting a single distinctive emblem for the medical services and field hospitals of all armies. However, it did recommend, among other matters, 'that a uniform distinctive sign be recognised for the Medical Corps of all armies', and 'that a uniform flag also be adopted in all countries for ambulances and hospitals'.[18]

The diplomatic conference, consisting of sixteen states (all European, plus the USA), which met the next year to adopt the 1864 Geneva Convention, decided that a red cross on a white ground should be the distinctive and uniform sign for army medical personnel, and for military ambulances and hospitals.[19] This prescription is found in subsequent treaties that amplified and updated the 1864 Convention.[20]

Why a red cross on a white background?

There is no definitive explanation for the selection of a red cross on a white ground as the uniform distinctive sign for the medical services of armed forces. Later versions of the original Geneva Convention (i.e. those of 1906, 1929 and 1949) refer to the connection between the heraldic emblem of the Swiss Confederation and the red cross

[16] The next international conference, the 29th, is scheduled to be held in 2007.

[17] Resolutions of the Geneva International Conference, 26–29 October 1863, Article 8.

[18] *Ibid.*, Recommendation (c). Also see Boissier, *History of the International Committee of the Red Cross*, p. 78.

[19] Article 7 of the 1864 Geneva Convention.

[20] See, as examples, the Hague Convention of 29 July 1899, for the Adaptation to Maritime Warfare of the Principles of the Geneva Convention of 22 August 1864 (Convention No. III of 1899), Article 5; the Geneva Convention of 6 July 1906, for the Amelioration of the Condition of the Wounded and Sick in Armies in the Field, Article 18; Geneva Convention I 1949, Article 38; Geneva Convention IV 1949, Article 18; Additional Protocol I, Article 8(l); Additional Protocol II 1977, Article 12.

emblem.[21] Both the 1929 and the 1949 Geneva Wounded and Sick Conventions contain an article which states: 'As a compliment to Switzerland, the heraldic emblem of the red cross on a white ground, formed by reversing the Federal colours, is retained as the emblem and distinctive sign of the Medical Service of armed forces'.[22] This seems logical given the integral role of the Swiss authorities in convening the diplomatic conference which led to the adoption of the 1864 Geneva Convention, and the essential role of Swiss citizens, notably, Henry Dunant and what became the International Committee of the Red Cross (ICRC), in promoting and preparing the original Convention, and its successors.

However, the records of the 1863 Geneva International Conference do not reveal who proposed use of a red cross on a white background[23] and also give no indication that the conference wished to honour Switzerland by choosing a sign formed by reversing the Federal colours. In fact, Boissier provides one piece of evidence which suggests that a representative of the Swiss Federal Council at the time, Dr Brière, was not pleased by the similarity between the red cross emblem and the Swiss cross; Dr Brière wrote that he preferred use of the St Andrew's cross, that is, a diagonal cross extending to each corner of the flag.[24]

Regardless of the original reason for selecting a red cross on a white ground, it seems clear that the participants at both the 1863 international conference and the 1864 diplomatic conference wished to adopt a single emblem which would attract universal support as the uniform and distinctive sign of protection for the officially authorized medical function on the battlefield.

[21] The ICRC Commentary to the relevant provision in Geneva Convention I 1949 (Article 38), records that the phrase was also intended 'to confirm officially and explicitly that the [red cross] emblem had no religious significance', Pictet, *Commentary to Geneva Convention I*, pp. 303, 304. This is relevant to the subsequent discussion above.

[22] Geneva Convention of 27 July 1929 for the Amelioration of the Condition of the Wounded and Sick in Armies in the Field, Article 19; Geneva Convention I 1949, Article 38.

[23] Pictet suggests that the Prussian delegate at the 1863 International Conference, Dr Loeffler, proposed use of the equal armed red cross on a white background. However, the matter was settled during a recess and the details of the discussion never recorded, J. Pictet, *Development and Principles of International Humanitarian Law* (Martinus Nijhoff, 1985), p. 30.

[24] Boissier, *History of the International Committee of the Red Cross*, pp. 77–8.

Not a religious symbol, but . . .

The red cross emblem was not intended to be a sign of Christianity. The founders of the Red Cross Movement, and the representatives at the 1864 diplomatic conference, may have been inspired by their personal religious convictions. The Swiss flag may have its origin in a representation of the Christian faith. However, as explained in the preceding section, the red cross emblem was intended to be a universal symbol, signifying neutrality and protection. It seems worth noting that, in 1855, Henry Dunant had been involved in establishing the World Alliance of Young Men's Christian Associations (YMCA). The YMCA has a specific Christian basis. However, this is not the case for the Red Cross Movement, whose founders, notably Dunant, wished to establish a universal humanitarian organization (relief network), whose voluntary medical personnel would use a universal neutral protective sign.[25]

Yet, it was not long after the red cross emblem was adopted in 1864 that the soldiers of Turkey took offence at the sign, reportedly because it reminded them of the badge of the Crusaders. Thus, during the Russo-Turkish War in 1876, the Turkish government said that its military medical services would use a red crescent on a white ground in place of the red cross emblem.[26] The Russian government initially protested, but eventually accepted the practice provided that Turkey would continue to respect Russia's use of the red cross. The ICRC made clear its concern[27] and preference for use of the red cross emblem. However, it acquiesced in the Turkish practice for the duration of the conflict. Among its concerns, the ICRC feared that opposition could result between the red cross, which the Turks wrongly considered a religious symbol, and the red crescent, which was Turkey's (the Ottoman Empire's) religious and national emblem. Historically, the ICRC was always against the adoption of a national or religious symbol as a neutral protective emblem.

Later, Egypt joined Turkey in using the red crescent emblem, and Persia (subsequently Iran) used the red lion and sun emblem. Other emblems were also proposed, such as the following. In 1877, Japan's

[25] See H. Haug (ed.), *Humanity for All: The International Red Cross and Red Crescent Movement* (Haupt, 1993), p. 39.

[26] Turkey had acceded to the 1864 Geneva Convention without reservation on 5 July 1865. Strictly speaking, Turkey first used the red crescent in her war with Serbia, earlier in 1876. As indicated previously, this account of the background to the emblem issue is a selective summary and is not intended to be exhaustive.

[27] Bugnion, *The Emblem of the Red Cross*, p. 17.

National Society used a sun above a red strip. At diplomatic conferences in 1899 and 1906, Siam (Thailand) sought recognition of the combined sign of the red cross emblem with the Buddhist symbol of the flame. In 1935, Afghanistan applied for recognition of the emblem of a red archway. After becoming independent states, India proposed the symbol of a red wheel on a white ground; Lebanon considered the sign of a red cedar tree; Sri Lanka suggested a red swastika (a symbol long common to Buddhism, Hinduism and Jainism), and Sudan, among other symbols, contemplated a red rhinoceros. Ultimately, the governments of all these countries decided to adopt one of the recognized emblems, either the red cross or the red crescent.[28]

The ICRC consistently made known its objections to these practices, believing they undermined the principle of a single universal emblem. However, the question of use of a distinctive emblem rested on the interpretation and application of the 1864 Geneva Convention and its successors and was thus ultimately a matter for the governments of the states parties to those Conventions. Although the ICRC voiced its concerns, and the states parties stressed the neutral, secular character of the red cross emblem, eventually the practices of Turkey, Egypt and Persia in using different emblems were recognized in the Geneva Wounded and Sick Convention of 1929, in the hope of preventing further exceptions.[29]

The same matter was raised at the diplomatic conference which adopted the four Geneva Conventions in 1949. At that time, it was also proposed to increase the number of exceptions by recognizing the red shield of David on a white ground (the Magen David Adom, used by the medical services of the armed forces of Israel), or even by allowing each country to choose any red symbol on a white ground. Others wished to revert to the use of the red cross as the only distinctive emblem, or to adopt a completely new symbol. The Conference decided to maintain the general arrangement agreed in 1929, whereby the red cross emblem is the accepted sign of the armed forces' medical services, but countries which used the red crescent or the red lion and sun before the adoption of the 1949 Convention could do so. In practice, since 1949, the states parties have not objected when additional countries have decided to use the red crescent.[30]

[28] See *ibid.*, pp. 61–6; colour illustrations at p. 70.

[29] Article 19 of the 1929 Geneva Wounded and Sick Convention.

[30] Also, on 4 September 1980, the Islamic Republic of Iran made a declaration stating that henceforth, it intended to use the red crescent as the emblem and distinctive sign in place of the red lion and sun emblem. At the same time, it reserved the right to return to

Israel's military medical services have continued to use the red shield of David emblem. Israel made a reservation to this effect when it signed the 1949 Geneva Conventions, which it maintained on ratification on 6 July 1951.[31] The Israeli government decided not to pursue formal recognition of the emblem during the diplomatic conference which adopted the 1977 Additional Protocols to the 1949 Geneva Conventions, withdrawing a proposed amendment before it could be considered.

Involvement of the National Red Cross and Red Crescent Societies

The International Red Cross and Red Crescent Movement has a close connection with the emblem issue by virtue of its historic and continuing association with the Geneva Conventions. As the names suggest, Red Cross and Red Crescent organizations use the emblems prescribed in the Geneva Conventions (indeed, as noted above, the red cross emblem was first agreed as the sign for voluntary medical personnel working under military command).

The Red Cross Movement and the Geneva Conventions have a common origin in the ideas of Henry Dunant. Dunant was a Swiss businessman who wrote a moving account of the suffering he witnessed following the Battle of Solferino, involving French, Italian and Austrian forces, in 1859. Many sick and wounded soldiers were left to die because of the insufficiency of the military medical services of the three armies. To address this problem, Dunant advocated two main ideas: first, in each country permanent relief societies should be formed in time of peace, which would be organized and ready to succour the wounded in time of war; second, countries should adopt a treaty providing an international basis for relief to the wounded.

The Geneva International Conference of 1863 agreed that each country should have what later became known as National Red Cross and Red Crescent Societies, thus, fulfilling Dunant's first proposal.[32] These Societies were auxiliary to the military medical service and, logically, used the same emblem. Thus, the distinctive emblems of the red cross and of the red crescent have two uses. The first, and the primary, use is as

use of the red lion and sun emblem should new emblems be recognized in future. For information, see (1980) 219 *International Review of the Red Cross* 316.

[31] This reservation is relevant to the later discussion of the draft Third Additional Protocol, Article 3 on indicative use of the new distinctive emblem.

[32] The 1864 Geneva Convention gave form to Dunant's second idea.

a protective sign, marking medical and religious personnel and objects entitled to respect and protection during armed conflicts. The second use is indicative, showing that persons or objects are linked to the Red Cross and Red Crescent Movement.[33]

In many armed conflicts, including during the First World War, these National Societies played a very useful role in support of the medical service of their country's armed forces. Especially since the 1920s, the role of National Societies has expanded to include humanitarian activities during peacetime, and in a number of countries, the Society no longer has a significant role in support of the medical service of its country's armed forces. Nevertheless, every National Society continues to be an auxiliary to the public authorities of its country in the humanitarian field, and to qualify for recognition as a member of the International Movement, it must use one of the distinctive emblems and names prescribed under the Geneva Conventions, namely, the red cross or red crescent.[34] This explains the reason for one of the main current problems surrounding the emblem, that is, there are certain National Societies which feel unable to adopt either of the emblems currently in use and, thus, cannot be recognized by the ICRC as a component of the Movement or admitted to membership of the International Federation of Red Cross and Red Crescent Societies.

Main current problems and the proposed solution

As mentioned in the preceding section, one of the main difficulties concerning the emblem issue is internal to the International Red Cross and Red Crescent Movement: that is, certain National Societies have a difficulty using one or other of the existing emblems. Two examples stand out: the Magen David Adom in Israel wishes to use its own emblem, the red shield of David, and the government of Eritrea wishes its National Society to use the red cross and the red crescent together

[33] Both uses are provided for in Geneva Convention I 1949, in Article 44. Any confusion between the two uses must be avoided; generally, the emblem is large in size when used for protection, and small when used as an indicative sign. The states parties to the Geneva Conventions and the components of the Movement have adopted Regulations to ensure that the emblems are used properly, in particular, by National Societies, and to uphold their integrity.

[34] Statutes of the International Red Cross and Red Crescent Movement, Article 4(5). These Statutes were adopted by the states parties to the Geneva Conventions and the components of the Movement at the 25th International Conference of the Red Cross in 1986.

(the so-called double emblem). The 1949 Geneva Conventions do not provide for the use of more than one emblem at the same time and for practical purposes of protection, the two emblems side-by-side are significantly less visible than a single sign.[35]

The inability of the Magen David Adom (MDA) to be recognized has been a long-standing source of concern to many. Some argue that the Red Cross and Red Crescent Movement cannot be neutral, impartial and universal while the MDA is excluded. In particular, the American Red Cross has for some four years been pressing for immediate recognition of the MDA and for approximately the same period, it has been withholding statutory payments to the International Federation of Red Cross and Red Crescent Societies to demonstrate its displeasure. The American Society has also stopped its voluntary contributions to the ICRC's headquarters budget and supported members of the US Congress who have called for United States government funding of the ICRC to be withheld until the MDA is recognized. Since 2002, the US Secretary of State has been required annually to certify to the Congress that the MDA is not being denied participation in the activities of the Movement before government funds can be used to support the ICRC and the Federation. Two such certifications have been made. In July 2003, the Director-General of the MDA, Avi Zohar, is reported to have said that the MDA cannot ask the American Red Cross to continue withholding funds from the ICRC for its humanitarian work.[36] This may, in part, be the result of increased operational cooperation between the ICRC and the MDA.

Another main problem, of perhaps even greater importance, is that the red cross and red crescent emblems have not been as well respected in certain recent armed conflicts, such as in Somali, Chechnya, Afghanistan and Iraq, a recent example being the attack on the ICRC's headquarters in Baghdad in October 2003 which led to a temporary reduction in the ICRC's humanitarian activities in Iraq. In at least some cases, this is felt to be due to the religious or national/ethnic significance attached to these emblems. They may be perceived as being identified with an enemy.

[35] See Geneva Convention I 1949, Article 38. The International Federation of Red Cross and Red Crescent Societies uses both emblems, inside a red rectangular box. However, this is exceptional, and may be considered to be an indicative use of the emblems (see Rules of Procedure of the International Federation, Rule 1.3).

[36] *Jerusalem Post*, 16 July 2003.

The International Red Cross and Red Crescent Movement began extensive study of these two problems in 1995, including consultation with representatives of the states parties to the Geneva Conventions. Two decades earlier, in 1977, a statutory body of the Movement, the Council of Delegates, set up a Working Group to examine all questions related to the emblem. Despite strenuous efforts, the Working Group was unable to reach an agreement and its activities were terminated by the Council of Delegates in 1981.[37] In the renewed study of 1995, it became clear that many states and National Societies would not wish to abandon their existing emblem in favour of an entirely new protective emblem. This was due not only to strong emotional ties to the existing sign, but also, to concern that it would take time for a new emblem to build up the necessary degree of understanding, among the armed forces and the general public, for it to provide the necessary protection. It was also concluded that it would be inappropriate to adopt additional emblems that could have religious, national, cultural, ethnic or political symbolism. Such symbols would not be universal and neutral, and could lead to a proliferation of emblems, thus compounding the difficulties.

The 27th International Conference of the Red Cross and Red Crescent in 1999 supported the establishment of a joint state/Movement working group to consider the emblem issue and to make a recommendation for a comprehensive solution, acceptable to all the parties concerned, both in terms of substance and procedure.[38] This Joint Working Group differed from the Working Group set up in 1977, among other reasons, because it included state representatives, and as noted earlier, only states can amend the 1949 Geneva Conventions. It also illustrated the shared responsibility of states and the Movement for the distinctive emblems established by the Geneva Conventions. The Joint Working Group recommended the adoption of a new distinctive emblem, which could be used by states and as a consequence, by their National Societies, which have a difficulty using the red cross or the red crescent. This new neutral, protective emblem would need to be established in a legally sound way, which means through the adoption of a Third Additional Protocol amending the 1949 Geneva Conventions.

[37] Decision 3; the Council is composed of delegations from all the components of the Movement; it considers 'matters which concern the Movement as a whole': Statutes of the Movement 1986, Articles 13 and 12 respectively; relevant sub-paragraphs in Articles 4 and 5 of the previous Statutes, dated 1952, are similar.

[38] Resolution 3 of the 27th International Conference.

Draft Third Additional Protocol

The ICRC, in consultation with the International Federation of Red Cross and Red Crescent Societies, has prepared a draft text of the Third Additional Protocol.[39] The draft takes account of the views of members of the Joint Working Group, and others. An overview follows.

The draft is in three parts: a Preamble, the main body (Articles 1–17) and an annex. The lengthy Preamble seeks to provide the necessary safeguards and reassurances. Significant provisions include the following: the High Contracting Parties reaffirm relevant provisions of the 1949 Geneva Conventions and, where applicable, their 1977 Additional Protocols concerning the use of distinctive emblems. States parties may continue to use their existing emblem in conformity with their obligations under the Geneva Conventions and, where applicable, the Additional Protocols. The Preamble recalls that protection of persons and objects is not dependent on use of a distinctive emblem but derives from their protected status under international law. It is stressed that the distinctive emblems are not intended to have any religious, ethnic, racial, regional or political significance.

The Preamble confirms the distinction between the protective use and the indicative use of a distinctive emblem. It also confirms that a National Society undertaking activities outside its territory must ensure that the emblem it intends to use may be used in the country where the activity takes place and in the country or countries of transit. Finally, it is noted that the ICRC, the International Federation and the International Red Cross and Red Crescent Movement intend to retain their current names and emblems.

Thus, the Preamble is quite carefully balanced: it reaffirms and is based upon existing law and practice, and makes clear that the adoption of a new distinctive emblem will not change usage by components of the Red Cross and Red Crescent Movement, or by the Movement itself.

Article 1 begins by stating the obligation to respect and to ensure respect for the Protocol in all circumstances. This reflects Common Article 1 of the four Geneva Conventions and their Additional Protocol I. The second paragraph specifies the material scope of application of the Protocol. The Protocol reaffirms and supplements the

[39] The formal title is the Draft Protocol additional to the Geneva Conventions of 12 August 1949, and relating to the Adoption of an Additional Distinctive Emblem (Protocol III). The present text is dated 12 October 2000.

provisions of the 1949 Geneva Conventions and their 1977 Additional Protocols concerning the distinctive emblems, and is to apply in the same situations as those provisions.

Article 2 defines the protective use of the new distinctive emblem. Paragraph 1 recognizes the new additional distinctive emblem, and states that all the distinctive emblems have equal status. The latter is significant since as mentioned previously, under Geneva Convention I 1949, the red cross emblem is the accepted sign for military medical services, the red crescent and the red lion and sun being exceptions.

Paragraph 2 defines the additional distinctive emblem: it is 'composed of a red frame in the shape of a square on edge on a white ground [and] shall conform to the illustration in the annex to [the] Protocol'. The distinctive emblem is referred to in the draft Protocol as the 'third Protocol emblem'. In an earlier version of the draft text, the emblem was described as, and called, the 'red diamond'. However, there were concerns about this designation, for example, given the negative connotations of diamonds in Africa, as a result of the conflicts fuelled by the diamond trade. Consequently, for the purposes of the draft text, a more neutral approach was followed, leaving the decision on the actual name of the new distinctive emblem to the diplomatic conference which would consider and adopt the final version of the Protocol. At the time of writing (January 2004), a name which seems to have some support is the 'red crystal'. A crystal is a sign of purity, and is associated with water, which is essential to all human life. The word 'crystal' begins with the same letters as 'cross' and 'crescent', and reportedly, translates satisfactorily into the official languages of the Geneva Conventions and their Additional Protocols, as well as in other languages.[40]

The graphic design of the new emblem has also changed. Previously, the emblem was completely red, whereas as illustrated in the annex to the Protocol (reproduced at the end of this chapter), there is now a white space in the centre. This adjustment was the result of visibility tests carried out by the Swiss army in August 2000 with support from the ICRC. Quite properly, tests were conducted to ensure that the design of the new emblem would be at least as visible as the existing distinctive emblems. Perhaps obviously, such visibility is essential for the new emblem to carry out its protective function.

Paragraph 3 of Article 2 provides that the conditions for use of and respect for the new emblem are identical to those established by the

[40] See e.g. Additional Protocol I 1977, Article 102.

Geneva Conventions and their 1977 Additional Protocols for the existing distinctive emblems. If the new emblem is given a name different from 'third Protocol emblem', then it may be necessary to include reference to the name in this provision, i.e. to ensure that the conditions for use, etc., of the name are identical to those established for the names of the distinctive emblems under the Geneva Conventions and where applicable, their Additional Protocols.

Article 2(4) would be helpful to British and other armed forces. It enables medical services and religious personnel of the armed forces of High Contracting Parties to make temporary use of any of the distinctive emblems where this may enhance protection. Such temporary use will be without prejudice to the emblem currently used by such personnel. At present, Geneva Convention I does not expressly provide for the medical service of armed forces to use a different distinctive emblem on a temporary basis. This draft text clarifies the position and permits flexibility in the interest of increased protection, thus benefiting the wounded and other victims in an armed conflict where use of the military medical service's usual emblem might prove unhelpful, and even dangerous. While the draft provision might be said to acquiesce to the view that the existing emblems are not neutral signs, a better view might be that it takes account of the reality that some people, in certain circumstances, do not perceive the current emblems to be neutral, and that it is important to try to ensure that the medical function remains protected on the battlefield in the interest of preserving human life.

Article 3 covers indicative use of the new emblem. This provision is one of the most sensitive in the draft Protocol. Paragraph 1 permits National Societies of High Contracting Parties to incorporate within the new emblem, for indicative purposes, one of the emblems recognized by the Geneva Conventions or a combination of these emblems. Thus, for example, a red cross emblem could appear within the third Protocol emblem, or the red cross and the red crescent emblems could appear together, within the new emblem. National Societies may also incorporate another emblem which they have effectively used for a number of years and which was the subject of a communication to the other High Contracting Parties and the ICRC through the depositary prior to the adoption of the Protocol. Such incorporation may be criticized on the basis that by placing an existing emblem or a combination thereof inside the new emblem, it conveys that the existing emblems are not neutral symbols. On the other hand, the possibility of incorporation may encourage more National Societies to use the new emblem, and help with efforts to raise awareness and understanding of the new sign. Article 3 addresses the situation of the MDA. A previous version of this text referred to a reservation to the Geneva Conventions but it has been amended to avoid too explicit a reference to Israel's reservation on its use of the red shield of David emblem.[41] The term 'communication' in the revised text serves the same purpose but without requiring states to take a position on Israel or its reservation.

Paragraph 1 ends by stating that '[i]ncorporation shall conform to the illustration in the Annex to [the] Protocol'. The illustration also confirms that the new emblem can be used indicatively without needing to have another emblem or a combination of emblems incorporated within it. Previously, the dimensions of the incorporated emblem were specified in the draft Protocol. This stipulation provoked debate and came to be regarded as unnecessary.

Paragraph 2 of Article 3 allows National Societies which incorporate another emblem within the new emblem to use that emblem and the corresponding name within its national territory. This must be in conformity with national legislation. The effect of this is that, within Israel, the MDA could continue to use its existing emblem and name on their own, and within Eritrea, the National Society could use the double emblem and name, i.e. Red Cross and Red Crescent Society, on their own. One assumes that this will be for indicative purposes only, and that such Societies will use the new distinctive emblem for protection. It is possible that both the new emblem and the Society's current emblem might be displayed simultaneously, e.g. the red shield of David might be shown separately from the new emblem. One might think that this might affect the protective object of the new distinctive emblem. Yet, the Geneva Conventions do provide that the distinctive emblem may be accompanied by the national flag, national colours or other insignia.[42] Therefore, there may not be a difficulty in practice. In addition, the international Regulations governing use of the emblem by National Societies also permit simultaneous use of the emblem as a protective and as an indicative device, albeit in such instances, the design of the emblem is the same.[43]

Paragraph 3 of Article 3 permits National Societies to make temporary use of the new distinctive emblem, 'in accordance with national

[41] See above n. 31.

[42] See e.g. Geneva Convention I 1949, Articles 36, 40 and 42.

[43] Article 14 of the 1991 Regulations. See above n. 33 and related text.

legislation and in exceptional circumstances and to facilitate their work'. This provision refers to National Societies which wish to continue to use their existing emblem, e.g. the red cross or the red crescent. Although this text appears in the article on indicative use, it would seem that these National Societies could make protective or indicative use of the new emblem, on a temporary basis, subject to the conditions noted above. For example, a Society which normally used the red crescent might wish to use the new emblem in an area of its country where the crescent is regarded with suspicion; such exceptional use might be in the context of a civil disturbance, such as a riot (when the new emblem might be used protectively), or in the context of a special event to recruit new members or raise funds (when indicative use would be made). Conceivably, a National Society, on the same basis, might make use of the new emblem outside its national territory, but this would also be subject to the relevant laws and practice of that foreign country.

Article 3(4) makes clear that the provisions of Article 3 do not affect the legal status of the distinctive emblems or the legal status of any particular emblem when incorporated within the new emblem for indicative purposes. This is intended to allay concerns about giving greater recognition to the red shield of David emblem or to the double emblem.

Article 4 enables the ICRC and the International Federation to use the new emblem in exceptional circumstances and to facilitate their work. This is more restrictive than the position governing their use of the existing distinctive emblems, which they may do at all times.[44] The limitation is intended to ensure that generally, the status quo is maintained. In practice, this restriction is unlikely to cause a difficulty for either institution, since they will be able to use the new emblem when they need it most.

Article 5 authorizes the medical services and religious personnel participating in operations under the auspices of the United Nations to use one of the distinctive emblems (including the new one), with the agreement of participating states. Originally this provision authorized the medical services of peace operations of the United Nations or of other international or regional organizations to use the new distinctive emblem. It was one of the most controversial articles in the previous version of the draft Protocol. This was due largely to the general concerns expressed by some states on the use of multinational forces, particularly outside the framework of the United Nations; the text has

[44] Geneva Convention I 1949, Article 44, para. 3.

been made more specific to seek to alleviate such concerns. Operations involving multinational forces, even those under UN auspices, have not become less controversial, however, and it may be that this provision will be modified further or even dropped from the final version of the Protocol. On the other hand, the object of the article may be achievable in practice without needing to be included in the Protocol.

Article 6 provides for prevention and repression of misuse of the new emblem. Paragraph 1 states that the relevant provisions of the Geneva Conventions and where applicable, their 1977 Additional Protocols, apply equally to the new emblem. It then, in effect, repeats the obligation on High Contracting Parties to take measures necessary to prevent and repress, at all times, misuse of the existing distinctive emblems and their names, as well as misuse of the new emblem, and goes further than existing law by saying expressly that this includes perfidious use.

Paragraph 2 permits prior users of the new emblem or of imitations of the new emblem, to continue to use their signs, on two conditions: first, that such use would not appear, in time of armed conflict, to confer the protection of the Geneva Conventions and where applicable, the Additional Protocols, and second, that the rights to such use were acquired before the adoption of the Protocol. In an earlier version of the Protocol, prior users of the new emblem or of an imitation thereof were given three years from the coming into force of the Protocol to discontinue such use. The more lenient approach was adopted in the light of concerns regarding trademark or similar pre-existing rights. In recent years, the ICRC has registered the current design of the new distinctive emblem as a trademark in certain jurisdictions in order to try to minimize such difficulties.

Article 7 requires the High Contracting Parties to disseminate knowledge of the Protocol as widely as possible in their respective countries. This dissemination must take place in peacetime as well as during armed conflict. In particular, the Protocol must be included in programmes of military instruction and the civilian population must be encouraged to study it. The wording of the text is nearly identical to the provision on general dissemination in Additional Protocol I 1977.[45] Unlike a previous text, there is no specific reference to ensuring that members of the armed forces and the civilian population are familiar with the new distinctive emblem and the existing distinctive emblems. However, this should be

[45] Additional Protocol I 1977, Article 83(1).

covered by the general reference to disseminating knowledge of the Protocol.

The final provisions of the draft Third Additional Protocol, Articles 8–17, are largely technical in nature. They are based on the equivalent provisions in Additional Protocol I 1977. Under Article 11(1), the new Additional Protocol III will enter into force six months after two instruments of ratification or accession have been deposited. Article 12 covers treaty relations upon entry into force of the Protocol. Article 13 provides for amendments: any High Contracting Party may make such a proposal, and all the High Contracting Parties, the ICRC and the International Federation will be consulted before a diplomatic conference is convened to consider a proposed amendment. This will be the only way to establish additional emblems. Any future proposals for a new emblem(s), or related matters, will be of great importance to National Societies. Thus, it was considered that they should be consulted before any diplomatic conference is convened. This will be done through the International Federation of Red Cross and Red Crescent Societies, which has a statutory function as the official representative of, in effect, the recognized National Societies, in the international field.[46]

The annex consists of two articles (and is reproduced at the end of this chapter). They illustrate the design of the new distinctive emblem for protective and indicative uses, as mentioned in Articles 2 and 3 of the draft Third Additional Protocol.

Current situation

The text of the draft Third Additional Protocol was sent to the states parties to the 1949 Geneva Conventions on 12 October 2000. A diplomatic conference was due to convene later that month for the purpose of adopting the Protocol. The governments of the United Kingdom, Israel and from other regions were fully in support. Regrettably this conference had to be postponed[47] because of the renewed outbreak of violence

[46] See 1986 Statutes of the Movement, Article 6(4)(k), and the 1999 Constitution of the Federation, Article 3(1)(j).

[47] An International Conference of the Red Cross and Red Crescent had been convened for 14 November 2000, following the planned adoption of the new Protocol by the diplomatic conference, in order to make consequential changes to the Statutes of the Movement, in particular, to the conditions for recognition of National Societies (Article 4(5); see above n. 34 and the related text). This International Conference also had to be postponed.

in the Middle East, and it is unlikely to be reinstated until the current situation improves.

In the meantime, the International Red Cross and Red Crescent Movement has taken steps to integrate the MDA and the Eritrean Society operationally into its activities. The Movement, in particular, the international institutions, has also continued consultations with governments with a view to promoting the adoption of the Third Additional Protocol as soon as circumstances allow. This two track approach, i.e. promotion of the new emblem/Third Protocol process and operational cooperation with the National Societies whose recognition depends on the adoption of the Third Protocol, is based on Resolution 6 of the 2001 session of the Council of Delegates.[48] Separate resolutions of the 2003 session of the Council of Delegates confirm support for the two track approach.[49] In November 2001, the President of the MDA was appointed as an expert to the Health and Community Services Commission of the International Federation, and in June 2003, the ICRC signed a cooperation agreement with the MDA, pledging significant financial support for some of its programmes. Similar contacts have been reinforced with the Eritrean National Society, and assistance provided.

Way forward

Moves towards a viable peace process in the Middle East raise the possibility, however remote, that a diplomatic conference to adopt the Third Additional Protocol to the 1949 Geneva Conventions can be convened. Failure to complete this work as quickly as possible has serious consequences:

- inadequate protection of armed forces' medical personnel and authorized humanitarian workers, and thereby, the victims of armed conflict, in situations where the red cross or red crescent emblems are not accepted as neutral protective signs;
- continued division within the Red Cross and Red Crescent Movement, as a result of contention over the status of those National Societies (Israel and Eritrea) which are not yet recognized members of the Movement; this may impair the capacity

[48] For an explanation about the Council, see above n. 37 and related texts.

[49] Resolution 5 for the Third Additional Protocol process, and Resolution 7 for operational cooperation, see also nn. 50 and 52, and the related texts.

of the Movement to continue to carry out the humanitarian mandate given to it by states;

- the affected National Societies are unable to play their full part in humanitarian action, and their potential to contribute to promoting peaceful relations and the rebuilding of civil society in their respective territories is significantly hampered.

The ICRC and the International Federation are strongly committed to the resolution of this difficult humanitarian issue, and strongly support the adoption of the Third Protocol. Consultations with states parties to the 1949 Geneva Conventions, and with National Societies, indicate that there continues to be a large measure of support for the adoption of this instrument. At the appropriate time, governments, with the support of their National Societies, can help significantly to progress the matter.

The two statutory bodies of the Movement most relevant to this issue, the Council of Delegates and the International Conference of the Red Cross and Red Crescent, met in December 2003. The Council of Delegates adopted a resolution on the emblem reaffirming support for the new emblem/Third Additional Protocol process, regretting the delay in bringing it to a successful conclusion and reaffirming the issue as a priority.[50] The 28th International Conference, meeting shortly after the Council of Delegates, passed a resolution adopting the earlier Council of Delegates resolution.[51]

These two resolutions are good outcomes. However, interventions were made at both meetings which indicate clearly that the situation in the region will need to improve before the necessary diplomatic conference can be held, and that concerns remain about the current draft text of the Protocol. This was the general significance of the statement made by the Algerian government representative on behalf of the Arab group following the adoption by consensus of Resolution 3 at the 28th International Conference.

Although the situation is difficult, the International Red Cross and Red Crescent Movement must resist attempting to short cut the new emblem/Third Additional Protocol process and engineer the admission of the MDA and the Eritrean National Society to the Movement by some

[50] Resolution 5 of the 2003 Council of Delegates, entitled 'Follow-up to Resolution 6 of the Council of Delegates in 2001 – Emblem'.

[51] Resolution 3 of the 28th International Conference of the Red Cross and Red Crescent, entitled 'Emblem'.

other means. It is unlikely that this would even be in the interest of the National Societies themselves. As an example, if National Societies were recognized by the ICRC or admitted to the International Federation in a way which did not conform to the existing rules, their standing within the Movement or the Federation could always be questioned. Alternative approaches have been considered but rejected. The Third Additional Protocol is, to date, the only solution which is legally sound, comprehensive, viable for the long term and acceptable to all parties.

As noted above, the draft Third Additional Protocol makes it perfectly clear that states and National Societies can continue to use their existing emblems. However, for idealists, another merit of the draft Protocol is that the establishment of a new neutral emblem would offer the possibility of a return to a single universal emblem, at some distant time. This is most unlikely to occur in the near future. A more immediate additional advantage is that it could offer assistance to those states and National Societies which, although they use one of the existing emblems, would find it helpful to use the new emblem, or for indicative purposes, the double emblem, or even a combination of emblems, given the traditions or multicultural composition of their country's population.

Increased operational cooperation with the MDA and the Eritrean Society should continue,[52] and these Societies should continue to take the actions necessary to meet all the conditions for recognition. The new emblem/Third Additional Protocol should remain a priority for the Red Cross and Red Crescent Movement. When appropriate, Red Cross and Red Crescent organizations should seek to remind governments of the matter, encouraging them to keep it on their agenda, and Movement organizations should be ready to press for the diplomatic conference to be convened as soon as it looks reasonable to expect a successful result. The new Third Additional Protocol to the 1949 Geneva Conventions does not necessarily need to be adopted by total unanimity of the states parties to the Geneva Conventions. However, support needs to be genuinely widespread, including members of all groupings, for the objectives to be achieved.

[52] This was, in effect, endorsed in a separate resolution at the 2003 session of the Council of Delegates. In Resolution 7, 'Strategy for the International Red Cross and Red Crescent Movement', the Council calls upon the International Federation and the ICRC 'to continue to extend operational cooperation also to National Societies awaiting recognition and admission with the aim of preparing for their membership in the Movement' (operative para. 3).

Annex: Third Protocol Emblem[53]

See Article 2, paragraph 2 and Article 3, paragraph 1 of the Protocol.

Article 1 Distinctive emblem

Article 2 Indicative use of the third Protocol emblem

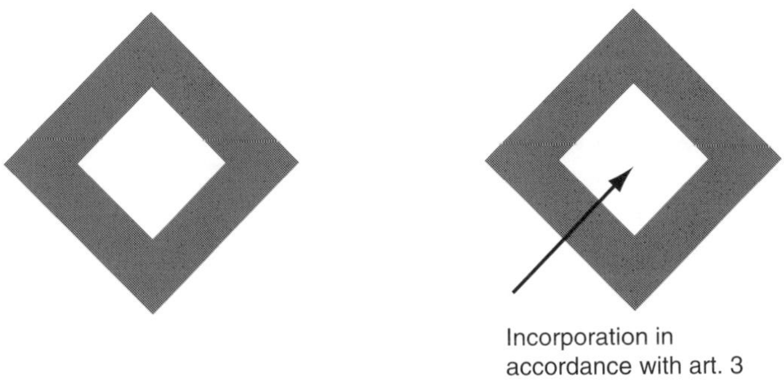

[53] This is the Annex to the Draft Protocol additional to the Geneva Conventions of 12 August 1949, and relating to the Adoption of an Additional Distinctive Emblem (Protocol III), dated 12 October 2000. It is reproduced with the kind permission of the International Committee of the Red Cross. The emblem (shown here in black) is red on a white background. A full colour version of the emblem may be viewed at the website of the International Committee of the Red Cross, www.icrc.org

7

Towards the unification of international humanitarian law?

LINDSAY MOIR

Introduction

The international laws of war have traditionally been divided strictly between those applicable to international armed conflicts, and those which are, in contrast, applicable to non-international, or internal, armed conflicts. On 22 March 1996, however, the President of the International Criminal Tribunal for the former Yugoslavia (ICTY), Antonio Cassese, sent a memorandum to the members of the Preparatory Committee for the Establishment of the International Criminal Court. The memorandum outlined the conclusions of the ICTY Appeals Chamber on this distinction, and asserted that:

> since the 1930s, there has been a gradual blurring of the distinction between the customary international law rules governing international conflicts and those governing internal conflicts. Put another way, there has been a convergence of two bodies of international law with the result that internal strife is now governed to a large extent by the rules and principles which had traditionally only applied to international conflicts. ... [R]egarding the formation of customary international law rules to protect those who are not taking part in the hostilities, ... this convergence has come about due largely to the following four factors: (1) the increase in the number of civil conflicts; (2) the increase in the level of cruelty of internal conflicts; (3) the increasing interdependence of States; and, (4) the influence of universal human rights standards. The Appeals Chamber then turned to the extension of the rules regarding methods and means of warfare to internal armed conflicts and concluded that a similar blurring had occurred. In short, ... certain norms apply as customary international law to internal and international armed conflicts alike.[1]

[1] United Nations Memorandum from President Cassese to Members of the Preparatory Committee on the Establishment of an International Criminal Court on the Definition of

This chapter examines the extent to which a blurring of the distinction has indeed occurred, and assesses whether future developments in international law might eventually lead to the situation whereby a single body of international humanitarian law can be applied to all armed conflicts, regardless of their character.

Traditional dichotomy in international humanitarian law

Historically, the notion that some measure of humanitarian restraint should be shown during internal armed conflicts was not widely disputed. Any such regulation was, however, commonly perceived to be a matter of domestic, rather than international, law.[2] Not until the scale and intensity of an internal uprising had reached a certain level of severity did the question of regulation by international law arise, with the relevant threshold being characterized – and identified – by the recognition of belligerency.

Following the initial stage of rebellion, and the intermediate stage of insurgency,[3] a recognition of belligerency represented an acceptance by the recognizing party (either the government of the afflicted state or of some third state) that hostilities had escalated to the level whereby both insurgent and state forces were entitled to be treated in the same way as opposing belligerents engaged in an international armed conflict. Recognition of belligerency by a third state rendered applicable the customary international law of neutrality between the recognizing state and the parties to the conflict. Recognition by the parent government brought into effect the entire *jus in bello* between government and insurgent forces. Not until the parent state had taken the step of recognizing belligerency on the part of insurgents did international humanitarian law apply to internal hostilities.[4]

Crimes and General Principles of Criminal Law as Reflected in the International Tribunal's Jurisprudence, 22 March 1996, para. 11.

2 See, e.g., T. Baty and J. H. Morgan, *War: Its Conduct and Legal Results* (Murray, 1915), p. 289, and W. L. Walker and F. T. Grey, *Pitt Cobbett's Leading Cases on International Law* (5th edn, Sweet and Maxwell, 1937) vol. II, p. 6.

3 See H. A. Wilson, *International Law and the Use of Force by National Liberation Movements* (Clarendon Press, 1988), pp. 22–9; R. P. Dhokalia, 'Civil Wars and International Law', (1971) 11 *Indian Journal of International Law* 219 at pp. 224–6; H. Lauterpacht, *Recognition in International Law* (Cambridge University Press, 1947), Part III; and L. Moir, *The Law of Internal Armed Conflict* (Cambridge University Press, 2002), pp. 4–11.

4 This would have been less problematic had belligerency been recognized as a matter of course in such situations by involved states. This was not the case, however. See Moir, *Internal Armed Conflict*, pp. 11–18.

That is not to say, however, that arguments were not made in favour of a more unified approach to the legal regulation of international and internal conflicts. As early as the eighteenth century, for example, Emmerich de Vattel had argued that civil war broke, or at least suspended, the bands of society and government, so that the parties to an internal conflict had to be treated in the same way as two nations in conflict. Accordingly, 'the common laws of war, those maxims of humanity, moderation and probity ... are in civil wars to be observed by both sides'.[5] The unification movement gained yet further momentum in the late nineteenth century when, in the aftermath of the American Civil War, a number of American scholars began to argue that the laws of war should be applicable to all armed conflicts, irrespective of their international or internal nature. Hannis Taylor, for example, asserted that, 'it is all war, whatever its cause or object, and should be conducted in a civilised way ... There is no distinction from a military view between a civil war and a foreign war until after the final decisive battle.'[6]

Indeed, during the American Civil War, a military manual had been drawn up by Dr Francis Lieber, setting out the legal regime applicable to Union forces for their conduct during hostilities.[7] Rosemary Abi-Saab explains that the Code was considered at the time to be of general application, or at least as a step in the direction of codifying the laws and customs of war in general. It was, in fact, 'taken as an example of how the laws and customs of war should be codified to apply to inter-State wars, in view of the great similarities between civil and inter-State wars'.[8] The majority of continental European scholars remained unconvinced, however, perceiving the Lieber Code as relevant only to the American Civil War, and stubbornly clinging to the notion of belligerent recognition.[9] The current situation is, then, precisely the opposite of that described by Abi-Saab above: 'we still emphasize

[5] E. de Vattel, *The Law of Nations*, Book III, (1760), ch. XVIII, pp. 109–10.

[6] H. Taylor, *A Treatise on International Public Law* (Callaghan and Co., 1901), p. 454.

[7] Instructions for the Government of Armies of the United States in the Field (known as the 'Lieber Code'), promulgated as General Orders No. 100 by President Lincoln on 24 April 1863. Reproduced in D. Schindler and J. Toman (eds.), *The Laws of Armed Conflicts. A Collection of Conventions, Resolutions and Other Documents* (3rd edn, Sijthoff, 1988), p. 3.

[8] R. Abi-Saab, 'Humanitarian Law and Internal Conflicts: The Evolution of Legal Concern', in A. J. M. Delissen and G. J. Tanja (eds.), *Humanitarian Law of Armed Conflict: Challenges Ahead* (Martinus Nijhoff, 1991), p. 209 at p. 210.

[9] Abi-Saab, 'Humanitarian Law', p. 210. See, e.g., A. Merignhac, *Droit Public International* (1912), vol. III, p. 19.

the similarities of international and non-international armed conflicts, but [we do so] in order to maintain the applicability of existing humanitarian law to internal conflicts as well'.[10]

In terms of international regulation of internal armed conflict, worse was to follow, as the doctrine of recognition of belligerency itself fell into a sharp decline and became virtually obsolete from the end of the nineteenth century onwards. Hans-Peter Gasser has claimed that the last recognition of belligerency granted by a parent state to insurgents operating within its own territory was that granted during the Boer War in 1902.[11] This trend, although largely welcomed by states, resulted in the absence of any international regulation for internal armed conflicts.

Recognizing the inherent danger in such a position, the International Committee of the Red Cross (ICRC) accordingly stepped in and began efforts to remedy the situation. The eventual outcome was Article 3 common to the Geneva Conventions adopted in 1949 – the first international provision designed specifically to regulate armed conflict of a non-international character.[12] The level of protection afforded to noncombatants by Common Article 3, however, falls significantly short of that applicable to international armed conflicts. Rather than require that the parties to an internal armed conflict meet the obligations of the Geneva Conventions in their entirety, Article 3 merely sets out a minimum standard of protection, incorporating what were perceived to be the underlying humanitarian principles of all four Conventions.[13] Furthermore, common Article 3 contains no regulation whatsoever of methods and means of warfare during internal conflict, a problem exacerbated by the fact that, following the decline of recognition of belligerency, the issue of whether there was any customary international law on the subject was far from clear.

A number of academics nevertheless maintained the argument for a closer union between the regulation of international and non-international

[10] Abi-Saab, 'Humanitarian Law', pp. 210–11.

[11] H. P. Gasser, 'International Humanitarian Law', in H. Haug (ed.), *Humanity for All: The International Red Cross and Red Crescent Movement* (Haupt, 1993), p. 491 at p. 559.

[12] For an examination of the process leading to the adoption of common Article 3, see Moir, *Internal Armed Conflict*, pp. 23–9.

[13] For a general outline of the level of humanitarian protection applicable to internal armed conflict, see H. McCoubrey, *International Humanitarian Law: The Regulation of Armed Conflicts* (1st edn, Dartmouth, 1990), pp. 171–86 and H. McCoubrey and N. D. White, *International Law and Armed Conflict* (Dartmouth, 1992), pp. 317–27.

conflict. Jean Pictet, for example, writing in 1956, expressed the desire that, 'one day the Powers will accord at all times and to all men the benefits they have already agreed to grant their enemies in time of war',[14] while Georg Schwarzenberger stated in 1968 that, 'the distinction between international and internal armed conflicts [was becoming] increasingly relative'.[15] When a diplomatic conference was held from 1974–7 to reaffirm and develop international humanitarian law, and resulting in the Additional Protocols to the four Geneva Conventions of 1949, the traditional distinction between international and internal armed conflicts nonetheless persisted to the extent that a separate Protocol was adopted for each category.

Article 1(4) of Additional Protocol I did reclassify those armed conflicts in which peoples are 'fighting against colonial domination and alien occupation and against racist regimes in the exercise of their right of self-determination', traditionally considered internal, as *international* armed conflicts.[16] At least one category of internal conflicts was therefore made subject to international humanitarian law in its entirety. Having achieved this largely political outcome, however, many delegations lost interest in the adoption of any further regulations for internal armed conflict. Only the last-minute intervention of Pakistan allowed the adoption of even a watered-down Additional Protocol II.[17]

During negotiations, a small number of delegations had supported a unification of humanitarian law. Norway, for example, argued strongly that:

> the protection of victims of armed conflicts should be the same regardless of their legal or political classification. The Conference should establish identical legislation for all victims of all armed conflicts. The distinction drawn between international and non-international conflicts, and the elaboration of two different protocols with different levels of protection

[14] J. Pictet, *Red Cross Principles* (1956), p. 29, n. 1.

[15] G. Schwarzenberger, 'From the Laws of War to the Law of Armed Conflict', (1968) 21 *Current Legal Problems* 239 at p. 255.

[16] This, in itself, was a controversial step in that the character of an armed conflict was accordingly to be determined by the objectives of one of the parties involved. See G. I. A. D. Draper, 'Wars of National Liberation and War Criminality', in M. Howard (ed.), *Restraints on War* (Oxford University Press, 1979), p. 135 at p. 150 and in M. A. Meyer and H. McCoubrey (eds.), *Reflections on Law and Armed Conflicts: The Selected Works on the Laws of War by the late Professor Colonel G. I. A. D. Draper* (Kluwer, 1998), p. 180 at pp. 185–6.

[17] For background to the adoption of Additional Protocol II, see Moir, *Internal Armed Conflict*, pp. 91–6.

for victims [would only lead] to discrimination or what has been called 'selective humanitarianism'.[18]

This view was regarded with scepticism by the vast majority of delegations, however, who remained wedded to distinguishing internal and international conflicts. Additional Protocol II was finally adopted, therefore, dealing specifically with conflicts not of an international character, and providing a high threshold of application in Article 1(1). Narrower and more restrictive in scope than common Article 3, the more detailed humanitarian protection contained in Additional Protocol II is applicable only to the most intense internal armed conflicts. Other than Article 4(1),[19] which states that, 'It is prohibited to order that there shall be no survivors', Additional Protocol II, like common Article 3, also contained no regulation of methods and means of warfare.

Despite the opportunities for reform presented in the 1970s, conventional international humanitarian law has, therefore, doggedly retained the traditional distinction between international and internal armed conflicts, and their regulation. Recent developments, however, have had a profound influence on the direction of customary international law in this respect.

Eroding the dichotomy

Theodor Meron has asserted that, 'Calamitous events and atrocities have repeatedly driven the development of international humanitarian law.'[20] From the American Civil War to the Second World War, to the conflicts in the former Yugoslavia and in Rwanda, history shows this to be true. Importantly for the present study, however, the vast majority of such 'calamitous events' in recent times have not actually been international in character:[21]

[18] *Official Records of the Diplomatic Conference on the Reaffirmation and Development of International Humanitarian Law Applicable in Armed Conflicts, Geneva 1974–1977* (1978), CDDH/I/SR. 23, vol. VIII, pp. 215, 217.

[19] And, to an extent, Articles 13–18, which outline the protection applicable to the civilian population, including the obligation not to launch attacks against the civilian population or against civilian objects. The provision on quarter in Article 4(1) is, however, the only provision in Additional Protocol II relevant to conduct between opposing combatants actively engaged in hostilities.

[20] T. Meron, 'The Humanization of Humanitarian Law', (2000) 94 *American Journal of International Law* 239 at p. 243.

[21] The precise legal characterization of the conflict(s) in the former Yugoslavia has, however, been the subject of much debate. See the *Tadic* jurisprudence for the

> The current changing nature of conflicts from international to internal is closely related to the normative developments. Internal conflicts have necessitated both new norms and reinterpretation of existing norms. The change in direction toward intrastate or mixed conflicts – the context of contemporary atrocities – has drawn humanitarian law in the direction of human rights law.[22]

Of course, the 'humanization' of humanitarian law is not exclusively a recent phenomenon. Concern for the protection of individuals in terms of avoiding unnecessary suffering and other limitations on the conduct of hostilities – concern easily placed in the broad sphere of human rights – has been evident from the very earliest incarnations of the laws of war.[23] Indeed, common Article 3 itself is widely considered to be a provision containing fundamental human rights. The Inter-American Commission on Human Rights has stated that, 'the provisions of common Article 3 are essentially pure human rights law',[24] and it has been described by the International Court of Justice as representing 'elementary considerations of humanity'.[25]

As Meron explains,[26] this is, perhaps, indicative of the change in the focus of humanitarian law from a state-centred and reciprocal approach to an approach concerned more with the individual. Such factors have had a major influence on customary international law and, as a consequence, on the legal distinction between international and non-international conflicts. This has manifested itself in a convergence of customary international law in two areas: (a) the protection of victims and (b) the conduct of hostilities.

development of the relevant arguments: *Prosecutor* v. *Tadić* (Case IT–94–1), Appeal on Jurisdiction, 2 October 1995, paras. 71–8; Opinion and Judgment, 7 May 1997, paras. 578–608 (and Separate and Dissenting Opinion of Judge McDonald); Appeals Chamber, judgment, 15 July 1999, paras. 83–162.

22 Meron, 'Humanization', pp. 243–4.

23 See McCoubrey, *International Humanitarian Law* (1st edn), pp. 1–21.

24 Report No. 55/97, Case 11.137 (*Abella* v. *Argentina*), 18 November 1997, IACHR *Annual Report 1997*, OEA/Ser. L/V/II. 98, Doc. 7 rev., 13 April 1998, para. 158, n. 19.

25 *Military and Paramilitary Activities in and Against Nicaragua* (*Nicaragua* v. *United States*), Merits, [1986] ICJ Reports 14 at 114. The precise nature of the relationship between human rights and humanitarian law has vexed commentators for some time, and the developing views of Draper on the subject are outlined in Meyer and McCoubrey, *Reflections*, pp. 121–50.

26 Meron, 'Humanization', pp. 247–53.

The protection of victims

The jurisprudence of the ad hoc criminal tribunals for the former Yugoslavia and Rwanda both demonstrate how human rights norms can impact upon the corresponding norms of humanitarian law. Taking torture as an example, the ICTY and ICTR have both applied the definition of torture contained in international human rights law to acts of torture being prosecuted under their respective Statutes. The ICTY therefore held in the *Celibici* case that, 'the definition of torture contained in the Torture Convention ... reflects a consensus which the Trial Chamber considers to be representative of customary international law'.[27]

As such cross-fertilization increases, then, 'through a process of osmosis or application by analogy, the recognition as customary of norms rooted in international human rights instruments [will affect] the interpretation, and eventually the status, of the parallel norms in instruments of humanitarian law'.[28] In this way, a growing number of human rights norms which are replicated in the provisions of humanitarian law (and vice versa) can receive recognition as customary international law. Continuing efforts at raising the level of humanitarian protection during internal conflicts are therefore likely to result in the wider acceptance of more humanitarian law provisions as applicable to all armed conflict, be it internal or international in character.

Such a convergence of the humanitarian norms protecting victims of armed conflicts is, however, dependent upon questions of interpretation. It is therefore necessarily limited to those provisions of humanitarian law contained either in common Article 3 or in Additional Protocol II,

[27] *Prosecutor* v. *Delalic, Mucic, Delic and Landzo* (Case IT–96–21), judgment, 16 November 1998, para. 459. See also *Prosecutor* v. *Furundzija* (Case IT–95–17/1), judgment, 10 December 1998, para. 159 and *Prosecutor* v. *Akayesu* (Case ICTR–96–4), judgment, 2 September 1998, para. 593.

[28] Meron, 'Humanization', p. 244. The same is equally true in reverse, with international adjudicative bodies accepting an important role for international humanitarian law norms as regards the interpretation and development of human rights law in times of conflict. The ICJ, for example, in its *Advisory Opinion on the Legality or Threat of Nuclear Weapons*, (1996) 35 *International Legal Materials* 809 para. 25, has accepted that the right to life continues to apply during armed conflict, but that 'The test of what is an arbitrary deprivation of life ... falls to be determined by the applicable *lex specialis*, namely the law applicable in armed conflict.' See also the approach of the Inter-American Commission on Human Rights in, for example, *Abella* v. *Argentina*, above n. 24 at para. 161.

or else codified in the Statutes of Criminal Tribunals. Since regulation of the conduct of hostilities – or methods and means of warfare – in internal armed conflict is absent from conventional international law, perhaps more important, then, is the second way in which the two branches of humanitarian law have begun to merge.

The conduct of hostilities

Fundamentally important in this regard was the decision of the ICTY Appeals Chamber in *Prosecutor* v. *Tadić* (*Appeal on Jurisdiction*).[29] It was the first judgment to suggest that there is a body of customary international humanitarian law which is applicable to internal armed conflict, and which includes a number of the norms applicable to international armed conflict.

Dealing first with the protection of civilians, the Appeals Chamber asserted that the relevant rules of international armed conflict have in fact been applied to internal armed conflicts since the Spanish Civil War, in the context of which the British Prime Minister, Neville Chamberlain, had stated that, 'it is against international law to bomb civilians as such and to make deliberate attacks upon civilian populations'.[30] The Chamber was able to cite further developments, both in terms of conventional international law and examples of state practice, in order to augment this stance.[31]

The ICTY went beyond the simple statement that civilians were not to be the object of attack during internal armed conflict, however, and asserted that a body of customary international law has also developed to regulate the methods and means of warfare. Starting from the position stated in Article 5(3) of the 1990 Turku Declaration of Minimum Humanitarian Standards,[32] that, 'weapons or other material or methods prohibited in international armed conflicts must not be employed in any circumstances', the Appeals Chamber held that:

[29] Case IT–94–1-AR72, (1996) 35 *International Legal Materials* 32.

[30] 337 House of Commons Debates, 21 June 1938, cols 937–8, as referred to by the Appeals Chamber in *Tadić* (Jurisdiction), above n. 21 at para. 100.

[31] *Tadić* (Jurisdiction), above n. 21 at paras 102–7.

[32] UN doc. E/CN. 4/1995/116 (1995). The Declaration is not legally binding, but it has been endorsed by the CSCE and by the United Nations Sub-commission on the Prevention of Discrimination and the Protection of Minorities. See *Tadić* (Jurisdiction), above n. 21 at para. 119.

> elementary considerations of humanity and common sense make it preposterous that the use by States of weapons prohibited in armed conflicts between themselves be allowed when States try to put down rebellion by their own nationals in their own territory. What is inhumane, and consequently proscribed, in international wars, cannot but be inhumane and inadmissible in civil strife.[33]

Further evidence that this is indeed the case can be found in recent developments in conventional international law as regards the legality or illegality of the use of certain weapons. Two excellent examples of this relate to the use of chemical weapons and land-mines. When it was alleged that the Iraqi government was engaged in the use of chemical weapons against its own Kurdish population, the action was widely condemned by the international community. Indeed, numerous governments issued statements demonstrating a clear acceptance that the use of such weapons was a violation of the customary international law applicable to both internal and international armed conflicts.[34] The Convention on the Prohibition of the Development, Production, Stockpiling and Use of Chemical Weapons and on their Destruction was accordingly agreed in 1993,[35] with Article I providing that chemical weapons may 'never [be used] under any circumstances'.

Likewise, after a concerted international campaign led by the ICRC, limitations on the use of land-mines were extended to cover internal armed conflicts by amending the Protocol on Prohibitions or Restrictions on the Use of Mines, Booby-Traps and Other Devices in May 1996.[36] The Convention on the Prohibition of the Use, Stockpiling, Production and Transfer of Anti-Personnel Mines and on their Destruction was duly adopted at Ottawa in 1997,[37] which prohibits their use 'under any circumstances'. The Second Protocol to the Hague Convention of 1954 for the Protection of Cultural Property in

[33] *Tadić* (Jurisdiction), above n. 21 at para. 119.

[34] As discussed in *ibid.*, para. 120–2. See the statements made by the European Union in (1988) 4 *European Political Co-operation Documentation Bulletin* 92, the United Kingdom in (1988) 59 *British Yearbook of International Law* 579, Germany in (1990) 50 *Zeitschrift für Auslandisches Offentliches Recht Und Volkerrecht* 382–3, and the USA in US Department of State Press Guidance (9 September 1988).

[35] (1993) 32 *International Legal Materials* 800.

[36] (1996) 35 *International Legal Materials* 1206, Protocol to the 1980 Convention on Prohibitions or Restrictions on the Use of Certain Conventional Weapons which may be Deemed to be Excessively Injurious or to have Indiscriminate Effects.

[37] (1997) 36 *International Legal Materials* 1507.

the Event of Armed Conflict,[38] adopted in 1999, also applies to all armed conflicts irrespective of their character.

The Appeals Chamber in *Tadić* was extremely careful to point out, however, that the emergence of these customary rules and principles for the regulation of internal armed conflicts did not mean that they are subject to the laws of international armed conflict in their entirety. In pointing to two particular limitations, the Chamber held that:

(i) only a number of rules and principles governing international armed conflicts have gradually been extended to apply to internal conflicts; and
(ii) this extension has not taken place in the form of a full and mechanical transplant of those rules to internal armed conflicts, rather, the general essence of those rules, and not the detailed regulation they may contain, has become applicable to internal conflicts.[39]

This attempt at limitation failed, however, to convince a number of scholars. Christopher Greenwood, for example, believed that the rules as set out by the Appeals Chamber went far beyond what had traditionally been seen as the regulation of internal conflict.[40] Peter Rowe went even further, arguing that the Chamber had driven 'a coach and four through the traditional distinctions between an international and a non-international conflict'.[41]

This was, however, the only possible outcome – probably even the intended outcome – in light of the Appeal Chamber's assertion that the distinction between internal and international armed conflicts was becoming outdated. As the Chamber argued:

> Why protect civilians from belligerent violence, or ban rape, torture or the wanton destruction of hospitals, churches, museums or private property, as well as proscribe weapons causing unnecessary suffering when two sovereign States are engaged in war, and yet refrain from enacting the same bans or providing the same protection when armed violence has erupted 'only' within the territory of a sovereign State? If international

[38] (1999) 38 *International Legal Materials* 769, Article 22.
[39] *Tadić* (Jurisdiction), above n. 21 at para. 126.
[40] C. J. Greenwood, 'International Humanitarian Law and the Tadic Case', (1996) 7 *European Journal of International Law* 265 at p. 278.
[41] C. Warbrick and P. Rowe, 'The International Criminal Tribunal for Yugoslavia: The Decision of the Appeals Chamber on the Interlocutory Appeal on Jurisdiction in the Tadic Case', (1996) 45 *International and Comparative Law Quarterly* 691 at p. 701.

> law, while of course duly safeguarding the legitimate interests of States, must gradually turn to the protection of human beings, it is only natural that the aforementioned dichotomy should gradually lose its weight.[42]

The precise methods employed by the Tribunal to achieve such an outcome may well be open to criticism,[43] but it is difficult to disagree with the end result.

Statute of the International Criminal Court

The adoption of a Statute of the International Criminal Court has been vitally important in terms of consolidating the progress made in the sphere of humanitarian law by the ICTY. Finally agreed in July 1998 in Rome,[44] its successful adoption following the involvement of such a large number of delegates can be seen as a clear manifestation of state practice. Importantly, then, it affirms a broad view of the customary law status afforded to much of the relevant legal regulation of internal conflict by the Criminal Tribunals for the former Yugoslavia and Rwanda. This is especially valuable given the guiding principle that those crimes within the jurisdiction of the International Criminal Court should be limited to 'the most serious crimes of concern to the international community as a whole',[45] i.e., that the ICC Statute should be reflective of customary international law, not developmental.

Among the participating states, there was a general consensus from the very beginning that serious violations of the laws and customs applicable in armed conflict should be included in the Rome Statute.[46] Whether this ought to include violations of the laws and customs of internal armed conflict was, however, much more controversial. The question remained open until the last stages of the drafting process, to the extent that even the final draft placed before the diplomatic conference retained the option of deleting those sections dealing with internal armed conflict.[47]

[42] *Tadić* (Jurisdiction), above n. 21 at para. 97.

[43] Indeed, they have been severely criticized in some quarters. See, e.g., T. Meron, 'The Continuing Role of Custom in the Formation of International Humanitarian Law', (1996) 90 *American Journal of International Law* 238 at pp. 242–4.

[44] Statute of the International Criminal Court, UN doc. A/Conf. 183/9, 17 July 1998, (1998) 37 *International Legal Materials* 1002.

[45] See *Report of the Preparatory Committee on the Establishment of an International Criminal Court*, vol. 1, UN doc. A/51/22, 13 September 1996, para. 51.

[46] *Ibid.*, para. 74.

[47] Option V ('Delete sections C and D') to the draft article on war crimes in the Draft Statute, UN doc. A/CONF. 183/2 (April 1998). For more detailed discussion of the

As part of the long, and often tortuous, process leading to the eventual creation of the International Criminal Court, the International Law Commission (ILC) had been heavily involved in the drawing up of its own Draft Statute. When this task was completed in 1994,[48] Article 20 of the ILC Draft Statute provided that the Court should have jurisdiction over, amongst other crimes, 'serious violations of the laws and customs applicable in armed conflict'.[49] No specific mention was made as to whether this included those violations committed during *internal* armed conflict. Theodor Meron believed that this must, nonetheless, have been the case, since the ILC Commentary stated that Article 20 reflected (at least partially) Article 22 of the ILC Draft Code of Crimes Against the Peace and Security of Mankind, which applies to both internal and international armed conflicts.[50] Christopher Greenwood, on the other hand, was less convinced. He believed that the question had been deliberately left open.[51]

In fact, the ILC had simply intended to refer to the customary law of war crimes in general, whatever that was or would become. Granted, the ILC Draft Statute did not provide for jurisdiction over breaches of Additional Protocol II (at least in terms of conventional international law),[52] although in the wake of *Tadić*, jurisdiction may have been possible over those provisions of Protocol II held to reflect custom. Of course, the ILC did not have the benefit of the ICTY's *Tadić* jurisprudence to draw on at the time. At any rate, the suggestion that Article 20(c) of the ILC Draft referred only to violations of the laws and customs

background to this, and commentary on the provisions as adopted, see H. von Hebel and D. Robinson, 'Crimes Within the Jurisdiction of the Court', in R. S. Lee (ed.), *The International Criminal Court: The Making of the Rome Statute, Issues, Negotiations, Results* (Kluwer, 1999), pp. 79, 104–5 and 119–22, and M. Cottier, W. J. Fenrick, P. V. Sellars and A. Zimmerman, 'War Crimes', in O. Triffterer (ed.), *Commentary on the Rome Statute of the International Criminal Court: Observers' Notes, Article by Article* (Nomos, 1999), pp. 173, 262–86 (Zimmerman).

48 See J. Crawford, 'ILC Adopts a Statute for an International Criminal Court', (1995) 89 *American Journal of International Law* 404.

49 For the ILC Commentary on Article 20 of its draft, see UN doc. A/49/10, pp. 29, 70–9.

50 T. Meron, 'International Criminalization of Internal Atrocities', (1995) 89 *American Journal of International Law* 554 at p. 574. See ILC Commentary, pp. 73–4.

51 Greenwood, 'Humanitarian Law and Tadic', p. 281.

52 Additional Protocol II is not listed in the Annex containing those treaties violations of which are crimes within the Court's jurisdiction. Treaties which merely regulate conduct, or which prohibit conduct but only on an inter-state basis, were excluded. Additional Protocol II was therefore ruled out, since 'it contains no clause dealing with grave breaches, nor any equivalent enforcement provision'. See ILC Commentary, pp. 141 and 145.

of international armed conflict does not seem easily tenable. This is especially so when one considers the importance attached by the ILC Commentary to Article 3 of the ICTY Statute,[53] the application of which to internal conflicts has been strongly affirmed.[54] The ILC further stated, in paragraph 10 of the Commentary to Article 20(c), that war crimes existed under customary international law, and the ICTY demonstrated in *Tadić* that these can, and do, apply equally to internal armed conflicts.

When the process reached the stage of government involvement, the majority of states duly supported the inclusion of internal armed conflict in the Statute of the International Criminal Court. This was for two main reasons: first, 'it was precisely in internal armed conflicts that national criminal justice systems were in all likelihood unable to adequately respond to violations of such norms',[55] and secondly, most of the conflicts since the Second World War had been internal in character. Unless war crimes in those cases were included, the Court would have been unable to act against those violations of humanitarian law which are now the most widespread. Indeed, as the Lawyers Committee for Human Rights stated in 1998, 'It is untenable to argue that the perpetrators of atrocities committed in non-international armed conflict should be shielded from international justice just because their victims were of the same nationality.'[56]

A minority of states nevertheless continued to make protestations.[57] Their arguments were advanced on the bases, first, that the inclusion of internal armed conflict would undermine the universal acceptance of the Court; secondly, that individual criminal responsibility was not clearly established for such violations; and thirdly, that customary international law had not changed in this respect since the adoption of the ICTR Statute in 1994.[58] Happily, the majority view prevailed, and the inclusion of violations of the laws of internal armed conflict was finally accepted. Article 8 of the Rome Statute sets out the relevant provisions in paragraph (2)(c)–(f).

[53] ILC Commentary, p. 73.

[54] See *Tadić* (Jurisdiction), above n. 21 at para. 87–9, *Tadić* (Judgment), paras 615–16.

[55] Von Hebel and Robinson, 'Crimes', p. 105.

[56] Lawyers Committee for Human Rights, *Establishing an International Criminal Court: Major Unresolved Issues in the Draft Statute* (International Criminal Court Briefing Series 1998), Vol. 1, No. 1, section IV.

[57] China, India, the Russian Federation, Turkey and a number of Asian and Arab states. See Von Hebel and Robinson, 'Crimes', p. 105, n. 87.

[58] *Report of the Preparatory Committee*, Vol. 1, para. 78.

Intimately connected to the question of whether internal conflicts should be covered by the Statute, however, and equally divisive, was the issue of exactly which humanitarian norms are applicable in such conflicts. This determination is pivotal in terms of examining the extent of any move towards the unification of international humanitarian law, and the two proposals initially submitted to the Working Group of the Preparatory Committee on the Definition of Crimes reflected the division of opinion. The first proposal, submitted by the USA,[59] limited those crimes in internal armed conflict to violations of common Article 3. The second proposal, drawn up by the International Committee of the Red Cross and submitted by New Zealand and Switzerland,[60] set out a much more extensive list.[61]

Ultimately, most delegations were reasonably happy to accept that common Article 3 represented customary international law, and Article 8 of the Rome Statute therefore asserts jurisdiction over violations of common Article 3, providing that:

> 1. The Court shall have jurisdiction in respect of war crimes in particular when committed as part of a plan or policy or as a large-scale commission of such crimes.
>
> 2. For the purpose of this Statute, 'war crimes' means: ...
>
> (c) In the case of an armed conflict not of an international character, serious violations of article 3 common to the four Geneva Conventions of 12 August 1949, namely any of the following acts committed against persons taking no active part in the hostilities, including members of armed forces who have laid down their arms and those placed *hors de combat* by sickness, wounds, detention or any other cause:
>
> (i) Violence to life and person, in particular murder of all kinds, mutilation, cruel treatment and torture;
>
> (ii) Committing outrages upon personal dignity, in particular humiliating and degrading treatment;
>
> (iii) Taking of hostages;
>
> (iv) The passing of sentences and the carrying out of executions without previous judgment pronounced by a regularly

[59] UN doc. A/AC. 249/1997/WG. 1/DP. 2.

[60] UN doc. A/AC. 249/1997/WG. 1/DP. 1.

[61] For an outline of this process, see Zimmerman, 'War Crimes', pp. 262–3. The consolidated draft text drawn up by the Working Group and incorporating both proposals (the second as an option) can be found at UN doc. A/AC. 249/1997/WG. 1/CRP. 2.

> constituted court, affording all judicial guarantees which are generally recognized as indispensible.

This is, perhaps, uncontroversial. The delegates also agreed, however, that a number of the provisions of Additional Protocol II should also be considered to reflect custom.[62] The Statute goes much further, then, than sub-paragraph (c), asserting in Article 8(2)(e) the Court's jurisdiction over:

> (e) Other serious violations of the laws and customs applicable in armed conflicts not of an international character, within the established framework of international law, namely, any of the following acts:
> (i) Intentionally directing attacks against the civilian population as such or against individual civilians not taking direct part in hostilities;
> (ii) Intentionally directing attacks against buildings, material, medical units and transport, and personnel using the distinctive emblems of the Geneva Conventions in conformity with international law;
> (iii) Intentionally directing attacks against personnel, installations, material, units or vehicles involved in a humanitarian assistance or peacekeeping mission in accordance with the Charter of the United Nations, as long as they are entitled to the protection given to civilians or civilian objects under the international law of armed conflict;
> (iv) Intentionally directing attacks against buildings dedicated to religion, education, art, science or charitable purposes, historic monuments, hospitals and places where the sick and wounded are collected, provided they are not military objectives;
> (v) Pillaging a town or place, even when taken by assault;
> (vi) Committing rape, sexual slavery, enforced prostitution, forced pregnancy, as defined in article 7, paragraph 2(f), enforced sterilization, and any other form of sexual violence also constituting a serious violation of article 3 common to the Geneva Conventions;
> (vii) Conscripting or enlisting children under the age of fifteen years into armed forces or groups or using them to participate actively in hostilities;
> (viii) Ordering the displacement of the civilian population for reasons related to the conflict, unless the security of the civilians involved or imperative military reasons so demand;

[62] Von Hebel and Robinson, 'Crimes', p. 105.

(ix) Killing or wounding treacherously a combatant adversary;
(x) Declaring that no quarter will be given;
(xi) Subjecting persons who are in the power of another party to the conflict to physical mutilation or to medical or scientific experiments of any kind which are neither justified by the medical, dental or hospital treatment of the person concerned nor carried out in his or her interest, and which cause death to or seriously endanger the health of such person or persons;
(xii) Destroying or seizing the property of an adversary unless such destruction or seizure be imperatively demanded by the necessities of the conflict.

This remarkably extensive list is drawn almost directly from Article 8(2)(b) of the Statute,[63] which lists violations of the laws and customs of *international* warfare, other than grave breaches of the Geneva Conventions. It is true that the majority of the provisions found in sub-paragraph (e) are also found in Additional Protocol II, but they are equally to be found in Additional Protocol I, in Geneva Convention IV, and indeed in the 1907 Hague Regulations, i.e. the law governing international conflicts. There are some innovations (e.g. the protection for those engaged in United Nations peacekeeping) and developments (e.g. the expanded list of sexual offences), which had not previously applied even to international conflicts,[64] but more important for the purposes of this chapter is the inclusion of provisions previously applicable only where a conflict was international in character. Perhaps the best example of this is Article 8(2)(e)(ix), prohibiting perfidy – a methods and means of warfare provision governing relations between combatants, and not previously applicable to internal conflict (or at least not in the context of conventional international law).[65]

Article 8(2)(e) clearly, then, goes beyond the level of regulation provided for internal armed conflict by common Article 3 and Additional

[63] Some modifications have been made to the list where necessary. References to grave breaches (as in Article 8(2)(b)(xxii)) were replaced by references to serious violations of common Article 3 (as in Article 8(2)(e)(vi)), for example. Some other provisions of para. (b) are not reproduced in para. (e), either because they are simply not relevant to internal armed conflict, or else because they were not considered to have attained customary status. See Zimmerman, 'War Crimes', p. 263.

[64] And which may, therefore, be susceptible to challenge on the grounds that they were not already part of customary international law.

[65] The same is true of Article 8(2)(e)(xii), regarding the destruction or seizure of enemy property.

Protocol II. The approach taken by the drafters of the Rome Statute – and indeed the effect of the Statute itself – is therefore consistent with 'the gradual blurring of the fundamental differences between international and internal armed conflicts'.[66]

The problem with unification

The position advanced by the ICTY Appeals Chamber in *Tadić*, along with that of Antonio Cassese as quoted in the introduction to this chapter and the impact of the adoption of the ICC Statute may, therefore, lead the reader to assume that international humanitarian law is indeed moving rapidly towards the situation whereby a single body of law – or at least a single body of customary international law – will be applicable to all armed conflicts, be they international or internal. It has even been suggested that conventional international law could eventually dispose of the traditional distinction altogether. Vitally important in terms of international legal regulation would therefore be not whether an armed conflict is considered international or internal, but simply whether an armed conflict per se exists or not.

This may appear to be the ideal situation as far as humanitarian protection is concerned. Such a unified approach to the regulation of armed conflict would have one major flaw, however. It relies upon a clear idea of when an armed conflict actually exists. This may initially seem of little consequence, after all, the absence of a widely accepted definition of 'armed conflict' has caused relatively few problems in the context of international armed conflict. States generally recognize one when they see it. Of course, there are some situations, such as low-intensity border incidents, where it can be difficult to determine with any certainty whether an armed conflict is occurring or not. Except at very low levels, however, such a determination is normally relatively straightforward.

The goal of a unified humanitarian law, however, is the extension of the laws of international conflict to cover internal armed conflicts. This, in contrast, is deeply problematic. The situation pertaining within a state is not analogous to its international relations. While it may be unusual for a state to use force against other states, force is constantly

[66] Von Hebel and Robinson, 'Crimes', p. 125.

employed within its territory against its own citizens.[67] Determining whether an internal conflict is in progress is therefore necessarily more difficult, and neither common Article 3 nor Additional Protocol II offer any assistance in this regard.[68] The Appeals Chamber in *Tadić*, however, besides dealing with the customary rules of internal armed conflict, did grapple with the definition of 'armed conflict', eventually concluding that:

> an armed conflict exists whenever there is a resort to armed force between States or protracted armed violence between governmental authorities and organized armed groups or between such groups within a State. International humanitarian law applies from the initiation of such conflicts and extends beyond the cessation of hostilities until a general conclusion of peace is reached; or, in the case of internal conflicts, a peaceful settlement is achieved.[69]

This represents a fairly broad interpretation, which has been relied upon in a number of subsequent ICTY cases. The ICTR Trial Chamber has since stated, however, that the definition offered in *Tadić* is still, 'termed in the abstract, and whether or not a situation can be described as an "armed conflict", meeting the criteria of Common Article 3, is to be decided upon on a case-by-case basis'.[70] Here we come to the crux of the problem. Absent an independent authority to decide on such matters, the question of whether an armed conflict exists or not will necessarily be left to the state concerned. It is unrealistic to expect – or even to hope – that such states will be either willing or capable of assessing the position objectively. Until it is in the state's own interests to apply humanitarian law, the likelihood must be that it will be disregarded. It makes no difference how precise, or how general, the definition of 'armed conflict' may be; as long as the definition contains criteria determining the existence or not of an armed conflict, it will be open to states to dismiss claims that the criteria have been met by insurgents. As Richard Baxter lamented, 'the first line of defense against international humanitarian law is to deny that it applies at all'.[71] This problem is always particularly acute with regard to internal situations,

67 This can range from everyday enforcement action against individual criminals to large-scale operations aimed at the quelling of riots or other civil disturbances.

68 See Moir, *Internal Armed Conflict*, pp. 31–42 and 99–109.

69 *Tadic* (Jurisdiction), above n. 21 at para. 70.

70 *Prosecutor* v. *Rutaganda* (Case ICTR–96–3), judgment, 6 December 1999, (2000) 39 *International Legal Materials* 557, para. 91.

71 R. R. Baxter, 'Some Existing Problems of Humanitarian Law', in *The Concept of International Armed Conflict: Further Outlook* (Proceedings of the International Symposium on Humanitarian Law, Brussels, 1974), pp. 1, 2.

and without careful management it could lead to the situation where the unified body of law would be applied only to high intensity conflicts, with the attendant danger that, once again, internal conflicts would be effectively excluded from the practical operation of humanitarian law.

Despite this practical difficulty, all is not lost, and it is still possible that international law could develop along the lines suggested. State practice is, after all, replete with violations of humanitarian law during internal armed conflict. Commentators, the ad hoc Criminal Tribunals and states themselves have, however, all accepted that certain rules *have* become a part of customary international law. Such attitudes are important since, as argued by Professor Baxter, 'The firm statement by the State of what it considers to be the rule is far better evidence of its position than what can be pieced together from the actions of that country at different times and in a variety of contexts.'[72] Were an affected state therefore publicly to accept a convergence in the international regulation of internal and international armed conflicts in principle, but to deny that the situation facing it at a particular moment in time was actually an armed conflict – even where, objectively, the opposite would clearly seem to be the case – while there may well be serious humanitarian consequences for the victims of that particular situation, this might not have any serious impact on the development of customary international humanitarian law into a single, unified body of rules.

Future prospects

As is clearly demonstrated by the *Tadić* jurisprudence and by the Statute of the International Criminal Court, it is incontrovertible that there has been a blurring of the distinction between international and internal armed conflicts in terms of their regulation by international humanitarian law. Despite this movement towards a unified legal regime for all armed conflict, however, a single body of humanitarian rules is still some way off. Indeed, Andreas Zimmerman points out that, despite the progress made by the Rome Statute, it still 'does not completely follow the approach by the ICTY which stated that "what is inhumane and consequently proscribed, in international wars, cannot but be inhumane and inadmissible in civil strife" '.[73]

[72] R. R. Baxter, 'Multilateral Treaties as Evidence of Customary International Law', (1965–6) 41 *British Yearbook of International Law* 275 at p. 300.

[73] Zimmerman, 'War Crimes', p. 263.

In truth, we are unlikely to see a completely unified legal regime in the near future. This is due largely to the unwillingness of states themselves. Several of those states that would be happy to see an increase in the level of humanitarian protection and regulation for internal conflicts are nonetheless unlikely to agree to the wholesale adoption in such cases of the rules for international conflicts. There remains a broad acceptance throughout the international community that internal and international armed conflicts are fundamentally different in character. As long as this view persists – and it is likely to do so for the foreseeable future – any attempt to abolish their separate legal regulation seems doomed to failure.

It would, then, seem premature to claim that the distinction between international and internal armed conflict has disappeared altogether. Indeed, in terms of conventional international law, there have been no developments towards even a convergence of their regulation. This will remain the position until – or unless – there is a re-appraisal of the Geneva Conventions and their Additional Protocols, should this ever occur. In the sphere of customary international law, however, Cassese's statement is irrefutable. The regulation of internal and international armed conflicts by customary humanitarian norms is clearly overlapping to an ever-greater extent. Furthermore, this has taken place without any disregard for the different characteristics of the two types of conflict. An acceptance that the relevant humanitarian rules of international conflict can, and should, be applied to internal conflicts does not require states to abandon the distinction between international and internal conflicts per se. It is to be hoped that these developments in the customary sphere will provide the blueprint for the future development of international law as a whole in this area.

8

Of vanishing points and paradoxes: terrorism and international humanitarian law

RICHARD BARNES

Introduction

Humanitarian law only applies in cases of armed conflict and, historically, this was limited to conflicts between states. However, as a response to increased instances of internal conflict, this evolved to include non-international conflict between states and insurgent or belligerent groups.[1] To this extent there has been an increased scope for the application of humanitarian law, and it must be conceded that humanitarian law may usefully control or mitigate violence involving non-state actors. Other legal regimes such as domestic and international criminal law and human rights law also apply to a limited extent during times of armed conflict, and more fully when international violence falls short of armed conflict. However, international violence in the form of terrorism is an increasing threat to contemporary international security, as incidents such as the bombing of the American embassies in Kenya and Tanzania in 1998, the strike against the USS Cole in October 2000, the attacks of 11 September 2001, the bombing of the British Consulate in Istanbul in 2003 and railway bombs in Madrid in March 2004 confirm. These incidents involve acts of violence by transnational armed groups and have led to calls for action by the victim states against the perpetrators: a so-called 'war on terror'. In such a war it is right to ask can, and should, international humanitarian law exert any controlling effect on the violence.

Concerned as he was with the application of humanitarian law to a widening range of conflicts, Hilaire McCoubrey was more reticent about the application of humanitarian norms to situations of terrorist violence. If the *jus in bello* was applicable to terrorists then it would

[1] See generally, L. Moir, *The Law of Internal Armed Conflict* (Cambridge University Press, 2002), ch. 1.

threaten the entire basis of international humanitarian law by collapsing the distinction between combatants and civilians, and, perhaps, legitimize the acts of the terrorists. These considerations led McCoubrey and White to conclude that although some aspects of humanitarian law can be applied to terrorist acts, the *jus in bello* does not provide an appropriate normative framework to regulate terrorist activities.[2] In a collection of essays in Hilaire's honour it seems appropriate to reflect upon this position, especially in light of the changing paradigm of international violence and the increased use of terrorism as a means of political coercion.[3]

Humanitarian law as codified by the Geneva Conventions of 1949 and the Additional Protocols of 1977 did not anticipate armed conflict in the form of modern terrorism and as such it may be regarded as inadequate to deal with modern forms of international violence. Yet, if the aims of humanitarian law are to mitigate the effects of hostilities and to provide a certain degree of protection to people in times of conflict, and these have been extended to new forms of international violence, then, arguably, there is some scope for using international humanitarian law to control terrorism. In this respect, ascertaining the true scope of international humanitarian law is crucial because international humanitarian law may also legitimize certain acts or actors that would otherwise be regarded as illegal. There are clear policy reasons for ensuring that those committing terrorist acts do not receive any form of approbation.

The application of humanitarian law to terrorism is beset by a number of problems, which may be understood in the context of two problematic and related paradigms: the vanishing point and the paradox. According to the former, terrorism is considered as an issue at the edge of international law's regulatory compass, which makes agreement about the law, and its application, difficult to reach. This leads to more fundamental structural problems when it comes to deciding how best to proceed with regulation. The latter theme questions the possibility of trying to regulate extra-legal activities, and more specifically, how to use the law to humanize inhumane conduct occurring in, or at a level amounting to, a state of armed conflict. By examining the way in which these obstacles affect the development and implementation of humanitarian law it is possible to assess how much of a controlling effect international humanitarian law may have on terrorist violence.

[2] See H. McCoubrey and N. D. White, *International Organizations and Civil Wars* (Dartmouth, 1995), pp. 68–71.

[3] The term international violence refers to any form of violence that threatens international peace and security and so potentially engages norms of international law.

In the next two sections the precise implications of these two themes are explored. When considering terrorism at the vanishing point, it is suggested that the marginal (i.e. at the limits of law/politics) status of terrorist regulation results in the development of narrowly focused, and sometimes unsophisticated, regulations on areas of core agreement. Thus, as one such focus area, humanitarian law should be narrowly construed so as to maintain its legitimacy when applied to terrorist activities. Furthermore, the paradox of trying to humanize inhumane conduct does not act as any logical bar to the regulation of terrorism through international humanitarian law. However, it does ensure that caution is required because of the potentially legitimising effect that humanitarian law exerts. A review of how humanitarian law actually regulates terrorist activities is used to test these conclusions, although it must also be conceded that certain deficiencies in humanitarian law mean that even the limited regulatory scope of humanitarian law does not present an entirely satisfactory approach to the regulation of terrorist activities in cases of armed conflict. Finally, there is a brief consideration of homologous areas of terrorist regulation. This is important, because if the regulation of terrorism proceeds on an atomized basis, then it is important to ensure that acts of terrorism do not fall into the interstices of the international regulatory framework.

Terrorism: at the vanishing point of international law

As Hersch Lauterpacht famously observed, 'if international law ... is the vanishing point of law, the law of war is even more conspicuously the vanishing point of international law'.[4] His point was that international law does not provide a categorical answer to difficult questions, such as the legality of nuclear weapons, and his viewpoint is often seized upon by the sceptic who, often with good cause, doubts the relevance or efficacy of international law.[5] This observation can be readily applied

[4] H. Lauterpacht, 'The Problem of the Revision of the Law of War', (1952) 29 *British Yearbook of International Law* 360 at pp. 381–2.

[5] Richard A. Falk echoes Lauterpacht's scepticism, in 'Rediscovering International Law after September 11th', (2002) 16 *Temple International and Comparative Law Journal* 359. Elsewhere, Sornarajah places international environmental law at the vanishing point of international law, being a subject full of 'pious prescriptions but little bite'. M. Sornarajah, 'The Haze over South East Asia', (1997) 1 *Singapore Journal of International and Comparative Law* 639 at p. 640. Fitzpatrick and Bennett have characterized immigration laws in the same manner. See J. Fitzpatrick and M. Bennett, 'A Lion in the Path? The Influence of International

to terrorism, which is undoubtedly a highly politicized issue. There are several possible reasons for this marginalization, some of which are noted below, but whatever these might be, such scepticism should not obscure the point that Lauterpacht was making: knowledge of such a regulatory limitation alone is a good reason for continued efforts to expound and elucidate the law. Upholding the law and ensuring its effectiveness is imperative, and just over fifty years on this observation seems particularly apposite to recent attempts at the international regulation of terrorism. If international law is at the edge of law and humanitarian law is at the edge of international law, then regulation of terrorism occurs at the vanishing point of humanitarian law. This then demands continued efforts to provide a suitable normative framework for tackling the problem.

Since 'September 11th' there has been a proliferation of writing on the subject of terrorism and international law, which demonstrates that it is easy to characterize the September 11th attacks as acts of terrorism.[6] However, as many eminent jurists have noted, it is much more difficult to provide an objective definition of terrorism suitable for legal purposes. Thus, Schachter has noted 'no single inclusive definition of international terrorism has been accepted by the United Nations or in a generally accepted multilateral treaty'.[7] And Professor Levitt, keenly aware of the difficulties, characterizes the search for a definition as resembling the quest for the Holy Grail.[8] More sceptical altogether was Judge Baxter who concluded that the concept was imprecise, ambiguous, and served no operative legal purpose.[9] What are the difficulties? Why is consensus so difficult to achieve? This may simply be because, as

Law on the Immigration Policy of the United States', (1995) 70 *Washington Law Journal* 589 at p. 621.

[6] The following are but the tip of the iceberg. See M. Cherif Bassiouni, 'Legal Control of International Terrorism: A Policy Orientated Assessment', (2002) 43 *Harvard International Law Journal* 83; Jonathan I. Charney, 'The Use of Force Against Terrorism and International Law', (2001) 95 *American Journal of International Law* 835; T. M. Franck, 'Terrorism and the Right of Self Defence', (2001) 95 *American Journal of International Law* 839; J. Strawson (ed.), *Law after Ground Zero* (GlassHouse Press, 2002). This is in addition to an already substantial body of literature on the topic. See, e.g., W. M. Reisman, 'International Legal Responses to Terrorism', (1999) 22 *Houston Journal of International Law* 3; R. Wedgwood, 'Responding to Terrorism: The Strikes against Bin Laden', (1999) 24 *Yale Journal of International Law* 559.

[7] O. Schachter, 'The Extraterritorial Use of Force Against Terrorist Bases', (1989) 11 *Houston Journal of International Law* 309.

[8] G. Levitt, 'Is Terrorism Worth Defining?', (1986) 13 *Ohio Northern University Law Review* 97.

[9] R. Baxter, 'A Skeptical Look at the Concept of Terrorism', (1974) 7 *Akron Law Review* 380.

the old cliché suggests, 'one man's terrorist is another man's freedom fighter'. Or it may be that too many grey areas inhere in the concept to which the sweeping application of a general rule on terrorism would not do justice. It may be that 'terrorism' is simply a powerful rhetorical device used by politicians to motivate political action or seize the populist initiative in response to anti-state activities, and which lacks any normative legal content. Or it may be that the term terrorism simply adds nothing to the litany of crimes that are already proscribed. It may be that some states are unwilling to denounce the acts of terrorists which further their shared political goals. Or it may be that the means of regulating terrorism are structurally deficient. What is certain is that many of these positions were articulated by states in the Secretary-General's *Report to the General Assembly on Measures to Eliminate International Terrorism.*[10] And it is likely that all are partially to explain the regulatory deadlock. However, for present purposes it is sufficient to conclude that there is not a common approach to terrorist regulation at the international level and no general law of terrorism. As Higgins concludes, it 'is a term without legal significance. It is merely a way of alluding to activities, whether of States or of individuals, widely disapproved of and in which either the methods used are unlawful, or the targets protected, or both.'[11]

Despite these difficulties, the search for an answer is compellingly driven by a collective desire to prevent future acts of terrorism and this at least requires us to establish a working definition of terrorism.[12] Although the choice of definition may be a somewhat arbitrary exercise, certain common elements can be ascertained from the various definitions that are sufficient for present purposes. Having reviewed the literature on terrorism, Arend and Beck claim that a terrorist act can be distinguished by reference to three specific qualities: '*violence,* whether actual or threatened; a '*political*' objective, however conceived; and an *intended audience,* typically though not exclusively a wide one.'[13] The concept is further distilled into the following definition: 'the threat or use

[10] UN doc. A/44/456, 25 August 1989.

[11] R. Higgins, 'The General International Law of Terrorism', in R. Higgins and M. Flory (eds.), *Terrorism and International Law* (Routledge, 1997), p. 28.

[12] Most commentators on terrorism accept such limitations but regard it as a hindrance rather than a bar. See A. C. Arend and R. J. Beck, *International Law and the Use of Force* (Routledge, 1993), p. 141; C. L. Blakesley, 'Ruminations on Terrorism and Anti-Terrorism Law and Literature', (2003) *University of Miami Law Review* 1041 at p. 1074.

[13] Arend and Beck, *Use Of Force*, p. 141.

of violence with the intent of causing fear in a target group, in order to achieve political objectives'.[14]

Significantly, Arend and Beck's definition shows that terrorism cannot be defined by the act alone. Thus, as Higgins points out, whilst hostage-taking, assassination, robbery, sabotage and indiscriminate bombing might constitute terrorism, not every such act automatically amounts to terrorism.[15] If the object, or target, of terrorism is not central to the definition of terrorism, as it surely isn't, then it seems that motive or intention must be crucial. Yet reliance on intention leads to significant problems. For example, where the intention behind the act of violence is the achievement of certain 'acceptable' political goals, then it may be claimed that the act was not illegal, but that it was in reality a legitimate act of self-determination. In short, do the ends justify the means?

Focus on intention also leads to other insuperable problems, because intention to cause fear or spread anxiety is not limited to the arsenal of the terrorist. States have also adopted policies with known psychological effects which are designed to bring other states into line with their, or community, objectives. Indeed, terror, fear and anxiety are often tools of war. For example, one retired US Army general has noted that the 'shock and awe' offensive with nuclear weapons against Japan during the Second World War had a decisive military impact.[16] Similarly, the 'shock and awe' strategy used against Iraq during the opening days of the Iraq campaign was designed to crush resistance both physically and psychologically.

In addition to these practical problems, efforts to regulate terrorism are affected by structural problems which flow from inherent deficiencies in regulatory approaches. To illustrate this issue, Franck provides us with two alternative approaches to regulating terrorism: 'idiots' law' and 'sophists' law'.[17] Sofaer, who attacks the tendency of contemporary international law to introduce exculpatory 'why' and 'whom' factors, which suggest that 'terrorism can be lawful in the pursuit of proper goals', is illustrative of the former approach.[18] According to this

[14] *Ibid.*

[15] R. Higgins, 'General International Law of Terrorism', p. 15.

[16] Charles A. Horner, 'Policy Considerations in Using Nuclear Weapons', (1997) 8 *Duke Journal of Comparative and International Law* 15.

[17] See Thomas M. Franck, 'Porfiry's Proposition: The Role of Legitimacy and Exculpation in Combating Terrorism', in Y. Dinstein (ed.), *International Law at a Time of Perplexity* (Martinus Nijhoff, 1989), p. 149.

[18] A. D. Sofaer, 'Terrorism and the Law', (1986) 64 *Foreign Affairs* 901 at p. 906.

approach a form of conduct is simply proscribed as unlawful in whatever form it takes. Thus, Sofaer would prefer a law such as the 1986 US–UK Extradition Treaty, which defines 'terrorist offences in terms of simple, inclusive *what* categories of activity', e.g. the taking of a hostage, or the bombing of a civic building.[19] In contrast, the sophists' position is taken by Pyle, who condemns the above treaty as 'simplistic and crude' for failing to take account of 'why' and 'whom' factors that might have justified an act.[20] The latter suggests that the conduct will be lawful depending on its context. For example, the act may be lawful if it is the only effective means by which a group can pursue certain well-established community goals such as self-determination.[21]

Underlying each position Franck perceives certain, yet unarticulated, value priorities.[22] Thus, the former prefers simplicity in the law whilst the latter prefers legal sophistication. However, what is crucial here is that neither approach can be defended through rational discourse because each approach has inherent advantages and disadvantages which cannot be measured against each other, and so no basis for choosing between them exists. Thus, if efforts at regulating terrorism follow either path they will run into unavoidable difficulties. This apparent stalemate can be side-stepped, but only once the limitations of each approach are realized and addressed.

The advantage of idiots' law is that it is easier to understand and apply than a law that takes complex phenomena such as motive and the qualities of the victim into account.[23] However, this quality is also its weakness. Its simplicity results in its rigid application, and this uncalibrated application may lead to patently unacceptable results.[24] For example, the rule 'murder is wrong' is simple and easy to apply in the sense that all that needs to be ascertained is the fact that a murder took place. No consideration of complicating factors, such as necessity or self-defence, is taken into account, and this means that morally acceptable conduct is not exculpated under the idiots' law.

If idiots' law is to be adopted then the above structural defects must be ameliorated. Franck suggests this is possible by deconstructing the category of conduct being regulated.[25] This deconstruction narrows

[19] Franck, 'Porfiry's Proposition', p. 170, referring to the Supplementary Treaty concerning the Extradition Treaty 1985, (1986) 24 *International Legal Materials* 1105.

[20] C. H. Pyle, 'Defining Terrorism', (1986) 64 *Foreign Affairs* 63 at p. 75.

[21] *Ibid.*, p. 75. [22] Franck, 'Porfiry's Proposition', p. 169. [23] *Ibid.*, p. 172.

[24] *Ibid.*, p. 182. [25] *Ibid.*

the scope of a particular law and helps build up consensus, which in turn generates legitimacy.[26] For example, terrorism can be broken down into component activities, such as hostage-taking, which are then subject to remedial action. Instead of a general rule outlawing terrorism, several more focused rules which prohibit attacks on women and children or against hospitals and schools are articulated. This also has the effect of facilitating the regulation of activities which are generally agreed to be unacceptable, whilst leaving unregulated those activities at the margins of acceptability. Of course, in the case of terrorism, this may not provide a solution for some of the most controversial activities, such as an oppressed people's use of suicide bombing against the civilians of a tyrant state.

The advantage of the sophists' position is that a calibrated set of rules will more closely accord with reasoned behaviour. A complex rule is capable of explaining and regulating complex social phenomena, and this renders sophists' law more appealing – or *legitimate*. However, the flaw of the sophists' rule is that as a finely calibrated system of regulations, its complexity renders its application difficult, if not impossible, and highly controvertible. Of course, sophists' law could claim to be the best approach if it could address its structural defects, i.e. if complex rules could be established on the basis of a 'genuine, shared set of community values underpinning the agreed norms', and if there was general agreement about the law being applied consistently in controversial cases by an impartial and binding decision-making process.[27] Clearly, sophists' law requires an effective judiciary, or other institutional mechanisms, for determining the content of the law and ascertaining its correct application in any given circumstances. At the level of domestic law this is not such an issue with a clearly defined and acceptable system of courts. However, at the level of international law, the absence of a comparable system of courts renders this defect critical. It means that any gains in legitimacy made by a calibrated law are dissipated by unilateral and self-serving applications of those rules by states.[28]

[26] Legitimacy is taken by Franck to be an essential component of law, i.e. law must be legitimate in the sense that it accords with the reasonable and decent expectations of the community. More particularly, legitimacy requires law, at the point of creation and enforcement, to be 'generally recognised as a basis for action'. *Ibid.*, p. 167. On the indicators of legitimacy more generally, see Thomas M. Franck, *Fairness in International Law and Institutions* (Oxford University Press, 1995), ch. 2.

[27] Franck, 'Porfiry's Proposition', p. 180.

[28] *Ibid.*, pp. 177, 178.

The point here is not to espouse the superiority of one approach over another, but rather to show that certain fundamental structural deficiencies exist within anti-terrorist discourse which must be overcome. Experience seems to confirm that the sophists' approach is unlikely to succeed because of systemic deficiencies in the international legal system; the absence of a sophists' anti-terrorist code seems to be proof of this. A brief survey of international law reveals the normative process to have been driven by a pragmatic response to individual instances of terrorist violence rather than a considered and planned normative response based on general consensus.[29] However, this has not always resulted in the exclusion of complicating factors such as motive from anti-terrorist agreements.[30] As noted above, terrorism may be defined according to both the act and the intent or motive behind it, and this militates against purely 'what' type categorizations of wrongful conduct. Anti-terrorist efforts have resulted in very narrow conduct orientated rules, such as prohibitions against hostage-taking and, more appositely, rules against acts of terrorism during the conduct of armed hostilities. Of course, this approach, which appears to follow a 'remedied idiots' law approach', may in the long-term contribute to sophists' law, in the sense that it forms part of a recognized process of syllogistic reasoning by inducing general rules of conduct from specific instances, i.e. a form of precedent.

If international law, or rather states, favour the pragmatic deconstructing of terrorism in order to facilitate regulation, then particular care must be taken to ensure that activities at the margins of the deconstructed activities are addressed. However, this position may prove difficult to achieve, especially where the boundaries of the deconstructed area of terrorism are unclear. For example, one needs to consider, as is done below, how acts of terrorism short of a full-scale armed attack, or occurring at the margins of an armed conflict, would fit within the scope of the deconstructed rules on terrorism as articulated in the form of humanitarian law. At this point it becomes important to

[29] See, e.g., the *Achille Lauro* incident of 1985 prompting the International Maritime Organisation to adopt the Convention on the Suppression of Unlawful Acts against the Safety of Maritime Navigation, (1988) 27 *International Legal Materials* 668.

[30] For example, most instruments that provide for extradition allow this to be qualified by a political offences exception, through the mechanism of subjecting extradition to the law of the extraditing state. On the problems this may cause see A. Cassese, 'The International Community's "Legal" Response to Terrorism', (1989) 38 *International and Comparative Law Quarterly* 589 at p. 593.

ascertain how and when other regimes control terrorism and how well they interlink with international humanitarian law.

In summary, it can be concluded that terrorism is presently at the vanishing point of international law because, at the level of normative discourse, terrorism is an intensely and, perhaps, essentially political problem. States disagree about terrorism and seek to maintain their right to disagree, and by doing so they maintain their authority and discretion over how best to deal with the problem. There are considerable moral, legal and political obstacles to an international law on terrorism. Even if agreement on how to tackle the issue is reached, these obstacles are buttressed by more profound structural problems inherent in regulatory discourse. If these are to be overcome then it seems that only narrowly focused 'idiot' rules on terrorist activities are likely to succeed in the short term.

Regulating extra-legal violence: a paradox?

The second theme is no less problematic. At the start of his monograph on humanitarian law, McCoubrey noted that there is a paradox with the application of law to what is essentially extra-legal violence.[31] Thus, states resorting to force are in a sense putting themselves beyond, or abandoning, ordinary legal relations. How then can law regulate extra-legal activities? This echoes the Clausewitzian precept, that 'to introduce into the philosophy of War itself a principle of moderation would be an absurdity'.[32] War is the negation of law and any attempt to regulate war is a logical contradiction.

However, this paradox is more apparent than real, or at least of abstract intellectual concern rather than of practical importance. As McCoubrey subsequently points out, states of violence are temporary phenomena and states will generally resume peaceful legal relations.[33] And even when violence occurs, it does so in social and political contexts that may moderate the violence. These social and political factors set the parameters to situations of violence. For example, the parties in conflict may refrain from acts of barbarism because this will tend to delegitimize

[31] H. McCoubrey, *International Humanitarian Law: The Regulation of Armed Conflicts* (1st edn, Dartmouth, 1990), p. 2.

[32] C. von Clausewitz, *On War* (1832; M. Howard and P. Paret (eds.), Princeton University Press, 1984), p. 76. Also reproduced in McCoubrey, *International Humanitarian Law* (1st edn), p. 3.

[33] *Ibid.*

any claim to be acting justly. There are a number of other factors that may compel the parties to adhere to humanitarian law during an armed conflict. Humanitarian law reduces the barbarity of the conflict and makes the process of normalization of relations more likely.[34] Also, the principle of reciprocity encourages the emergence of certain minimum standards i.e. the parties in conflict will mutually respect each other's prisoners of war and civilians.[35] Indeed, if humanitarian laws are regarded as a general good, then they should be respected for this reason alone.[36] Rules which provide for immediate and necessary palliative measures are essential or fundamental in the same way that human rights are fundamental. So, just as the murderer who is wounded during an arrest is entitled to medical treatment, so is the enemy combatant who is rendered *hors de combat*.

At all times, and this is increasingly so in our contemporary media-driven society, the violence of the parties is subject to a high degree of scrutiny and evaluation by both the parties in conflict and the wider by-standing society. It is now very difficult for states to escape the critical scrutiny of the global community and so there are strong pragmatic reasons, in addition to humanitarian reasons, for adhering to a generally accepted code of humanitarian law.

Although international humanitarian law does not justify or comment upon resort to force, it is arguable that it does legitimize certain forms or means of conflict. Yet to the extent that law actually regulates conflict then the paradox is diminished because the extra-legal aspect of the situation is diminished. Thus, international humanitarian law is somewhat an answer to the paradox stated. This may be objectionable from a moral standpoint, because it accepts that forms of violence are acceptable or legal. However, it represents a realist compromise by accepting the inevitability of violence within society; violence which must be controlled when it arises. By recognizing and providing a calibrated structure for the conduct of hostilities international law exerts an important normative control over the conduct of states and individuals.

34 *Ibid.*, p. 4.

35 It should be noted that this idea of reciprocity does not suggest that the operation of humanitarian law is somehow reciprocal in a strict legal sense. On this see *Prosecutor* v. *Kupreskic and others* (Case IT–95–16–T), judgment, 14 January 2000, para. 511.

36 Although the exact status of humanitarian law may be debated, the claim that it is fundamental has received strong support. See the *Nicaragua* case [1986] ICJ Rep. 14, para. 218; *Prosecutor* v. *Kupreskic*, above n. 35 at para. 520.

To this extent the general existence and application of humanitarian law has not been challenged.[37] However, within the laws of war, and probably for international law generally, the view is that terrorism is a more fundamental negation of law and social order and so it ought to be considered differently.[38] States are willing to accept that armed conflict can be regulated and 'legitimated' by international law, but unwilling to characterize terrorism in the same way.[39] Armed conflict may not be desirable, but it is acceptable. Terrorism is neither. This may be a sweeping claim, but certainly at the rhetorical level the term terrorism is characterized as completely anathema to global social order against which all states are united, whereas most states have participated directly or indirectly in the use of force.

Terrorism and international humanitarian law

International armed conflict

International humanitarian law deals with acts of terrorism only in so far as they occur in cases of armed conflict. In this context, terrorism may arise, either as an illegal means of warfare, or as the deliberate targeting of civilians.[40] The humanitarian law applicable to inter-state armed conflict is primarily contained in the four Geneva Conventions of 1949 and Additional Protocol I of 1977, which are, of course, supplemented by customary international law.[41] Common Article 2 determines

37 As is noted below, there may be particular disputes concerning the particular application of humanitarian law.

38 W. H. Taft IV, 'The Law of Armed Conflict after 9/11: Some Salient Features', (2003) 28 *Yale Journal of International Law* 319 at p. 323; D. Held, 'What Hope for the Future?: Learning the Lessons of the Past', (2002) 9 *Indiana Journal of Global Legal Studies* 381 at p. 391.

39 On the condemnation of terrorism, see e.g. Security Council Resolution 1377, UN doc. S/RES/1377, 12 November 2001. Between December 1972 and March 2004 there have been over thirty General Assembly Resolutions adopted on the subject matter of terrorism. To these we can add twenty-one global or regional Conventions designed to tackle various facets of terrorist activities. See below on humanitarian law and its relationship to other anti-terrorist rules.

40 Reisman, 'International Legal Responses', pp. 11–12.

41 Geneva Convention I for the Amelioration of the Condition of the Wounded and Sick in Armed Forces in the Field, Geneva, 12 August 1949, (1949) 75 UNTS 31; Geneva Convention II for the Amelioration of the Condition of Wounded, Sick and Shipwrecked Members of Armed Forces at Sea, Geneva, 12 August 1949, (1950) 75 UNTS 85; Geneva Convention III relative to the Treatment of Prisoners of War, Geneva, 12 August 1949, (1950) 75 UNTS 135; Geneva Convention IV relative to the Protection

the scope of these rules as applicable to 'all cases of declared war or of any other armed conflict which may arise between two or more of the High Contracting Parties'. This is further extended to situations of partial or total occupation of the territory of a High Contracting Party. However, it should be noted that the application of the rules of the Geneva Conventions are limited to the territories of the states parties, and this means that the protection afforded is not generally applicable unless a wider rule of customary international law is established.

Terrorist acts may be controlled by international humanitarian law in three ways: first, by restricting the right to use force to lawful combatants; secondly, by restricting the legitimate targets of military attacks, and thirdly, by limiting the actual methods and means of warfare.

Only lawful combatants are entitled to use force, and where they do so this must be in accordance with limits imposed by international law.[42] This is an integral part of the *quid pro quo* of humanitarian law; that in return for certain humanitarian guarantees, killing and other acts which would ordinarily be regarded as criminal are accepted as legitimate acts of war. Nothing in the Conventions permits civilians to use force and any person doing so may be prosecuted.[43] This precept maintains the strict limits of humanitarian law by rendering hostile actions of civilians subject to distinct regulation, i.e. domestic criminal law or military penal sanctions outside the limits of humanitarian law. This reinforces the point that approaches to terrorism are deconstructed, or streamlined, to ensure maximum legitimacy and respect for the law. It also circumscribes the legitimating effect of humanitarian law. However, because such acts are placed beyond the scope of humanitarian law it is important that the controlling ambit of non-humanitarian laws is clearly established. This point becomes even more crucial when it is recalled that the question of the status of a combatant is not always clear-cut and may complicate the application of humanitarian law. Criticisms of the USA over its

of Civilian Persons in Time of War, Geneva, 12 August 1949, (entered into force 21 October 1950) 75 UNTS 287; Protocol Additional to the Geneva Conventions of 12 August 1949, and relating to the Protection of Victims of International Armed Conflicts 1977, (entered into force 7 December 1978) 1125 UNTS 3.

42 Additional Protocol I, Article 43(1). See further Y. Sandoz, C. Swinarski and B. Zimmermann (eds.), *Commentary on the Additional Protocols of 8 June 1977 to the Geneva Convention of 12 August 1949* (Martinus Nijhoff, 1987), commentary to Article 43, para. 1675, p. 513. Hereinafter, *ICRC Commentary*.

43 See *Ex parte Quirin* 317 U.S. 1, 31 (1942).

treatment of the persons detained at Guantanamo Bay illustrate just this point.

At the heart of humanitarian law is the pivotal distinction between civilians and combatants. Terrorists often seek to betray this. Thus, humanitarian law is necessarily concerned with certain acts of terrorism and to this end there is a clear prohibition of attacks on civilians and civilian objects.[44] Where such acts are committed they are regarded as grave breaches and may be prosecuted as war crimes.[45] Although this seems unproblematic, difficulties arise because this application of humanitarian law proceeds on the basis that so-called acts of terrorism are always directed against civilian targets. However, as the attack on the USS Cole or the car bomb attacks on security installations in Iraq during the 2004 occupation suggest, this is not always the case. One simply cannot characterize all attacks on military targets as acts of war, and all attacks on civilian targets as terrorism. For example, when attacks are carried out against mixed targets, or when there are collateral effects on civilian targets, it will be difficult to distinguish acts of terrorism, which are primarily directed at spreading terror, from legitimate military attacks, which incidentally do the same. Moreover, not all attacks on civilians are intentional, and neither are all attacks on military targets always in accordance with the rules of war (i.e. perfidious attacks).[46] Clearly, ascertaining the nature of such acts often requires us to have regard to motive and intention, and at this point the controlling mechanisms of international humanitarian law become snared in the difficulties of proving intent and securing claims of political legitimacy for the act – the freedom fighter/terrorist dichotomy.

Another difficulty inherent in this area of humanitarian law is the relationship between military necessity and the principle of distinction. The much debated concept of military necessity provides that states are only authorized to use such destructive force as is 'necessary, relevant and proportionate to the prompt realization of legitimate belligerent objectives'.[47] The difficulty inherent in this concept is how to quantify the factors in the equation and this leads McDougal and Feliciano to

[44] Additional Protocol I, Articles 51(2) and 52.

[45] Additional Protocol I, Article 85(2).

[46] To illustrate this, one may recall the accidental targeting and bombing of a Red Cross warehouse facility in Kabul on 16 October 2001 during the military campaign in Afghanistan.

[47] M. S. McDougal and F. P. Feliciano, 'International Coercion and World Public Order: The General Principles of the Laws of War', (1958) 67 *Yale Law Journal* 771 at pp. 826–7.

conclude that because it is not feasible to quantify military force, then the principle must be expressed more modestly as the 'minimizing of unnecessary destruction'.[48] The military tribunal at Nuremburg was careful to note that military necessity does not justify a violation of a positive rule of law. Accordingly, it would seem that a narrow definition of military necessity prevails.[49] However, as noted below, many of the positive rules on the means and methods of force are couched in less than absolute terms which allow room for manoeuvre. Also, although military necessity originated as a constraint on the use of force, this seems to have been forgotten.[50] There are numerous instances where states appear to have disregarded the principle and it has, on occasion, been used to justify more excessive acts of warfare.[51] Unless military necessity is properly articulated as a restraint upon action, then the flexibility and ambiguity inherent in the concept mean that it may be used to justify considerable and potentially indiscriminate force where this appears to have a sufficiently well-defined military justification.

Although the principle of distinction is regarded as fundamental, it is not absolute, and Lauterpacht was wise to question its sacrosanctity.[52] Thus, it is highly doubtful that one could establish that the aerial bombardment of civilian centres during the Second World War was contrary to international law:

> although belligerents have often yielded to considerations of humanity and chivalry in matters which did not affect the supreme purpose of the war, they have refused to follow them when they threatened to assume the complexion of a decisive limitation of their freedom of action bent upon achieving victory.[53]

It is evident that there is a risk that a broad application of military necessity combined with a less rigorous application of the principle of distinction could result in potential acts of terrorist violence being regarded as legitimate military acts.

[48] *Ibid.*, p. 827.

[49] Having reviewed the relevant authorities, Nardin is of the view that a narrow definition of military necessity prevails. T. Nardin, 'The Laws of War and Moral Judgement', in R. Falk, F. Kratochwil and S. Mendlovitz (eds.), *International Law: A Contemporary Perspective* (Westview Press, 1985), p. 437 at p. 447.

[50] Burrus M. Carnahan, 'Lincoln, Lieber and the Laws of War: The Origins and Limits of Military Necessity', (1998) 92 *American Journal of International Law* 213 at pp. 216–17.

[51] Thus it was used as a defence during the Nuremburg trials. See, e.g., *Re Von Leeb*, 15 ILR 376 at 397, and *Re List and others* (1948) 15 ILR 635 at 646–7.

[52] Lauterpacht, 'The Problem of Revision', pp. 365–6.

[53] *Ibid.*, p. 366.

If we turn to the methods and means of inter-state warfare, Article 35 of Additional Protocol I provides that 'the right of the Parties to the conflict to choose methods and means is not unlimited'. Furthermore, the parties cannot employ methods or means of warfare that cause superfluous injury or unnecessary suffering.[54] To the extent that terrorist acts cause unnecessary suffering, Article 35 implicitly prohibits certain types of terrorist attack. However, there are only two specific references to terrorism in the whole of the Geneva Conventions and Additional Protocol I. Article 33 of Geneva Convention IV 1949 contains a general prohibition on acts of terrorism and Article 51(2) of Additional Protocol I prohibits acts or threats of violence, the primary purpose of which is to spread terror among the civilian population. However, some acts which may be regarded as terrorist acts are specifically prohibited. These include indiscriminate attacks,[55] reprisals on civilian targets,[56] attacks on works and installations containing dangerous forces,[57] attacks on places of worship,[58] the taking of hostages,[59] and the murder of persons not taking part in the hostilities.[60] Although such acts are prohibited, the fact that they are committed does not automatically entail a charge of terrorism. This is because the prohibition is in many instances to be balanced with military necessity. Thus, dams may be destroyed as legitimate military targets and civilian property subject to collateral damage. Moreover, a simple assimilation of these acts with terrorism fails to address the point made above about gauging intent to spread fear which is a central feature of terrorism.

In the context of the war in Iraq, the difficulty of distinguishing acts of terrorism from (illegal) acts of war is illustrated by the suicide bombing of a military checkpoint. On 29th March 2003, an Iraqi non-commissioned officer reportedly posed as a taxi driver in order to deliver a car bomb to a military checkpoint manned by American soldiers, four of whom were killed in the subsequent blast. Although the *modus operandi* may appear to resemble that of the atypical terrorist, the action is best cast as perfidy – an attack launched by a combatant who has led the opposing forces to believe that they are a non-combatant.[61] Thus, when considering the means and methods of war it is worth asking whether a focus on 'terrorism' actually adds anything to the content of

[54] Additional Protocol I, Article 35(2). [55] Additional Protocol I, Article 51(4).
[56] Additional Protocol I, Article 51(6). [57] Additional Protocol I, Article 56.
[58] Additional Protocol I, Article 53.
[59] Additional Protocol I, Article 75 and common Article 3. [60] *Ibid.*
[61] Additional Protocol I, Article 37.

humanitarian law. This point is important. Here we may recollect Baxter's criticism of terrorism – that it confuses and over-politicizes the application of law.[62] Characterizing the act as one of terrorism only serves to indicate that the act was viewed as particularly heinous rather than establish the basic illegality of the action.

Before considering non-international conflicts it is worth commenting on the extended scope of international humanitarian law. Article 1(4) of Additional Protocol I widens the definition of an international armed conflict to include 'armed conflict in which peoples are fighting against colonial domination and alien occupation and against racist regimes in the exercise of their right of self-determination'. Any authority representing such a people may undertake to apply the Geneva Conventions and Additional Protocol I by making a unilateral declaration addressed to the depositary of the treaty.[63] Expanding the scope of humanitarian law thus has resulted in complications, and fear that this provision would legitimize the acts of terrorist organizations, and, *inter alia*, led to the well-documented refusal of the USA to ratify Protocol I.[64] Article 1(4) was regarded as providing recognition and international legal status to groups engaged in terrorism, and legitimizing the use of force by such groups. Although this view is misguided in strict legal terms, because Article 4 provides that nothing in the rules shall affect the legal status of the parties to the conflict, and because of a well-established rule of humanitarian law that nothing in the rules of humanitarian law affects the legitimacy of any recourse to force, the fear that this provision would provide political capital to non-state belligerent groups is understandable.

The American stance and the resulting debate has heightened relief the tension between ensuring the fullest application of humanitarian law to situations of conflict and the incidental legitimacy that international humanitarian law gives to the belligerents. In the 'war on terror' it is clear that law in general, and humanitarian law in particular, should not afford those engaged in terrorism any degree of support. However, the claim that international humanitarian law legitimizes recourse to force has been overstated, and there are a number of compelling arguments in favour of the extended scope of humanitarian law. Thus, humanitarian

[62] See above n. 9. [63] See Article 96(3).

[64] See the 'Letter of Transmittal', (1987) 81 *American Journal of International Law* 910. A. Sofaer, 'The United States Decision not to Ratify Protocol I', (1988) 82 *American Journal of International Law* 784; H.-P. Gasser, 'An Appeal for Ratification by the United States', (1987) 81 *American Journal of International Law* 912.

law applies to both sides to a conflict regardless of which side is the aggressor or victim. It has already been conceded that force may be used to achieve self-determination, or national liberation, and Additional Protocol I should not be used to reignite this debate.[65] There is a clear distinction between the *jus ad bellum* and the *jus in bello* and this should not be distorted, not least by states claiming to uphold the rule of law. Moreover, as the above commentary suggests, Additional Protocol I actually strengthens the distinction between combatants and civilians as targets. Finally, it must be remembered that acceptance of the application of international humanitarian law to national liberation groups does not entail any acceptance of terrorist tactics. As Greenwood notes, the US President's message to the US Senate conflates the aims and practices of groups described as terrorist, by suggesting that acceptance of a national liberation group must imply acceptance of its methods and means.[66] Just as an acceptance of the application of humanitarian law to the armed forces of a state does not amount to an acceptance of any use of terrorist methods, neither does an acceptance of the application of humanitarian law to a national liberation group imply an acceptance of any terrorist practices by that group.[67]

Non-international armed conflict

Non-international armed conflict is typified as conflict involving organized armed groups within a state struggling against the state or against other organized armed groups.[68] Humanitarian and security concerns mean that such conflicts are not the exclusive concern of the state in whose territory the conflict occurs. To this end international law, by virtue of common Article 3 of the Geneva Conventions and Additional Protocol II, sets down minimum standards regulating the scope and conduct of hostilities in non-international armed conflicts.[69] These instruments impose obligations not only on the states parties, but also on the non-state combatants who

[65] See G. Abi-Saab, 'Wars of National Liberation in the Geneva Conventions and Protocols', (1979-IV) 165 *Hague Recueil* 353.

[66] C. Greenwood, 'Terrorism and Humanitarian Law: The Debate over Additional Protocol I', (1989) 19 *Israel Yearbook on Human Rights* 187 at p. 199.

[67] *Ibid.*, pp. 199–200.

[68] See *Prosecutor* v. *Tadić* (Case IT–94–1), decision on the defence motion for interlocutory appeal on jurisdiction, 2 October 1995, para. 70.

[69] 1977 Geneva Protocol II Additional to the Geneva Conventions of 12 August 1949, and relating to the Protection of Victims of Non-International Armed Conflicts, (1979) 1125 UNTS 609.

comprise the rebel or insurgent groups.[70] Indeed, the binding nature of these obligations may provide the primary advantage that this branch of international humanitarian law has over other branches of international law in the 'war on terrorism'. Of course, any optimism here must be qualified in light of the fact that any organization committed to terrorist means and methods is unlikely to comply with these norms.

Before examining the substance of the rules on non-international armed conflict, it is important to highlight the limited scope of these rules because they do not automatically apply to all forms of internal violence. Certain threshold criteria must be satisfied before the rules become applicable, which in many instances render this branch of international humanitarian law impotent to regulate terrorism. An oft-quoted starting point here is Pictet's suggestions for determining the application of common Article 3.[71] However, only two of these criteria are properly determinative: the existence of a state of armed conflict, and the ability of the non-state parties to implement the provisions of international humanitarian law.[72]

The application of international humanitarian law depends on the existence of a particular quality of violence that amounts to armed conflict.[73] This may be easy to determine in respect of inter-state conflicts, where the actual intervention of armed forces may amount to armed

[70] This position is generally accepted by commentators and states. For an excellent discussion of this issue see A. Cassese, 'The Status of Rebels under the 1977 Geneva Protocol on Non-International Armed Conflicts' (1981) 30 *International and Comparative Law Quarterly* 416.

[71] '(1) That the Party in revolt against the *de jure* Government possesses an organized military force, an authority responsible for its acts, acting within a determinate territory and having the means of respecting and ensuring respect for the Convention. (2) That the legal Government is obliged to have recourse to the regular military forces against the insurgents organized as military and in possession of a part of the national territory. (3)(a) That the *de jure* Government has recognized the insurgents as belligerents; or (b) that it has claimed for itself the right of a belligerent; or (c) that it has accorded the insurgents recognition as belligerents for the purposes of the present Convention; or (d) that the dispute has been admitted to the agenda of the Security Council of the General Assembly of the United Nations as being a threat to international peace, or an act of aggression. (4)(a) That the insurgents have an organization purporting to have the characteristics of a State. (b) That the insurgent civil authority exercises *de facto* authority over persons within a determinate territory. (c) That the armed forces act under the direction of the organized civil authority and are prepared to observe the ordinary laws of war. (d) That the insurgent civil authority agrees to be bound by the provisions of the Convention.' Jean S. Pictet (ed.), *Commentary, The Geneva Convention for the Amelioration of the Wounded and Sick in Armed Forces in the Field* (1952), pp. 49–50.

[72] See Moir, *Internal Armed Conflict*, pp. 36–40.

[73] See common Articles 2 and 3.

conflict, but much more difficult to ascertain in internal armed conflicts.[74] What level of violence amounts to an internal armed conflict and so becomes subject to international humanitarian law? Common Article 3 is silent on this matter, other than to exclude armed conflict of an 'international character'. There is the view that common Article 3 was only intended to apply to internal armed conflicts that closely resemble inter-state conflicts.[75] However, as Jinks notes, this would be inconsistent with the proposal put forward at the time.[76] Perhaps more precisely, the matter was simply left open.[77] This, of course, suggests that no clear boundary can be drawn and the precise scope of humanitarian law is left uncertain. This is crucial because recent history suggests it is in precisely this grey area between conflict and peace that many acts of terrorist violence take place.

A clearer distinction appears to be drawn in Article 1(2) of Additional Protocol II, which excludes from its scope of application 'situations of internal disturbances and tensions, such as riots, isolated and sporadic acts of violence and other acts of a similar nature'. In addition to Article 1(2), Additional Protocol II has the cumulative requirement that the non-state armed forces exercise control over a part of a state's territory.[78] This provision can be contrasted with common Article 3, which merely requires that the conflict occur within the territory of the High Contracting States.[79] Thus, it is generally accepted that the scope of Additional Protocol II is narrower than common Article 3.[80] However, although this test may seem to clarify the scope of humanitarian law, the divergent tests may actually complicate the application of humanitarian law by rendering some conflicts subject to common Article 3 and not Additional Protocol II.

[74] See, e.g., the Resolution on the Definition of Aggression, GA Res. 3314(XXIX), 14 December 1974.

[75] M. Greenspan, *The Modern Law of Land Warfare* (University of California Press, 1959), p. 619 *et seq*.

[76] D. Jinks, 'September 11 and the Laws of War', (2003) *Yale Journal of International Law* 1 at pp. 39–40.

[77] See the comments of Pictet noted in Howard S. Levie, *The Law of Non-International Armed Conflict* (Martinus Nijhoff, 1987), p. 41.

[78] Article 1(1). [79] See Moir, *Internal Armed Conflict*, p. 31.

[80] See M. Bothe *et al.*, *New Rules for Victims of Armed Conflicts: Commentary on the Two 1977 Additional Protocols to the Geneva Conventions* (Martinus Nijhoff, 1982), pp. 623–4; Moir, *Internal Armed Conflict*, p. 100 *et seq*; C. Lysaght, 'The Scope of Protocol II and its Relation to Common Article 3 of the Geneva Conventions of 1949 and other Human Rights Instruments', (1983) 33 *American University Law Review* 9 at p. 21; William A. Schabas, 'Punishment of Non-State Actors in Non-International Armed Conflict', (2003) 26 *Fordham Journal of International Law* 907 at p. 922.

Furthermore, those conflicts arising out of a struggle for national liberation are subject to the rules on inter-state armed conflict, even though they may more closely resemble a non-international armed conflict.[81]

The scope of Additional Protocol II is also limited by reference to the quality of organization of the non-state armed forces. Such groups must be 'under responsible command ... as to enable them to carry out sustained and concerted military operations and to implement this Protocol'.[82] The problem is not with this requirement per se, which seems logical and reasonable, but whether, as Moir points out, the required degree of organization can actually be ascertained.[83] For many insurgent groups, this requirement would preclude the application of humanitarian law. It may also be the case that the particular form of organization taken on by the group, i.e. a cellular decentralized arrangement, might also preclude the application of rules.

This delineation between armed conflict and purely domestic incidents of violence may be contrasted with the definition of non-international armed conflict adopted in the Rome Statute, which focuses on '*protracted* armed conflict between governmental authorities and organized armed groups or between such groups'.[84] The requirement of protracted violence has also been required by the ICTR and ICTY.[85] However, this has been done with a degree of flexibility. Thus, in the former, a period of violence extending over a few months was regarded as sufficient given the intensity of the levels of violence. In the latter, a degree of intensity and certain organizational requirements were further required.[86] However, in the *Tadić* and *Celebici* trials it was noted that the emphasis on protraction was necessary in order to distinguish armed conflict from the instances of civil unrest or terrorism.[87] Clearly, the

[81] See above nn. 63 to 67 and the accompanying text. [82] Article 1(1).

[83] Moir, *Internal Armed Conflict*, p. 36.

[84] Rome Statute of the International Criminal Court, UN doc. A/CONF. 183/9, Article 8(2)(f) (emphasis added).

[85] See *Prosecutor* v. *Jean Paul Akayesu* (Case No. ICTR–96–4–T), 2 September 1998, para. 619; *Tadić*, above n. 68, para. 70.

[86] *Prosecutor* v. *Tadić* (Case No. IT–94–1), opinion and judgment, 7 May 1997, para. 562. The tribunal noted that the factors relevant to determining this are addressed by the ICRC, although it did not explain exactly how these were to be evaluated. See *ICRC Commentary*, Article 3, which provides non-mandatory guidance for identifying the degree of military organization necessary. See Pictet, above n. 71.

[87] *Prosecutor* v. *Tadić*, *ibid.*, *Prosecutor* v. *Mucic and others* (Case No. IT–96–21–T), judgment, 16 November 1998, para. 184.

tribunal was guarding against the creeping extension of international humanitarian law to situations for which it was not designed. That said, beyond noting this distinction, little was done to clarify it.

This position may be further contrasted with the view of the Inter-American Commission on Human Rights, that a short but intense period of violence will suffice to found the application of the law of armed conflict rather than international human rights law.[88] In all cases the existence of an armed conflict must be objectively determined irrespective of any motivation underlying the conflict, or the views of the parties; otherwise the application of international humanitarian law may be distorted by the political self-interest of states. Although the views of the Inter-American Commission on Human Rights may not be regarded as an authoritative interpretation of international humanitarian law, the flexible approach inherent in this view seems well-suited to the vagaries of modern conflict. However, this flexibility should not result in the extension of humanitarian law beyond the scope intended by states as this would likely result in its delegitimization.

Common Article 3 of the Geneva Conventions extends the fundamental principle of distinction to such conflicts, by requiring the humane treatment of non-combatants:

> To this end the following acts are and shall remain prohibited at any time and in any place whatsoever with respect to the above-mentioned persons:
>
> a. Violence to life and person, in particular murders of all kinds, mutilation, cruel treatment and torture;
> b. Taking of hostages;
> c. Outrages upon personal dignity, in particular humiliating and degrading treatment.

There is no express reference to terrorism in common Article 3, but in the same way that those rules applicable to international armed conflict can be applied to the means and techniques associated with terrorism, so too can the provisions of common Article 3. These provisions are developed under Additional Protocol II. Article 4 establishes certain fundamental guarantees for those not taking part in the conflict. Thus, paragraph (2)(a) prohibits the

[88] *Juan Carlos Abella* v. *Argentina*, Report 5/97, Case 11.137. Here a carefully planned, coordinated and executed attack by an organized armed group against a military base, confronted by military action, constituted an armed attack, its short duration notwithstanding (at p. 152).

murder of persons not, or no longer, taking part in hostilities and paragraph (2)(b) prohibits the taking of hostages. Furthermore, Additional Protocol II specifically provides that acts of terrorism[89] and 'acts or threats of violence the primary purpose of which is to spread terror among the civilian population' are prohibited.[90] It then continues to specify that those prohibitions which are operative in inter-state conflicts, namely, attacks on civilians and civilian objects,[91] attacks on works and installations containing dangerous forces,[92] and attacks on places of worship, are operative in non-international conflicts.[93]

Gasser has recently argued that the norms prohibiting terrorism in an internal armed conflict are basically the same as those applicable to international armed conflict.[94] This may be broadly true but there are some important limitations. First, there is no express limitation on the right of the parties to a conflict to choose the methods and means of warfare. To some extent this may be rendered immaterial by the existence of a customary rule limiting the methods and means of warfare during non-international armed conflict. Thus, the Appeals Chamber in *Tadić* asserted, in reference to the means used by a state to put down a rebellion, that what is 'inhumane, and consequently proscribed, in international wars, cannot but be inhumane and inadmissible in civil strife'.[95] Whether this amounts to an exhaustive replication of the rule found in Article 35 of Additional Protocol II to non-international conflicts is open to debate, but it certainly marks a trend towards the extension of rules of international armed conflict to non-international conflicts.

A second limitation is the absence of any provisions on individual criminal responsibility in common Article 3 or Additional Protocol II. However, the ICTY in the *Tadić* case has since confirmed that certain crimes committed during an internal armed conflict are to be regarded as international crimes.[96]

Limits of humanitarian law

International humanitarian law is limited to situations of armed conflict and herein is the major difficulty; the relevance of international

[89] Article 4(2)(d). [90] Article 13(2). [91] *Ibid.* [92] Article 15. [93] Article 16.

[94] H.-P. Gasser, 'Acts of Terror, "Terrorism" and International Humanitarian Law', (2002) 84 *International Review of the Red Cross* 547 at p. 560.

[95] *Prosecutor* v. *Tadić* (Case No. IT–94–1), decision on the defence motion for interlocutory appeal on jurisdiction, Judgment, 2 October 1995, para. 119.

[96] *Ibid.*, paras. 128 and 134. See also *Prosecutor* v. *Mucic*, above n. 87, para. 316.

humanitarian law to incidents of terrorism is necessarily limited because these acts do not typically occur as a part of the hostilities in the scope of armed conflict as currently accepted. It is likely that acts of terrorism do not satisfy the requisite degree of intensity or protraction that international law requires to trigger the application of humanitarian law. And unless a state of armed conflict already persists, then humanitarian law will not apply. Thus, although attacks like those of September 11th were unquestionably crimes under domestic law, and, possibly, international law, commentators are in agreement that they were not violations of the laws of war.[97]

Humanitarian law is no panacea for the problem of contemporary international terrorism and it is no surprise that some commentators claim that the *jus in bello* does not apply to terrorist activities.[98] This position is often based on the assumption that the application of humanitarian law would confer a measure of recognition and status to groups practising terrorist activities.[99] It may even be argued that humanitarian law legitimizes the use of force by such groups. However, as Gasser points out, neither of these claims is correct because Article 4 of Additional Protocol I expressly precludes any impact on the status of the parties to a conflict.[100] As he states, emphatically, 'humanitarian law never legitimizes any recourse to force'.[101] In strict legal terms, this question of legitimacy has already been conceded elsewhere and it is generally accepted that in certain limited circumstances, i.e. where force

[97] See J. Fitzpatrick, 'Jurisdiction of Military Commissions and the Ambiguous War on Terrorism', (2002) 96 *American Journal of International Law* 345 at pp. 346–9; J. J. Paust, 'Antiterrorism Military Commissions: Courting Illegality', (2001) 23 *Michigan Journal of International Law* 1, n. 16 and 'Antiterrorism Military Commissions: The Ad Hoc Rules of Procedure', (2001) 23 *Michigan Journal of International Law* 677 at p. 683. Paust derives his argument from the fact that al-Qaeda is a non-state, non-belligerent and non-insurgent actor, with which the USA cannot be at war. See further *Pan American Airways, Inc* v. *Aetna Casualty* & *Surety Co*, 505 F. 2d 989, 1013–15 (2d Cir. 1974), where the court regarded the PLO similarly.

[98] T. Stein, 'How Much Humanity do Terrorists Deserve', in A. J. M. Delissen and G. J. Tanja (eds.), *Humanitarian Law of Armed Conflict: Challenges Ahead: Essays in Honour of Frits Karlshoven* (Martinus Nijhoff, 1991), p. 567 at p. 573.

[99] These points were expressed by President Reagan's Letter of Transmittal explaining why the USA should refuse to ratify Additional Protocol I. Reprinted in (1987) 81 *American Journal of International Law* 910.

[100] H.-P. Gasser, 'An Appeal for the Ratification by the United States', (1987) 81 *American Journal of International Law* 912 at pp. 917–18.

[101] *Ibid.*, p. 917. These views on the neutral application of humanitarian law are echoed elsewhere. See Greenwood, 'Terrorism and Humanitarian Law'.

is the tool of oppression, force may be used as a means of self-determination.[102] Thus, certain non-state actors may have legitimate recourse to force.

States have insisted on maintaining maximum discretion in how to deal with all forms of international violence, but, in particular, violence falling short of international armed conflict. The moderating control of humanitarian law is frequently hampered by the potential legitimacy it bestows upon the non-state actors which is often contrary to the political aims of the states involved. As Meron points out, states have refused to be 'reassured by treaty language, such as Article 3(2) common to the Geneva Conventions for the Protection of Victims of War, which explicitly states that application of the listed protective norms will not affect the legal status of the parties'.[103] As a result, the extension of humanitarian law to new forms of international violence is a continual struggle against the sovereign authority of states.

Despite these problems it is clear that certain acts of terrorism carried out during an armed conflict, whether international or non-international, may be regulated by the laws of war. States have a legal duty, apart from any self-interest, in monitoring compliance with international humanitarian law and prosecuting offenders' violations of the same.[104] Acts of terrorism, when they take the form of such violations, may amount to grave breaches of the Geneva Conventions or violations of common Article 3. Although states are under an obligation to prosecute the former, they only enjoy a right and not an obligation to prosecute the latter. Unfortunately, in either case, although the ad hoc tribunals for Rwanda and the former Yugoslavia represent a significant step in the right direction of controlling international violence, the overall commitment of states to prosecuting law-breakers is sadly to be found wanting.[105] This is particularly so when it is recalled that much of humanitarian law is directed at state actors and agents.

[102] W. Reisman, 'Criteria for the Lawful Use of Force in International Law', (1985) 10 *Yale Journal of International Law* 279 at pp. 282–3.

[103] T. Meron, 'International Criminalisation of Internal Atrocities', (1995) 89 *American Journal of International Law* 554.

[104] See common Article 1.

[105] See Moir, *Internal Armed Conflict*, ch. 6; Meron, 'International Criminalisation of Internal Atrocities', pp. 554–5.

Humanitarian law and its relationship to other anti-terrorist rules

The only universal treaty attempting to regulate terrorism in all circumstances, the Convention for the Prevention and Punishment of Terrorism 1937, has never entered into force.[106] Two further attempts to establish a comprehensive regime against terrorism have also failed, demonstrating the difficulty of reaching agreement on terrorist regulation.[107] In the wake of these attempts an array of conventions dealing with various acts of terrorism in peacetime has been developed and implemented on an ad hoc basis. Such agreements deal with, *inter alia*, unlawful acts against the safety of maritime navigation,[108] hijacking and unlawful acts against aircraft,[109] hostage-taking,[110] crimes against internationally protected persons,[111] the suppression of terrorist financing activities,[112] and the suppression of terrorist bombings.[113] The report of the UN Secretary-General on measures to eliminate international terrorism indicates that there are twenty-one instruments in force that purport to deal with various facets of international terrorism.[114] These multilateral instruments have been supplemented by hundreds of bilateral agreements that typically provide for extradition and inter-state cooperation for the purpose of suppressing such activities.[115]

A comprehensive review of these instruments is not necessary to illustrate the argument pursued in this chapter, that international law has followed the 'idiots' path' to regulation and that this requires a high degree of coordination between the various strands of 'idiots' law' in

106 (1938) 19 *League of Nations OJ* 23.

107 United States Draft Convention on Terrorism 1972, (1972) 11 *International Legal Materials* 1382, and the Model American Convention on the Prevention and Punishment of Serious Forms of Violence (American Bar Association, 1983).

108 Convention for the Suppression of Unlawful Acts against the Safety of Maritime Navigation 1988, (1988) 27 *International Legal Materials* 668.

109 Tokyo Convention on Offences and Certain Other Acts Committed on Board Aircraft 1963, 704 UNTS 219; Hague Convention for the Suppression of Unlawful Seizure of Aircraft 1970, 860 UNTS 105; Montreal Convention for the Suppression of Unlawful Acts against the Safety of Civil Aviation 1971, 974 UNTS 177.

110 International Convention against the Taking of Hostages 1979, 1316 UNTS 205.

111 Convention on the Prevention and Punishment of Crimes against Internationally Protected Persons, including Diplomatic Agents 1973, 1035 UNTS 167.

112 Convention for the Suppression of the Financing of Terrorism 1999, (2000) 39 *International Legal Materials* 270.

113 Convention for the Suppression of Terrorist Bombings 1997, (1998) 37 *International Legal Materials* 251.

114 UN doc. A/58/116 and Add. 1.

115 See generally G. Gilbert, *Aspects of Extradition Law* (Martinus Nijhoff, 1991).

order to ensure an effective response to terrorist atrocities. The first point may be inferred from the simple fact that no general agreement on terrorism exists and that a sophists' rule on terrorism remains beyond the grasp of states. At the regional level there has been limited success with the European Convention on the Suppression of Terrorism 1977.[116] However, this remains exceptional, and in any case a review of some of the key aspects of these instruments reveals that an atomized approach has other weaknesses.

The aim of these agreements is to ensure that terrorists are brought to justice somewhere, and this is facilitated through the use of the principle *aut dedare aut judicare*: the duty to extradite or prosecute.[117] Thus, states on whose territory persons who are reasonably suspected of committing an act of terrorism happen to be must either try those persons or hand them over to other contracting states who are seeking the extradition of those persons. This is further supplemented by a 'universal' jurisdiction clause which permits all contracting states to try those suspected of committing acts of terrorism whether or not they occurred in the territory of the states, and whether or not the victims or their property were nationals of that state, as long as the offender is present in the territory of the state.[118] Any prosecution would take place under the domestic laws of the state concerned.

There is a degree of convergence between these instruments and humanitarian law. For example, Article 12 of the Hostages Convention provides that 'in so far as the Geneva Conventions ... are applicable to a particular act of hostage-taking ... the present Convention shall not apply to an act of hostage-taking committed in the course of armed conflicts as defined in the Geneva Conventions'. This means that where the provisions of the Geneva Convention fall short of the Hostages Convention, the latter prevails.[119] This is important because in an internal armed conflict situation, although hostage-taking violates common Article 3, this does not establish a duty to prosecute or extradite. In such a situation, the Hostages Convention will control. In contrast, in an

[116] (1976) 15 *International Legal Materials* 1972.

[117] See further M. Cherif Bassiouni and Edward M. Wise, *Aut Dedere aut Judicare: The Duty to Extradite or Prosecute in International Law* (Martinus Nijhoff, 1995).

[118] See, e.g., Article 4(2) of the Hague Convention 1970; Article 5(2) of the Montreal Convention 1971; Article 6(4) of the Rome Convention 1988; Article 7(4) of the International Convention for the Suppression of the Financing of Terrorism 1999.

[119] Of course, this interpretation turns on whether the Geneva Conventions are seen to be applicable, despite the absence of an obligation to prosecute or extradite.

international armed conflict situation, hostage-taking violates Article 34 of Geneva Convention IV 1949, which is an explicit grave breach giving rise to an obligation to prosecute or extradite.[120]

Although this basic approach may seem to provide, or at least contribute to, a seamless approach, it does not. Cassese points out a number of deficiencies with these responses to terrorism.[121] First, not enough states are parties to these instruments, and, more particularly, as Cassese points out, not 'enough States that actually *count* in this field are parties – that is, those States on whose territories terrorists seem consistently to end up'.[122] Not enough states are parties to these agreements and in particular the multilateral agreements. For example, although the USA is a party to over 100 bilateral agreements it is only party to one multilateral agreement.[123] This may be contrasted to the near universal participation in the humanitarian agreements.

Secondly, most of the above instruments fail to exclude terrorist type offences from the 'political offences' exception which operates under most extradition laws.[124] However, it should also be noted that there appears to be a trend towards the depoliticizing of serious terrorist crimes in this respect.[125] The European Convention on the Suppression of Terrorism is a useful model in this respect, whereby Article 1 provides that a number of offences shall not be regarded as political offences.[126] However, it does subsequently allow states to reserve the right to refuse extradition for those offences if it regards the offence to be political.[127] Although the state remains under an obligation to prosecute, this reservation, and the political offences exception, serve to weaken peacetime control of terrorist activities.

[120] Geneva Convention IV 1949, Article 147.

[121] Cassese, 'The International Community's Legal Response', pp. 593–6.

[122] *Ibid.*, p. 593.

[123] This being the Montevideo Convention on Extradition 1933, 165 LNTS 45.

[124] For example, Article 10 of the Italian Constitution prohibits the extradition of a foreigner for political offences.

[125] See J. Fitzpatrick, 'Rendition and Transfer in the War against Terrorism: Guantanamo and Beyond', (2003) 25 *Loyola of Los Angeles International and Comparative Law Review* 457 at p. 474.

[126] See generally, O. Lagodny, 'The European Convention on the Suppression of Terrorism: A Substantial Step to Combat Terrorism?', (1989) 60 *University of Colorado Law Review* 583. Also Cassese, 'The International Community's Legal Response', pp. 594–5.

[127] Article 13.

A third problem is that none of these agreements contain effective enforcement provisions, whereby a defaulting state can be compelled to comply with the treaty. If a state fails to prosecute or extradite, then other states parties can only apply the ordinary peaceful sanction permitted by international law to the recalcitrant state. As Cassese notes in the aftermath of the *Achille Lauro* incident, neither Egypt, who failed to comply with their obligations under the Hostages Convention, nor Italy, who failed to comply with their obligations under a bilateral extradition agreement with the USA, was subject to any significant action.[128] Of course, this criticism may be levelled at humanitarian law, and may be regarded as a systemic weakness, rather than one peculiar to the regulation of terrorism. Finally, there is the related problem of ensuring that states take adequate steps to search for and arrest suspects. There are no effective rules requiring states to take these steps, and clearly, any failure to do so renders the obligations to prosecute or extradite meaningless.

Despite the need for a coherent and systematic response to terrorism, it is quite clear that responses to terrorism outside humanitarian law are both disparate and flawed. Of course, most of these agreements were concluded as a reaction to specific events, such as the *Achille Lauro* incident, and were not intended to provide a systematic regime for the regulation of terrorism. This is consonant with the claim that responses to complex and inherently political phenomena like terrorism are likely to develop in the form of 'idiots' or 'remedied idiots' rules. Unlike humanitarian law, where there are compelling moral grounds, and well-established legal principles, underpinning the system of regulation, these regimes are comparatively 'immature'. That said, at the same time they purport to import a degree of sophistication through the use of the political offence exception. However, the viability of this is clearly contingent on a reliable and effective system for determining the legitimacy of any such defence. In many cases this is absent, disputed or simply abused, and this may seriously hamper any efforts to regulate terrorist activities.

Concluding thoughts

Although Hilaire McCoubrey was quite sceptical about using humanitarian law to regulate terrorist activities, it is quite clear that humanitarian law

[128] Cassese, 'The International Community's "Legal" Response', p. 593.

specifically prohibits a range of acts that can be considered as terrorist in nature. Indeed, it is quite plausible that had the September 11th attacks on the USA occurred during an armed conflict they would have been adequately covered by the laws of war. However, we should be careful about expecting too much of humanitarian law in any 'war on terror'. This is primarily because humanitarian law has a limited scope, but also because some of the rules of humanitarian law are not a satisfactory response to acts of terrorism.

Humanitarian law was not designed to deal with a war on terror when that war does not amount to an armed conflict. As Rona observes, 'it is not that humanitarian law is inadequate, but rather that its application is inappropriate'.[129] It is quite clear that when tackling complex phenomena like terrorism, political and structural considerations have forced international law to develop rules with a narrow focus in order to maintain their legitimacy. To extend the scope of such rules to novel situations is likely to undermine international law's effectiveness. This is also likely to have 'unhumanitarian' consequences because if humanitarian law permits violence prohibited by domestic law, then a premature application of humanitarian law may actually result in a net increase in human suffering.[130] For these reasons, humanitarian law is necessarily limited to situations of armed conflict and claims that it should be extended to meet new forms of international violence should be rejected.

However, it is not always easy to clearly categorize outbreaks of violence as inter-state, intra-state, or non-state, and states may try to blur such boundaries to suit their needs. To this extent it is crucial that there is a seamless normative framework covering all the various forms of international violence. This is because law plays a role in channelling disputes and it is important that disputes are dealt with by the appropriate frameworks and according to appropriate rules. Law has a role to play in mitigating levels of violence, ensuring adherence to basic conditions of respect for persons and facilitating the return to non-violent relations. It may even be that law has to play a strategic role in providing the protagonists with a claim to political legitimacy as the 'law-abiding good guys'. In any event, what has been shown is that in the

[129] G. Rona, 'Interesting Tomes for International Humanitarian Law: Challenges from the "War on Terror" ', (2003) 27 *Fletcher Forum of World Affairs* 55 at p. 58.

[130] W. J. Fenrick, 'Should the Laws of War Apply to Terrorists?', (1985) 79 *American Society of International Law Proceedings* 112.

absence of a general regime against terrorism, focused 'idiots' laws' must knit together in order to ensure that lacunae or complications do not arise.[131] Any such failure may lead to the type of problem faced by the USA as a result of its ill-advised detention of the prisoners at Guantanamo Bay.

[131] This conclusion in respect of terrorism parallels the argument by a number of commentators that there should be a convergence of humanitarian and human rights norms, which prevent any lacunae arising. See, e.g., M. Draper, 'The Relationship between the Human Rights Regime and the Law of Armed Conflicts', (1971) 1 *Israeli Yearbook of Human Rights* 191; M. J. Peterson, 'On the Inadequate Reach of Humanitarian and Human Rights Law and the Need for a New Instrument', (1983) *American Journal of International Law* 589; George H. Aldrich, 'New Life for the Laws of War', (1981) 75 *American Journal of International Law* 764; T. Meron, 'The Humanization of Humanitarian Law', (2000) 94 *American Journal of International Law* 239 at pp. 266–73.

9

What is a legitimate military target?

A. P. V. ROGERS

Military objectives

It is evident from media reports of recent conflicts, from the letter pages of the newspapers and even from the pronouncements of politicians, that people are not very well informed about what may legitimately be attacked in an armed conflict. In fact, the law of armed conflict is quite clear and simple: it permits attacks on military objectives; it prohibits attacks on civilian persons and civilian objects. The law also recognizes that attacks on military objectives are likely to cause incidental loss or damage to civilians or civilian property, and so requires attacks to be cancelled, suspended or replanned if it becomes apparent that the incidental loss or damage is going to be out of proportion to the military advantage expected. This is known as the rule of proportionality.

Since the law limits attacks to military objectives, it is vital to know what these are.[1] Military objectives are defined as follows:

> In so far as objects are concerned, military objects are limited to those objects which by their nature, location, purpose or use make an effective contribution to military action and whose total or partial destruction, capture or neutralization, in the circumstances ruling at the time, offers a definite military advantage.[2]

The chapter was revised for publication on 15 January 2004. The author's book, *Law on the Battlefield* (2nd edn, Manchester University Press, 2004), owed a lot to Hilaire McCoubrey, whose work is much quoted, because it was based on an LLM thesis of the same name for which Hilaire was the external examiner.

[1] The question was discussed in some detail at the seminar on 'Targeting and International Law' at San Remo, Italy, in October 2000 (hereinafter 'San Remo seminar'). Unfortunately, opinions differed markedly on the subject. This chapter started life as a draft article designed to reach some conclusions from the San Remo discussions.

[2] 1977 Geneva Protocol I Additional to the Geneva Conventions of 12 August 1949, and relating to the Protection of Victims of International Armed Conflicts, (1979) 1125

This definition is limited to objects so does not cover areas of land, personnel or intangible things like morale, the legitimacy of attacking which falls to be determined according to the laws and customs of war. Further, the definition is rather legalistic and, inevitably, begs the question: 'what can we legitimately attack?' The purpose of this chapter is to review recent practice to ascertain whether an answer to this question can be provided.[3]

1990–1991 Gulf War

One of the main criticisms of the coalition air campaign related to the attacks on what became known as 'dual-use facilities', that is those that were of importance both to the Iraqi armed forces and to the civilian population. It is easy enough to enumerate military objectives that are of a purely military nature, for example, the enemy's armed forces, warships, military airfields, missile sites, military equipment and factories producing armaments. However, in order to defeat the enemy armed forces, it is also necessary to deny them the supplies on which they depend: ammunition, military spares and fuel, of course, but also supply routes, electrical power and telecommunications. The latter items serve the needs of both the armed forces and the civilian population and it is difficult to cut off supplies to the armed forces without at the same time harming the civilian population.

Dual-use facilities attacked during the Gulf War included the Iraqi intelligence service headquarters; refined oil production installations; nuclear, chemical and biological sites; bridges; communications towers, exchanges and lines; supply lines, including railway and road bridges; radio and television installations and electricity production facilities.[4] Roads, railways, bridges, airports and ports were attacked to hinder the deployment of enemy military forces and the movement of military supplies, and to cut off communications. Microwave towers were attacked because they can be used as part of the military command and control system. It was considered that because of the highly centralized Iraqi command arrangements, the communications system was

UNTS 3, Article 52(2). Although Additional Protocol I is not binding on some leading states such as the USA, this definition provides useful guidance in practice.

[3] This chapter is based mainly on the NATO practice in the Kosovo air campaign of 1999. There have, of course, been more recent conflicts in Afghanistan and Iraq, but there is so far little information in the public domain about targeting issues in those conflicts.

[4] A. P. V. Rogers, *Law on the Battlefield* (2nd edn, Manchester University Press, 2004) p. 72.

a very important target since if it were rendered inoperative, the Iraqi leaders would be unable to direct their forces. Electric power installations were attacked because modern armed forces depend heavily on electricity for their effectiveness.

There has been some criticism of the attacks on the Iraqi electrical system because of the suffering that this caused to the civilian population. According to DeSaussure,[5] 215 sorties were flown against Iraqi electrical plants, destroying 75 per cent of electrical generating plants and four of five hydroelectric plants. Incidental effects included lack of refrigeration for food storage, resulting in food shortages; medical facilities were affected; and the sewage system was severely impaired, with sewage in the Tigris causing disease. The justification for these attacks was that the weapons industry and communications were dependent on electric power. They were hit several times to keep them out of action. For example, the Al-Hartha power plant was hit thirteen times. The first strike hit all four steam boilers, the water treatment systems and the administration building, cutting power to 1.5 million people and halting water flow and sewage pumps.

Sometimes, civilian factories were used as a cover for military production. The fact that a building is used for both civilian and military purposes does not mean that its military element cannot be attacked; as far as it can be isolated and attacked separately, it should be – otherwise, subject to proportionality, the whole building can be attacked.

1999 Kosovo Air Campaign

News reports and the daily NATO press briefings at the time, as well as official reports published later, indicate that the air campaign followed the pattern that had been adopted in the Gulf War. The emphasis, at the outset, was on cutting off supplies and communications to the forces operating in Kosovo, before attention was turned to those forces themselves. This policy included attacks on targets in Belgrade, precision guidance being used to minimize incidental damage and casualties.

According to the US Department of Defense Report,[6] the campaign phases were:

[5] Major A. L. DeSaussure, 'The Role of the Law of Armed Conflict During the Persian Gulf War: An Overview', (1994) 37 *Air Force Law Review* 62.

[6] United States Report to Congress, *Kosovo/Operation Allied Force After-Action Report* (31 January 2000) (hereinafter 'US Kosovo Report').

(a) establishing air superiority over Kosovo and degrading command and control and the integrated air-defence system over the whole of the Federal Republic of Yugoslavia;
(b) attacking military targets in Kosovo and those Yugoslav forces south of 44° north that were providing reinforcement to Serbian forces in Kosovo;
(c) expanding air operations against high-value military and security force targets throughout the Federal Republic of Yugoslavia.[7]

On 23 April 1999, NATO leaders expanded the target list to include the military-industrial infrastructure, media responsible for promulgating propaganda and other strategic targets.[8]

The UK Defence Ministry Report[9] is not very specific about targets. It states that the initial phase of the air operation was designed to degrade the Yugoslav integrated air defence system, the Yugoslav/Serbian command and control infrastructure, airfields and deployed heavy weapons in Kosovo. The subsequent phase widened the operation to include targets of high military value across Yugoslavia.[10] The air operation was pursued on two axes: against strategic targets of high military value, for example, headquarters buildings in Belgrade, and tactical targets in and around Kosovo, such as military vehicles and heavy weapons.[11]

Targets attacked

More concrete information about targets attacked can be gleaned from the Department of Defense Report. They included:

(a) bridges and electric power systems;[12]
(b) coastal defence radar sites;[13]
(c) fixed-wing aircraft, bridges, television and radio stations, petroleum and oil facilities, underground command and control bunkers;[14]
(d) Yugoslav Ministry of Interior and regular army garrisons and headquarters;[15]

[7] US Kosovo Report, pp. 7–8. [8] *Ibid.*, p. 8.
[9] UK Ministry of Defence, *Kosovo, Lessons from the Crisis* (Cm 4724, The Stationery Office, June 2000) (hereinafter 'MOD Report'), especially ch. 7 on air operations.
[10] MOD Report, para. 7.3. [11] *Ibid.*, para. 7.5. [12] US Kosovo Report, p. 9.
[13] *Ibid.*, p. 57. [14] *Ibid.*, p. 67. [15] *Ibid.*, pp. 83 and A-7.

(e) communications targets, which fell into two categories: military specific targets, such as radio-relay sites and air-defence control and reporting posts; and dual-use facilities such as telephone systems and television and radio broadcasting facilities;[16]
(f) air defence radars, armour, artillery and personnel;[17]
(g) the Serbian state television building in central Belgrade, 'a facility used for propaganda purposes';[18]
(h) the Yugoslav electricity grid, 'creating a major disruption of power affecting many military related activities and water supplies'.[19]

Journalists reported the following among specific military objectives attacked: MiG-21 aircraft, ammunition dumps, air bases, communications sites, tanks, artillery positions, SA-6 sites, oil refineries, bridges,[20] electrical transmission stations in the Belgrade suburbs of Resnik and Batanica and the Telekom building in Uzice. Later, operations were concentrated on the 3rd Army in Kosovo with attacks by bombers and anti-tank aircraft. All of these have traditionally been regarded as legitimate military targets.

Selecting military objectives for attack is one thing but operational planners then have to go on and consider the likely incidental effects of the attacks and the question of proportionality, especially in the case of bridges, refineries and electricity installations. All four Danube bridges at Novi Sad were destroyed and this was likely to stop river traffic for a considerable period. The pollution effects of the attack on Pancevo refinery north east of Belgrade would have to be taken into account.

Dual-use facilities

According to media reports, other static targets attacked in the NATO bombing campaign included the Belgrade heating plant[21] and part of the

[16] *Ibid.*, p. 83. [17] *Ibid.*, p. 92. [18] *Ibid.*, p. A-8.

[19] *Ibid.*, p. A-10. It is to be hoped that the water supplies were not attacked but that they were affected by the attacks on the electrical power supply. According to one report, Belgrade was down to less than 10 per cent of its water reserves: Steven Erlanger in the *International Herald Tribune*, 25 May 1999.

[20] On 30 May 1999, for example, NATO attacks on the bridge over the Morava River at Varvarin at 12.53 p.m. and again at 1.07 p.m. resulted in civilian deaths: *The Independent*, 31 May 1999.

[21] One civilian night watchman killed, see Human Rights Watch, *Report*: *The Crisis in Kosovo* (February 2000) (hereinafter 'Human Rights Watch Report'), p. 9. This report is reproduced in H. Krieger (ed.), *The Kosovo Conflict and International Law* (Cambridge International Documents Series, Cambridge University Press, 2001) vol. 11, p. 317.

Zastava car factory used for weapons production.[22] At first sight, the first is not a military objective, so one would need to know why this object was of military importance. The second is clearly a military objective. There were also reports of attacks on army headquarters, defence ministry and police headquarters[23] and the Ministry of Interior.[24] Defence ministries are legitimate targets. An interior ministry would not normally be a legitimate target unless the ministry was involved in the conduct or control of military operations. The justification in this case, apparently, was that the ministry was responsible for controlling the unlawful activities of the special police in Kosovo. That gives rise to an interesting question. Were the special police members of the armed forces? Were they involved in an armed conflict? This issue is addressed later in the chapter.

Targeting results

In the course of 10,484 air strike sorties, static targets destroyed or significantly damaged included: 14 command posts, 10 military airfields, over 100 military aircraft, 34 road bridges, 11 railway bridges, 29 per cent of all Yugoslav/Serbian ammunition storage capacity, 57 per cent of petroleum reserve capacity, all Yugoslav oil refineries.[25]

Accurate estimates of mobile targets struck are more difficult to make. At the NATO briefing on 6 May 1999, General Jertz reported that at that stage 300 pieces of military equipment had been attacked, representing 20 per cent of heavy forces in Kosovo, and that Serb military movement had been restricted.[26] It later turned out that a number of items of 'military hardware' struck were, in fact, dummies, the use of dummy military equipment being a legitimate ruse of war.[27]

22 Robert Fisk, *The Independent*, 10 April 1999: 'it is the fate of Yugoslav industry that, thanks to Tito, hundreds of its factories have dual production facilities'.
23 *The Times*, 2 May 1999.
24 See the NATO website, www.nato.int, and the record of the press briefings on 30 April and 1 May 1999.
25 US Kosovo Report, p. 82; MOD Report, para. 7.16.
26 *The Independent*, 7 May 1999.
27 NATO website, record of press briefing on 16 September 1999.

Incidental effects

There were several cases of guidance systems failing, or missiles or bombs going astray, killing many civilians and even damaging hospitals in the process. In the case of the Chinese Embassy, completely the wrong building was attacked in error.[28] Sometimes incidental losses were high. While most regrettable, these incidents do not make those responsible war criminals so long as they were doing their best in difficult circumstances to comply with the law of armed conflict. Given the number of sorties flown, the incidental loss and damage seems not to have been disproportionate. Human Rights Watch estimated civilian deaths at between 489 and 528 in 90 separate incidents,[29] while according to NATO spokesman, Jamie Shea, of 8,988 sorties flown, 12 attacks went astray.[30]

The mere fact that a civilian object is destroyed or damaged does not necessarily mean that the object was actually targeted or that a war crime has been committed. There were, inevitably, cases of civilian casualties and incidental damage, for example, bombs that fell 800 metres short of a target at Aleksinac, for which there was an apology from Air Commodore David Wilby of the NATO staff. There were allegations of civilian deaths at Surdulica on 27 April 1999 when homes were destroyed and a hospital damaged. On 31 May 1999, it was reported in the press that the NATO attack on Surdulica resulted in the destruction of a hospital despite, according to Robert Fisk, the absence of a military objective nearby except a radio repeater station 1km away.[31] NATO expressed regret that one bomb went astray when they attacked a barracks. According to Human Rights Watch, this was an error, the complex being mistaken for a military location in the same town. NATO apologized for bomb damage to the Swiss Embassy in Belgrade but said that twelve NATO targeting errors amounted to less than 0.1 per cent of the missiles fired.[32]

Journalists wrote of other attacks that caused collateral death and damage: in the centre of Pristina when one of three bombs aimed at the main telephone exchange in Pristina missed and landed in a residential

[28] See the letter from Secretary of State Madeleine Albright to the Minister of Foreign Affairs of the People's Republic of China set out in (2000) 3 *Yearbook of International Humanitarian Law* 653.

[29] Human Rights Watch Report, p. 4. [30] *The Independent*, 10 May 1999.

[31] Robert Fisk, *The Independent*, 1 June 1999. [32] *The Independent*, 22 May 1999.

area[33] and at Cuprija when homes were damaged in an attack on the local army barracks.[34] Robert Fisk, one of NATO's fiercest critics, referred to collateral damage as 'that obscene cliché'.[35] But collateral damage is the unfortunate reality of war. It does not mean that civilian objects are being deliberately targeted. However carefully attacks are aimed at military objectives, incidental damage is going to be caused in some cases because of the proximity of civilian objects to military objectives, or because of flaws in the plan of attack, mechanical failure,[36] deflection by defensive measures or human error in the heat of the moment.

Just such a case occurred on 12 April when two missiles were fired at the Grdelica bridge near Leskovac, just as train 393, on its way from Belgrade, via Skopje to Thessalonika, crossed it. Apparently, the pilot fired a second missile, even after he became aware of the presence of the train. A NATO spokesman expressed regret about the civilian casualties but said that the track was an important military supply line.[37] The case was examined by the committee of experts appointed by the Prosecutor of the International Criminal Tribunal for the former Yugoslavia (ICTY). Their report[38] indicates that the committee considered the bridge to be a legitimate target and, though having reservations about the second missile, decided that the case should not be investigated by the Prosecutor. They must have considered the first missile strike to be a legitimate action against a military objective, the inference being that any civilian casualties of that strike were not disproportionate, and that the firing of the second missile was an error of judgment in the heat of the moment. It seems clear to me that the aircrew were concentrating on hitting the bridge but did not reach classroom levels of perfection in the agony of the moment. A similar case was reported to have occurred on 1 May when two laser-guided bombs were fired at a bridge at Luzane, 20km north of Pristina, moments before a bus crossed the bridge resulting in civilian casualties. NATO reported that in bombing the

[33] John Davison, *The Independent*, 10 April 1999.

[34] Robert Fisk, *The Independent*, 10 April 1999.

[35] Robert Fisk, *The Independent*, 10 April 1999 and 14 April 1999.

[36] According to *The Times*, 30 April 1999, an F-16 missile fired at a Serbian surface-to-air missile site strayed from its target after the ground radar was switched off and hit a house in Sofia, Bulgaria. Nobody was hurt.

[37] *The Independent*, 13 April 1999.

[38] Final Report to the Prosecutor by the Committee established to Review the NATO Bombing Campaign against the Federal Republic of Yugoslavia (hereinafter 'ICTY Report'), para. 62, (2000) 39 *International Legal Materials* 1257 at p. 1275.

bridge the pilot did not see the bus.[39] Errors of judgement such as these are not the stuff of criminal prosecutions.

It was reported that on 7 May 1999, NATO cluster bombs aimed at an airfield at Nis hit a hospital and a marketplace causing deaths and many injuries. Sub-munitions fell near the pathology building of the Nis medical centre, in the town centre near the Nis University rector's office, including the area of the central city marketplace, the bus station and a health centre, and near a car dealership and the Nis express parking lot. The NATO spokesman explained that the cluster bomb container opened right after release, projecting sub-munitions into the city. This was evidently a malfunction. The use of cluster bombs has come in for some criticism in the press. The UK Foreign Secretary had this to say on the subject:

> UK armed forces use the most effective weapons systems available, subject to compliance with international humanitarian law. Cluster bombs are an effective weapon against targets such as soft skinned military vehicles. The cluster bomb used by UK armed forces is not banned by any international agreement. It is not an anti-personnel mine as defined by the Ottawa Convention, nor is it prohibited under that Convention, under UK national legislation on land mines or by the 1977 Additional Protocol I to the Geneva Conventions. All feasible precautions are always taken with a view to avoiding, and in any event, minimising collateral damage.[40]

The ICTY Prosecutor decided not to commence an investigation into the use of cluster bombs by NATO. In the Rule 61 hearing of the ICTY Trial Chamber in the *Martic* case, it was decided that there was no formal provision of the law of armed conflict that prohibited the use of cluster bombs as such.[41] Apart from cluster bombs, the use of depleted uranium has also been criticized. On this matter the UK Foreign Secretary stated:

> Depleted uranium (DU)-based ammunition is used because of its unique capability against the most modern types of main battle tank armour. At present, no alternative material currently exists which achieves the levels of penetration necessary to defeat modern tanks. The level of chemical toxicity of DU is similar to that of other heavy metals such as lead, and the

39 *Sky News*, 2 May 1999, confirmed in *The Independent*, 3 May 1999. The NATO explanation can be found at www.nato.int/kosovo/press/p990502b.htm

40 See Response of the Secretary of State for Foreign and Commonwealth Affairs to the Foreign Affairs Committee Fourth Report (Cm 4825, The Stationery Office, August 2000).

41 See *Martic* case, 8 March 1996, (1998) 108 ILR 39 at 47.

> health risks from exposure to DU are assessed as low. Its use is not prohibited under any international agreements and the International Committee on Radiation Protection does not list DU as a health hazard. British forces did not use DU-based ammunition during the Kosovo campaign, but, given the effectiveness of DU weapons against certain types of targets, the Government retains the option of UK forces using DU ammunition in appropriate circumstances.[42]

Voluntary human shields

An interesting aspect of the campaign was the gathering on bridges of volunteers wearing target emblems to act as 'human shields', and the effect that had on targeting. The fact is that, if a bridge is a legitimate target, the presence on the bridge of civilians would not render it immune from attack. Their presence would go to the issue of proportionality, that is, the importance of the target in military terms as against the expected loss of civilian life. The fact that they were there as volunteers, knowing full well that the bridge was likely to be attacked, would, it is suggested, reduce the weight on the humanity side of the scale. Nevertheless, the operational planners would have had to consider how urgent it was to attack the bridge at the time when civilians were congregated on it and whether the attack could be postponed.

Questionable targets

Some targets that appear questionable to the outside observer were the 'Black Building' (the headquarters of Milosevic's ruling socialist party),[43] Milosevic's villa at 15 Uzicka Street in the Belgrade suburb of Dedinje[44] and the tobacco factory at Vranje.[45] It is impossible to comment on these incidents without knowing the full facts and the extent to

[42] See above n. 40.

[43] This was mentioned at the NATO press briefing on 21 April 1999. The justification advanced was that it was collocated with a communications transmitter and that the headquarters was part of the command and control system in respect of the operations in Kosovo. See also SACEUR's briefing to the press on 27 April 1999.

[44] At the NATO press conference on 23 April 1999, there was mention of an attack on 'one of Milosevic's bunker systems in the suburbs'. This may have been the incident referred to in the press.

[45] An attack on a cigarette factory was mentioned at the NATO press briefings on 20 and 21 April 1999 and the fact that the factory was associated with the production of ammunition.

which these objects were of strategic or tactical military importance or were dual-use facilities. The justification might have been in the case of the first (and this is pure speculation) that it was from here that operations in Kosovo were being conducted. As for the second, it was said to be equipped with command and control facilities. Apparently the third was attacked without loss of life. It has been said that the tobacco factory could be converted to a bullet factory.

Television station

The television station in Belgrade was hit at 2 a.m. on 23 April, killing and injuring members of the civilian night staff. The Human Rights Watch report condemns the attack if its purpose was merely to silence a propaganda tool of the Milosevic government[46] and because there was no need to attack an urban studio as opposed to transmitters. However, media installations were included as potential targets in the ICRC draft rules of 1956 which refer to means and lines of communication, broadcasting and television stations, telephone and telegraph installations, in so far as all of these are of fundamental military importance.[47]

The only specific targeting issue (apart from the Chinese Embassy in Belgrade, which was clearly not a military objective and which was attacked in error)[48] addressed by the UK Foreign Affairs Committee in their report,[49] was that of the legality of attacking broadcasting stations. They had the benefit of opinions from various experts but concluded that they did not have evidence either to confirm or deny the proposition that the Serbian radio or television stations were being used for military purposes or to incite ethnic cleansing. Professor Christopher Greenwood, in his evidence to the Foreign Affairs Committee, said that in the case of *Radio Mille Collines* in Rwanda, which in 1994 had incited ethnic cleansing, he would have had no difficulty in justifying an attack on the radio station. The inference is that, had the broadcasting stations been broadcasting such material, they would have been legitimate

[46] Human Rights Watch Report, p. 12.

[47] See Y. Sandoz, C. Swinarski and B. Zimmermann (eds.), *Commentary on the Additional Protocols of 8 June 1977 to the Geneva Convention of 12 August 1949* (Martinus Nijhoff, 1987), para. 2002 (hereinafter '*ICRC Commentary*').

[48] See below n. 62 and related text.

[49] Foreign Affairs Committee Session 1999–2000, Fourth Report, *Kosovo*, vol. 1 (The Stationery Office, 23 May 2000). This report is abstracted in Krieger, *The Kosovo Conflict*, p. 336.

targets. The committee did not, it seems, consider the question of whether media stations, per se, are military targets. The point about incitement to racial violence is interesting because that would fall within the *jus ad bellum*; it is not a normal purpose of the *jus in bello* to permit attacks on targets unless for military reasons. In that respect, if the station is being used to collect or process military intelligence, or to pass on military information to the armed forces or for the purposes of calling-out reservists, that would make it a military objective, possibly even if it was being used for putting out war propaganda – but not normal peacetime broadcasts.

The UK Foreign Secretary responded to this report as follows:

> This matter has been examined in some detail by the ICTY Prosecutor's Office. The report by ICTY experts on allegations made against NATO concerning the Kosovo air campaign examined the rationale given for the attack on the RTS station in Belgrade. Having considered the report, the Prosecutor informed the UN Security Council on 2 June that, in ICTY's view, there was no basis for further investigation by ICTY of this or any other incident during the campaign and that she was satisfied that 'there was no deliberate targeting of civilians or unlawful military targets by NATO during the bombing campaign'.[50]

The ICTY report stated that 'insofar as the attack actually was aimed at disrupting the communications network, it was legally acceptable. If, however, the attack was made because . . . the station was part of the propaganda machinery, the legal basis was more debatable.'[51] The report refers, in this regard, to the judgment of the IMT at Nuremberg in the case of *Hans Fritzsche*, where the tribunal found that the accused, though making strong statements of a propagandistic nature, did not incite the commission of atrocities. On the basis that this may have been an attack on the integrated communications network, the ICTY report recommended that no investigation be carried out by the Office of the Prosecutor. The report also stated that:

> Everyone will agree that a munitions factory is a military objective and an unoccupied church is a civilian object. When the definition is applied to dual-use objects which have some civilian uses and some actual or potential military use (communications systems, transportation systems, petrochemical complexes, manufacturing plants of some types), opinions may differ.[52]

[50] See above n. 40 . [51] ICTY Report, paras. 75 and 76. [52] *Ibid.*, para. 37.

The report went on to state that the precise scope of 'military-industrial infrastructure, media and other strategic targets ... is unclear. Whether the media constitutes a legitimate target group is a debatable issue. If the media is used to incite crimes, as in Rwanda, then it is a legitimate target. If it is merely disseminating propaganda to generate support for the war effort, it is not a legitimate target'.[53] Further it stated that 'to the extent particular media components are part of C3 (command, control and communications) network they are military objectives'.[54]

An application was made to the European Court of Human Rights by the relatives of those who were killed in this attack and by survivors who were injured. This did not result in any enlightenment on the legitimacy of the target, however, as the application was declared inadmissible. The Court held that the applicants did not come within the jurisdiction of the respondent states. In other words: you cannot apply human rights law from the air.[55]

Hostages

In some cases it seems that civilians were deliberately placed near to military objectives so that their deaths could be blamed on NATO. On 13 May 1999, NATO carried out an attack at Korisa in which civilians were killed. Burnt-out tractors were shown in television reports. At the Pentagon briefing on 15 May, it was said that F-16s had attacked an artillery site, two 500lb laser-guided bombs hitting a command post and several 500lb gravity bombs hitting artillery positions. The BBC reported[56] a survivor as saying that refugees who had been hiding in the hills were directed to that place by Serb police. On 2 June, Haxhere Palushi was reported as saying that the bombing took place soon after several hundred refugees had been herded into the farm compound by Serb soldiers and padlocked in. The allegation of use of human shields is supported, to some extent, by the Human Rights Watch report.

The ICTY committee also recommended that NATO involvement in the Korisa incident should not be further investigated by the Office of the Prosecutor. If the allegation is true that civilians were deliberately

53 *Ibid.*, para. 47. 54 Ibid., para. 55.

55 *Banković* v. *Belgium and others*, Grand Chamber decision, 12 December 2001, (2003) 123 ILR 94. The German state court (*Landgericht*), Bonn, came to a similar conclusion on 10 December 2003 in respect of a case of a victim of the NATO attack on a bridge at Varvarin on 30 May 1999 (Case No. 1 O 361/02).

56 On 16 May, on the 9 a.m. news broadcast.

placed close to a military site with a view to giving it immunity from attack, or in the event of attack, to hold NATO responsible for their deaths, a serious war crime was committed.

On 22 May 1999, it was reported that NATO had hit a jail at Istok in Kosovo in the course of attacking military objectives in the vicinity of the prison. Although some deaths may have been caused by the bombing, Human Rights Watch said that seventy-six of the deaths at the prison were extra-judicial executions carried out by Yugoslav forces after the bombing.[57] Extra-judicial executions are, of course, also serious war crimes.

Mobile targets

At a later stage in the air campaign, NATO aircraft started to attack troops on the ground.[58] According to *The Independent*, General Short, the NATO air commander, announced in late May that his operation was concentrating on destroying the Yugoslav 3rd Army in Kosovo with intensified attacks by B-1 and B-52 bombers and the arrival of a second squadron of A-10 ground attack aircraft. But as one airforce expert at the San Remo seminar[59] commented, pilots are reluctant to attack mobile targets because of the difficulty of hitting them accurately. In the case of the unfortunate attack on a column of Kosovo-Albanian refugees near Djakovica on 14 April, it was not accuracy of attack but accuracy of target verification that let NATO down. Laser-guided bombs were delivered from an altitude of 15,000 feet at what was thought to be a military column. Once doubts began to creep in, lower flying aircraft were sent in to investigate and, realizing there had been a mistake, the controllers called off the attack. The author dealt more fully with this incident elsewhere and concluded:

> The law does not demand that there be no casualties in armed conflict. However, the law, political expediency and public sentiment combine to demand that casualties, whether among members of the armed forces or among the civilian population, should be reduced to the maximum extent that the exigencies of armed conflict will allow. An important element of this endeavour is verification of the target because attacking the wrong target is likely to lead to unnecessary casualties. Target verification requires reasonable care to be exercised. The precise degree of

[57] Human Rights Watch Report, p. 12.
[58] *The Independent*, 25 May 1999. [59] See above n. 1.

> care required depends on the circumstances, especially the time available for making a decision. In the event of doubt about the nature of the target, an attack should not be carried out, with a possible exception where failure to prosecute the attack would put attacking forces in immediate danger.[60]

The ICTY report states the opinion of the committee that civilians were not deliberately attacked in this incident and that, while the air-crews could have benefited from lower altitude scrutiny of the target at an earlier stage, the committee considered that those concerned did not display the degree of recklessness that would sustain criminal charges.[61]

Chinese embassy

On 7 May it was reported that NATO had hit the Chinese Embassy in Belgrade causing death and injuries.[62] The US Defence Secretary, William Cohen, and Central Intelligence Agency Director, George Tenet, explained that this was due to faulty CIA intelligence that occurred at the planning stage and went unnoticed through subsequent checks. They thought they were attacking a weapons supply and procurement centre, the Federal Directorate of Supply and Procurement. Cohen confirmed that the map consulted by the Pentagon target planners that dated from 1992 had been revised in 1997 and 1998, but the revisions did not include the move of the Chinese Embassy to its new building. The UK Foreign Secretary summed the matter up as follows:

> The American Government presented the results of its review to the Chinese Government on 18 June 1999. The text of that presentation was made publicly available on 6 July 1999 on the State Department website. The Government has seen nothing to suggest that the attack was anything other than a tragic error.[63]

This was a mistake of fact by those carrying out the mission. Mistake of fact is a defence to war crimes charges.[64]

60 A. P. V. Rogers, 'Zero-casualty Warfare', (2000) 82 *International Review of the Red Cross* 165.
61 ICTY Report, paras. 69 and 70.
62 *BBC News*, 7 May 1999; *The Independent*, 8 May 1999; *Sky News*, 8 May 1999.
63 See above n. 40.
64 Rome Statute of the International Criminal Court 1998, Article. 32(1).

Strike sortie: casualty ratio

Human Rights Watch put the civilian death toll of this operation at around 500.[65] One legal expert at the San Remo seminar expressed the view that this was too high a figure for a limited operation of this kind. However, while every civilian death is a matter of great regret, it must be said that the casualty rate was low in relation to the number of strike sorties flown. The UK Defence Ministry concluded:

> If this figure [i.e. the estimate of 500] is correct, out of a total of some 10,500 strike sorties conducted by NATO forces during the course of which some 23,600 pieces of ordnance were delivered, less than one per cent of all missions led to unintended fatalities.[66]

Problem areas

At the San Remo seminar, the environmental and economic targeting group commented that the definition of military objectives in Additional Protocol I suits close battle rather than deep battle situations. It is of interest, therefore, to examine some of the targeting issues that arose in the Kosovo conflict to see if there is any merit in this comment.

Armed civilians

Before the NATO intervention, there were news reports of civilians arming themselves with hunting rifles to protect their families. By doing so did they become combatants? There is nothing in the law of war that prohibits the carrying of arms by civilians and they do not thereby forfeit their non-combatant status. They lose that status by taking a direct part in hostilities. Using reasonable force in self-defence of one's family does not amount to taking a direct part in hostilities. However, armed civilians run the risk of being mistaken for combatants and attacked. A member of the armed forces who mistakenly attacks an armed civilian believing him to be a combatant would not commit a war crime.

[65] Human Rights Watch Report, p. 4. [66] MOD Report, para 7.10.

Special police

Another interesting issue is whether, after the NATO intervention had started, special police taking part in 'ethnic cleansing' operations could be said to be either combatants or civilians directly participating in hostilities and, therefore, legitimate targets. Rowe seems to think that they could be attacked, but only when they were actually actively involved in ethnic cleansing, although he accepts that there might have been identification problems from the air.[67] It follows that he must regard ethnic cleansing as 'taking a direct part in hostilities' or combat activity. Accepting for the moment that it is, this seems a rather narrow construction of Additional Protocol I: 'Civilians shall enjoy the protection afforded by this Section, unless and for such time as they take a direct part in hostilities.'[68] It seems to the author that loss of protection would have subsisted for the entire period of the special police's deployment on the ethnic cleansing operations in Kosovo, not merely during each individual action. More problematic is whether ethnic cleansing, however reprehensible, is taking 'a direct part in hostilities'. It is certainly not a normal combat activity. On the other hand, the law of war, which is designed to protect human beings from the effects of war without impeding lawful military activity, would fail if the term were narrowly construed. In those circumstances, despite the fact that it seems at odds with the presumption of civilian status,[69] one is driven to concede that the line taken by Rowe on that aspect of the problem may be correct.

As a legal expert pointed out at the San Remo seminar, the rule of doubt seems to conflict with the presumption of innocence in a criminal trial; in the case of a criminal trial, the presumption of innocence will, no doubt, prevail.

Assassination

Another point of interest is whether the political leaders of an enemy state may be targeted. The older textbooks say that assassination is not a lawful act of war. The authority given for this is Article 23(b) of the

[67] P. Rowe, 'Kosovo 1999: The Air Campaign', (2000) 82 *International Review of the Red Cross* 147 at p. 151. I take issue with Rowe's assertion in this article that Additional Protocol I has made no difference to the conduct of military operations. It has been hugely influential in operational planning, even for states not party to it.

[68] Additional Protocol I, Article 51(3).

[69] 'In case of doubt whether a person is a civilian, that person shall be considered to be a civilian': Additional Protocol I, Article 50(1).

Hague Regulations 1907, which provides: 'it is forbidden to kill or wound by treachery individuals belonging to a hostile nation or army'. The dictionary definition of 'assassinate' is: 'to kill by treacherous violence'. The emphasis here is on treachery. The *United Kingdom Manual*[70] said there was nothing wrong with the attempt on Rommel's life by members of the British special forces in 1943 because it was carried out by military personnel in uniform and was aimed at enemy personnel in an operational headquarters. So killing a member of the enemy armed forces is permissible, whether by dropping a bomb on his command post, using a sniper to fire at him or sending in a commando party, provided it is not done perfidiously, that is, killing him by inviting his confidence that he is entitled to give or receive protection under the law of war and then abusing that confidence.[71] The issue of fact for determination, therefore, is whether the enemy political leader is a member of the armed forces or, at least, commands and controls the operations of the armed forces.[72] If he is, he can be attacked; if not, he cannot be attacked because he is entitled to civilian immunity.[73]

Military utility

The law of war permits only actions that have a military purpose, so the commander always has to ask himself: what military purpose is going to be achieved by this action? As Greenwood puts it, 'the principle of necessity operates as an additional level of restraint by prohibiting acts which are not otherwise illegal, as long as they are not necessary for the achievement of legitimate goals'.[74] This can have an effect even in relation to targets that otherwise fall within the definition of 'military objective'. David[75] states that it is illegitimate to carry out attacks, even on military objects, that have no purpose. He condemns on this basis the 1991 attack on retreating Iraqi troops on the Basra Road, which he thinks was a plain massacre. The author would not go so far. So long as those forces had not surrendered and posed a threat to coalition forces, there was a military purpose in attacking them.

70 *The Law of War on Land*, Part III of the *Manual of Military Law* (HMSO, 1958), p. 42.

71 See Additional Protocol I, Article 37.

72 See Rogers, *Law on the Battlefield*, p. 46.

73 For combatant status, see Additional Protocol I, Articles 43 and 44.

74 C. Greenwood, 'Historical Development and Legal Basis', in D. Fleck (ed.), *The Handbook of Humanitarian Law in Armed Conflicts* (Oxford University Press, 1995), pp. 1–38 at p. 33.

75 E. David, *Le Droit des Conflits Armés* (3rd edn, Bruylant, 2002), p. 273.

Anticipatory attacks

At the San Remo seminar, the environmental and economic targeting group were divided on the question of whether it was legally permissible to attack a facility that could be converted to military production. After the Second World War a French court decided that a lighthouse attacked by German forces was a military objective because it could have provided navigational assistance to allied forces.[76] One of the legal experts at the San Remo seminar, pointed out that the definition of 'military objective' in Additional Protocol I must cover potential military objectives since it was generally accepted that the tactic of area denial was in order. However, as it was also necessary to comply with rule of doubt,[77] there was a need for specific rules on the concept of imminence in connection with military objectives. Rowe, in particular, counsels caution.[78] He indicates the danger of thinking that merely because the military may make use of an object, that object becomes a military objective. That would mean having to destroy all objects of a category, for example, all telecommunications centres and all power-generating facilities, in order to achieve the military advantage. This concern is reflected by Oeter,[79] who asks whether, if main supply routes are legitimate targets and the enemy switches to other routes, this does not make all potential supply routes targets. He says that the practice in Desert Storm indicates that for military effectiveness the total telecommunication network (at least its central connection points) must be destroyed. David,[80] referring to the oil tanker and lighthouse cases,[81] comes to the interim conclusion that, according to the letter of the law, preventative destruction is prohibited: unless an object makes a real contribution to military action it may not be destroyed. However, he questions the realism of this interpretation since nobody queried the legality of attacking oil wells and installations in the Gulf war (except on environmental grounds). In considering dual use, such as bridges, highways or

[76] See the case of *Gross-Brauckmann*, (1948) 15 AD 687.

[77] 'In cases of doubt whether an object which is normally dedicated to civilian purposes, such as a place of worship, a house or other dwelling or a school, is being used to make an effective contribution to military action, it shall be presumed not to be so used': Additional Protocol I, Article 52(3).

[78] Rowe, 'Kosovo 1999', p. 151.

[79] S. Oeter, 'Methods and Means of Combat', in Fleck, *Handbook*, pp. 105–204 at p. 161.

[80] David, *Le Droit des Conflits Armés*, p. 271.

[81] *US–Germany Mixed Claims Commission* (1924) 2 AD 405.

microwave towers, he cites the *List* case where the court considered it permissible to attack property that might be utilized by the enemy.[82] The authors of the *San Remo Manual*, by using the words 'not at some hypothetical future time', also considered that there must be some time limitation on anticipatory attacks, writing:

> Provided the objects meet the two-pronged test, under the circumstances ruling at the time (not at some hypothetical future time), military objectives include activities providing administrative and logistical support to military operations such as transportation and communications systems, railroads, airfields, port facilities and industries of fundamental importance for the conduct of the armed conflict.[83]

The drafters of Additional Protocol I certainly made room for anticipatory attacks in their definition of 'military objectives'. 'Purpose' means future intended use of an object, while 'use' means its present function.[84]

Nevertheless, this does not give attackers *carte blanche* to attack anything on the basis that it might be used for military purposes. The justification must be more definite than that. It is hard to think of an example of a case where 'purpose' will be the deciding factor, especially given the limitation of 'in the circumstances ruling at the time'. If, for example, a military commander received intelligence that the enemy were about to use a school as a munitions depot, it is unlikely, subject to the question of proportionality, that he would want to attack it until the munitions had been moved in. On the other hand, if there were reliable intelligence that a tractor factory was fitted with machine tools for the alternative production of tanks, that would probably be sufficient justification for attacking the factory.

Electrical installations

Because these are so important to the functioning of military forces, electrical installations remain military objectives, despite the effects that attacking these installations will have on, for example, food storage and

[82] (1948) 15 AD 646. However, see *Manstein*, (1949) 16 AD 509 at 522.

[83] L. Doswald-Beck (ed.), *San Remo Manual on International Law Applicable to Armed Conflicts at Sea* (Cambridge University Press, 1995), para. 40.11.

[84] *ICRC Commentary*, para. 2022.

water supply. Those effects have to be considered under the heading of 'proportionality', as have the longer-term effects of attacks. According to an airforce expert at the San Remo seminar, it is possible to use carbon-based weapons that cause short-out and attacks can be concentrated on relay switches, thus reducing incidental damage and long-term disruption of the electricity supply.

Bridges

An airforce expert at the San Remo seminar explained that bridges were important targets because they carried fibre optic communication cables and were the weakest link in the command and control system. The Human Rights Watch report[85] refers to the bombing of the 'Marshall Tito' Petrovaradin (Varadinski) Bridge in Novi Sad in 1999 and questions the legitimacy of the target.[86] They query the military utility of attacking the bridge and quote American military sources as saying that bridges were often attacked for other than their transportation role (for example, they were conduits for communications cables, or because they were symbolic and psychologically lucrative, as in the case of the bridge over the Danube in Novi Sad).

The law of war does not permit objects to be attacked purely for symbolic or psychological reasons. However, there is nothing wrong in obtaining a psychological boost by attacking a target that, for other reasons, is a legitimate military objective.[87]

Industry

Although dismissed as 'panacea targets' by Harris, an advocate of the bombing of industrial towns,[88] some experts consider that the most effective part of the Second World War bombing was against targets such as synthetic oil plants and key transport facilities. They consider

85 Human Rights Watch Report, p. 8.

86 Human Rights Watch Report, Incident no. 2. Apparently, civilians were killed in six other road bridge attacks. It is not clear how many civilians were killed in these strikes.

87 Rogers, *Law on the Battlefield*, pp. 46, 104.

88 Sir Arthur Harris, *Bomber Offensive* (Greenhill, 1990), p. 220. Of course, both the law and targeting technology has moved on a lot since 1947.

that the offensive against German towns neither broke morale nor lowered war production.[89]

Industry producing goods used by the armed forces and facilities supporting those factories are military objectives, but the precise extent to which general industry can be made the object of attack is the subject of heated debate. Oeter[90] states that the armaments industry is a legitimate target but also the heavy industries delivering the metallurgical, engineering and chemical products on which that industry relies, as well as storage and transport serving those industries; also electricity production installations serving the military (problem of dual use) and research and development in the armaments sector. He expresses concern that sub-contracting and decentralization of defence industries can easily lead to an erosion of the regulatory system and a return to 'total war'.

It is clear that, for an industrial installation to be a legitimate target, there must be a nexus between the industry in question and the enemy's ability to conduct military operations. Rather like civilians who forfeit their immunity if they take a direct part in hostilities, industry is not immune from attack if it directly supports the conduct of military operations.

Economic targets

At the San Remo seminar, the environmental and economic targeting subgroup was divided about whether a bank that finances military operations is a legitimate target. The British–American Claims Commission recognized the justification for destroying Confederate cotton during the American civil war, since cotton sales provided funds for importing almost all Confederate arms and ammunition.[91] German submarine warfare against the United Kingdom during the Second World War was aimed at preventing all manner of supplies from crossing the Atlantic and there were no post-war convictions relating to unrestricted submarine warfare. Nevertheless, the current definition of 'military objective' seems to exclude economic targets. The author adheres to the view that:

[89] E.g., T. D. Biddle, 'Air Power', in M. Howard, G. J. Adreopoulos and M. R. Shulman (eds.), *The Laws of War: Constraints on Warfare in the Western World* (Yale University Press, 1994), p. 158.

[90] Oeter, 'Methods and Means of Combat', p. 161.

[91] See discussion of *Cotton Claims* (1871) 4 Moore, *International Arbitrations*, 1894, 3679 in L. C. Green, *The Contemporary Law of Armed Conflict* (2nd edn, Manchester University Press, 2000), p. 191.

If a country relies almost entirely on, say, the export of coffee beans or bananas for its income and even if this income is used to a great extent to support its war effort, the opinion of the author is that it would not be legitimate to attack banana or coffee bean plantations or warehouses. The reason for this is that such plants would not make an *effective* contribution to *military* action nor would their destruction offer a *definite* military advantage. The definition of military objectives thus excludes the general industrial and agricultural potential of the enemy. Targets must offer a more specific military advantage. Green puts it as economic targets that indirectly but effectively support enemy operations.[92] None of this, however, would prevent attacks on military objectives, such as means of transportation or ports, which would indirectly affect the export of agricultural products.[93]

Conclusions[94]

Taking into account the practice of states and past attempts at codification, the following examples of military objectives are tentatively given. It is important to stress that:

(a) the list is by no means exhaustive;
(b) the mere fact that an object, such as a bridge or a communications installation, is in the list does not mean that it is necessarily a military objective; it must make an effective contribution to military action and its neutralization must offer a definite military advantage;[95]
(c) when attacking these targets the proportionality rule must be respected and the natural environment protected against widespread, long-term and severe damage.

Military objectives

Examples of military objectives include:

(a) military personnel and persons who take part in the fighting without being members of the armed forces;[96]

92 *Ibid.* 93 Rogers, *Law on the Battlefield*, p. 70.
94 These conclusions are reproduced from *ibid.*, p. 83.
95 Additional Protocol I, Article 52(2).
96 *ICRC Commentary*, p. 632.

(b) military facilities, military equipment, including military vehicles, weapons, munitions and stores of fuel,[97] military works, including defensive works and fortifications,[98] military depots and establishments, including defence and military supply ministries;[99]
(c) works producing or developing military supplies and other supplies of military value, including metallurgical, engineering and chemical industries supporting the war effort;[100]
(d) areas of land of military significance such as hills, defiles and bridgeheads;[101]
(e) railways, ports, airfields, bridges, roads, tunnels and canals used for troop movement or military logistic purposes;[102]
(f) oil and other power installations;
(g) communications installations, including broadcasting, television, telephone and telegraph facilities, used for military communications.[103]

Objects protected from attack

It follows that attacks on certain types of targets are *prohibited*. These include:

(a) cities, towns and villages as such;[104]
(b) buildings used by civilians such as houses, schools, museums, places of worship, shops, markets, agricultural and other buildings without military significance;

[97] See M. Bothe, K. J. Partsch and W. Solf, *New Rules for the Victims of Armed Conflicts: Commentary on the Two 1977 Protocols Additional to the Geneva Conventions of 1949* (Martinus Nijhoff, 1982), p. 323.

[98] *Ibid.*, p. 323. [99] See *ICRC Commentary*, p. 632. [100] *Ibid.*

[101] The United Kingdom made a statement on ratification of Additional Protocol I to the effect that an area of land could be a military objective. A similar statement was made on ratification by Canada, Germany, Italy, the Netherlands, New Zealand and Spain, see A. Roberts and R. Guelff, *Documents on the Laws of War* (3rd edn, Oxford University Press, 2000), pp. 499–512.

[102] See *ICRC Commentary*, p. 632.

[103] See *ibid.* Fleck, *Handbook*, includes as military objectives (at para. 443): 'economic objectives which make an effective contribution to military action (transport facilities, industrial plants etc.)'.

[104] That means that the morale of the civilian population may not be used as a justification, see L. Doswald-Beck, 'The Value of the 1977 Protocols', in M. A. Meyer (ed.), *Armed Conflict and the New Law* (British Institute of International and Comparative Law, 1989), p. 155.

(c) agriculture, foodstuffs and food storage, distribution and supply; water sources and water supply;[105]
(d) cultural property;
(e) central and local government buildings (except those that are military-related);
(f) civilian transportation, such as passenger trains, ferries and civil aircraft,[106] buses, trams and private cars, not being used for military purposes;
(g) civilian industrial, commercial and financial institutions not directly supporting the war effort;
(h) zones under special protection,[107] specially protected installations, such as dams, dykes and nuclear electrical-generating stations,[108] and installations and transports relating to medical services,[109] prisoners of war and civil defence.

Objects in categories (b), (c), (d), (e) and (g) lose their protection if they are used for military purposes. There are special provisions relating to military activity in connection with zones and installations under special protection.

105 Food, food producing areas and water are specifically dealt with in Article 54 of Additional Protocol I. This prohibition does not include sustenance solely for members of the armed forces or objects used in direct support of military action.
106 Subject to the special rules on naval and air warfare, see, e.g. , the *San Remo Manual*.
107 Hague Regulations 1907, Article 25; see Geneva Convention I 1949, Article 23; Geneva Convention IV 1949, Articles 14 and 15; Additional Protocol I, Articles 59 and 60.
108 Additional Protocol I, Article 56.
109 Such as hospitals and ambulances.

10

The application of the European Convention on Human Rights during an international armed conflict

PETER ROWE

> We are in danger [because of the European Convention on Human Rights] of producing servicemen whose only purpose will be to deliver tea and sympathy, rather than carry out their proper combat duties.[1]

This chapter will consider how the European Convention on Human Rights (ECHR) impacts upon military operations during an international armed conflict. It will, therefore, confine itself to those situations to which international humanitarian law applies concurrently with it in order to determine how far the ECHR affects the obligations assumed by states during such an armed conflict.

Introduction

A state party to the ECHR may find itself involved in an international armed conflict occurring on its territory, on the territory of another state, on the high seas, or in the airspace over such areas. It may send its armed forces under United Nations or NATO auspices to the territory of a state which is, itself, involved in an international armed conflict. Before considering these various situations it is necessary to analyse the scope of the ECHR to assess its impact upon an international armed conflict.

None of the states parties to the ECHR has entered a reservation as to its applicability should it become involved in an international armed conflict. France, however, has entered a reservation to Article 15(1) whereby a proclamation of a state of siege or emergency by the French

[1] Ian Duncan-Smith, MP, Shadow Defence Secretary (as he then was), *The Times*, 5 December 2000.

government is to be understood as being compliant with Article 15(1), and ten states (Czech Republic, France, Lithuania, Moldova, Portugal, Russian Federation, Slovakia, Spain, Turkey, Ukraine) have made a reservation to a greater or lesser extent of the non-applicability of ECHR obligations to discipline within their armed forces. A state which has been a party to the Convention for five years is permitted to denounce it, but only after giving six months' notice. No recent denunciations have been made.

If faced with an international armed conflict to which its armed forces are committed a state may wish to derogate from some of its obligations under the ECHR. It may do so 'to the extent strictly required by the exigencies of the situation, provided that such measures are not inconsistent with its other obligations under international law ... in time of war or other public emergency threatening the life of the nation'.[2] The European Court of Human Rights (ECtHR) has taken the view that 'the State is afforded a wide margin of appreciation in assessing the existence of an emergency and the measures necessary to deal with it'.[3] The state may not, however, derogate from Article 2, except in respect of deaths resulting from lawful acts of war, or from Articles 3, 4(1) and 7.[4] A derogation notice was issued by the United Kingdom in respect of Article 5(3) and the questioning of suspects in Northern Ireland. It was withdrawn as of 26 February 2001.[5] A further derogation was made on 18 December 2001.[6] It is open to any state to make a permitted derogation but it must inform the Secretary-General of the Council of Europe of any such derogation and the reasons for it.[7] None can be implied from the circumstances in which a state finds itself. Indeed, the European Commission stated in *Cyprus* v. *Turkey* that Article 15 'requires some formal and public act of derogation, such as a declaration of martial law or a state of emergency ... where no such act has been proclaimed by the High Contracting Party concerned ... Article 15

[2] Article 15(1). See generally, D. Harris, M. O'Boyle and C. Warbrick, *Law of the European Convention on Human Rights* (Butterworths, 1995) ch. 16; R. Higgins, 'Derogations under the Human Rights Treaties', (1976–7) 48 *British Yearbook of International Law* 281; R. Macdonald, 'Derogations under Article 15 of the European Convention on Human Rights', (1997) 36 *Columbia Journal of Transnational Law* 225.

[3] *Aksoy* v. *Turkey* (1997) 23 EHRR 553, para. 173. [4] Article 15(2).

[5] Council of Europe Press Release, 22 February 2001.

[6] See the Human Rights (Designated Derogation) Order 2001, SI 2001/3644, in force 13 November 2001; Human Rights Act 1998 (Amendment No. 2) Order 2001, SI 2001/4032, in force 19 December 2001.

[7] Article 15(3).

could not apply'.[8] It is worth noting that no derogations were made by any member of the Council of Europe involved in the Falklands conflict (the United Kingdom alone), the Gulf War 1990–1, the military action carried out in the former Yugoslavia, or the war in Iraq (2003).

A notice of derogation is an act imbued with political significance, rather than a mere administrative procedure. A government considering such an act will have to weigh carefully whether the issue of a notice to the Secretary-General of the Council of Europe will be likely to cause more political damage than by retaining the status quo. The more serious the effects of the situation affecting the state, the easier it will be to make an extensive derogation. Thus, if it is faced with 'war' on its territory the issue of a derogation notice will be relatively easy and more difficult where its citizens are not directly threatened.

The principal argument in favour of making a permitted derogation from the ECHR is likely to be that the state concerned is able to tailor its obligations to the fact that it is involved in an international conflict, a situation foreseen by the framers of the ECHR. Depending upon the nature of the armed conflict such action might attract popular support, certainly if the conflict proves to be of other than short duration. Similarly, it may see the need at some time during the armed conflict to have the wider latitude permitted, for instance, to act in breach of the right to life,[9] to circumvent some of the requirements set out in Articles 5 and 6, to impose compulsory labour (Article 4(2)), to interfere with the right to private and family life (Article 8), to restrict freedom of expression (Article 10) and of assembly and association (Article 11).[10] It may issue a derogation notice by way of reciprocity if the enemy state has done so. Since the ECHR obligations are reduced by any permitted derogation, the legal constraints upon the state in the pursuit of its political goals in relation to the armed conflict may also be perceived to be reduced. A purported derogation notice which is inconsistent with

8 (1976) 4 EHRR 482, para. 527. *Quaere* where there is a proclamation or declaration of martial law but no formal notice of the derogation is given to the Secretary-General under Article 15(3) and see para. 526.

9 Including restoring the death penalty under its national law for 'acts committed in time of war or of imminent threat of war', see Protocol 6 (1983) to the Convention for the Protection of Human Rights and Fundamental Freedoms concerning the Abolition of the Death Penalty, as amended by Protocol 11, Article 2. Compare, however, Protocol 13 (2002) concerning the Abolition of the Death Penalty in All Circumstances.

10 See also Protocol 4 (1963) Articles 2 (freedom of movement) and 4 (collective expulsion of aliens); Protocol 7 (1984) Article 1 (procedural safeguards relating to the expulsion of aliens).

the state's other obligations under international law will be likely to be judged to be invalid. In practice, therefore, a state could not issue a valid derogation notice which had the effect of excluding its liability under international humanitarian law.

The arguments against derogation are likely also to be political in nature. The government may well have to explain in Parliament why it wishes to reduce the human rights of individuals at a time when the whole concept of human rights is of increasing significance. Finally, the very act of derogation may be subject to legal challenge before the ECtHR[11] or under national jurisdiction.[12] The fact that no extensive derogation notices of the type under discussion have been made is, perhaps, not surprising if the political consequences of inaction are deemed to outweigh those of action in pursuing a permitted derogation. Moreover, it may be argued that up to the present time, no such derogation was considered necessary by any state since in no case has an international armed conflict been fought within the territory of a member state and 'no State has indicated a belief that its extra-territorial actions involved an exercise of jurisdiction within the meaning of Article 1 of the Convention by making a derogation pursuant to Article 15'.[13] There is a clear link drawn by the ECtHR between the reach of the ECHR under Article 1 and the need to issue a derogation notice under Article 15.

A further issue for exploration is the relationship between the ECHR and international humanitarian law during an international armed conflict. The fact that the ECHR permits a state to issue a derogation notice in respect of the right to life under Article 2 for 'lawful acts of war'[14] implies that the Convention continues to apply, as it would do in peacetime, during an international armed conflict, subject to any

[11] See *Brannigan and McBride* v. *United Kingdom* (1993) 17 EHRR 539, paras. 43–9.

[12] By way of a challenge, in the United Kingdom, under the Human Rights Act 1998. This would amount to a challenge to the actual derogation made under s. 14 and its compatibility with Article 15 of the ECHR. Although the latter Article is not a part of English law, a court or tribunal must take it into account when interpreting the law of England and Wales. See *A* v. *Secretary of State for the Home Department* (Sp. Imm. App. Comm., decision of 30 July 2002); *A, X and Y* v. *Secretary of State for the Home Department* [2002] HRLR 45.

[13] See *Bankovic, Belgium and others*, 12 December 2001, para. 62, (2002) 41 *International Legal Materials* 517. For an application brought in respect of the sinking of the *General Belgrano* in the Falklands conflict 1982, see *Luisa de Ibanez* v. *United Kingdom* (Application No. 58692/00), decision on admissibility, 19 July 2000.

[14] In addition to the right to make provision in law for the death penalty 'in time of war', Protocol 6 (1983) to the ECHR, Article 2, unless the state concerned is a party to Protocol 13 (2002).

permitted derogations. In *Bankovic* v. *Belgium and others*, the respondent states had argued that 'international humanitarian law, the ICTY [International Criminal Tribunal for the former Yugoslavia] and, most recently, the International Criminal Court ... exist to regulate such state conduct'.[15] This line of reasoning would tend to suggest that, in the view of such states, international humanitarian law replaces the ECHR during an international armed conflict. The ECtHR did not express a view on the relationship between these two branches of law, given its conclusion that the ECHR could not extend to the bombing by air of a television station in Belgrade in 1999 since it decided that the victims of that attack were not then within the jurisdiction of a Convention state. The International Court of Justice had, however, expressed a view in *Legality of the Threat or Use of Nuclear Weapons*, Advisory Opinion, 8 July 1996.[16] It had concluded that 'the protection of the International Covenant on Civil and Political Rights [1966] does not cease in times of war, except by operation of Article 4 of the Covenant whereby certain provisions may be derogated from in time of national emergency'.[17] It is likely that the ECtHR would take the same view. This relationship between international humanitarian law and the ECHR will now be explored. It is assumed that no derogation notice has been issued by any state involved.

Limits of the term 'within their jurisdiction' when armed forces are acting outside national territory

High Contracting Parties to the ECHR are required by Article 1 to 'secure[18] to everyone within their jurisdiction the rights and freedoms

[15] Application No. 52207/99, decision, 12 December 2001, para. 43. The observations of the United Kingdom regarding admissibility of the application were adopted by all the respondent states, although some of the respondent states made observations on particular issues. For a discussion of the effects of this case see C. Greenwood in 'Bombing for Peace: Collateral Damage and Human Rights', [2002] *American Society International Law Proceedings* 95 at p. 100 and compare with H. Hannum, *ibid.*, p. 96; D. McGoldrick, 'The Extra-Territorial Application of the International Covenant on Civil and Political Rights', in F. Coomans and M. Kamminga (eds.), *The Extra-Territorial Application of Human Rights Treaties* (Intersentia, 2004), ch. 4.

[16] [1996] ICJ Reports 265.

[17] *Ibid.*, para. 25. See also *Coard et al* v. *United States of America*, Report No.109/99, Case 10.951, 29 September 1999, para. 39.

[18] This obligation is reinforced by Article 19. An earlier version of Article 1 read 'the High Contracting Parties shall undertake to secure ... ': *W* v. *United Kingdom*, Application No. 9348/81, 32 D & R 190 at 195.

defined ... in this Convention'. Where the state is engaged in an international armed conflict on the territory of another state the issue of whether an enemy national is 'within' that state's 'jurisdiction' will arise. Whether a state's armed forces take the jurisdiction of their state with them whenever they operate outside national territory has been addressed by the ECtHR in *Loizidou* v. *Turkey (Preliminary Objections)* (1995)[19] in a case concerning the rights of a Cypriot national who was prevented by Turkish soldiers[20] from gaining access to her property situated in the Turkish occupied part of Cyprus. The Court concluded that:

> the responsibility of a contracting party may also arise when, as a consequence of military action–lawful or unlawful–it exercises effective control of an area outside its national territory. The obligation to secure, in such an area, the rights and freedoms set out in the Convention derives from the fact of such control whether it be exercised directly, through its armed forces, or through a subordinate local administration.[21]

Does this passage mean that the nationals of one state are considered to be within the 'jurisdiction' of the state to which the armed forces belong whenever (a) there is any military action affecting them or (b) where they are within an area under the 'effective control' of those armed forces, whether by occupation of territory or otherwise, or (c) when they come under the physical control of those armed forces even in territory not under their effective control? Further, is there any geographical limit to the protection of the ECHR in these circumstances?

If it is assumed that all the states concerned are parties to the ECHR it is suggested that the actions of the armed forces of a state will bring

[19] (1995) 20 EHRR 99, para. 62; *Loizidou* v. *Turkey* (1997) 23 EHRR 513, para. 52; *Cyprus* v. *Turkey* (2002) 35 EHRR 731, para. 77.

[20] Turkey had argued that its armed forces had acted 'on behalf of the TRNC [Turkish Republic of Northern Cyprus], and see *Loizidou* v. *Turkey* (1997) EHRR 513, para. 54; *Djavit An* v. *Turkey*, Application No. 20652/92, judgment, 20 February 2003, para. 23.

[21] At para. 62. The ECtHR drew upon the analogy of 'the extradition or expulsion of a person by a Contracting State [which] may engage the responsibility of that State under the Convention ... [and the responsibility of a Contracting Party] because of acts of their authorities, whether performed within or outside national boundaries, which produce effects outside their own territory', *ibid.* See also *Drozd and Janousek* v. *France and Spain* (1992) 14 EHRR 745, para. 91. Compare *Bankovic* v. *Belgium and others*, Application No. 52207/99, judgment, 12 December 2001, (2002) 41 *International Legal Materials* 517, para. 68.

persons located in another state within the 'jurisdiction' when they are in an area under the 'effective control' of that state (whether through the occupation of territory or otherwise) or where they come under the physical control of those forces. This interpretation is consistent with Geneva Convention IV 1949, Article 4. It is also consistent with the view of the ECtHR in *Cyprus* v. *Turkey* that 'having assumed control over a given individual, it is incumbent on the authorities to account for his or her whereabouts'[22] and of the Commission in *Cyprus* v. *Turkey*.[23] The armed forces of the state must, in other words, have effective control over foreign territory or effective control over a foreign national. Although the ECtHR in *Loizidou* did not discuss directly the latter of these two propositions, no sensible distinction can be drawn between situations where the foreign armed forces are in effective control of an area and where non-nationals come within the physical control of the armed forces in an area where effective control has not been established.[24] It is only when such control is exercised that it can equate with jurisdiction over national territory. In these circumstances the state is able to 'secure' to individuals all (i.e. not merely those rights which can be secured through non-action, e.g. the right to life)[25] the rights given in section 1 of the Convention.[26]

Once a person comes within the 'jurisdiction' of a Convention state, he or she is owed all the obligations of the ECHR, including a right to an effective remedy before a national authority under Article 13. The insistence on 'effective control' over territory or over individuals is designed to draw in all those obligations of the state under the ECHR to those over whom it has a responsibility simply because its jurisdiction runs to this limited extra-territorial extent. If a state has no effective

22 *Cyprus* v. *Turkey* (2002) 35 EHRR 30, para. 147.

23 *Cyprus* v. *Turkey* (1976) 4 EHRR 482, para. 83.

24 Individuals may come under the effective control of the armed forces of a Convention state before effective control is established over territory and then remain in such control thereafter. For the concentration by the ECtHR on the fact that the state had 'assumed control over a given individual' see *Cyprus* v. *Turkey* (2002) 35 EHRR 30, para. 147. See also *Ocalan* v. *Turkey (Judgment, Merits and Just Satisfaction)*, 12 March 2003, para. 93, where the applicant, a national of Turkey, was handed over to Turkish officials in Kenya. The ECtHR held that he was within the jurisdiction of Turkey at that moment.

25 See *Bankovic* v. *Belgium and others*, above n. 21, replies of the applicants to the observations of the United Kingdom regarding the admissibility of the application, para. 120. The state holding a non-national can secure to *him or her* all the Convention rights although it could not secure these to all persons within the territory of the foreign state.

26 A point made in *Ergi* v. *Turkey* (2001) 32 EHRR 18 at para. 83.

control over territory or of individuals outside its national boundaries, any imposition of obligations under the ECHR would sound in theory rather than in practical rights of individuals.

It cannot, therefore, be the position that a state brings individuals located in another state within its jurisdiction simply because its armed forces act in a way to deny them what would be considered to be an ECHR right.[27] Given, however, the ECtHR's view of 'the Convention's special character as a human rights treaty'[28] it might be argued that the acts of the armed forces can travel across borders and thus bring persons on the territory of another state within the 'jurisdiction' of that state. In *W* v. *United Kingdom*, however, the Commission considered, *obiter*, 'whether any *active* measures of the UK authorities could have contributed to the death of the applicant's husband in the Republic of Ireland [by terrorists]'.[29] Had the British Army, for instance, shot and killed the applicant's husband from the territory of Northern Ireland might it then be argued that the 'direct' victim[30] had been brought within the 'jurisdiction' of the United Kingdom? If the answer is in the affirmative it would be difficult to distinguish from this the firing of a missile or the launch of an air strike from the territory of one state onto the territory of another. Any purported distinction, such as limiting the transferability of 'jurisdiction' to the acts carried out by individual soldiers, would seem chimerical. Nor does it appear satisfactory to argue that if a missile is fired from the territory of one state it would bring the victims of its impact within the 'jurisdiction' of the launching state but not if those victims are injured or killed as the result of the launching of airborne munitions from aircraft flying within the airspace of another state. The statement of the ECtHR in *Drozd and Janousek* v. *France and Spain*[31]

[27] The comment in Harris *et al.*, *Law of the European Convention*, p. 643, that 'it has now been placed beyond doubt that the Convention is applicable to army operations abroad' must be too sweeping. The view that jurisdiction attaches where 'a State's conduct has consequences beyond its territory' is argued by A. Orakhelashvili, 'Restrictive Interpretation of Human Rights Treaties in the Recent Jurisprudence of the European Court of Human Rights', (2003) 14 *European Journal of International Law* 529 at p. 546, who appears to overlook the words other than 'jurisdiction' in Article 1.

[28] *Loizidou* v. *Turkey* (1997) 23 EHRR 513, para. 43.

[29] Application No. 9348/81, 32 D & R 190 at 199.

[30] The applicant (the wife) was described as the 'indirect victim', who at all relevant times was within the United Kingdom. See also *Cyprus* v. *Turkey* (2002), above n. 22 at paras. 156–7 and for the loss of 'victim' status, see *Ilascu and others* v. *Moldova and the Russian Federation*, decision (Admissibility), 4 July 2001, para. III.

[31] (1992) 14 EHRR 745, para. 91.

that the responsibility of states can be 'involved because of acts of their authorities producing effects abroad' must be taken to refer to situations where their armed forces act outside national territory through exercising effective control over a particular area, or by taking individuals under its control. It must be accepted that a person located in the territory outside the control of the attacking state would have an advantage over an inhabitant of that state since the former's obligation to exhaust domestic remedies[32] would be largely meaningless. For practical reasons (such as the difficulties of travel or obtaining visas) he may not be able to commence an action in the courts of the attacking state.[33]

The view of jurisdiction taken previously by the ECtHR and the Commission might be thought to be inconsistent with *Bankovic* v. *Belgium* where the Grand Chamber of the ECtHR declared inadmissible a claim by the victims of the bombing of Radio Televizije Srbije in Belgrade on 23 April 1999 by NATO aircraft. In interpreting Article 1 the Court recalled that:

> the case law of the Court demonstrates that its recognition of the exercise of extra-territorial jurisdiction by a Contracting State is exceptional: it has done so when the respondent state, through the effective control of the relevant territory and its inhabitants abroad as a consequence of military occupation ... exercises all or some of the public powers normally to be exercised by that Government.[34]

This statement, which concentrates upon the existence of military occupation, must be considered an *obiter dictum*. The ECtHR was actually concerned with the argument, *inter alia*, that since NATO forces had effective control over the airspace of the Federal Republic of Yugoslavia, those affected by its actions came within the 'jurisdiction' of the individual states of NATO. Its decision was based, not upon the

[32] Article 35(1).

[33] See *Bankovic*, above n. 21, Application, para. 98; *Ilascu and others* v. *Moldova and the Russian Federation*, decision (Admissibility), 4 July 2001, para. IV; *Cyprus* v. *Turkey* (2002), above n. 22 at paras. 102, 194; *Issa* v. *Turkey*, decision (Admissibility), 30 May 2000.

[34] *Bankovic*, above n. 21 at para. 71. There would appear to be a distinction drawn by the ECtHR between the term 'within jurisdiction' and state responsibility, where the actions of a state actor (the armed forces) outside national territory would attract the responsibility of the state. I am grateful to Professor Francoise Hampson for drawing my attention to this point. See also Orakhelashvili, 'Restrictive Interpretation of Human Rights Treaties', pp. 539–46.

reach of the ECHR as between or among contracting states but on the fact that the Federal Republic of Yugoslavia, not a party to the ECHR, was not therefore within 'the legal space' of it.[35] The ECtHR had, previously, declared admissible a number of cases where the issue was whether a contracting state had brought individuals, whom it had arrested outside its territory, within its jurisdiction. Such individuals were under the effective control of the armed forces of a foreign state. In none of these cases was the territory of the foreign state occupied.[36]

The ECtHR in *Bankovic* was being invited to go far beyond the existing jurisprudence of the ECHR.[37] Had it decided that the victims of the bombing of the television station were within the jurisdiction of the NATO states through their control of the airspace of the territory of the Federal Republic of Yugoslavia, the Court would have accepted a number of novel developments. First, the ECtHR would have had to make a distinction between, on the one hand, munitions delivered by aircraft over-flying the territory of the attacked state and, on the other, missiles or artillery shells launched from the territory of a state or from the high seas. Whilst the flying by military aircraft without hindrance over the territory of the attacked state might show control over the latter's airspace,[38] it would be difficult to argue that the firing of such missiles or artillery shells through that airspace did so. Secondly (and as shown above) the reach of the ECHR would have been extended to

[35] *Bankovic*, above n. 21 at para. 80. Had the issue of control of territory been part of the *ratio decidendi* of the case, the ECtHR would have had to decide whether, on the facts, the claimed control of airspace was adequate for this purpose. The ECtHR made no such findings. This interpretation of *Bankovic* appears to have been adopted by Burnton J in *R* v. *Secretary of State for Work and Pensions* (unreported) 22 May 2002, para. 21, who also draws attention to the French version of Article 1. This appears to be wider than the English version but it is not referred to by the ECtHR in *Bankovic*.

[36] See *Issa and others* v. *Turkey*; *Ocalan* v. *Turkey* (unreported) Application No. 46221/99, decision (Admissibility), 14 December 2000 and see *ibid. (Judgment, Merits and Just Satisfaction)*, 12 March 2003. It is difficult to accept that in *Ocalan* v. *Turkey*, Turkish forces controlled any territory in Kenya. In *Issa*, jurisdiction was not raised as a contentious issue. *Quaere* whether *Ocalan* is authority for the proposition that the reach of the Convention extends beyond the '*espace juridique* of the Contracting States'. The applicant was of the same nationality as the respondent state and the Kenyan authorities cooperated with those of Turkey.

[37] Compare Orakhelashvili, 'Restrictive Interpretation of Human Rights Treaties', p. 545.

[38] This was disputed, see *Bankovic*, above n. 21, observations of the United Kingdom regarding the admissibility of the application, para. 50. The ECtHR made no finding on the imputability of the actions of any individual NATO state through the use of NATO aircraft to any other member state.

activities carried out by the organs of one state in the territory of a non-contracting state. This seems now, however, to have been accepted.[39]

Where a state imposes 'effective control' over an area outside its national territory

The requirement of 'effective control' as set out in the *Loizidou* case is consistent with the test in the Hague Regulations 1907 for determining the stage at which a state becomes an occupying power. Thus, territory 'is considered occupied when it is actually placed under the authority of the hostile army. The occupation extends only to the territory where such authority has been established and can be exercised.'[40] The reasoning behind this Article is that because the occupying army has established its authority over the territory it has temporarily replaced the lawful sovereign and it must assume some at least of the obligations towards the inhabitants and property within that state. Thus, the 1907 Regulations require that the occupier '*shall* take all measures in his power to restore, and ensure, as far as possible public order and safety'.[41] It is precisely because the occupier can carry out these obligations towards the inhabitants that they are imposed on him. Once territory is occupied, the occupier will owe obligations to all those individuals protected by the Geneva Conventions of 1949 and Additional Protocol I.[42] Assuming that both the occupying state and the state occupied are parties to the ECHR the former will also, subject to any permitted derogations, owe such individuals rights under that Convention. The fact of a military occupation of territory was the situation envisaged by *Bankovic*,[43] as bringing the inhabitants of that territory within the jurisdiction, for the purposes of the ECHR, of the occupying state. Where there is no derogation, the rights of the ECHR will be more

[39] In *Ocalan* v. *Turkey (Judgment, Merits and Satisfaction)*, 12 March 2003, the acts of Turkish officials took place (partly) in Kenya, a state not party to the ECHR.

[40] Regulations annexed to Hague Convention IV 1907, Article 42.

[41] *Ibid.*, Article 43.

[42] Other treaties may also apply when occupation of territory has taken place during an international armed conflict. See, e.g., the Convention for the Protection of Cultural Property in the Event of Armed Conflict 1954, Article 5; Second Protocol to the Hague Convention of 1954 for the Protection of Cultural Property in the Event of Armed Conflict 1999, Article 9.

[43] See above n. 15 at para. 71.

extensive in some respects than those guaranteed under the 1949 Geneva Conventions.[44]

It is, perhaps, much more likely that a state party to the ECHR will derogate, where permissible, if it actually occupies territory during an international armed conflict. This may, however, depend upon the reasons for the occupation. There is, for example, a considerable difference in fact between an occupation of territory for nationalistic purposes and an occupation for the purposes of restoring democracy to a state.[45] The occupation of territory has not, however, been a common feature of international armed conflicts between states both of which are parties to the ECHR.[46]

Where a state does not have effective control of an area outside its national territory

It is common during land warfare for the armed forces of a state to be engaged in combat outside their national territory without occupying territory or taking effective control of an area. Armed forces of one state may be fighting to drive an occupying force from the territory of a third state or to prevent it from establishing occupation. Alternatively, armed forces may be engaged in attempting to prevent a state harming an ethnic group of its own citizens. In none of these situations will there be any occupation of territory or even the exercise of 'effective control' over an area, since fighting will be continuing. It is, however, very likely that individuals will come within the control of the foreign armed forces. Prisoners of war and civilian protected persons may find themselves in its hands. It is argued above that rights under the ECHR will be owed to such individuals during the armed conflict, since the detaining state is able to exercise effective control over them.

[44] As extended by Additional Protocol I 1977. For an example of the breach of various Articles of the ECHR following the occupation of northern Cyprus by Turkish forces from 1974, see *Cyprus* v. *Turkey* (2002) 35 EHRR 30.

[45] See, generally, A. Roberts, 'What is a Military Occupation?', (1984) 55 *British Yearbook of International Law* 249. For an argument that UN peacekeeping forces may 'occupy' territory and thus bring into operation Geneva Convention IV 1949, see M. Kelly, *Restoring and Maintaining Order in Complex Peace Operations: the Search for a Legal Framework* (Kluwer, 1999).

[46] See the 'occupation' of the northern part of Cyprus by Turkish forces in 1974; *Cyprus* v. *Turkey* (2002) 35 EHRR 30 at para. 13 *et seq*. It has been common for states to deny that a formal occupation of territory is taking place, although compare Iraq in 2003, as to which see UN Security Council Resolution 1472, 28 March 2003.

Where the Convention state's armed forces remain on its own territory

The acts of a military group organized into a military structure may be attributed to a ECHR state where that state keeps its own armed forces within its borders but 'wields overall control over the group, not only by equipping and financing [it], but also by co-ordinating or helping in the general planning of its military activity'.[47] The acts of the military group in another state may then cause the ECHR state not only to become a party to the armed conflict but also to be responsible for the acts of that group. It is as if the military group is treated as part of the armed forces of the state which 'wields overall control' over it. By a process of constructive liability the group must then bring those under its control 'within the jurisdiction' of the ECHR state. Thus, Turkey was held responsible by the ECtHR for the acts of the Turkish Republic in Northern Cyprus (TRNC) following its invasion of this territory in July 1994. Since Turkey had 'effective control over northern Cyprus, its responsibility', said the Court:

> cannot be confined to the acts of its own soldiers or officials in northern Cyprus but must also be engaged by virtue of the acts of the local administration which survives by virtue of Turkish military and other support.[48]

In the Bosnian context, the ICTY decided that the Bosnian Serbs were within the overall control of the Federal Republic of Yugoslavia (FRY).[49] Had FRY been a party to the ECHR it would have owed Convention rights to those coming under the control of the Bosnian Serb forces.

Where the ECHR state is taking part in a UN peace support operation

In many peace support operations there will not be an international armed conflict taking place. Armed conflict may, however, break out at

[47] *Prosecutor* v. *Tadić*, judgment of the ICTY Appeals Chamber, 15 July 1999, para. 131; *Prosecutor* v. *Aleksovski*, judgment of the ICTY Appeals Chamber, 24 March 2000, para. 143.

[48] *Cyprus* v. *Turkey* (2002) 35 EHRR 731, para. 77. The Convention state may also be responsible for the acts of private individuals if it acquiesces or connives in such acts, para. 81.

[49] *Prosecutor* v. *Tadić* (1999) 38 *International Legal Materials* 1518, para. 145. The Appeals Chamber went on to say that 'clear evidence of a chain of military command between Belgrade and Pale was presented to the Trial Chamber', para. 152.

any time. Two common situations may arise. First, the peace support forces are attacked and they respond by way of self-defence. Secondly, although their mandate does not involve engagement in the conflict they operate in an area where an armed conflict is taking place and they take military action to defend those for whom they are responsible. It is suggested that in neither situation will the UN force become parties to the armed conflict. The effect, however, of the Secretary-General's Bulletin, *Observance by United Nations Forces of International Humanitarian Law* (1999)[50] is that the 'fundamental principles and rules of international humanitarian law ... are applicable to United Nations forces when in situations of armed conflict they are actively engaged therein as combatants'.[51] These principles and rules are 'applicable in enforcement actions, or in peacekeeping operations when the use of force is permitted in self-defence'.[52] A consequence of the application of the Bulletin is that those who come into the hands of the armed forces of a state providing peace support outside its territory will be owed rights[53] similar to those under international humanitarian law and also under the ECHR (assuming the relevant state is a party to the ECHR) since they will come within the effective control of that state's armed forces.

It would be difficult for a state to argue that it is required to make a derogation under Article 15 of the ECHR when it is involved in a UN support operation since it will be unlikely to be able to show that it is engaged in 'war or other public emergency threatening the life of the nation'.

Role of national law

It is not uncommon for the national law of the state to apply to the members of its armed forces whilst taking part in an armed conflict beyond the territorial limits of the state.[54] Such law may be enforced by military discipline systems or by the courts of the territory when the alleged wrongdoer is returned to that state. Of particular relevance in this connection is whether the ECHR is a part of the national law of the

[50] (1999) 38 *International Legal Materials* 1656.
[51] At s. 1, 1.1. [52] *Ibid.*
[53] See, e.g., s. 8 dealing with the treatment of detained persons.
[54] In relation to the United Kingdom see Criminal Justice Act 1988, s. 134, International Criminal Court Act 2001, s. 51; Army Act 1955, s. 70; Air Force Act 1970, s. 70; Naval Discipline Act 1957, s. 42.

state. In the United Kingdom this is now the case, with the coming into force of the Human Rights Act (HRA) 1998 in October 2000. Thus, by section 6 of the Act it is 'unlawful for a public authority [which term would include the armed forces] to act in a way which is incompatible with a Convention right'. The armed forces will not have acted unlawfully if they could not have acted differently because of their compliance with primary legislation.[55] Where there is no legislation to compel them to act otherwise, members of the armed forces must therefore respect Convention rights. Although the HRA 1998 does not refer to Article 1 of the ECHR it seems clear that by a combination of that Act and the relevant service discipline Act,[56] the British armed forces will be required to act in compliance with section 6 (subject to any derogations made under HRA 1998, section 14) when they are taking part in an armed conflict or are involved in UN peace support operations outside the territorial limits of the United Kingdom. A victim[57] of any breach of ECHR rights by a member of the armed forces may be permitted by a state party to the ECHR to bring a civil action in its domestic courts on the basis of such a breach.

Application of the ECHR during an international armed conflict

This chapter has attempted to show when a person may be considered to be 'within the jurisdiction' of a ECHR state. The circumstances under which a state takes part in an international armed conflict, and the effects on individuals caught up in such events, can vary considerably. The most relevant articles applicable during such an armed conflict are Articles 2–11 of the ECHR, Article 1 of the First Protocol, Articles 2 and 4 of the Fourth Protocol, Articles 1 and 2 of the Sixth Protocol (along with the Thirteenth Protocol, 2002) and Articles 1 to 4 of the Seventh Protocol.[58] The concurrent applicability of these Articles with the

[55] Section 6(2) or where primary legislation 'cannot be given effect to in a way which is incompatible with the Convention rights'.

[56] Including other Acts of Parliament conferring extra-territorial jurisdiction. For the view that a British national detained by American authorities in Guantanamo Bay was not within the jurisdiction of the UK authorities see *R (Abassi)* v. *Secretary of State for Foreign and Commonwealth Affairs and Secretary of State for the Home Department* [2002] EWCA Civ. 1598, para. 77.

[57] Defined in terms of Article 34 of the ECHR, s. 7(7) of the 1998 Act. For the concept of 'direct' and 'indirect' victims see *W* v. *United Kingdom*, above n. 18 at 198.

[58] For an extensive application of many of these Articles see *Cyprus* v. *Turkey* (2002) 35 EHRR 731.

relevant principles of international humanitarian law will now be considered. Reasons of space prevent discussion of the protection of property and the treatment of aliens.

Killing during an international armed conflict

Article 2 of the ECHR is, perhaps, the most significant right applicable during an armed conflict. In the absence of a derogation, a person may not be deprived of his life unless it 'results from the use of force which is no more than absolutely necessary (a) in defence of a person from unlawful violence; (b) in order to effect a lawful arrest or to prevent the escape of a person lawfully detained; (c) in action lawfully taken for the purpose of quelling a riot or insurrection'.[59] On the other hand, international humanitarian law (IHL) permits a lawful combatant to kill other combatants, provided the methods and means of doing so are not, in themselves, unlawful. Examples of unlawful killing include killing through causing superfluous injury or unnecessary suffering, by perfidy, through misuse of the distinctive emblems, by declaring no quarter, by killing an enemy combatant who is *hors de combat*, or who has parachuted from an aircraft in distress, by failing to distinguish oneself at the appropriate time from the civilian population or by using a prohibited weapon.[60] IHL even accepts that civilians may be killed lawfully provided the attack on combatants or military objectives is 'not expected to cause incidental loss of civilian life ... which would be excessive in relation to the concrete and direct military advantage anticipated'.[61] Moreover, in international humanitarian law there is no requirement that the killing should be 'absolutely necessary' as required by the ECHR in the absence of a permitted derogation. Any requirement that during an international armed conflict combatants could only kill enemy combatants where this was 'absolutely necessary' would be quite unrealistic.

[59] Compare the International Covenant on Civil and Political Rights 1966, Article 6 which provides that 'No one shall be *arbitrarily* deprived of his life' (emphasis supplied). See generally, A. Reidy, 'The Approach of the European Commission and Court of Human Rights to International Humanitarian Law', (1998) 324 *International Review of the Red Cross* 513.

[60] See, generally, H. McCoubrey, *International Humanitarian Law: The Regulation of Armed Conflicts* (1st edn, Dartmouth, 1990), pp. 147–52. Compare whether a state may deprive its own soldiers of their right to life.

[61] Additional Protocol I 1977, Article 51(5)(b). See, generally, R. Normand and C. Jochnick, 'The Legitimation of Violence: A Critical Analysis of the Gulf War', (1994) 35 *Harvard International Law Journal* 387.

Where a derogation notice is issued under Article 15 of the ECHR a state will not be in breach of Article 2 if the deaths result from 'lawful acts of war'. There must, therefore, be a distinction between the justifications for causing death when there is, and when there is not, a derogation from Article 2 of the ECHR.

Where no derogation from Article 2 has been made and assuming that enemy forces are brought within the jurisdiction[62] of the ECHR, state force can only[63] be used in order to achieve the objectives set out in that Article. The link between the use of force and the need to defend a person from unlawful violence must not be too remote. It is difficult to accept that the life of a person may be taken on the ground that he might on some later occasion impose unlawful violence upon another person.

A state is clearly under an obligation to treat protected persons, such as prisoners of war or civilians, humanely.[64] The former will, by definition, come within the effective control and, therefore, the jurisdiction of the detaining state. Once they have done so they are owed the right to life as set out in Article 2. Since they will be detained, the ECHR state should have little difficulty in complying with that Article. This will also be the case with any civilians detained under Geneva Convention IV 1949. Weapons can be used against escaping prisoners of war, if preceded by suitable warnings, and the ECHR allows for the use of force which is 'absolutely necessary' to 'prevent the escape of a person lawfully detained'.[65] The death of a prisoner of war must lead to an inquiry by the detaining power,[66] a similar requirement to that under the ECHR, Article 2 for an effective investigation into the death of a person (whether prisoner of war or civilian) caused by state organs.[67]

Prohibition against torture, inhuman or degrading treatment or punishment

The right not to be treated in one of these prohibited ways, granted by ECHR, Article 3, has a counterpart in the grave breach provisions of each of the four Geneva Conventions of 1949 and Additional Protocol

62 For example, the state is occupying territory and engages in armed conflict.

63 See *McCann* v. *United Kingdom* (1995) 21 EHRR 97, para. 149; *Gul* v. *Turkey*, judgment, 14 December 2000, para. 82.

64 See Geneva Convention III 1949, Article 13; Geneva Convention IV 1949, Article 27.

65 Geneva Convention III 1949, Article 39 and ECHR, Article 42 respectively.

66 Geneva Convention III 1949, Article 121.

67 See *Cyprus* v. *Turkey* (2002) 35 EHRR 731, para. 131.

I of 1977.[68] In addition, all those protected by the Geneva Conventions must be treated humanely.[69] Since no derogation may be made from ECHR, Article 3,[70] it and IHL lay down similar obligations applicable during an international armed conflict.

Rights when detained

During an international armed conflict, prisoners of war are likely to be, and civilians[71] may be, detained by the armed forces. Where there has been no derogation under Article 15 the full rights of the ECHR will be owed to such individuals. Article 5 provides that 'No one shall be deprived of his liberty save in the following cases and in accordance with a procedure established by law.' The 'following cases' do not make provision for the deprivation of liberty of prisoners of war or detained civilians unless the detention can be said to be 'in order to secure the fulfilment of any obligation prescribed by law'.[72] The term, 'prescribed by law' must then be interpreted as including a ECHR state's other obligations imposed under international law. The 'obligation prescribed by law' is the duty to treat prisoners of war in accordance with Geneva Convention III 1949[73] and detained civilians in accordance with Geneva Convention IV 1949.

Such a conclusion does, however, place the prisoner of war and the detained civilian in a position which would not be tolerated under the ECHR in the absence of an international armed conflict. Prisoners of war may be detained without any judicial intervention for an indefinite period, i.e. until the cessation of active hostilities.[74] Civilian protected persons[75]

[68] See Articles 50, 51, 130, 147 respectively of the Geneva Conventions 1949 and Articles 11(4) and 85 of Additional Protocol I 1977. For examples see *Cyprus* v. *Turkey* (1976). See also the European Convention for the Prevention of Torture and Inhuman or Degrading Treatment or Punishment 1987.

[69] Articles 12, 13, 27 respectively of the Geneva Conventions 1949. Compare 'degrading' treatment, to which no reference is made in these Articles.

[70] Article 15(2) ECHR, see *Cyprus* v. *Turkey* (2002) 35 EHRR 731, para. 154; *Ocalan* v. *Turkey* (2003) 37 EHRR 10, para. 220.

[71] See the Fourth Geneva Convention 1949, Articles 5 and 66–76.

[72] See Vienna Convention on the Law of Treaties 1969, Article 31(3)(c). For the need to consult other treaty obligations as a means of interpretation see *Coard* v. *United States*, Inter-American Commission on Human Rights, Report No.109/99, 29 September 1999, para. 43.

[73] See *Cyprus* v. *Turkey* (1976), above n. 23 at para. 313.

[74] Geneva Convention III 1949, Article 118.

[75] Protected persons may only be interned in the circumstances envisaged by Geneva Convention IV 1949, Articles 41 and 42.

may also be interned for an indefinite period in occupied territory without a judicial decision, although they are given a right of appeal.[76]

Article 5(4) of the ECHR goes on to provide that a person who has been deprived of his liberty may take proceedings 'by which the lawfulness of his detention [is to be] decided speedily by a court'. In this connection, a court must refer to a judicial process established by national law. In practice, it is unlikely that such a right would be invoked by many members of the armed forces who have fallen into the power of the enemy,[77] simply because the detention of prisoners of war is well understood. It may be, however, that a person detained seeks to argue that he is entitled to be treated as a prisoner of war and not, for example, as an 'unlawful combatant' or as a mercenary. Without denying his status as a civilian he may wish to argue that he has been wrongly detained or that he is not being treated in accordance with his rights under the ECHR. The 'lawfulness of his detention' must then be argued to include the regime under which he is detained as well as whether there are grounds for his detention at all. Under the law of the United Kingdom, for instance, the only 'court' available outside territorial limits to determine these issues is a board of inquiry convened under the Prisoner of War (Determination of Status) Regulations 1958.[78] Since the 1958 Regulations apply only to those 'in custody ... who have committed a belligerent act prior to capture'[79] it is unlikely to be available as a means of testing the lawfulness of the detention of civilians. For the reasons indicated in the following section it is unlikely that such a board of inquiry would comply with ECHR, Article 6(1).

The conclusion must be drawn that a state party which does not provide a court for the purposes of ECHR, Article 5(4) would be in breach of its obligations under that Article in time of an international armed conflict. Those whose ECHR rights are affected will have an enforceable right to compensation.[80]

[76] Geneva Convention IV 1949, Article 78. For the position of protected persons not in occupied territory see *ibid.*, Articles 42 and 43.

[77] Geneva Convention III 1949, Article 4.

[78] Schedule 1 to the Royal Warrant Governing the Maintenance of Discipline Among Prisoners of War (1958) (as amended).

[79] Regulation 1(1). This was interpreted more widely in 1990–1. See G. Risius, 'Prisoners of War in the United Kingdom', in P. Rowe (ed.), *The Gulf War 1990–91 in International and English Law* (Routledge, 1993), ch. 14.

[80] ECHR, Article 5(5).

International humanitarian law permits a state to transfer prisoners of war to another state party to Geneva Convention III 1949. Where ground fighting is carried out by a coalition of states modern practice has shown that one or more of these states will assume responsibility for the detention of prisoners of war. A state which transfers prisoners of war retains an obligation towards them to request their return if the transferee state fails to carry out its obligations under that Convention. Should a 'real risk of treatment going beyond the threshold set by [any of the substantive articles of the ECHR]'[81] exist were the transfer to take place, the transferor state would be in breach of its ECHR obligations to the prisoner of war if it were to transfer him. The prisoner of war might then be said to have a right not to be transferred. Should this risk be perceived only when the transfer has actually taken place, the prisoner of war will no longer be within the jurisdiction of the transferring state and may not be within the jurisdiction of another ECHR state. In these circumstances it is difficult to accept that he would have a right to invoke the machinery of the ECHR since the failure of the transferor state (a party to the ECHR) is in not securing his return from the transferee state whilst the individual is clearly beyond the jurisdiction of the former state.

Under both international humanitarian law[82] and the ECHR, the detaining state is under an obligation to account for those whom it detains.[83] The effect of non-compliance with this may be to give a relative a right to bring a claim under the ECHR as a victim.[84]

Right to a fair trial

The right to a fair trial is to be found in all human rights instruments. In the absence of any derogation, Article 6 of the ECHR will apply during an international armed conflict. Again, difficulties may be experienced where the operations of armed forces outside the territorial limits of the state bring individuals within the jurisdiction of that state.

The armed forces may capture an alleged spy, who is not to be 'punished without previous trial'.[85] In addition, prisoners of war may

[81] *Soering* v. *United Kingdom* (1989) 11 EHRR 439 at para. 111.

[82] For prisoners of war see Geneva Convention III 1949, Article 122 and for protected civilians, Geneva Convention IV 1949, Article 136.

[83] See *Cyprus* v. *Turkey* (2002), above n. 22 at para. 147.

[84] *Ibid.*, paras. 156–7. A curfew did not involve a breach of Article 5 in *Cyprus* v. *Turkey* (1976), above n. 23 at para. 235.

[85] Article 30 of the Hague Regulations annexed to Hague Convention IV 1907.

be subject to a hearing for disciplinary offences committed whilst detained or tried for crimes committed before or after capture[86] and civilians may be tried by an occupying power.[87] It is likely that any court in these situations will be a military court. Indeed, in respect of prisoners of war, Geneva Convention III 1949 requires a prisoner of war to be tried by the same type of court as the members of the armed forces of the detaining power.[88] This may be a military court. A civilian protected person against whom is alleged a breach of the penal provisions promulgated by an occupying state must be handed over to that state's 'non-political military courts'.[89]

International humanitarian treaties provide some very basic fair trial safeguards. In relation to disciplinary offences committed by prisoners of war, Geneva Convention III 1949, Article 96, requires that the prisoner of war be told of the offence of which he is accused, be given an opportunity to explain himself, to call witnesses and to have the services of a qualified interpreter. Where a prisoner of war, or any other person (be they a civilian protected person or a member of the armed forces of an enemy state who is not entitled to be treated as a prisoner of war), is to be tried for a penal offence, Article 75 of Additional Protocol I lays down substantial fair trial procedures, which are in many ways similar to ECHR, Article 6. Two points can be made here. First, the list of the rights of an accused is preceded by an obligation on the part of the regularly constituted court to respect 'the generally recognised principles of regular judicial procedure'. Secondly, it has been suggested that since 'Article 75 is not subject to any possibility of derogation or suspension ... consequently it is these provisions which will play a decisive role in the case of armed conflicts'.[90] To accept this conclusion one would have to find that in modern international armed conflicts, states involved have been in the practice of derogating from ECHR,

[86] Geneva Convention III 1949, Articles 82–108.

[87] Geneva Convention IV 1949, Articles 66–75.

[88] Article 84. The detaining state may provide for a civil court to assume jurisdiction for members of its own armed forces in relation to all or some offences. Under the law of the United Kingdom a soldier who commits any crime against English law outside the United Kingdom may be tried by a court-martial sitting anywhere in the world, Army Act 1955, ss. 70 and 91. Thus, a prisoner of war should also be subject to the same regime.

[89] Geneva Convention IV 1949, Article 66.

[90] Y. Sandoz, C. Swinarski and B. Zimmermann (eds.), *Commentary on the Additional Protocols of 8 June 1977 to the Geneva Convention of 12 August 1949* (Martinus Nijhoff, 1987), para. 3092.

Article 6. This has not proved to be the case. Both sets of fair trial provisions will apply during an international armed conflict where neither ECHR state involved has issued a relevant derogation notice. Although 'the provisions in all these instruments are more or less equivalent',[91] those given by the ECHR are of much greater value to an accused since he has a means of enforcing them by procedures that may well be implemented within the law of the ECHR state or by bringing a case before the ECtHR, rather than having to rely upon a subsequent criminal trial of those charged with, for example, a grave breach of the Geneva Conventions.[92]

Where ECHR rights continue to apply in the absence of an effective derogation, the state will need to ensure that it is able to provide an independent and impartial tribunal to try those who have been brought within its jurisdiction. This may prove difficult if the court is, as it is likely to be, a military one.[93] Such a court may have to sit outside the borders of the state itself where the armed conflict is, itself, occurring outside those borders. Where territory is occupied, a state may not transfer protected persons to its territory for trial or for any other reason.[94] The consequence of this is that the ECHR state will be required to have in place facilities for an extra-territorial court to conduct trials (and appeals if necessary) in accordance with ECHR, Article 6 of persons involved in conduct related to the armed conflict and where the individuals concerned cannot (or where it is impractical to do so) be transferred to the territory of the detaining state for trial. The transfer of a civilian from the custody of the armed forces of the occupying state

[91] *Ibid. Quaere* whether this is so, at least between the ECHR and Additional Protocol I 1977. Thus, the latter does not require an 'independent' court (a matter upon which the ECtHR has been much exercised in relation to military courts) nor does it require the provision of an interpreter or legal assistance (although see Articles 95 and 105 of Geneva Convention III 1949, in respect of prisoners of war, Articles 72 and 123 of Geneva Convention IV 1949 in respect of protected civilians) nor does it give a general right of appeal. On this right to appeal see Geneva Convention III 1949, Article 106; Geneva Convention IV 1949, Article 73 and for the relevant human rights treaties, Protocol 7 (1984), Article 2, to the ECHR and the International Covenant on Civil and Political Rights 1966, Article 14.

[92] See Article 85(4)(e) of Additional Protocol I; Article 8.2(a)(vi) of the Rome Statute 1998, the grave breach of 'wilfully ... depriving a person [protected by the Geneva Conventions 1949] of the rights of fair and regular trial'.

[93] See, e.g., *Findlay* v. *United Kingdom* (1997) 24 EHRR 221; *Incal* v. *Turkey* (2000) 29 EHRR 449; *Cyprus* v. *Turkey* (2002) 35 EHRR 731 at para. 358.

[94] Geneva Convention IV 1949, Article 49. This does not apply to prisoners of war, who may be transferred to the territory of the detaining state for trial.

to the civilian authorities in the occupied state is another possibility, subject, however, to where a real risk is foreseen that to do so would involve a breach of a person's Convention rights.

Conclusion

Even where no derogation notice is issued by a state engaged in an international armed conflict, the obligations on that state will not actually be extensive unless foreign nationals come within the hands of the armed forces or other organs of the state (through their exercise of control over territory or over individuals). Moreover, the well-established obligation on the part of a ECHR state to conduct an investigation into the facts surrounding a breach of the Convention will often not be difficult to apply during an international armed conflict. The killing of a prisoner of war, for example, should lead to little difficulty in conducting an investigation since this will, in reality, be little different from an investigation of an alleged breach of the ECHR towards a prisoner during peacetime.[95]

It has been assumed that all states involved in an international armed conflict are parties to the ECHR. If they are not, a further issue arises, namely, whether the ECHR can nevertheless apply to individuals within the jurisdiction (as discussed above) of a ECHR state engaged in an armed conflict with a non-ECHR state. There would appear to be no logical reason for distinguishing these situations and, indeed, this has been established.[96] This is quite different from arguing that an armed conflict between a ECHR state and a non-ECHR state would impose Convention obligations on the latter. The ECtHR in *Soering* v. *United Kingdom* concluded that 'The Convention does not govern the actions of States not Parties to it, nor does it purport to be a means of requiring the Contracting States to impose Convention standards on other States.'[97] If the result of this conclusion is that states will be more likely

[95] Investigations where a war crime is alleged may, in practice, be dealt with as criminal investigations, especially where the state concerned is a party to the Rome Statute 1998.

[96] See *Ocalan* v. *Turkey (Judgment, Merits and Satisfaction)* (2003) 37 EHRR 10 where the acts of Turkish officials in Kenya brought the applicant within the jurisdiction of Turkey, although no breach of Convention rights was held to have taken place in Kenya. In *Bankovic* v. *Belgium*, above n. 21, the Court was keen to stress that the reason for the extra-territorial jurisdiction set out in *Cyprus* v. *Turkey* (2002), above n. 22 at para. 78 was to prevent the applicant from losing her opportunity to enforce her Convention right against a state.

[97] (1989) 11 EHRR 439 at para. 86, relied upon by the Court in *Bankovic* v. *Belgium*, above n. 21. UK armed forces 'could not, for example, hand over Iraqis to the USA if they faced

to issue a derogation notice, the consequence is therefore to bring the law of the ECHR into a realistic frame given that an armed conflict is taking place.[98] To decide that, in these circumstances, the ECHR does not apply is to deny a person who has actually come within the jurisdiction (as discussed above) of a ECHR state the right to enforce his or her ECHR rights.[99] These rights may, as explained above, be of much greater value to the person than would be the opportunity to seek 'justice' through the trial of a defendant for a breach of international humanitarian law. To accept the author's conclusion would also tend to induce state organs to exercise greater care to avoid a breach of the ECHR and thus give a further opportunity to deny impunity to those who would breach the concurrently applicable rules of international humanitarian law.

Postscript

Since completing this chapter some important developments have occurred. In *Ilascu* v. *Moldova and the Russian Federation*, Judgment, 8 July 2004 and in *Issa* v. *Turkey*, Judgment, 16 November 2004, the ECtHR has considered further the meaning of 'within their jurisdiction' contained in Article 1 of the ECHR. The High Court in England in *R (Al Skeini and others)* v. *Secretary of State for Defence* [2004] EWHC 2911, has dealt with the applicability of the Human Rights Act 1998 to the treatment of various Iraqi nationals by British forces in Iraq.

the death penalty at the hands of the Americans', V. Lowe, 'The Iraqi Crisis: What Now?', (2003) 52 *International Legal and Comparative Quarterly* 859 at p. 869.

98 An important issue will be the timing of the derogation notice since it will not have retrospective effect, as to which see N. Mole, 'Who Guards the Guards: the Rule of Law in Kosovo', [2001] *European Human Rights Law Review* 280 at p. 292.

99 The ECtHR has a responsibility to 'ensure the observance of the engagements undertaken by the High Contracting Parties' independently of the states concerned or of the victim, Article 19; *Cyprus* v. *Turkey* (2002), above n. 22 at para. 78.

11

Regional organizations and the promotion and protection of democracy as a contribution to international peace and security

RICHARD BURCHILL

In what, unfortunately, would be his final book, Hilaire, along with Justin Morris, engaged in a study entitled *Regional Peacekeeping in the Post-Cold War Era.*[1] In that volume they presented a wide-ranging analysis of the potential contributions and limitations of regional arrangements as peace support actors. Their foray into this area was significant, for regionalism is pervasive in the international system but a neglected area of study in international law. In both theory and practice, regionalism creates a dilemma for today's international law which is commonly understood and conceived as a global, universal system of law. By its very definition, regionalism poses a challenge to a global, universal system of international law as it advocates the recognition of diversity. At the same time, the realities of the international system and international relations demonstrate that regional arrangements have an important role to play in a wide variety of activities. Hilaire and Justin rightly identified that regional arrangements can act in cooperation with universal arrangements in dealing with specific problems faced by the international system and furthermore regional arrangements play an 'enhanced and powerful role' in addressing a range of issues.[2]

This contribution intends to add to the debate stimulated by Hilaire and Justin in viewing how regional arrangements may contribute to international peace and security. Their study examined the role of regional arrangements in the field of peacekeeping and security; this contribution will look at the role of regional arrangements in the promotion and

[1] H. McCoubrey and J. Morris, *Regional Peacekeeping in the Post Cold-War Era* (Kluwer, 2000).
[2] *Ibid.*, p. 228.

protection of democracy as part of the global pursuit of international peace and security. Since the end of the Cold War the promotion and protection of democracy has become a central feature in the development of international law and has proven to be an integral element in the pursuit and maintenance of international peace and security.[3] Our understanding of security now includes matters beyond the traditional area of political-military matters to involve issues such as human rights, democracy, social issues and the protection of the environment. The conceptual and practical shifts in what constitute security considerations have been broadly recognized by the United Nations with democracy being a major priority in addressing the protection and maintenance of peace and security.[4]

It is in the area of democracy promotion and protection that regional arrangements have demonstrated the ability to develop and implement standards well above what has been possible for a global organization such as the United Nations. In doing so, regional arrangements have not undermined the United Nations but have instead shown the way forward and worked with the United Nations in pursuit of common goals and objectives which ultimately prove beneficial for the whole of the international system.

Regionalism and international law

The definition of a regional arrangement is open to a variety of interpretations. The most common definition of a regional arrangement is a grouping of geographically contingent states linked by some common purpose. However, geographical proximity can be stretched, as evidenced by the Organisation for Security and Cooperation in Europe (OSCE) which includes two non-European states in the USA and Canada, or the Commonwealth which has member states all over the world. A precise definition of a regional arrangement is absent from the United Nations Charter and it is the practice of some regional arrangements to declare

[3] McCoubrey and Morris raise the question as to whether or not it is desirable to broaden the security agenda, *ibid.*, p. 88, but it will be the contention here that such a broadening is necessary and desirable.

[4] See Note by the President of the Security Council, UN SCOR, 47th Sess., 3046th mtg. at 3, UN doc. S/23500 (1992); United Nations, *Report of the Panel on United Nations Peace Operations* (Brahimi Report) UN doc. A/55/305-S/2000/809 (21 August 2000) paras. 37–42; ICISS, *The Responsibility to Protect* (International Development Research Centre, 2001), paras. 2.21–2.23.

themselves a regional arrangement for the purposes of Chapter VIII of the Charter, while others do not make this point. Defining what is, or is not, a regional arrangement is not wholly essential as it is the nature of the functions undertaken and the relationship of the regional arrangement with the United Nations that is more important.[5] For the purposes here, regional arrangements will be understood as collectives of states that have voluntarily come together in cooperative arrangements in the pursuit of common goals or objectives and in doing so have created specific institutional structures at the level above the state but not open to universal membership.

In viewing regional arrangements as an important aspect of international law and relations, a range of pros and cons can be identified.[6] On the positive side, regional arrangements often have the possibility of being more conducive for action as the states in an arrangement will often possess a common history, traditions, culture and characteristics that give rise to greater levels of cooperation and interaction, something distinctly lacking at the global level.[7] Such commonalities will contribute to a similarity of views that over time will help to eliminate physical conflict and give rise to greater cooperation, a point McCoubrey and Morris note at the outset as being obvious but often overlooked.[8] Due to size, proximity and shared beliefs and values, regional arrangements possess a higher degree of cohesion in the pursuit of activities which may be missing from the actions of a global body.[9] Commonly, the relatively small geographical area involved with a regional arrangement allows for a more efficient allocation of resources and delegating of tasks when it comes to problem-solving procedures.[10] Governments will

[5] C. Gray, *International Law and the Use of Force* (Oxford University Press, 2000), p. 206.

[6] See A. Leroy Bennett, *International Organizations: Principles and Issues* (6th edn, Prentice Hall, 1995), pp. 230–1; M. Pugh and W. Singh Sidhu (eds.), *The United Nations and Regional Security: Europe and Beyond* (Lynne Reinner, 2003), Part 1.

[7] H. Levie, 'Some Constitutional Aspects of Selected Regional Organizations: A Comparative Study', (1966) 16 *Columbia Journal of Transnational Law* 15; E. Frey-Wouters, 'The Prospect for Regionalism in World Affairs', in C. Black and R. Falk, *The Future of the International Legal Order* (Princeton University Press, 1969), vol. 1, pp. 553–4.

[8] McCoubrey and Morris, *Regional Peacekeeping*, p. 1. Also N. MacFarlane and T. Weiss, 'The United Nations, Regional Organisations and Human Security: Building Theory in Central America', (1994) 15 *Third World Quarterly* 283.

[9] D. Jividen, 'It Takes a Region: A Proposal for an Alternative Regional Approach to UN Collective Force Humanitarian Intervention', (1999/2000) 10 *USAF Journal of Legal Studies* 123.

[10] R. Schema, 'The OAS and the Quest for International Co-operation: American Vision or Mirage', (1981) 13 *Case Western Reserve Journal of International Law* 101.

likely be more inclined to follow the directives of a regional arrangement since the supervisory bodies created will possess greater legitimacy, being seen as having a greater understanding of the more localized situation.[11] The inability of a universal arrangement to understand or take into consideration the particularities unique to the members of a regional arrangement often results in action by the larger entity being seen as outside interference.[12] The existence of regional arrangements increases the possible range of options available to address particular problems and the presence of a regional arrangement can ensure a lasting commitment to the issues and problems facing the region.[13]

While these are the attractive possibilities of regional arrangements, there are equally a number of negative factors to consider:[14] within regions, the actual commitment of the member states is not always as deep as perceived, for states may selectively use regional or universal procedures depending upon individual needs; homogeneity among states and societies is not a given within any region and the closeness of states may result in deep-seated antagonisms and continued physical conflict;[15] regional powers may be able to manipulate the regional arrangement in the pursuit of their own self-interested goals and[16] in turn other states in a region may prefer global arrangements as an attempt to avoid manipulation by a regional power;[17] regional arrangements may not always possess the necessary resources and knowledge that would be available to a universal body;[18] the range of experience, knowledge and resources that global arrangements may possess could help to fill the gaps that a regional arrangement is unable to cover; and the creation and existence of a number of regional blocs could easily threaten world peace as the regional arrangements may engage in

[11] A. H. Robertson and J. G. Merrills, *Human Rights in the World* (3rd edn, Manchester University Press, 1992), pp. 223–4; MacFarlane and Weiss, 'The United Nations, Regional Organisations and Human Security', p. 283.

[12] J. Donnelly, 'International Human Rights: A Regime Analysis', (1986) 40 *International Organization* 637.

[13] McCoubrey and Morris, *Regional Peacekeeping*, pp. 212 and 224.

[14] See J. Nye, 'Regional Institutions', in C. Black and R. Falk (eds.), *The Future of the International Legal Order* (Princeton University Press, 1972), vol. 4, pp. 433–6.

[15] I. Claude, *Swords into Ploughshares: The Problems and Progress of International Organization* (4th edn, Random House, 1964), p. 105; C. Schreuer, 'Regionalism v Universalism', (1995) 6 *European Journal of International Law* 479.

[16] McCoubrey and Morris, *Regional Peacekeeping*, p. 39 discussing the *Nicaragua* case (*Nicaragua* v. *United States*).

[17] McCoubrey and Morris, *Regional Peacekeeping*, p. 54.

[18] Schreuer, 'Regionalism v Universalism', p. 479.

political, military or ideological rivalry leading to animosity and possibly conflict. By bringing states together under a single global body, local and regional animosity can be minimized.

The universal/regional debate is too often presented as a zero-sum situation where the international system is either organized under a single global, universal system, or it is to fragment into various regional groupings with potentially violent results. Regional arrangements, by definition, give rise to fragmentation of a sort and could easily be seen to be contrary to a singular universal global project. However, a better approach to the topic is to see regional and global arrangements as being able to coexist and work together in addressing problems faced by the international system. The relation between regional and universal arrangements should not be seen as one of competition but rather as complementarity. Hilaire and Justin identified no one particular model of cooperation as regional arrangements will differ in scope, character and ability and the context within which both regional and universal arrangements work differs greatly. The challenge is to ensure that the resources and capabilities which are available are used to their best potential for meeting the needs of the international system, regardless of whether those needs are confined to a region or are universal issues. As McCoubrey and Morris discuss, we are not faced with a crude choice between global and regional mechanisms. Instead, it is a question of making appropriate choices 'amongst potential actors in order to secure the optimum balance between both modes of operation'.[19] The post-Cold War environment has been described as a 'resource-driven crisis' in the international system which makes greater use of regional organizations 'inevitable'.[20] The necessary first step is to see regional arrangements as integral and complementary to the efforts of the United Nations.

Regional arrangements and the United Nations

The creation of the United Nations following the Second World War was a clear statement that the future of international law was to be based on a singular, global organization uniting all members of the international system. The United Nations' predecessor, the League of Nations, also faced the regional/global debate but the situation was less acute due to the overall impact of the organization. Articles 20 and 21 of the

[19] McCoubrey and Morris, *Regional Peacekeeping*, p. 229. [20] *Ibid.*, p. 214.

League's Covenant addressed the issue, with Article 20 giving the League a primary position as a global organization, but Article 21 recognizing that the Covenant would not affect the 'validity of international engagements, such as treaties of arbitration or regional understandings like the Monroe doctrine, for securing the maintenance of peace'. An early proposal from France concerning the creation of the League set out a clear statement that the scope of the organization was to be universal.[21]

Since the creation of the United Nations, international law has constantly strived to be 'universal' in character, avoiding the dangers and pitfalls of a fragmented international system. The creation and subsequent development of the United Nations has been based on the belief that international peace and security is best maintained by a global body uniting all states and avoiding regional groupings that could only lead to animosity and eventually conflict. In the debates during the drafting of the UN Charter, various organizational models were proposed giving regional arrangements a lesser or greater role in the organization of the international system. In its final form, the Charter recognizes the existence of regional arrangements but in a clearly subordinate manner, the global, universal concept being seen as the best way to ensure international peace and security. As Inis Claude has explained:

> The finished UN Charter conferred general approval upon existing and anticipated regional organisations, but contained provisions indicating the purpose of making them serve as adjuncts to the United Nations and subjecting them in considerable measure to the direction and control of the central organisation. The Charter reflected the premise that the United Nations should be supreme, and accepted regionalism conditionally, with evidence of anxious concern that lesser agencies should be subordinated to and harmonised with the United Nations.[22]

McCoubrey and Morris view the inclusion of regional arrangements in the protection of peace and security in Article 51 as more of an afterthought of the drafters.[23] This cautious and conditional approach to the existence of regional arrangements has persisted despite the fact that regional arrangements have long been part and parcel of the

[21] See F. Knipping, H. von Mangoldt and V. Rittberger (eds), *The UN System and its Predecessors* (Oxford University Press, 1997), p. 185.

[22] Claude, *Swords into Ploughshares*, p. 114, quoted in McCoubrey and Morris, *Regional Peacekeeping*, p. 213.

[23] McCoubrey and Morris, *Regional Peacekeeping*, p. 37.

international system and more recently have become more prolific in number and activities.[24]

In the final version of the UN Charter, Chapter VIII covers 'Regional Arrangements'. Article 52(1) states:

> Nothing in the present Charter precludes the existence of regional arrangements or agencies for dealing with such matters relating to the maintenance of international peace and security as are appropriate for regional action provided that such arrangements or agencies and their activities are consistent with the Purposes and Principles of the United Nations.

Article 52(2) places an obligation on states to utilize regional arrangements, where they exist, to achieve a peaceful settlement to a local dispute before referring it to the UN Security Council, and Article 52(3) provides that the Security Council shall encourage the use of regional arrangements in this way. Under Article 53, the Security Council is, in appropriate circumstances, to make use of regional arrangements for enforcement actions and no regional arrangement may undertake enforcement action in the absence of Security Council authorization. Finally, Article 54 states that the Security Council will be kept fully informed of any activities undertaken by regional arrangements in the maintenance of international peace and security.

Commentators are in agreement that even though the UN Charter does recognize the existence and importance of regional arrangements, they remain subordinate to the universal UN system.[25] Over time it has been recognized that regional arrangements are 'fundamental' features of the international system,[26] making cooperation between regional arrangements and the United Nations 'crucial'.[27] The coexistence between global and regional arrangements is becoming accepted as a

[24] See generally B. Andemicael (ed.), *Regionalism and the United Nations* (Oceana, 1979); Richard Falk and S. Mendlovitz (eds.), *Regional Politics and World Order* (Freeman, 1973); L. Fawcett and A. Hurrell (eds.), *Regionalism in World Politics: Regional Organization and International Order* (Oxford University Press, 1995); A. Gamble and A. Payne (eds.), *Regionalism and World Order* (MacMillan, 1996); Pugh and Singh Sidhu, *The United Nations and Regional Security* (2003).

[25] See B. Simma *et al.*, *The Charter of the United Nations: A Commentary* (Oxford University Press, 1994), p. 679.

[26] UN GA Res. 51/102 GAOR 51st Sess., Supp. 49, p. 207.

[27] Report of the Secretary-General, *Regional Arrangements for the Promotion and Protection of Human Rights*, UN doc. A/51/480 (11 October 1996), para. 3.

practical way forward for international law [28] and in a number of areas the United Nations and regional arrangements have effectively worked together.[29] A significant recognition of the role and importance of regional arrangements in maintaining peace and security came when the then Secretary-General of the United Nations, Boutros Boutros-Ghali, presented his report, *An Agenda for Peace*, in 1992.[30] In this report, regional arrangements were at the forefront in terms of possible solutions to the challenges faced by the United Nations in the maintenance of peace and security. It was explained:

> regional arrangements or agencies in many cases possess a potential that should be utilized ... Under the Charter the Security Council has and will continue to have primary responsibility for maintaining international peace and security, but regional action as a matter of decentralisation, delegation and co-operation with United Nation efforts could not only lighten the burden of the Council, but also contribute to a deeper sense of participation, consensus, and democratisation of international affairs.[31]

The Secretary-General's view of regional arrangements maintains their subordinate role to the universal body but does recognize the possibility of regional arrangements playing a much more significant role in the international system. This was recognized in the follow-up to *An Agenda for Peace*, where the Secretary-General took a more cautious approach but still clearly supported the idea of regional arrangements being actively involved in the international system.[32]

[28] W. Lang, 'New Regionalism in a Changing World Order', in K. Wellens (ed.), *International Law Theory and Practice, Essays in Honour of Eric Suy* (Martinus Nijhoff, 1998), p. 32.

[29] In the maintenance of peace and security: see McCoubrey and Morris, *Regional Peacekeeping*, ch. 3; in economic and social programmes: see P. Newman, 'Regionalism in Developing Areas: UN Regional Economic Commissions and their Relations with Regional Organizations', in Andemicael, *Regionalism and the United Nations*, p. 339; E. Haas, 'The UN and Regionalism', (1970) 3 *International Relations* 796; and in environmental protection: see D. Freestone, *The Road to Rio* (University of Hull Press, 1994), pp. 8–9.

[30] *An Agenda for Peace: Preventive Diplomacy, Peacemaking and Peacekeeping*, UN doc. A/47/277-S/24111 (17 June 1992), available at www.un.org/documents/secretariat.htm

[31] *An Agenda for Peace*, para. 64.

[32] *An Agenda for Peace*, Supplement, UN doc. A/50/60-S/1995/1 (3 January 1995) available at www.un.org/documents/secretariat.htm. Information concerning cooperation between the United Nations and regional arrangements in the area of conflict prevention and peace building may be found at www.un.org/Depts/dpa/prev_dip/fr_un_cooperation.htm

There has been an increase in the number and actions of regional arrangements but international practice has not developed clear or coherent legal relationships between the regional bodies and the United Nations, with most action being described as 'improvised'.[33] As Gray explains:

> Recent practice shows a significant increase in regional activity and a new awareness of the possibilities offered by regional organizations, but some legal uncertainties remain and the problems with regional operations have become even more apparent outside the Cold War context.[34]

This problem is down to the fact that even though regional arrangements are more commonly utilized by the United Nations and seen in their own right as an important part of the international system, the idea persists that regional arrangements are somehow contrary to the United Nations' universal system. McCoubrey and Morris commented that the debate about regionalism has not changed much from the birth of the United Nations to the post-Cold War era of today, with the exception of a change in context.[35] Even though, over time, regional arrangements have achieved greater acceptance either by default, or by design, the primacy of the UN Charter is continually stressed in order to maintain the view that international law is a universal global order.[36] Suspicion remains that it is competition and not cooperation that best describes the relationship between the United Nations and regional arrangements. Given the limited resources of the United Nations and the political conflicts among members which determine its ability and direction, the United Nations cannot be expected to ensure peace and security comprehensively throughout the world.[37] Therefore, regional arrangements have to be viewed not as competitors or elements of fragmentation but rather as a means of finding the most appropriate solutions to problems faced by the international system.

[33] M. Pugh and W. Singh Sidhu, 'Introduction: The United Nations and Regional Actors', in Pugh and Singh Sidhu, *The United Nations and Regional Security*, p. 1.

[34] Gray, *International Law*, p. 201.

[35] McCoubrey and Morris, *Regional Peacekeeping*, pp. 213, 229.

[36] *An Agenda for Peace*, para. 88, quoted in McCoubrey and Morris, *Regional Peacekeeping*, p. 215.

[37] As demonstrated in the actions taken by the Economic Community of West African States (ECOWAS) with respect to events in Sierra Leone, see K. Samuels, 'Jus ad Bellum and Civil Conflicts: A Case Study of the International Community's Approach to Violence in the Conflict in Sierra Leone', (2003) 8 *Journal of Conflict and Security Law* 315.

An example of how regional arrangements can make direct and constructive contributions to universal issues can be seen in the promotion and protection of human rights. Human rights protection is an integral part of the UN system but the global body was unable in its early stages to achieve much progress in this area. During the drafting of the UN Charter, suggestions for specifically recognizing regional human rights arrangements in the Charter were rejected and proponents of this idea were accused of deviating from the purposes of the United Nations by trying to undermine the belief in the equal worth of all of humanity.[38] The concern seemed to be that different regions would recognize differing substantive norms which in turn would result in differing mechanisms for protection. However, the lack of substantive agreement at the universal level over human rights issues resulted in regional arrangements pursuing their own developments in human rights protection and eventually forced the United Nations to become more open to regional arrangements in this area.

Regional arrangements for human rights protection in Europe and the Western hemisphere were created around the same time the United Nations was struggling with its own institutions for human rights protection. In the Western hemisphere, the Organization of American States (OAS) had taken early action in the promotion and protection of human rights, adopting the American Declaration on Human Rights before the United Nations adopted the Universal Declaration on Human Rights in 1948. In both regions, Europe and the Western hemisphere, efforts concerning the promotion and protection of human rights have become well developed, demonstrating how regional arrangements can make a positive contribution in the region and for the international system as a whole.[39] In these regions the lack of agreement at the global level led directly to action at the regional level but not in a way which resulted in the undermining of the universal goals of the human rights project as expressed in the Universal Declaration on Human Rights. In both Europe and the Western hemisphere, the human rights systems which were formed explicitly trace their basis to the Universal Declaration, creating a direct link between the regional and universal.[40]

[38] B. Weston, *et al.*, 'Regional Human Rights Regimes: A Comparison and Appraisal', (1987) 20 *Vanderbilt Journal of Transnational Law* 588.

[39] *Ibid.*, p. 588.

[40] See the Preambles to the American Convention on Human Rights and the European Convention on Human Rights.

The efforts of regional arrangements in Europe and the Western hemisphere in the promotion and protection of human rights has demonstrated that universal norms can be developed and improved upon in a regional setting and are able to achieve workable and acceptable principles of actual application.[41] In turn, the work of the United Nations in the area of human rights protection has greatly benefited from the lessons learned in the regional systems, demonstrating the need for complimentary coordination and cooperation rather than competition.[42] We are able to see a similar development in the promotion and protection of democracy within international law. In the Western hemisphere and Europe, democracy has long been a condition of membership for the regional arrangements, at least in rhetoric. This rhetoric has gained strength over time, leading to the creation of mechanisms to ensure member states meet a variety of obligations concerning democracy. At the UN level, democracy has only very recently been mentioned in the work of the organization and does not have any explicit legal status in the UN framework.[43] The United Nations is developing mechanisms for the promotion and protection of democracy, primarily through the work of its human rights bodies and election-monitoring activities, but it does not have any specific enforcement or monitoring mechanisms in place.[44] As the United Nations attempts to broaden its institutional capacity in this area, the work of regional organizations which have preceded it will be useful guides and an area for inter-institutional cooperation in attempting to

[41] T. Meron, 'Norm Making and Supervision in International Human Rights: Reflections on Institutional Order', (1982) 76 *American Journal of International Law* 761.

[42] A. A. Cançado Trindade, 'Co-ordination of Mechanisms of International Protection of Human Rights (at Global and Regional Levels)', (1987-II) 202 *Hague Academy Collected Courses* 122. A point recognized by Boutros-Ghali while he was Secretary-General of the United Nations, see B. Boutros-Ghali, 'The UN and Democracy', (1995) 4 *Law and Public Policy* 12.

[43] The ICCPR protects self-determination and political participation but there is no requirement for a state to be democratic, even though some commentators contend that a state must be democratic in order to meet its obligations under the Covenant, see M. Nowak, *United Nations Covenant on Civil and Political Rights: CCPR Commentary* (Engel, 1993), p. 441. At the same time, UN treaty-monitoring bodies have stated that the treaties are ideologically neutral, see UN Committee on Economic, Social and Cultural Rights, General Comment No. 3 (1990), UN doc. E/1991/23.

[44] For an overview see N. D. White, 'The UN and Democracy Assistance: Developing Practice within a Constitutional Framework', in P. Burnell (ed.), *Democracy Assistance: International Co-operation for Democratization* (Frank Cass, 2000), p. 67.

address a specific issue in the international system which contributes to international peace and security.

Regional arrangements in the Western hemisphere and Europe have identified the promotion and protection of democracy as an important aspect of peace and security in the region. In what follows the work of two regional organizations, the Organization of American States (OAS), and the Organization for Security and Co-operation in Europe (OSCE), in the field of the promotion and protection of democracy will be examined. This examination will demonstrate how regional arrangements have been able to foster the necessary cooperation and agreement in addressing a particular area that the United Nations has been unable to act upon.

Organization of American States

The current OAS has evolved out of a long history of regional cooperation that predates the United Nations and even the League of Nations. Every state of the Western hemisphere is a member of the OAS, but the government of Cuba was excluded from participation in 1962, a move obviously connected with the political inclinations of the regional superpower.[45] The member states of the OAS possess a great deal of diversity within and between themselves but they also share numerous common traits. From the earliest attempts at inter-American regional cooperation there has been a concern with democracy.[46] Institutions and mechanisms for the promotion and protection of democracy have long been a part of inter-American relations but these measures have also been unable to make any substantial impact until most recently. This history of the OAS is marked more by rhetorical support for democracy and human rights than substantive efforts to ensure their promotion and protection. Even today, the existence of democracy in the region is extremely fragile, making the presence of a regional arrangement essential in the ongoing struggle to further democracy as an element of peace and security in the region.

[45] The exclusion of Cuba for a lack of democracy did not set a precedent for action as the principle was not applied to subsequent authoritarian regimes, see A. Thomas and A. Thomas, *The Organization of American States* (SMU Press, 1963), p. 221.

[46] Inter-American Institute, *The Inter-American System: Its Development and Strengthening* (Oceana, 1966), p. xv.

The promotion and protection of democracy in the region begins with the OAS Charter[47] which entered into force in 1951 and has been amended by the Protocol of Buenos Aires (1967), the Protocol of Cartagena de Indias (1985), the Protocol of Washington (1992) and the Protocol of Managua (1993). These changes to the OAS Charter have come in response to events occurring in the region as the OAS has tried to keep pace with the shifting political, social and economic environment, attempting to consolidate further democracy, human rights and economic and social progress.[48] Prior to the Protocol of Cartagena de Indias, references to democracy in the OAS Charter were minimal even though the overall aims of the organization were linked to the effective exercise of political democracy.[49] The Protocol of Cartagena de Indias introduced the promotion of democracy as a purpose of the OAS as well as granting the Secretary-General the authorization to bring to the attention of the General Assembly matters which may affect peace and security in the region. At the same time the Protocol also reinforced the provisions in the OAS Charter dealing with non-intervention and the inability of the OAS to take substantive action with regard to the member states.[50] In the context of the overall mood in favour of democracy in the early 1990s, the OAS adopted the Protocol of Washington introducing into the OAS Charter specific legal commitments to democracy along with procedures for enforcement.

In its current form the Preamble to the Charter articulates the idea that 'representative democracy is an indispensable condition for the stability, peace and development of the region' and relations in the region are based upon efforts to consolidate and develop democracy. Article 2 contains the purposes of the OAS, first and foremost of which is to strengthen peace and security in the region, followed by the promotion and consolidation of representative democracy. Also included as a purpose is the promotion of economic, social and cultural development and the eradication of extreme poverty, which is said to constitute an obstacle to full democratic development. Article 3 outlines the principles

[47] OAS Treaty Series No. 1-E, OEA/Ser.A/2, Rev.5.

[48] S. Davidson, *The Inter-American Human Rights System* (Dartmouth, 1997), pp. 3–4; J. Arrighi, 'Les Reformes à la Charte de L'Organisation des Etats Americains: Problemes de Droit des Traites', (1997) 43 *Annuaire Francais de Droit International* 93.

[49] See D. Shelton, 'Representative Democracy and Human Rights in the Western Hemisphere', (1991) 12 *Human Rights Law Journal* 353.

[50] *Ibid.*, p. 354.

to which the member states are to adhere. These include the condemnation of wars of aggression, the use of peaceful procedures to settle disputes and the requirement that the political organization of member states is based on the effective exercise of representative democracy. Also contained in Article 3 is the right of every member state to choose, without external interference, political, economic and social systems in a way best suited to it and that other members have a duty to abstain from intervening in the affairs of another state. Finally, the elimination of extreme poverty, the promotion and consolidation of representative democracy and social justice are seen as means to lasting peace and cooperation in the region.

Article 3 sets the basis for a requirement of democracy for OAS members and Article 9 further develops this. In Article 9 it is stipulated that '[a] Member of the Organisation whose democratically constituted government has been overthrown by force may be suspended from the exercise of the right to participate' in the workings of the OAS. Article 9 further specifies the action to be taken against an offending state, including diplomatic measures to restore democracy and ultimately exclusion from the organization. Exclusion is to be as a last resort for continued efforts will be made by the OAS to ensure the suspended state fulfils its obligations in relation to democracy and any member state that is suspended will continue to be bound by commitments agreed to in the OAS Charter framework. Any decision in relation to suspension is to be taken by the General Assembly of the OAS through an affirmative vote in favour of suspension adopted by two-thirds of the member states. The provisions of Article 9 and their legal force have been disputed. Mexico has declared that 'democracy is a process which comes from the sovereign will of the people, and cannot be imposed from outside'. The government expressed the belief that 'it is unacceptable to give to regional organizations supranational powers and instruments for intervening in the internal affairs of our states'.[51] Regardless of the views of Mexico, the OAS has expanded upon Article 9 of the OAS Charter to further enhance the ability of the organization to promote and protect democracy.

This expansion has come in the form of resolutions accepted by the OAS General Assembly, based upon the commitments agreed to in the OAS Charter, establishing further specific procedures empowering the organization to take direct action in the promotion and protection

[51] OEA Ser.A/2 Add.3, General Information of the Treaty A-56.

of democracy in the region. The Santiago Commitment to Democracy,[52] issued in 1991, declared the dedication of the OAS to the defence and promotion of democracy as a necessary advancement in the region and recognized the importance of efforts at consolidating democracy in the region.[53] This led to the adoption of Resolution 1080 by the OAS General Assembly in 1991.[54] In its Preamble, the Resolution declares that the Charter of the OAS 'establishes that representative democracy is an indispensable condition for the stability, peace, and development of the region'. Resolution 1080 states that the interruption of legitimately elected government in the region is grounds for collective action taken by the OAS in order to re-establish a democratic government in line with the obligations of the OAS Charter. The Resolution calls for the convocation of the Permanent Council of the OAS in the event of 'sudden, or irregular interruption of the democratic political institutional process' with a view to finding a solution and ensuring the continuance of democracy. The role of the Permanent Council is to find a peaceful negotiated settlement but if that fails action may be taken under Article 9 of the OAS Charter.

The process set up by Resolution 1080 was further supported through the Declaration of Quebec City (2001) where it was stated that the values and practices of democracy are fundamental to the region and any disruption of a democracy will put into motion the regional response mechanisms. The Declaration places a good deal of importance on the existence of democracy as an essential element of peaceful and cooperative relations in the region. The Declaration of Quebec City led to the Inter-American Democratic Charter adopted by the OAS General Assembly in Peru on 11 September 2001. As with Resolution 1080, the Democratic Charter recognizes that democracy is 'indispensable for the stability, peace, and development of the region'. The Democratic Charter further elaborates on the procedures to be followed when democracy is under threat. Articles 17 and 18 provide that any government which feels that its democratic institutional process is under threat may request assistance from the OAS. In the event of an unconstitutional interruption of democracy in a member state, Articles 19 to 22 detail procedures which will be followed. These include possible suspension of the state in question from the workings of the organization, convocation of

52 OEA/Ser. P AG/DOC.2734/91.

53 V. Vaky, *The Future of the Organization of American States* (Twentieth Century Fund, 1993), p. 13.

54 AG/RES. 1080 (XXI-0/91).

the Permanent Council and possibly the OAS General Assembly in order to pursue diplomatic initiatives to restore democracy.

The measures developed by the OAS for the promotion and protection of democracy have not been confined to rhetorical support for democracy. The organization has taken direct action in the cases of Haiti (1991), Peru (1992), Guatemala (1993), Paraguay (1996), Ecuador (2000) and Venezuela (2002).[55] In each situation a range of factors, domestic, regional and international, contributed to the lessening or ending of the crisis where democracy was under threat. In Haiti, despite differences of opinion as to the nature and degree of action that should be taken to protect democracy, the OAS and United Nations demonstrated that regional and universal arrangements are able to cooperate in the pursuit of common goals related to the maintenance of international peace and security.[56]

In each case where the OAS has taken direct action to protect democracy in a member state, the democratic system that is in place is fragile at best and in many respects remains under threat. While the action of the OAS was by no means decisive and as recent events in Haiti have demonstrated, the regional arrangement cannot guarantee the long-term existence of democracy, its efforts in this area have made a positive contribution to peace and security in the region. The democracy which exists in many of the member states is far from ideal but there is an ongoing commitment to improve upon and support these democratic structures. The OAS has made it clear for the region that non-democratic forms of government are unacceptable. On the basis of the OAS Charter commitments and General Assembly resolutions, institutions like the Unit for the Promotion of Democracy (UPD) and the Inter-American Commission and Court on Human Rights are able actively to engage in the promotion and protection of democracy as well.[57] These support activities are crucial for preventing possible future conflict when

[55] See the discussion in McCoubrey and Morris, *Regional Peacekeeping*, pp. 108–21. Also 'The Role of the OAS is Underscored in the Defense and Promotion of Democracy in the Hemisphere', OAS Press Release E-039/01 (21 February 2001) available from www.oas.org

[56] See M. Herz, 'Managing Security in the Western Hemisphere: The OAS's New Activism', in Pugh and Singh Sidhu, *The United Nations and Regional Security*, pp. 219–24.

[57] See e.g. the discussion in *Constitutional Court* case, Inter-American Court of Human Rights, Series C, No. 71, judgment of 31 January 2001. Also R. Burchill, 'The Role of Democracy in the Protection of Human Rights: Lessons from the European and Inter-American Human Rights Systems', in David Forsythe and Patrice McMahon (eds.), *Human Rights and Diversity: Area Studies Revisited* (University of Nebraska Press, 2003), pp. 137–56.

democratic structures break down as they attempt to deal with matters before the democratic process collapses and peaceful settlement becomes remote. The work of the UPD is extensive involving support for the building of democratic institutions, assisting in all aspects of the electoral process, acting as a centre for information and dialogue on democracy issues and hosting and participating in specific programmes aimed at democratization efforts in particular states.[58]

The actions of the OAS in promoting and protecting democracy have demonstrated that Mexico's position discussed above concerning the involvement of an external entity in what are considered solely domestic affairs has been overcome. Mexico's belief that the OAS's support for democracy is contrary to the principle of non-intervention in the domestic affairs of states is not surprising given the interventionist position of the USA in the region.[59] The principle of non-intervention is equally enshrined in the OAS Charter, in Article 19, but this has not prevented the ability of the OAS to take action for the promotion and protection of democracy in the region. Article 23 of the OAS Charter provides that the principle of non-intervention does not apply when measures are taken 'for the maintenance of peace and security in accordance with existing treaties'. Articles 2 and 3 of the Charter make a direct link between the effective functioning of representative democracy and peace and security for the region. This is a significant development within the idea of comprehensive security as it prevents states from utilizing the non-intervention provisions in order to frustrate the work of the OAS in relation to the promotion and protection of democracy.

Critics would rightly note that the OAS has not been wholly successful in its efforts to promote and protect democracy in the region, as a good deal of instability remains as a result of weak democratic systems. The rhetoric in favour of democracy has been strong, but effective practice has been rare in the region with a major factor being the influence and dominance of a superpower in the region.[60] However, with the end of

[58] Full details of the UPD can be found at www.upd.oas.org/lab/main.html Also see R. Burchill, 'Consolidating Transitions: The Role of the OAS in Support for Democracy in the Western Hemisphere' available at www.psa.ac.uk/cps/1999/burchill.pdf

[59] See the remarks by the Minister of Foreign Affairs for Trinidad and Tobago, Statement made during the Dialogue of Heads of Delegation of the XXXII Regular Session of the OAS General Assembly, Barbados, 4 June 2002, available at www.oas.org/XXXIIGA/english/speeches/speech_Trinidad2.htm

[60] See McCoubrey and Morris, *Regional Peacekeeping*, p. 96.

the Cold War the desire for democracy in the region has gradually evolved from rhetoric to actual action as the OAS has found a variety of ways to promote and protect democracy in the region.[61] The OAS has made substantial progress in overcoming the strict adherence of states to the principle of non-intervention in domestic affairs and developing collective responses to the promotion and protection of democracy as a means of ensuring peace and security in the region.[62] The institutional arrangements in place for the OAS may act as models to be examined and considered by other regional arrangements interested in the promotion and protection of democracy as well as the United Nations, if it is ever able to consider such mechanisms as part of its efforts to further international peace and security.

The OSCE and the High Commissioner on National Minorities

Europe possesses a high level of integration with a number of regional arrangements existing across a range of competences. The positive elements of regionalism discussed above have been demonstrated in the regional organizations of Europe. In this section only one of these organizations, the OSCE, will be examined and even then only one particular institution, the High Commission on National Minorities (HCNM) will be discussed. The OSCE has outpaced international law in relation to minority rights and remains at the forefront in developing and implementing minority protection regimes as an integral part of efforts to bolster peace and security in the region. A central element to the OSCE's minority protection regime has been the promotion and protection of democracy as it has proven to be essential to the lessening of tensions between minority groups and the state within which they are located. While democracy is commonly equated to majority rule, it is this same aspect that leads to tensions between the majority and minorities which in turn has a direct impact on state and regional security as evidenced by events in the former Yugoslavia. The OSCE and HCNM have recognized that fully inclusive democratic systems are crucial for

[61] T. Farer, 'Collectively Defending Democracy in the Western Hemisphere: Introduction and Overview', in T. Farer (ed.), *Beyond Sovereignty: Collectively Defending Democracy in the Americas* (John Hopkins University Press, 1996), pp. 9–11.

[62] See J. Dominguez and A. Lowenthal (eds.), *Constructing Democratic Governance: Latin America and the Caribbean in the 1990s* (John Hopkins University Press, 1996), p. 5.

security in the region as they work to prevent tensions between groups escalating into violent conflict.

The current OSCE has fifty-five members ranging from the USA and Canada, all states of Europe and many of the former Soviet republics in Central Asia. The membership is highly diverse but there is a common concern for security in the region. The original CSCE was a product of the Cold War and its development into the OSCE has reflected the changing nature of peace and security in Europe as the organization has expanded its institutional competences and resources.[63] With the end of Communist-led regimes in Europe the OSCE moved to take a larger role in the area of security and conflict prevention in Europe based on the idea that preventing human rights abuses and ensuring democracy are essential to peace and security in the region. The OSCE strives to support a system of comprehensive security whereby peace and security is understood as relating to conventional political and military concerns but also incorporates concern for human rights and democracy as key features of conflict prevention.[64]

The OSCE's approach to the promotion and protection of democracy as a key aspect of comprehensive security in the region began in earnest with the 1990 Copenhagen Concluding Document.[65] The Copenhagen Document states that full respect for human rights, fundamental freedoms, pluralistic democracy and the rule of law are prerequisites for establishing peace and security in Europe.[66] Through the Copenhagen Document the OSCE states have committed themselves to multiparty democracy based on free, periodic and genuine elections, the rule of law and equal protection under the law for all based on respect for human rights and effective, accessible and just legal systems. The Document recognizes the need for the active involvement of all persons, groups, organizations and institutions to ensure the continual progress of the democratization process. It goes on to make specific mention of the position of national minorities within democratic systems[67] and

[63] For a review of OSCE developments see Arie Bloed (ed.), *The Challenges of Change: The Helsinki Summit and its Aftermath* (Martinus Nijhoff, 1994); M. Lucas (ed.), *The CSCE in the 1990s: Constructing European Security and Cooperation* (Nomos, 1993).

[64] See *OSCE Handbook* (3rd edn, Vienna, 2000), pp. 1–2.

[65] T. Buergenthal, 'The Copenhagen CSCE Meeting: A New Public Order for Europe', (1990) 11 *Human Rights Law Journal* 221; M. Halberstam, 'The Copenhagen Document: Intervention in Support of Democracy', (1993) 34 *Harvard International Law Journal* 164. The Copenhagen Concluding Document is available at www.osce.org/docs/english/1990–1999/hd/cope90e.htm

[66] Copenhagen Concluding Document, Preamble. [67] *Ibid.*, para. 30.

the need to ensure constructive cooperation on questions relating to national minorities as a means of promoting friendly and good-neighbourly relations, international peace and security.[68]

The Copenhagen Document was further strengthened by the Charter of Paris for a New Europe agreed to by the OSCE Heads of State and Government later in 1991.[69] In the Charter of Paris, the participating states agree that peace and security in the region depend upon 'the advancement of democracy, and respect for and effective exercise of human rights'. With the Cold War over, the OSCE steadily expanded its areas of concern in relation to security issues in the region and a major element of these activities was minority protection. The events in the former Yugoslavia quickly demonstrated that the new Europe was not an area of peace or security and that the position of minority groups was a key factor in security. The OSCE recognized the need for an institutional arrangement that would be able to address and hopefully settle the underlying problems related to ethnic tensions in the region and prevent escalation into outright violence. At the Helsinki Summit Meeting of 1992 it was agreed to establish the post of the High Commissioner on National Minorities as a conflict prevention tool contributing to peace and security in the region.[70]

The mandate of the HCNM was included under the security provisions of the 1992 Helsinki Document as the participating states acknowledged that the tensions and problems involving national minorities could develop into insecurity and potentially violent conflict.[71] The HCNM's responsibility is to identify and seek early resolution of ethnic tensions that might endanger peace, stability or friendly relations between the participating states of the OSCE.[72] The HCNM is described as 'an instrument of conflict prevention' that will:

> provide 'early warning' and, as appropriate, 'early action' at the earliest possible stage in regard to tensions involving national minority issues which have not yet developed beyond an early warning stage, but, in the judgement of the High Commissioner, have the potential to develop into a conflict within the [OSCE] area, affecting peace, stability or relations between participating States.[73]

[68] *Ibid.* [69] Available at www.osce.org/docs/english/summite.htm

[70] Helsinki Summit Declaration, 'The Challenges of Change', 9–10 July 1992, available at www.osce.org/docs/english/1990–1999/summits/hels92e.htm

[71] F. Timmermans, 'The Activities of the OSCE High Commissioner on National Minorities in Conflict Prevention', (1995/6) 1/2 *OSCE Yearbook* 365 at p. 366.

[72] The Mandate of the HCNM is included in the Helsinki Summit Declaration.

[73] Mandate, para. 3.

The HCNM was created as and remains an instrument of security promotion and conflict prevention. However, in doing so it works within the expanded understanding of comprehensive security making the promotion and protection of democracy an important aspect of its efforts to lessen tensions involving minorities.

The HCNM works in confidence and independent of all the parties concerned, and will not become involved in situations where violence is already being used by any of the parties concerned.[74] In approaching any situation where the HCNM has decided to become involved, account will be taken of 'the availability of democratic means and international instruments' in order to address the causes of the existing tensions.[75] To this end, the HCNM uses a wide range of existing international standards concerning the position of minorities in society, both regional and universal, regardless of the source.[76] The HCNM does not attempt to 'enforce' these standards, instead they are used in discussions mainly with governments to remind them of the obligations they have agreed to under international law and how adherence to these obligations will help to ensure open conflict is avoided.[77] The international standards will also act as a framework for resolving tensions so their use by the HCNM will vary depending upon the particular circumstances faced.[78] The HCNM has remarked:

> While one must not go below minimum international standards, it is important to apply these standards in the specific context of the states concerned ... One must be sensitive to the local conditions in order to best explain to the parties the reasons and possibilities for applying the relevant norms and standards.[79]

[74] *Ibid.*, para. 5b. [75] *Ibid.*, para. 6.

[76] W. Kemp (ed.), *Quiet Diplomacy in Action: The OSCE High Commissioner on National Minorities* (Kluwer, 2001), p. 25.

[77] See e.g. REF. 359/97/L, Letter to the Minister for Foreign Affairs of the Republic of Estonia, where there is an extensive discussion on the application of the UN Convention on the Rights of the Child in relation to Estonian naturalization laws, available at www.osce.org/hcnm/documents/recommendations/estonia/index.php

[78] Report of HCNM to the OSCE Implementation Meeting on Human Dimension Issues, Warsaw (2 October 1995), available at www.osce.org/hcnm/documents/speeches/1995/ See also Kemp, *Quiet Diplomacy in Action*, p. 26.

[79] 'Rapid Pro-action: Identifying and Addressing Sources of Conflict', address to Wilton Park Conference, London (1 July 2002) available at www.osce.org/hcnm/documents/speeches/2002/

This demonstrates the importance of international and regional standards working together in order to address specific problems in particular circumstances and the futility of trying to impose singular models, either universal or regional, upon all situations.

Quite often the cause of tensions involving minority groups includes issues of rights, participation and inclusion, essential elements to democracy.[80] This is why the Mandate of the HCNM makes clear it is necessary to take 'into account the availability of democratic means' in order to resolve a situation.[81] The importance of democracy in trying to resolve tensions involving national minorities has been confirmed by the HCNM, who stated that 'the democratic functioning of effective public institutions can increase popular trust in government and lessen the basis for ethnic conflict'.[82] It has also been explained that minority protection is to be the litmus test of democratization: if states are not prepared to grant special rights to minority communities populating their territory, their commitment to democracy appears doubtful.[83] The HCNM has demonstrated a firm belief in democracy as it is 'the pivotal element in [the OSCE's] mandate as a co-operative security organisation'.[84] Often the work of the HCNM will focus on language or education rights for minorities, areas many would feel are not connected to the promotion and protection of democracy. But as the HCNM has explained, language and education rights are matters of good governance in a democratic state, which, if ignored, can easily lead to ethnic tensions.[85] Overall it is the role of the HCNM 'to support the participation

[80] 'Early Warning and Early Action: Preventing Inter-Ethnic Conflict', speech by HCNM at the Royal Institute of International Affairs, London, 9 July 1999, available at www.osce.org/hcnm/documents/speeches/1999/

[81] Mandate, para. 6.

[82] 'International Response to Ethnic Conflicts: Focusing on Prevention', address to Martin Ennals Memorial Symposium, Saskatoon, 6 March 1993, available at www.osce.org/hcnm/documents/speeches/1993/

[83] 'Controlling Ethnic Tensions in Europe: the Experience of the CSCE High Commissioner on National Minorities', address to the Oxford University civil liberties society, 28 October 1994, available at www.osce.org/hcnm/documents/speeches/1994/

[84] 'Expectations of Future Cooperation between the OSCE High Commissioner on National Minorities and Latvia', address to Conference 'OSCE and Latvia: Past, Present and Future', Riga, 20 March 2002, available at www.osce.org/hcnm/documents/speeches/2002/

[85] See the Oslo Recommendations regarding the Linguistic Rights of National Minorities (February 1998), the Hague Recommendations regarding the Education Rights of National Minorities (October 1996) available at www.osce.org/hcnm/documents/recommendations/

of minorities, citizens or non-citizens, in the political and social life of their country of residence, to the extent laid down in international law and developed as democratic practice in a European context'.[86]

The HCNM has been actively involved in over fourteen states, mainly in Central and Eastern Europe. Sometimes the involvement is brief; in other cases a more protracted commitment is necessary. As the work of the HCNM is carried out in confidence there is little evidence available by which to evaluate the impact of the office. The HCNM does publish formal recommendations given to the states it has been involved in and these provide at least a glimpse as to what the HCNM is trying to achieve in a particular situation.[87] Often a central concern in the recommendations is the ability of minority groups to be active participants in the states in which they live and not to be subjected to arbitrary or discriminatory laws, central features of any democratic system and an effective means for ensuring peace and security.[88] To assist in this the HCNM commissioned a series of meetings by experts which resulted in the *Lund Recommendations on the Effective Participation of National Minorities in Public Life.*[89] The Lund Recommendations build upon existing international standards related to minority rights and set out twenty-four individual recommendations for ensuring effective minority participation in matters of governance relating to the state as a whole and in relation to aspects of self-governance for minority groups. Fostering and maintaining democratic systems responsive to minorities is crucial in Europe, as explained in the first principle of the Lund Recommendations:

> Effective participation of national minorities in public life is an essential component of a peaceful and democratic society. Experience in Europe and elsewhere has shown that, in order to promote such participation, governments often need to establish specific arrangements for national minorities.

86 See 'Expectations of Future Cooperation between the OSCE High Commissioner on National Minorities and Latvia'.

87 A full list of recommendations can be found at www.osce.org/hcnm/documents/recommendations/

88 'Human Rights, the Prevention of Conflict and the International Protection of Minorities: A Contemporary Paradigm for Contemporary Challenges', speech at the London School of Economics, 19 October 1999, available at www.osce.org/hcnm/documents/speeches/1999/

89 The Lund Recommendations on the Effective Participation of National Minorities in Public Life and Explanatory Note, Foundation on Inter-Ethnic Relations, September 1999, available at www.osce.org/hcnm/documents/recommendations/

The Recommendations directly link effective democratic structures responsive to the situation of minority groups with the protection of peace.[90] The Lund Recommendations bring together international and regional developments relating to minorities and democracy, another clear example as to how the regional and the universal can cooperate in addressing specific issues.

The office of the HCNM is undoubtedly unique. It is well known that conflict prevention is more desirable than conflict management but successful conflict prevention mechanisms are rare in international law.[91] The creation of the HCNM was in response to particular events in Europe but in pursuing its mandate the HCNM has relied upon both regional and international standards. Getting states to agree on any aspect of minority rights is difficult. The UN General Assembly adopted in 1992 the Declaration on the Rights of Persons Belonging to National or Ethnic, Religious and Linguistic Minorities, which remains the only UN instrument that directly addresses minority rights in a separate document. In 1995, a UN Working Group on Minorities was created but this is as far as it goes at the global level.

The HCNM demonstrates the ability of a regional arrangement to agree upon basic standards and implementation mechanisms in an area that has proven too difficult to foster agreement and action at the global level. The key feature to the success of the HCNM is its role in conflict prevention, which provides clear lessons for similar efforts by both regional and universal arrangements.[92] It has been asserted that having early warning mechanisms in place that deal with issues related to democracy is essential to the maintenance of peace and security.[93] The experiences of the HCNM have demonstrated that efforts to secure comprehensive security with the promotion and protection of

[90] See General Principle I and Explanatory Notes.

[91] 'Editor's Preface', in W. Zellner and F. Lange (eds.), *Peace and Stability Through Human and Minority Rights: Speeches by the OSCE High Commissioner on National Minorities* (Nomos Verlagsgesellschaft, 1999), p. 9. Also in *An Agenda for Peace* it is explained 'The most desirable and efficient employment of diplomacy is to ease tensions before they result in conflict – or, if conflict breaks out, to act swiftly to contain it and resolve its underlying causes', at para. 23.

[92] J. Packer, 'Conflict Prevention by the OAU: The Relevance of the OSCE High Commissioner on National Minorities', (1996) 4 *African Yearbook of International Law* 279.

[93] B. G. Ramcharan, *The International Law and Practice of Early-Warning and Preventative Diplomacy: The Emerging Global Watch* (Martinus Nijhoff, 1991), pp. 32 and 35–6.

democracy as a major factor directly contribute to peace and security, regionally and globally.

Conclusion

Helping to ensure the maintenance of international peace and security through the promotion and protection of democracy relies upon efforts at all levels of the international system, an area that remains full of potential in fostering cooperation among regional and global arrangements. By focusing on regional arrangements we are able to derive both theoretical and practical mechanisms allowing for action which falls between the 'discreteness of the State and the undifferentiated international system'.[94] Any effective system for the promotion and protection of democracy in international law will depend upon the various contributions to be made by regional and universal arrangements; allowing for difference but at the same time preventing abuses justified by diversity. In the promotion and protection of democracy, diversity should not be seen as a threat to the coherence of the international system, instead it needs to be seen as strengthening a universal approach by providing deeper understandings as to the meaning of democracy in differing contexts.

Since the end of the Cold War, the promotion and protection of democracy has come to be seen as an essential element of peace and security in the international system.[95] The OAS and OSCE promote democracy as an essential part of peace and security for their particular region, which in turn makes a direct contribution to the efforts of the United Nations in the maintenance of international peace and security. The ability of these two regional arrangements to foster agreement and create mechanisms in support of democracy is directly related to the nature of the particular regional arrangements where there exists broad consensus, a similarity of views in addressing common problems, and an effective use of resources. Issues of size, diversity and widespread

[94] L. Cantori and S. Spiegel, 'The Analysis of Regional International Politics: The Integration versus the Empirical Systems Approach', (1973) 27 *International Organization* 467; H. Bull, *The Anarchical Society: A Study in World Politics* (1st edn, MacMillan, 1977), p. 305.

[95] See e.g. the various declarations by Commission on Human Rights, 58th Session, 18 March – 26 April 2002, Declaration 2002/12 'Situation of Human Rights in Burundi', Declaration 2002/13 'Situation of Human Rights in Parts of South-eastern Europe', Declaration 2002/16 'Situation of Human Rights in the Sudan', available at www.unhchr.ch

animosity among neighbours have significantly hindered the development and contribution of regional arrangements in other parts of the world but the possibility for closer cooperation remains.[96] The ongoing success of the OAS and the OSCE in strengthening international peace and security through the promotion and protection of democracy is down to the fact that cooperation is fairly commonplace in each of the regions and occurs not in competition with the universal body of the United Nations, but for the most part in the spirit of cooperation.

The work of the OAS and HCNM in the promotion and protection of democracy demonstrates that there is no such thing as a 'one size fits all' solution to the issues facing the international system. In both cases, the regional arrangements have been able to develop principles and mechanisms in support of democracy that are unlikely to be seen at the global level anytime soon. McCoubrey and Morris felt that recourse to regional arrangements provides neither a simple nor a singular solution to the problems faced in ensuring peace and security[97] and the discussion above clearly demonstrates this. The future, then, needs to be based not on competition between the regional and the global nor on stark choices in favour of one approach or the other. Constructive solutions must be pursued making full use of the wide range of resources available for the ongoing maintenance of international peace and security. The promotion and protection of democracy is a key element in the maintenance of international peace and security and regional arrangements have demonstrated an ability to make significant developments in this regard. Their efforts undoubtedly contribute to international peace and security without undermining the global project of the United Nations, demonstrating there is no need to make stark choices between regional or universal. Instead, efforts need to be seen as complementing the pursuit of shared goals and objectives and not competition leading to fragmentation.

[96] McCoubrey and Morris, *Regional Peacekeeping*, p. 150; they discuss the potential for regional cooperation in Africa, Asia and the Arab region in chs. 6–8.

[97] McCoubrey and Morris, *Regional Peacekeeping*, p. 243.

12

Self-defence, Security Council authority and Iraq

NIGEL D. WHITE

Introduction

It is not possible to understand the threat and then the use of force against Iraq by the USA and the United Kingdom in 2003 without understanding the developments that have occurred in state practice since the Gulf Conflict of 1991. In the period after 1993, the USA and the United Kingdom, sometimes with other states, have placed incredible pressure on the legal framework governing the use of force contained in the UN Charter in a concerted effort to widen both exceptions to the ban on the threat or use of force in Article 2(4), namely the right of self-defence contained in Article 51, and military action taken under the authority of the Security Council derived from Article 42. While in 1991, Operation Desert Storm conducted by the Coalition of states against Iraq, under American command, but with UN Security Council authority, was generally viewed as lawful (by Hilaire and myself amongst many others),[1] the military action taken against Iraq commencing on 20 March 2003 was much more controversial. After the adoption of Resolution 1441 on 8 November 2002, the USA and the United Kingdom brought the above-mentioned pressures to bear by making claims that the resolution was by itself sufficient to justify the use of force against Iraq, even though it did not contain clear authorizing language. Furthermore, the USA claimed that even if the resolution did not authorize force, and in the absence of a further clearer resolution, it still had the right to use force in self-defence against the threat

I would like to thank Neil Boister, Robert Cryer, Robert McCorquodale and Eric Myjer for their helpful comments on an earlier draft. This chapter is based on papers given at the British International Studies Conference in London, December 2002, and a symposium on the Iraq Crisis held at the University of West of England, March 2003.

[1] See N. D. White and H. McCoubrey, 'International Law and the Use of Force in the Gulf', (1991) *International Relations* 347.

posed against it by Iraq. According to this view, the use of force against Iraq was justified under either or both exceptions to the ban on the use of force, despite the fact that Resolution 1441 did not authorize measures necessary against Iraq (the accepted mode of delegation under Article 42) and the fact that there had been no armed attack against the USA by Iraq within the meaning of Article 51. This chapter examines the process by which this position was reached and considers its legality.

Pre-emptive defence

The starting point of this chapter is the Bush Doctrine, or more formally 'The National Security Strategy of the United States of America', promulgated on 17 September 2002.[2] It represents the latest in a long line of US Presidential doctrines going back to the Monroe Doctrine of 1823.[3] Specifically on the issue of using force, and in response to the events of 11 September 2001, the Doctrine focuses on the recent and continuing threat posed by 'terrorist organizations of global reach and any terrorist or state sponsor of terrorism which attempts to gain or use weapons of mass destruction (WMD) or their precursors'. This signifies that the USA is committed to 'identifying and destroying the threat before it reaches' American borders, acting alone if necessary, 'to exercise our right of self-defense by acting preemptively against such terrorists, to prevent them from doing harm against our people and our country'. Further, the USA is prepared 'to stop rogue states and their terrorist clients before they are able to threaten or use weapons of mass destruction against the United States and [its] allies and friends'. This sort of pre-emptive strike is viewed by the USA as an adaptation of the doctrine of anticipatory self-defence stated to be recognized by international law, allowing nations 'to defend themselves against forces that present an imminent danger of attack'. The adaptation signifies that the emphasis is no longer on the imminence of the attack but the magnitude of the threat. 'The greater the threat, the greater is the risk of inaction – and the more compelling the case for taking anticipatory action to defend ourselves, even if uncertainty remains as to the time and place of the enemy's attack.' Deterrence, it is claimed, cannot be relied upon as the

[2] The National Security Strategy of the United States of America, September 2002, available at www.whitehouse.gov/nsc/nss.pdf

[3] See generally H. McCoubrey and N. D. White, *International Law and Armed Conflict* (Dartmouth, 1992), pp. 26–30.

mechanism for securing peace, positive action is posited as 'the only path to peace and security'.[4]

Unlike the previous post-1945 Presidential doctrines that juxtaposed a statement of political intent against an acceptance of the narrower strictures of international law, the Bush Doctrine not only constitutes a statement of political intent, it also constitutes an exposition on the conditions under which the USA views the use of force as acceptable under international law. Between the end of the Second World War and the announcement of the Bush Doctrine it was common for the political statements of the incumbent President on issues of power to be balanced by more legal statements of American representatives, for example in the Security Council.[5]

International lawyers would concede that Article 2(4) was not always adhered to during the Cold War since, despite the legal protestations of the USA and the USSR, both direct hemispheric and indirect extra-hemispheric interventions regularly occurred that were clearly breaches of that norm. However, Article 2(4) survived for, to paraphrase the words of the International Court of Justice in the *Nicaragua* case, all the relevant actors – the victim states and the intervening states – appealed to the rule and its exceptions, and the general attitude of the rest of the world was one of condemnation for breach of the rule.[6] Law did not prevent superpower interventions but it did appear to play a significant role. Debates and controversy centred around the applicability of the rules governing the use of force but the presence of the legal rules and principles signified that the 'controversy [was] normative not [simply] empirical'.[7]

It is not the aim of this chapter to argue for the uncritical application of a strict interpretation of Articles 2(4) and 51 of the UN Charter – a straightforward application of the formal rules embodied in the Charter

4 National Security Strategy, v, 6, 14, 15, 30.

5 See e.g. the doctrine of President Johnson – 'the American nation cannot permit the establishment of another Communist dictatorship in the Western hemisphere' – as a justification for the American intervention in the Dominican Republic ((1965) 52 *US Dept of State Bulletin* 745). Contrast this with the statements of the US representative in the Security Council who argued that the legal basis for the intervention was to be found in the doctrine of protection of nationals and in the involvement of the OAS – (SC 1196th mtg (1965)). See M. E. O'Connell, 'The Myth of Preemptive Self-Defense' (*American Society of International Law (ASIL) Task Force Papers*, 17 August 2000).

6 [1986] ICJ Rep. 14 at 98.

7 M. Koskenniemi, 'The Place of Law in Collective Security', (1996) 17 *Michigan Journal of International Law* 455 at pp. 469, 490.

to factual circumstances. This would ignore the dynamic built into both treaty law and customary law by the role of (subsequent) practice which, if combined with an acceptance of the legality of that practice (*opinio juris*), may modify the treaty rules or create new customary law. States using force, or proposing to use force, normally attempt to justify their actions either as actually coming within the treaty framework, or they try to stretch that framework, or they claim a customary basis for their action, or sometimes they admit that their actions are exceptional and not precedential. Law is either confirmed or reshaped by these claims and the responses of other states and actors to them. In effect, the legal rules claimed to be applicable in any given conflict or dispute are put into the international spotlight and either survive intact or are modified. This analysis focuses on the attempts by powerful states to stretch the treaty exceptions to the ban on the use of force and, in the case of self-defence, to recognize or create wider customary rules. However, we must not be too ready to assume that the law has changed when we are faced with behaviour that appears to disregard laws even if that behaviour is claimed to be reflective of a new law. While it is true that in issues of high politics, exemplified by the decision to threaten or use force in international relations, politics may (always) be in the ascendancy and also that politics influences the development of international law – laws, particularly fundamental ones, are not easily swept aside by the rise and fall of political tides.

The Bush Doctrine presents us with a new controversy because it is not predicated on the separation or indeed the dismissal[8] of the relevance of law to the issue of 'ultimate power', it is an attempt to bring power and law together, to reshape international law. In effect this would take us back to the Monroe Doctrine which seemed to achieve acceptance in international law as exemplified by its preservation in the Covenant of the League of Nations.[9] The Monroe Doctrine of 1823 was, of course, adopted against the background of a virtually unregulated right to use force in international relations, a situation in which self-defence as discussed in the Caroline incident of 1837 was simply one of many justifications for the use of force. The League of Nations Covenant may have been an attempt to restrict a state's sovereign right to go to war, but it was flawed in many ways, including the acceptance of the

[8] See statement of Dean Acheson on the Cuban Missile Crisis: 'law simply does not deal with ... questions of ultimate power' (1961–63) 14 *ASIL Proc.* 14.

[9] Article 21 of the Covenant of the League of Nations (1919).

Monroe Doctrine and other similar 'regional understandings', which was a reference to the so-called British Monroe Doctrine.[10] In the post-Cold War era, again it is the combination of the USA and United Kingdom seeking to gain acceptance of their understandings of the international order. However, in contrast to the Monroe Doctrine which was adopted against a background of lawlessness, the Bush Doctrine of 2002 is adopted against the background of a post-1945 order based on a ban on the use of force in Article 2(4), a norm that is generally accepted as *jus cogens*,[11] and allowing of only two exceptions. The exceptions permitted in the UN Charter are actions in individual or collective self-defence in response to an 'armed attack' embodied in Article 51, or military enforcement actions undertaken with Security Council authority under Chapters VII and VIII of the UN Charter.[12]

The Bush Doctrine represents the high point of a concerted effort by the USA to both undermine and change this order. It is aimed at widening the right of self-defence as embodied in the UN Charter, or perhaps more accurately in recognizing a wider customary right of self-defence than the treaty right embodied in the Charter since it harks back to, though it greatly widens, the doctrine of anticipatory self-defence embodied in the Caroline incident of 1837. But this is only one part of a three-pronged assault on the order contained in the UN Charter. The other two prongs consist of first, an effort to widen the circumstances in which it is deemed that the Security Council has sanctioned military action, and secondly, the resurrection of other customary rights to use force, principally the doctrine of humanitarian intervention.[13] The Bush Doctrine and the most recent post-Cold War military actions against Yugoslavia, Afghanistan and Iraq together seem to represent an assault on the order regulating the use of force contained in the UN Charter. Focus will be on the attempts to widen the two exceptions to the ban on the use of force contained in the UN Charter, namely authorization by the Security Council and the right of

[10] L. Lloyd, *Peace Through Law: Britain and the International Court in the 1920s* (Boydell, 1997), pp. 126–30.

[11] See e.g. B. Simma, 'NATO, the UN and the Use of Force', (1999) 10 *European Journal of International Law* 1.

[12] For arguments that the General Assembly has residual competence to recommend military action, see N. D. White, 'The Legality of Bombing in the Name of Humanity', (2000) 5 *Journal of Conflict and Security Law* 27.

[13] M. Byers, 'The Shifting Foundations of International Law: A Decade of Forceful Measures Against Iraq', (2002) 13 *European Journal of International Law* 21 at p. 22.

self-defence, which have come together in the current Iraq crisis. States have in the main concentrated on attempting to widen these exceptions rather than trying to create new exceptions, a difficult feat when faced with a prohibition that is recognized as *jus cogens*.

Nevertheless, the controversy over recognition of the legality of humanitarian intervention has been heightened in the wake of the Kosovo crisis of 1999. There is a perception that the pendulum has swung toward the legality of humanitarian intervention. Stripped of legal justifications based on spurious interpretations of Security Council resolutions, how could the bombing of the Federal Republic of Yugoslavia (FRY) be anything other than a clear instance of humanitarian intervention? However, the absence of anything like a consensus among those states intervening as well as the rest of the world immediately raises the previously oft-repeated question about the presence of sufficient *opinio juris* in favour of military intervention to prevent serious human rights abuses. Kosovo highlighted the divide among academics and politicians as to the legality of humanitarian intervention, it did not produce any definite conclusions.[14] Debates over humanitarian intervention have obscured the more concerted efforts, witnessed in the Kosovo episode itself, to claim Security Council authority, to widen the recognized exceptions to the ban on the use of force. Furthermore, such debates over the legality of the *use* of force have also almost presumed that the *threat* of the use of force is now acceptable in international relations – an issue that will be returned to at the end of the chapter.

Military actions

Since the end of the Gulf Conflict in 1991 there have been many instances of military action against Iraq, taken in the main by the USA and the United Kingdom, culminating in the threat of overwhelming force if Iraq did not comply with Resolution 1441 of 8 November 2002, and the subsequent use of force against Iraq commencing on 20 March 2003. In between March and June 1999, NATO states, primarily the USA with United Kingdom support, undertook the concerted bombing of the

[14] For a comprehensive re-evaluation see B. D. Lepard, *Rethinking Humanitarian Intervention: A Fresh Legal Approach Based on Fundamental Ethical Principles in International Law and World Religions* (Penn State Press, 2002).

Federal Republic of Yugoslavia (FRY) in order to prevent crimes against humanity being committed by FRY forces against the ethnic Albanian majority in Kosovo. In between October and December 2001 (although lower level action has continued thereafter), the USA with some British support and the significant involvement of the Northern Alliance undertook military action against the Taliban regime and their Al-Qaeda allies in Afghanistan in response to the attacks on the USA of 11 September 2001. All of these military actions are problematic when considering the rules governing the use of force in the UN Charter. None were clearly authorized by the Security Council and none were clearly responses in self-defence, at least in Charter terms, though Operation Enduring Freedom comes closest.[15] However, before concluding that they constituted violations of Article 2(4) as illegal uses of force, it is essential to evaluate the legal justifications put forward by those states using force and the responses of other states to those claims.

This chapter will consider the two main aspects of the three-pronged assault on the UN Charter, though it is worth noting here that each of the conflicts can be used in varying degrees to support all three. Violations of Security Council resolutions by Iraq have been a constant refrain by those states threatening or using force against Iraq since April 1991. This has been the main justification, though on occasions there have been references to the rights of humanitarian intervention and self-defence. Indeed, the latter seems to be increasing in importance in the shape of pre-emptive self-defence enunciated in the Bush Doctrine as the USA sought to justify carrying out its latest threat to use force against Iraq. The justification for the use of force against the FRY was again breach of Security Council resolutions, though the impression was more that it was a clear expression of the right of humanitarian intervention.[16] Self-defence played a minor role, though it has been invoked both by politicians[17] and in the literature.[18] In the case of

15 See J. I. Charney, 'The Use of Force Against Terrorism and International Law', (2001) 95 *American Journal of International Law* 835, questioning the claim of self-defence. But see T. M. Franck, 'Terrorism and the Right of Self-Defense', (2001) 95 *American Journal of International Law* 839 at p. 840; and A. Randelzhofer, in B. Simma (ed.), *The Charter of the United Nations* (2nd edn, Oxford University Press, 2002), p. 802, supporting the claim of self-defence.

16 But see Lepard, *Rethinking Humanitarian Intervention*, pp. 369–70.

17 See President Clinton's speech on Kosovo of 25 March 1999, *New York Times*, 25 March 1999, p. A15.

18 P. T. Egan, 'The Kosovo Intervention and Collective Self-Defence', (2001) 8 *International Peacekeeping* 39.

Afghanistan, the facts led to an exclusive reliance on the right of self-defence with some reference to Security Council resolutions. Reference to humanitarian intervention in this case tended to take the form of criticism of the users of force for not invoking it as a basis of the action given the oppressive denial of human rights to at least half of the population of Afghanistan.

The Security Council and the use of force

When considering the above military actions, there does seem to be significant practice by some states that lends credence to the idea that force can be taken in support of Security Council resolutions; especially (and probably only) those that have made a crucial finding of a threat to or breach of the peace under Article 39 of the UN Charter, though they do not contain an express 'authorization' to take 'necessary measures' (the Security Council's euphemism for military action). It is interesting that in the three main conflicts examined, reliance on this ground was strongest in two (Kosovo and Iraq), suggesting a preference for uses of force that can be justified under the UN collective security umbrella rather than customary rights that are exercised unilaterally. Indeed, in Afghanistan, much is made of the fact that the Security Council apparently endorsed the exercise of the right of self-defence.[19] The greater legitimacy that UN authority brings[20] has created tremendous pressures within the Security Council and on its resolutions.

The desire to bring actions under the authority of the United Nations reflects an acceptance of this as a mechanism for lawfully using force, but it also inevitably results in spurious claims by some states to be acting

[19] SC Res. 1368, 12 September 2001; SC Res. 1373, 28 September 2001. Although both resolutions affirmed the right of self-defence, neither determined that the terrorist atrocities of 11 September constituted an 'armed attack' or indeed 'breach of the peace' or 'act of aggression', preferring instead to find a 'threat to the peace'. See in contrast SC Res. 660 and 661, 2 and 6 August 1990 on Iraq. The latter made a clear affirmation of the 'inherent right of individual or collective self-defence, in response to the armed attack by Iraq against Kuwait, in accordance with Article 51 of the UN Charter'. See E. P. J. Myjer and N. D. White, 'The Twin Towers Attack: An Unlimited Right to Self-Defence', (2002) 7 *Journal of Conflict and Security Law* 5 at pp. 9–11. But see M. Byers, 'Terrorism, the Use of Force and International Law after 11 September', (2002) 51 *International and Comparative Law Quarterly* 401 at pp. 403, 409 – NATO and the OAS both categorized the terrorist atrocities of 11 September as an 'armed attack'.

[20] C. Gray, 'From Unity to Polarization: International Law and the Use of Force Against Iraq', (2002) 13 *European Journal of International Law* 1 at p. 8.

under UN authority. It is also telling that despite the invocation of the Bush Doctrine in September 2002,[21] the USA was persuaded, at least temporarily, not to invade Iraq on the basis of a claim to pre-emptive self-defence but on the basis of a Security Council resolution. The negotiation of Resolution 1441 took many weeks, and even then the result was not a clear authorization to use force. Nevertheless, the fact that the USA in the build-up to conflict was prepared to proceed on the basis of a not completely satisfactory resolution is telling. It initially at least showed a lack of belief in the certainty displayed in the Bush Doctrine as to the existence of a wide right of pre-emptive defence. The pressure put on the USA by the United Kingdom, its chief ally, to go to the Security Council is perhaps reflective of the lack of belief within the UK government in pre-emptive self-defence.

Despite the lack of clear authority in Resolution 1441, it will be shown that the United Kingdom in particular subsequently claimed that the Resolution's reference to 'serious consequences' in the face of a further 'material breach' of the disarmament regime imposed on Iraq were sufficient to justify the use of force against that country. Interpretations of Security Council resolutions based on a purposive approach,[22] or more accurately the principle of effectiveness,[23] may be acceptable if the interpretation reflects the views of the Security Council as a body. The 'interpretive task is to ascertain what the text means to the parties collectively rather than to each individually'.[24] Subsequent practice can be relied on to (re)interpret a resolution when it reflects a shared

[21] See also the British government's assessment of the threat posed by Iraq in 'Iraq's Weapons of Mass Destruction: The Assessment of the British Government', 24 September 2002, available at www.fco.gov.uk/Files/kfile/iraqdosier.pdf

[22] Byers, 'Shifting Foundations', p. 25.

[23] Though the two approaches are viewed as coterminous in A. Aust, *Modern Treaty Law and Practice* (Cambridge University Press, 2000), p. 185.

[24] See I. Johnstone, 'Treaty Interpretation: The Authority of Interpretative Communities', (1991) 12 *Michigan Journal of International Law* 371 at p. 381, where he characterizes the interpretative process as 'intersubjective interpretation'. But see C. F. Amerasinghe, *Principles of the Institutional Law of International Organizations* (Cambridge University Press, 1996), p. 63, where he states that 'there are many instances of the preparatory work being resorted to in the interpretation of decisions of organs. In the case of decision such as these it is arguable that there is a reason legitimately to refer to them, because the intention of the framer may be more relevant. But this argument may lack cogency, if such decisions are regarded as objective texts that have an existence of their own, independent of their creators.' This analysis seems to focus on the negotiations that went into the text, while the point here is that clear statements at the time of the adoption of the text – the intention of those voting for it – is of primary importance.

understanding.[25] Such practice has to be checked against the limitations contained in the Charter and must be undertaken in fulfilment of the purposes of the United Nations.[26] Subject to these limitations, if the Security Council members agree that a resolution referring to 'serious consequences' in the face of a further 'material breach' amounts to an authority to use force then that is what it means. If they disagree and some view it as granting such authority and others that it does not, this does not signify that it grants authority, at least in attributing meaning to the Security Council as a whole.

Interpreting a resolution of a body like the Security Council requires careful consideration of the text and the discussions that led up to it.[27] To interpret the words of a resolution in a way that is directly contrary to the consensus (which may be an agreement to disagree) underlying the resolution would undermine the Council as a forum for achieving compromise. Military action undertaken with Security Council authority is only permitted when there is agreement[28] in that body that such action is being authorized. Agreement to the effect that the Council is authorizing the use of force has been achieved in the past by a formula that combines the phrase 'necessary measures' with an 'authorization'. This has clearly been recognized in UN practice as authorizing the use of force in many instances.[29] However, there is no need to stick to this formula if all the members agree (especially the P5) that a threat of serious consequences in the face of a material breach signifies the authorization of necessary measures or the use of force. But clearly there was no such consensus.[30]

Even Resolution 1441, upon which the USA placed the maximum possible pressure, resulted in an apparent consensus at the meeting that

[25] S. Rosenne, *Developments in the Law of Treaties 1945–1986* (Cambridge University Press, 1989), p. 244.

[26] *Expenses* case [1962] ICJ Rep. 167.

[27] *Namibia* case [1971] ICJ Rep. 15 at 53. See further M. C. Wood, 'The Interpretation of Security Council Resolutions', (1998) 2 *Max Planck Yearbook of UN Law* 73 at pp. 74–5, 79, 95.

[28] In accordance with the voting rules contained in Article 27 of the UN Charter.

[29] See generally N. M. Blokker, 'Is the Authorization Authorized? Powers and Practice of the UN Security Council to Authorize the Use of Force by "Coalitions of the Able and Willing"', (2000) 11 *European Journal of International Law* 541.

[30] Gray, "From Unity", p. 9: 'It is no longer simply a case of interpreting euphemisms such as "all necessary measures" to allow for the use of force when it is clear from the preceding debate that force is envisaged; the USA, the UK and others have gone far beyond this to distort the words of resolutions and to ignore the preceding debates in order to claim to be acting on behalf of the international community.'

the Resolution did not automatically authorize the use of force if Iraq was in material breach. Indeed, the USA and the United Kingdom asserted to the other members in the meeting that no 'automaticity' was contained in the Resolution, but then outside the meeting repeatedly stated that there was no legal need for another resolution on the basis that Resolution 1441 was sufficient by itself, statements directed primarily at Iraq.[31] Clearly, the USA and the United Kingdom were speaking to different audiences in making these contradictory statements. On 8 November in the Security Council chamber, the USA and the United Kingdom were careful not to contradict their statements to the effect that the resolution did not authorize the use of force. However, the USA made it clear at the time that this did not undermine its rights of self-defence in the face of the threat posed by Iraq.[32] Subsequently though, both the USA and the United Kingdom engaged in unilateral interpretations of Resolution 1441 as permitting them to use force against Iraq. This is based on the fact that the Resolution not only invoked the concept of 'material breach' at several points but also stated that Iraq failed to take the final opportunity to comply with its disarmament obligations granted in the Resolution, and thus must face the 'serious consequences' warned of. This argument built on the previous justifications put forward by the USA and the United Kingdom for using force against Iraq to enforce its disarmament obligations since 1991 (for example in January 1993 and December 1998). Indeed, they could argue that Resolution 1441 signifies that the Security Council endorsed their position that material breach of the disarmament provisions of Security Council Resolutions from 687 of 3 April 1991 to 1441,[33] suspends the

[31] 'And, like almost every other country [on the Council] Syria ... had voted yes because it had been promised by Washington and London that the resolution was in no way a green light for American military action and contained no "triggers" or "automaticity" in regard to waging war. It was a promise restated by both Mr Negroponte and Sir Jeremy [Greenstock] in the chamber. "We heard loud and clear during the negotiations the concerns about automaticity and hidden triggers", Sir Jeremy intoned. "There is no automaticity in this resolution" '. Outside of the Security Council Mr Blair stated 'Defy the UN's will and we will disarm you by force. Be in no doubt whatever about that.' Mr Bush stated: 'The outcome of this crisis is already determined. The full disarmament of weapons of mass destruction will occur. The only question for the Iraqi regime is to decide how. His cooperation must be unconditional or he will face severest consequences': *The Independent*, 9 November 2002, pp. 1 and 5.

[32] Mr Negroponte (the US representative) stated that nothing in the resolution constrained the right of any member state from acting to defend itself from the threat posed by Iraq (SC 4644th mtg, 8 November 2002).

[33] See e.g. prior to the 1998 airstrikes, *The Times*, 19 February 1998.

operation of the ceasefire Resolution 687, thus allowing states to use force under the open-ended provisions of Resolution 678 of 29 November 1990. However, it is clear from the debates preceding the adoption of Resolution 1441 that it was not the intention of the Council to endorse that argument, and that any response to a material breach of the Resolution would come from the Security Council not individual member states, in other words that the 'serious consequences' were to be determined by the Council. The fact that the final version of the Resolution left out the words of the original American and UK draft authorizing member states 'to use all necessary means to restore international peace and security in the area' is telling.[34]

Further, it is also clear from the meeting at which Resolution 1441 was adopted as well as the history of Security Council diplomacy that a combination of 'material breach' and 'serious consequences' in the Resolution is not understood by the Security Council to include the use of armed force,[35] though that may be the subsequent interpretation put on the phrase by the USA and United Kingdom. 'Serious consequences' and 'material breach' were clearly put in the Resolution by the USA and the United Kingdom to enable them to make these arguments, as was the recollection of previous Resolutions including 678, but the non-acceptance of this position by the rest of the Council signified that the use of force had not been authorized by the Security Council as a reflection of its will.[36] In reality, in the absence of a further mandating resolution, the USA and United Kingdom relied on a combination of alleged Security Council authority and the not yet accepted Bush Doctrine of pre-emptive self-defence as justifications to use force against Iraq. It is true that Resolution 1441 came closer to the American and UK position than previous Resolutions dealing with Iraqi breach of Resolution 687,[37] but it does not meet the agreed requirements that

[34] See N. Grief, 'The Iraq Hearing', www.bbc.co.uk/radio4/today, 19 December 2002.

[35] But see F. L. Kirgis, 'Security Council Resolution 1441 on Iraq's Final Opportunity to Comply with Disarmament Obligations,' *ASIL Insights* (November 2002).

[36] The USA argued that para. 8 of Resolution 1441 prohibited Iraq from firing on American and UK planes enforcing the no-fly zones over Iraq. Paragraph 8 decides that 'Iraq shall not take or threaten hostile acts directed against any representative or personnel of the United Nations or the IAEA or of any Member State taking action to uphold any Council resolution'. The USA seemed to admit, though, that its interpretation was open to question given the doubt about the lack of authority for establishment of the no-fly zones: statement by Colin Powell, US Secretary of State, *Washington Post* in *Guardian Weekly*, 21–27 November 2002, p. 29.

[37] See e.g. SC Res. 1154, 2 March 1998; 1194, 9 September 1998; 1205, 5 November 1998.

for states to take military action under the auspices of Chapter VII there must be a clear and unambiguous mandate in the form of an authorization to use force.[38]

In the crucial meeting of the Security Council on 8 November when Resolution 1441 was adopted,[39] the US representative clearly accepted that the resolution did not contain any '"hidden triggers" and no "automaticity" with respect to the use of force'. He added that 'further Iraqi breach, reported to the Security Council by UNMOVIC, the IAEA, or Member State will lead to the matter returning to the Council'. This clearly indicates an acceptance of the interpretation of the Resolution shared by virtually all the other members of the Security Council. The UK representative's statement on this point was virtually the same except that he concluded that when the matter was returned to the Council, 'we would expect the Council to then meet its responsibilities'. Other members spoke about the lack of the automatic right to use force in the Resolution (Mexico, Russia, Bulgaria, Syria, Cameroon, China), labelled the 'two stage approach' by France; and the clear assurances about the lack of basis in the Resolution for the use of force (Ireland, Columbia); while Norway referred to the Council's responsibility recognized in the Resolution to secure international peace. Singapore, Guinea and Mauritius made statements that cannot be said to favour one interpretation over another.

The sense of the meeting is best summed up by the representative of Ireland when he thanked the sponsors of the resolution (USA and United Kingdom) for their assurances that the purpose of the 'resolution was to achieve disarmament through inspections, and not to establish the basis for the use of force'. Thus, the resolution did not authorize the use of force. This is made clear by the US representative when he stated 'if the Security Council fails to act decisively in the event of further Iraqi violations, this resolution does not constrain any Member State from acting to defend itself against the threat posed by Iraq or to enforce relevant United Nations resolutions to protect world peace and security'. By this statement, the USA was making it clear that despite the lack of authority in the Resolution itself, the USA claimed the right to defend itself against threats as outlined in the Bush Doctrine, as well as the right

[38] J. Lobel and M. Ratner, 'Bypassing the Security Council: Ambiguous Authorization to Use Force, Cease-Fires and the Iraqi Inspection Regime', (1999) 93 *American Journal of International Law* 124.

[39] S/PV 4644 mtg, 8 November 2002.

to enforce UN resolutions. The latter seems superfluous but follows from practice in Kosovo and against Iraq, where the argument has not been so much as to interpret the relevant Security Council resolutions as authorizing the use of force, but more the claim to be able to enforce Security Council resolutions. The fact that no other member of the Council made a similar claim in the debate reflects the lack of support for such a view. The debates of the Council show that only a clear resolution mandating the use of force is sufficient to enable military action to be undertaken under the authority of the United Nations. All other arguments – unilateral interpretations and claims to a right of enforcement – fall short, for the simple fact is that if the Security Council wants to authorize the use of force it will do so using clearly accepted language. It has not done so in the case of Iraq since the end of the conflict in 1991.

While maintaining the position subsequently adopted outside the Council that force was legally justified against Iraq without a further Council resolution, in January and February 2003 the United Kingdom in particular moved towards the position that a further resolution was politically desirable, though an 'unreasonable veto' would not deter the United Kingdom from using force.[40] Even then, the resolution being mooted in early February by the United Kingdom still did not envisage a clear authorization to use force, because in the absence of clear evidence of Iraqi armaments this was thought by the United Kingdom to be unachievable though it contained a further determination of a 'material breach'. British officials insisted that this would constitute authority to use force.[41] The contradiction in this argument is manifest, unless the members of the Security Council indicated that they had changed their minds and that such language now signified authorization to use force. The unconvincing evidence of WMD in Iraq, apparent from the critical but not damning reports from the Heads of the UN Monitoring, Verification and Inspection Commission (UNMOVIC) and the IAEA of 27 January,[42]

[40] A. Grice, 'Defiant Blair Says UN has No Veto on War', *The Independent,* 14 January 2003, p. 1. For discussion of the notion of the 'unreasonable' veto, see N. D. White, 'Security Council: An Impediment to International Justice?', (2004) *Amicus Curiae* (January/February).

[41] D. Usborne, J. Lichfield, P. Waugh and A. Penketh, 'Tony Blair, A Man with his Hands Full', *The Independent*, 8 February 2003, p. 1.

[42] S/PV 4692 mtg, 27 January 2003. Hans Blix (UNMOVIC) concluded (p. 8) that there were serious gaps in knowledge about Iraq's chemical and bacteriological weapons programmes, and that Iraq was not fully cooperating. He noted that UNMOVIC capability had increased over a short period of time, inferring that more time was

14 February,[43] 28 February,[44] and 7 March 2003[45] as well as the limited evidence presented to the Council by the US Secretary of State on 5 February, failed to persuade most members of the Council to change their view that the use of force was not yet justified. On 14 February, the US Secretary of State stated that it was not UNMOVIC's job to produce evidence of Iraqi breach, rather it was the responsibility of Iraq to disarm, which it clearly had not done. According to the USA this was a further material breach and a failure by Iraq to take the final opportunity afforded to them in Resolution 1441 and should have led to the serious consequences called for in that Resolution.[46] The United Kingdom made it clear that it would support the US military action even without a further resolution. On 17 February, the UK Foreign Secretary stated that 'in terms of mandate resolution 1441 gives us the authority we need, but in terms of political desirability we have always said that we would prefer a second resolution'.[47] Further, on 21 February he stated that 'diplomatic parlance is notoriously ambiguous, but in this case the terminology had one meaning: disarmament by force'.[48]

On 24 February the USA and the United Kingdom introduced a draft second resolution into the Security Council, though they made it clear that it was for discussion and would not be voted on until after further reports from the weapons inspectors. Legally, it seemed to add little to Resolution 1441. There was no explicit authorization to use necessary measures. After invoking Chapter VII, the initial draft had one operative paragraph where it 'decides that Iraq has failed to take the final opportunity afforded to it in Resolution 1441'. The Preamble recalled 1441's reference to material breach and warning of serious consequences. In

needed. Mr El Baradei (IAEA) concluded by saying (p. 12) that 'we have to date found no evidence that Iraq has revived its nuclear weapons programme since the elimination of the programme in 1990' but that a more definite conclusion could be provided in the next few months if the inspection process was allowed to continue.

43 S/PV 4708 mtg, 14 February 2003.

44 UN doc. S/2003/232. This report by UNMOVIC was critical of Iraq stating that it should show greater credible evidence of disarmament. On 28 February, Iraq started destroying missiles that exceeded the 150 km permitted range. UNMOVIC's Chairman Hans Blix stated this was a 'very significant piece of real disarmament': *UN News Centre*, 28 February 2003.

45 S/PV 4714, 7 March 2003. Dr Blix referred to the destruction of missiles by saying 'we are not watching the breaking of toothpicks. Lethal weapons are being destroyed.'

46 S/PV 4708 mtg, 14 February 2003, p. 21.

47 S. Castle, 'France Set to Block Second UN Resolution Against Iraq', *The Independent*, 18 February 2003, p. 1.

48 *The Independent*, 22 February 2003, p. 4.

effect, it found that Iraq had breached that Resolution by 'noting that Iraq has submitted a declaration ... containing false statements and omissions and has failed to comply with, and to cooperate fully in the implementation of' Resolution 1441.[49] In last ditch attempts to make this draft acceptable and thus to avoid the threatened vetoes of Russia and France as well as other probable negative votes, the United Kingdom amended the draft to provide for a further short deadline for Iraqi compliance of 17 March, and finally to list the various actions Iraq must undertake to demonstrate compliance.[50] This did not persuade Russia and France who insisted that the inspection process was working and should therefore be given several months to work through.[51] Furthermore, they were probably concerned that the second resolution had become of such symbolic significance for world opinion that its adoption would be seen as giving a green light for war despite the fact that it was not viewed as so doing by the Security Council as a whole. More importantly for the USA and the United Kingdom, a second resolution would have served domestic purposes, particularly in the United Kingdom where the public was much more willing to support the use of force if a second resolution could have been adopted.

The failed efforts to obtain a second iconic resolution in the Security Council meant that when full-scale conflict was engaged in Iraq on 20 March, the USA had already made it clear that the legal basis was self-defence, by reiterating its reliance on pre-emptive action. President Bush made this clear on 7 March 2003 when the debates in the Council were going against the draft. He stated that 'we don't really need the United Nations' approval to act ... When it comes to our security, we do not need anyone's permission.'[52] Further, on 18 March he outlined the nature of the threat: 'The danger is clear. Using chemical, biological or, one day, nuclear weapons obtained with the help of Iraq, the terrorists could fulfil their stated ambitions and kill thousands or hundreds of thousands of innocent people in our country or any other.'[53] The United Kingdom preferred to argue that it was legally justified on the basis of existing Security Council resolutions. In a

49 http://news.bbc.co.uk/go/pr/fr/-/hi/world/europe/2795747.stm
50 UN doc. S/2003/215, 7 March 2003.
51 See D. Usborne, 'On the Brink of War', *The Independent*, 8 March 2003, p. 1.
52 R. Cornwell, 'The Quiet Man', *The Independent,* 8 March 2003, p. 3.
53 http://news.bbc.co.uk/1/hi/world/middle_east/2858965.stm. But see United States' letter to Security Council on the day hostilities against Iraq commenced: UN doc. S/2003/351, 20 March 2003.

parliamentary written answer on 17 March 2003, the Attorney-General stated that the basis for force was Resolution 678 of 1990 containing the original authority to use force, which was reactivated in the light of material breach of Resolution 687 of 1991 and all subsequent disarmament resolutions up to and including Resolution 1441. He concluded that 'all that resolution 1441 requires is reporting to and discussion by the Security Council of Iraq's failures, but not an express further decision to authorise force',[54] since there was original authority in 678. The weakness of this argument has been demonstrated by the fact that it has not been accepted by other members of the Council shown above, but also by the fact that the authority of Resolution 678 does not extend beyond Resolution 687 when the Security Council declared in the final paragraph that the Council 'decides to remain seized of the matter and to take such further steps as may be required for the implementation of this resolution and to secure peace and security to the area'. The delegation of power to take military action that occurred in Resolution 678 was effectively revoked by Resolution 687, including the authority in Resolution 678 to restore 'international peace and security to the area'.[55] For the Attorney-General to state that 'material breach of resolution 687 revives the authority to use force under resolution 678', which is the crucial step in his reasoning back to Resolution 678, has no basis in those resolutions and thus no basis in law. It represents an unconvincing attempt to unlock Resolution 678, which was the only resolution in which the Security Council authorized necessary measures against Iraq.

The critical reaction of many states and other actors to the decision of the USA and the United Kingdom to use force without Security Council authority is of course significant in evaluating the legality of that action.

[54] http://news.bbc.co.uk/1/hi/uk_politics/2857347.stm, also found in (2003) 52 *International and Comparative Law Quarterly* 811. See further C. Greenwood, 'International Law and the Pre-Emptive Use of Force: Afghanistan, Al-Qaida, and Iraq', (2003) 4 *San Diego International Law Journal* 7 at pp. 35–6.

[55] SC Res. 678, 29 November 1990 authorized member states 'to use all necessary means to uphold and implement resolution 660 (1990) and all subsequent resolutions and to restore international peace and security to the area'. The Council meeting at which the resolution was adopted showed that states viewed this as giving the Coalition authority to push Iraq out of Kuwait and to restore peace between the two states (S/PV 2963, 29 November 1990, p. 78 (United Kingdom), p. 101 (USA)) not to take any wider action. The meeting at which SC Res. 687, 3 April 1991 was adopted showed that member states viewed the authority to authorize further measures as belonging to the Security Council, not to those states acting under 678 (S/PV 2981, 3 April 1991, p. 85 (USA), p. 111 (United Kingdom), p. 95 (China), p. 98 (USSR)).

On 10 March, before the outbreak of war, the Secretary-General was clearly of the opinion that it would be unlawful when he warned that 'if the US and others were to go outside the Council and take military action it would not be in conformity with the Charter'.[56] Criticisms of the impending war and warnings of illegality were voiced by the majority of members of the Council when meeting on the eve of the war.[57] After full-scale force was unleashed by the USA and United Kingdom on 20 March 2003, there were immediate statements condemning it as a violation of international law by China, Russia, France, Iran, Pakistan, India, Indonesia and Malaysia, while support was given by Australia, the Philippines, Japan and South Korea.[58]

The Security Council debates on Iraq and the reactions of states to the unauthorized use of force of 20 March 2003 show that to argue that a new purposive interpretative rule has been accepted that allows individual states to unilaterally interpret and enforce Security Council resolutions and even the UN Charter[59] is a *non sequitur*. The fact that the same minority of states that seek to justify the above interventions argue for the emergence of a new rule of interpretation is sufficient to show that such arguments are self-serving and are not accepted by the majority of states. In reality, a Security Council resolution is not a treaty text to be pulled this way and that over many years, it is a document of an executive body charged with taking action within its competence to fulfil the purposes of the UN Charter. As a piece of subsequent practice adopted under the auspices of a treaty, each resolution exists primarily as a reflection of the will of the Security Council.[60] That will can change;

56 UN News Service, 10 March 2003 available at www.un.org/apps/news/printnews.asp?nid=6399

57 S/PV 4721 mtg, 19 March 2003. Statements by Germany, France, Russia, Syria, Pakistan, Mexico, Chile, Angola, China. See also open meeting of Security Council S/PV 4717, 12 March 2003, when fifty-one states spoke.

58 http://news.bbc.co.uk/1/hi/world/middle_east/2867027.stm. The USA claimed that thirty countries were supporting the military action. 'Under the standards used by the current Bush administration, the size of the 1991 coalition is likely to have been more than 100 countries': E. MacAskill, 'US Lists Coalition of the Willing', BBC News, 27 March–2 April 2003, p. 5. In fact thirty-four countries contributed militarily to the 1991 campaign, while four countries contributed to the 2003 campaign (USA: 200,000; United Kingdom: 45,000; Australia: 200; Poland: 200). In 1991, the American-led coalition acted under a UN resolution and had broad support not only in the Security Council, but also in the General Assembly: see GA Res. 46/135, 17 December 1991.

59 Byers, 'Shifting Foundations', p. 27.

60 Wood, 'Interpretation', pp. 77, 95. See also H. Thirlway, 'The Law and Procedure of the International Court of Justice', (1996) 67 *British Yearbook of International Law* 29.

for example, the Council could decide that Resolution 242 (1967) on the Middle East is clearly binding on Israel but that would require a further resolution or statement by the Security Council as a whole.

Self-defence

Turning again to the other exception to the ban on the threat or use of force, the right of self-defence, Afghanistan, Iraq and the Bush Doctrine show pressure to develop the law of self-defence to allow for more flexibility in responding to terrorist attacks as well as threats from terrorism and weapons of mass destruction. Often the desire to respond to a terrorist attack is combined with a desire to prevent future attacks from occurring. Operation Enduring Freedom against Afghanistan is in part a response to the attacks of 11 September 2001 and in part an anticipatory action based on the continuing threat of terrorist attacks emanating from that country.[61] Some writers have analysed Enduring Freedom as purely anticipatory while others have seen it as solely reactive to a specific armed attack.

O'Connell argues that Operation Enduring Freedom against Afghanistan is justified under a narrow doctrine of anticipatory self-defence, where a 'state need not wait to suffer the actual blow before defending itself, so long as it is certain that the blow is coming'.[62] However, she then argues that there has been no acceptance of a wider right of pre-emptive self-defence as embodied in the Bush Doctrine. In other words, no state 'has the right to use force to prevent possible, as distinct from actual, armed attacks'.[63] The universal rejection of the legality of Israel's 1981 strike against the Iraqi nuclear reactor at Osirik is clear evidence of this.[64] Proponents of the doctrine of pre-emptive strikes rely primarily on the word 'inherent' in Article 51 to suggest the preservation of a much wider right than that contained in the UN Charter, one that pre-existed in customary law. Ironically though, the

[61] Greenwood, 'International Law', p. 10.

[62] O'Connell, 'The Myth', pp. 8, 10. Citing the terrorist strikes against the USA going back to 1993 (World Trade Center), the 1998 embassy bombings in Africa, the attack on the USS Cole in 2000, and continuing with the attacks on 11 September 2001, O'Connell states that there was plenty of evidence of further imminent attacks on the USA and the United Kingdom justifying anticipatory self-defence against Al-Qaeda and their supporters (including the Taliban) in Afghanistan. For a narrow interpretation of anticipatory (interceptive) self-defence see Y. Dinstein, *War, Aggression and Self-Defence* (3rd edn, Cambridge University Press, 2001), pp. 169–73.

[63] O'Connell, 'The Myth', p. 3. [64] See SC Res. 487, 19 June 1981.

Caroline Doctrine which is said to be the basis of the customary right can only really be read as justifying a very narrow doctrine of anticipatory self-defence, since the threat of attack has to be 'instant, overwhelming, and leaving no choice of means, and no moment for deliberation'.[65] Indeed, '[e]ven if earlier custom allowed pre-emptive self-defense, arguing that it persisted after 1945 for UN members requires privileging the word "inherent" over the plain terms of Article 2(4) and the words "armed attack" in Article 51. Indeed, it requires privileging one word over the whole purpose and structure of the UN Charter.'[66] Furthermore, O'Connell rightly points out that pre-emptive self-defence is 'not a right that the United States wants others to have'. It can 'hardly wish to see an anarchic regime in which every state is entitled to initiate the use of force against its adversaries in pre-emptive self-defense'.[67] To claim that the USA has this right but not other states,[68] not only goes against the whole nature of sovereign equality (at least in law-making) but simply will not work.[69] If the Bush Doctrine constitutes an offer to the rest of the world to agree to a wholly new view of self-defence that is inconsistent with previous understandings of the law, then it is problematic to assume that even if there is acceptance, it is acceptance to the effect that only the USA has this right.

In contrast to O'Connell who argues that Operation Enduring Freedom is an acceptable extension of the right of self-defence to include anticipatory though not pre-emptive action, Byers argues that it amounts to an acceptance of the Schultz Doctrine of 1986, namely the right to attack terrorists on the territory of other states as a response to terrorist attacks such as the 1986 Berlin bombing, or the response to 11 September. This is narrower than the Bush Doctrine that does not depend upon there having been a previous attack.[70] Both Byers and O'Connell agree, however, that although it is an extension of the right of self-defence, the Afghan precedent is much narrower than the Bush Doctrine of pre-emptive strikes. There certainly seems to have been an uncritical reaction by states to Operation Enduring Freedom in

[65] Letter from Mr Webster to Mr Fox (24 April 1841) 29 *British and Foreign State Papers* 1137–8; 30 *British and Foreign State Papers* 195–6.

[66] O'Connell, 'The Myth', p. 13.

[67] O'Connell, 'The Myth', pp. 15–16. O' Connell also points to the fact that pre-emptive strikes are very unlikely to be proportionate responses, at p. 19.

[68] See Byers, 'Shifting Foundations'.

[69] O'Connell, 'The Myth', p. 19.

[70] M. Byers, 'Pre-emptive Self-Defence: Hegemony, Equality and Strategies of Legal Change', (2003) 11 *Journal of Political Philosophy* 171.

Afghanistan, but the question remains whether this amounted to an endorsement of the Schultz Doctrine that was rejected fifteen years earlier. While the *prima facie* case for the legality of responses like Operation Enduring Freedom looks promising, the signs are that the Bush Doctrine has received a negative reception, not least from most European states.[71] The Australian Prime Minister has warned of Australian pre-emptive action against terrorists in the wake of the Bali bombings of 12 October 2002, though he more straightforwardly appealed for a change in international law governing self-defence to allow for such action to occur lawfully. It is worth noting that the claim to pre-emptive action was rejected by the states in the region.[72] Thus, there appears to be no acceptance as yet of the Bush Doctrine. There is strong evidence that the majority of states will be resistant to such a large-scale extension of the right of self-defence that allows a state to take military action based solely upon its perception of a threat.

However, we must be wary of simply accepting the legality of military actions based on the precedent of Operation Enduring Freedom. This was not a straightforward application of Article 51, or of the customary rules of immediacy and proportionality. In essence, the armed attack had ceased by the time the USA came to respond on 7 October. That there were good reasons for this delay is clear enough, but there no longer remained an aggression that had to be remedied as with the invasion of the Falkland Islands by Argentina in 1982. In essence, then, what was being claimed in the operation in Afghanistan was a wider right of self-defence, a right to respond to terrorist attacks within a reasonable period of time in the territory of other states where the government has harboured or possibly supported terrorists, the aim being to prevent future such attacks occurring. The Bush Doctrine goes further since it does not require the occurrence of an armed attack, military force can be triggered by the perception of a threat.

The Bush Doctrine has not been accepted, that is true, but protestations are fairly muted and it may be argued that it is a matter of time before it is (grudgingly) accepted by states. Furthermore, if Operation Enduring Freedom has been accepted as a precedent for a wider right of self-defence, then there may not be such a great leap between it and the Bush Doctrine.[73] Operation Enduring Freedom was only in part a

[71] *Keesing's Record of World Events* (2002), 144832.

[72] *Canberra Times*, 2 December 2002.

[73] See Greenwood, 'International Law', pp. 15–16, 37.

response for the attack of 11 September. Its purpose was not simply to respond to those terrorists behind the attacks of 11 September, but it was an attempt to try to remove terrorists and their supporters from Afghanistan, which would probably be a source of a future attack. The imminence of such a future attack would determine whether the action was *anticipatory* in the sense of the Caroline incident, or a *pre-emptive* strike in the sense of the Bush Doctrine.[74] There has been debate on whether a future attack was imminent, but that seems to have been of little importance in state practice that seems to have accepted the legality of Operation Enduring Freedom.

In this light, an acceptance of Operation Enduring Freedom could amount to a recognition that the Israeli practice of reprisals, and the American retaliations against Libya in 1986 (in response to the Berlin bombing), Iraq in 1993 (in response to the attempted assassination of Bush Senior), and the Sudan and Afghanistan in 1998 (in response to the embassy bombings), now constitute a line of practice that has finally been accepted as lawful with the uncritical reaction to the use of force in Afghanistan. While most of those responses were linked to past terrorist acts, the link was sometimes tenuous, and on other occasions (Libya and Sudan for instance) was shown not to exist.[75] As with the response to 11 September, these military actions were both punitive in response to an attack and anticipatory or pre-emptive to prevent future attacks. Their general disproportionality can only be explained by the existence of an anticipatory or pre-emptive element. Operation Enduring Freedom was a disproportionate response to the attacks of 11 September against the USA but may be viewed as proportionate if the purpose is also seen as anticipatory or pre-emptive (depending on the imminence of the threat). By their nature, anticipatory, and more so pre-emptive, strikes aim to eliminate not only perceived threats but also all possible sources of future threats and therefore tend to be overwhelming. Thus, Enduring Freedom and those retaliatory acts that have gone before are not far removed from the Bush Doctrine, since even under that Doctrine there must be some evidence of terrorist activities or weapons of mass

[74] Myjer and White, 'The Twin Towers Attack', pp. 6–9; but see M. E. O'Connell, 'Evidence of Terror', (2002) 7 *Journal of Conflict and Security Law* 19. See letter to the Security Council of 7 September 2001, UN doc. S/2002/946 in which the USA explained its action in self-defence as a response to the 'attacks on 11 September and the ongoing threat to the United States and its nationals posed by the Al-Qaeda organization'.

[75] Similarly, the pre-emptive strike against Iraq in 2003 appears to have been based on a misperception of the threat of weapons of mass destruction.

destruction. In fact, the USA itself linked its actions taken in self-defence against Afghanistan starting on 7 October 2001 with a wider and continuing right to defend itself against other threats.[76] Thus, Operation Enduring Freedom and the claimed right to take pre-emptive strikes are not seen as separate by the USA but as part of a defensive war against terrorism.[77]

The dangers of anticipatory, and more significantly pre-emptive, self-defence are clear but international lawyers may have to accept them if they become part of state practice. Kirgis states that customary international law is not static: 'it may be modified over time by new assertions of rights, if other states acquiesce in those assertions'.[78] Further, Byers claims that 'current evidence suggests that the customary process is in fact changing ... weakening those aspects of the law that disfavour the powerful while maintaining and strengthening those aspects, such as the rules concerning acquiescence, that operate in their favour'.[79] While acquiescence does play a role in the formation of customary international law, one must not assume it.[80] As Byers states, little publicity was given to the rejection of humanitarian intervention by the Non Aligned States in 2000 but their statement was a clear rejection of the somewhat half-hearted attempts to reinvent the doctrine in the Kosovo episode.[81]

Is it the case in this area governing the use of force that custom can be formed by assertions of new rights that are acquiesced to by other states? Two question marks can be raised in the context of claimed new rights to use force in international relations. First: what if the assertions of new rights appear to violate a norm of *jus cogens*? Secondly: what if the silence of the majority is not indicative of assent to the proposed change? The former will be returned to later when considering acquiescence in the face of threats of force. Gaining acquiescence by the use of pressure is an issue in the case of the war against terrorism following 11 September. There has not been a clear instance of collective rejection

[76] United States' letter to Security Council, UN doc. S/2001/946, 7 October 2001: 'we may find that our self-defense requires further actions with respect to other organizations and states'.

[77] W. M. Reisman, 'In Defense of World Public Order', (2001) 95 *American Journal of International Law* 833.

[78] F. L. Kirgis, 'Pre-emptive Action to Forestall Terrorism' *ASIL Insights* (June 2002).

[79] Byers, 'Shifting Foundations', p. 36.

[80] C. Gray, *International Law and the Use of Force* (Oxford University Press, 2000), p. 16.

[81] Declaration of the Group of 77 South Summit, Havana, Cuba, 10–14 April 2000, para. 54 available at www.g77.org/Docs/Declaration_G77Summit.htm

of the application of self-defence in Operation Enduring Freedom. It seems that in the absence of clear protestations, powerful states can properly take the opportunity to claim that there is acquiescence to and therefore acceptance of the asserted right to self-defence.[82] However, we must be careful in analyzing the quality of that acceptance. We need to ask and answer the question of why would less developed and weak states accept the dismantling of the collective security structure that at least provides them with rules that purport to protect their vulnerability? In seeking an answer we must take account of the pressure being exerted on them not to criticize military action being taken against terrorist organizations or rogue states by powerful states. President Bush sounded a warning against such criticism on 6 November 2001, when he stated that those nations not 'for' the USA were 'against us'.[83] While acquiescence can be viewed as acceptance, one must be careful not to assume this. As Brownlie states, 'the real problem is to determine the value of abstention from protest by a substantial number of states in face of a practice followed by some others. Silence may denote either tacit agreement or a simple lack of interest in the issue.'[84] Clearly, the latter does not constitute acceptance, and if this is the case acceptance cannot be presumed when the silence is a result of fear of the potential political and economic consequences of protest.

Threat of force

The above analysis has been concerned with the uses of force but it is argued here that the same analysis is applicable to the threat of force, though the issue is more problematic. Each military action discussed above was preceded by the threat of force unless something was done – disarmament by Iraq, the cessation of killings and evictions by the FRY, and the handing over of terrorists by the Taliban regime in Afghanistan. The fact that Security Council resolutions had demanded that these actions be done in binding Chapter VII Resolutions does not justify the use of force to enforce them in the absence of Security Council authority nor does it justify the threat of force. A threat may be issued

[82] Byers, 'Terrorism after September 11', p. 412: 'State sponsored terrorism on this scale now also constitutes an armed attack' within the meaning of Article 51.

[83] BBC News, 'Bush Urges Anti-Terror Allies to Act', 6 November 2001, available at http://news.bbc.co.uk/2/hi/world/europe/1642130.stm

[84] I. Brownlie, *Principles of Public International Law* (Oxford University Press, 2003), pp. 7–8.

by the Security Council that if the target state does not comply it will face 'serious consequences',[85] but the interpretation and application of those consequences must lie in the hands of the Security Council as the issuer of that particular threat, not in the hands of individual members. The Security Council must decide if the resolution has not been complied with before it decides whether to carry out its threat, and in what manner.

In the conflicts discussed, the threat of force by individual states has provided the context in which the Security Council has debated and often adopted resolutions. Admittedly, it is at this point that one may argue that the role of acquiescence is being ignored, for it seems that states (and the Council) are more willing to tolerate threats of force than uses of force. It may seem justifiable to tolerate threats of force as opposed to uses of force,[86] but this ignores the fact that threat and use are not so easily separated. Inevitably, if threats are to be credible they must be carried through in the face of intransigence. Threats are not somehow stand alone devices. To make the recent threats of force against Iraq credible there was a huge build-up of forces in the Gulf creating a momentum towards war that was difficult to stop. Indeed, the slide from threat of war to war itself is seen by the escalation of air strikes against Iraq early in March 2003 by the USA and United Kingdom even though diplomatically the decision to cross the threshold from threat to use of force was not made until 20 March.[87]

The fact that states are less willing to condemn threats should not readily be interpreted as acceptance of their legality for if states do not accept uses of force they are also rejecting the threat of those uses of force.[88] Furthermore (and this applies to arguments in favour of widening the right of self-defence to include acts that are both retaliatory and anticipatory, and pre-emptive strikes), one should not quickly assume acceptance in the face of rules that are peremptory such as that prohibiting the threat or use of force in Article 2(4). Threats of force, retaliatory/anticipatory and pre-emptive strikes are all uses of force *prima facie* contrary to Article 2(4). Although they may constitute attempts to

[85] See e.g. SC Res. 1441, 8 November 2002, para. 13: 'Recalls ... that the Council has repeatedly warned Iraq that it will face serious consequences as a result of its continued violations of its obligations'.

[86] R. Sadurska, 'Threats of Force', (1988) 65 *American Journal of International Law* 239.

[87] R. Cornwell, 'US Hits Roadblock in Push to War', *The Independent*, 4 March 2003, p. 1.

[88] N.D. White and R. Cryer, 'Unilateral Enforcement of Resolution 687: A Threat too Far?', (1999) 29 *California Western International Law Journal* 243 at 244–55.

widen the exceptions to that rule found in Chapter VII of the UN Charter, this does not by itself absolve them of their violative character. When practice is apparently violative of a peremptory norm, it is not enough to have acquiescence in the face of the violation in order to establish a new or extended right. It is argued that there needs to be more positive acceptance of the claim, positive proof that states have accepted the modification of the peremptory norm, proof in other words of *opinio juris*. Arguments about acquiescence seem to assume the emergence of new rights in a legal vacuum, but that is not the case. Brownlie puts this clearly when he states that 'the major distinguishing feature of such [peremptory] rules is their relative indelibility. They are rules of customary law which cannot be set aside by treaty or acquiescence but only by the formation of a subsequent customary rule to contrary effect'.[89]

To overcome objections based on the peremptory nature of the customary rule prohibiting the threat or use of force, arguments must be made that only parts of Article 2(4) are *jus cogens*,[90] or that the rule as a whole is dead through constant breach.[91] Admittedly, in the face of regular breach even of fundamental rules, states in the UN General Assembly and other fora must affirm allegiance to the rule, for even peremptory norms may eventually be eroded. There is a pressing need for a declaratory General Assembly resolution reaffirming the rules on the use of force in the post-Cold War era. While there has been no recent resolution along the lines of the 1970 Declaration on Friendly Relations[92] or the 1987 Declaration on the Non Use of Force[93] for instance, there have been references to the prohibition of the threat and use of force in

[89] Brownlie, *Principles*, p. 488. Alternatively, setting aside the *jus cogens* issue for the moment, to concentrate on the treaty rule in Article 2(4) and its exceptions. In this context, the legal arguments of states wishing to use force as attempts to widen the treaty exceptions to the prohibition on the threat or use of force, as well as eroding the content of the treaty rule itself, can be viewed as purported subsequent practice. Under treaty law, such practice can be taken into account in interpreting the text of a treaty (Vienna Convention on the Law of Treaties 1969, Article 31(3)(b)). However, to establish that such practice has amended the treaty provisions it is necessary to establish more than acquiescence. As Amerasinghe states '[e]ven if every party might not itself have actively participated in the practice, [the practice] must be such as to establish the agreement of the parties as a whole to the modification in question': Amerasinghe, *Principles*, p. 419.

[90] R. Müllerson, 'Plus Ça Change (Le Monde) Plus C'est La Même Chose (Le Droit)?', (2002) 7 *Journal of Conflict and Security Law* 149 at p. 169.

[91] T. M. Franck, 'Who Killed Article 2(4) or Changing Norms Governing the Use of Force by States', (1970) 64 *American Journal of International Law* 809.

[92] GA Res. 2625, 24 October 1970. [93] GA Res. 42/22, 18 November 1987.

resolutions supported by the majority of states since 11 September,[94] as well as some encouraging statements by the International Court of Justice in the *Oil Platforms* case of 2003.[95]

Furthermore, the Security Council, in its handling of the Iraq crisis in 2002–3 against the background of the threat of force by the USA and the United Kingdom, did not endorse the threat of force. There is some evidence that the threat of force that formed the background to the inspection process after the adoption of Resolution 1441 in November 1992 was not ignored by the Security Council members, but there was no clear position taken on it by that body. There was no doubt that the threat of force by the USA and the United Kingdom in this period led to Iraq's acceptance of a new inspection process and grudgingly slow cooperation with UNMOVIC and the IAEA. It can be blandly stated that all the Security Council was doing was taking advantage of this threat without endorsing it, and that the Council, if it had decided to authorize the use of force in a second resolution, would have been accepting the threat only for the purpose of enforcing its will. The failure to authorize the use of force could then be seen as a rejection of that threat that preceded it. However, the evidence is that those states opposing a second resolution authorizing force in February and March 2003 (principally France, Russia and Germany) would have been content for the inspection process to have continued, a process that was only possible due to a threat of force. This could be seen as an acceptance of the legality of a *threat of force* to enforce a resolution (1441) obliging Iraq to accept inspections, a position that potentially undermines those states' rejection of the argument that *use of force* can be used to enforce that resolution. The ambivalent attitude of states and the Security Council to threats of force, or what has been called 'diplomacy backed by force', apparently endorsed by the Secretary-General in 1998 in relation to Iraq,[96] has potentially erosive effects on the integrity of Article 2(4). The United Kingdom in particular pointed to this

[94] GA Res. 56/151, 19 December 2001, on the promotion of a democratic and equitable international order adopted by a vote of 109 to 53 with 6 abstentions; GA Res. 56/152, 19 December 2001, on respect for the purposes and principles contained in the Charter of the United Nations to achieve international cooperation in promoting and encouraging respect for human rights and for fundamental freedoms and in solving international problems of a humanitarian character, adopted by a vote of 100 to 54 with 15 abstentions.

[95] [2003] ICJ Reports paras. 46–78. See further Judge Simma's separate opinion.

[96] White and Cryer, 'Unilateral Enforcement', p. 281.

weakness in the position of those states opposed to force when the Foreign Secretary stated on 7 March 2003 that 'the paradox we face is that the only way we are going to achieve disarmament by peace of a rogue regime – which all of us know has been in defiance of this Council for the past 12 years – the only way we can achieve disarmament of their weapons of mass destruction, which the Council has said poses a threat to international peace and security, is by backing our diplomacy with a credible threat of force'.[97] While there is clearly a problem with the Council taking advantage of a threat of force by states, it is not possible to say that this amounts to an endorsement of such threats, since states are very well aware that this would potentially remove the barrier to accepting that actual force can be deployed by states to enforce Council resolutions. Nevertheless, by not rejecting the threat of force, states can be seen to have compromised Article 2(4) in practice, if not yet in law. Again, the Iraq crisis shows that the very integrity and normative status of Article 2(4) is under attack.

Conclusion

Far from witnessing new rules of interpretation, new rules of customary law, or possibly 'one set of legal processes [that] pertain to the single superpower, and another set to all other states',[98] we are witnessing breaches of international law by powerful democratic liberal states. However, they also constitute a very concerted attempt to change the legal order governing the use of force in international relations. While some flexibility is necessary for developing a legal order that is capable of dealing with terrorist violence as well as upholding human rights,[99] we must be careful not to remove the legal brakes on the use of force in international relations. The idea that Hilaire dedicated a large part of his life to – that peace can be achieved through law – should not be forgotten.

Purposive and unilateral interpretations of Security Council resolutions and unilateral adaptations of customary international law will, if accepted, lead to the collapse of the legal order contained in the UN Charter. Rules governing the use of force in the UN Charter, and its subsequent interpretations in General Assembly resolutions and in the

[97] S/PV 4714 mtg, 7 March 2003. [98] Byers, 'Shifting Foundations', p. 39.
[99] See H. McCoubrey, 'Kosovo, NATO and International Law', (1999) 14 *International Relations* 29.

ICJ, are premised on the need to prevent an escalation of conflict. Escalation will lead to further chaos and more devastating destruction. That is why both the threat and use of force are prohibited by Article 2(4); that is why self-defence is only permitted in response to certain breaches of Article 2(4); that is why the ICJ and the General Assembly have made it clear that Article 2(4) should be interpreted to mean that force cannot be used against any of the sovereign rights of a state;[100] and that is why the ICJ in the *Nicaragua* case did not permit the American arguments of counter-intervention even though they were offered as arguments of collective self-defence.[101] Individual interpretations of the UN Charter and of Security Council resolutions, the occasional inconsistent resurrection of the right of humanitarian intervention, and ever-widening claims to a right to take pre-emptive military action, will lead to an escalation of violence. To accept these claims and interpretations as lawful would remove the brakes on escalation. The world will descend into a remorseless and endless cycle of violence with blows followed by even more devastating counter-blows. Farer anticipated this when commenting on the developing Bush Doctrine and the gradual victory of the unilateralists:

> Signaling their triumph would be preemptive and punitive acts or threats of force increasingly unrelated to the specific events of 9/11 and an endorsement of the unrestrained use of violence by client regimes themselves acting in the name of counterterrorism. Battered by these initiatives and the intense opposition they would induce, the basic force-regulating provisions of the UN Charter, the frame of international relations for the past half century, would break along with the restraints on the use of terror by states against their own populations.
>
> Once the frame of order is broken, we can reasonably anticipate increasingly norm-less violence, pitiless blows followed by monstrous retaliation in a descending spiral of hardly imaginable depths. The Israeli experience could well prove a microcosmic anticipation of the global system's future.[102]

Farer is using the term 'unilateralists' here to signify those in the Bush Administration advocating the unilateral use of force under the Bush

[100] *Corfu Channel* case, [1949] ICJ Rep. 4; General Assembly Resolution on Non-Intervention, GA Res. 2131, 21 December 1965.
[101] *Nicaragua* case, [1986] ICJ Rep. 14 at 119.
[102] T. J. Farer, 'Beyond the Charter Frame: Unilateralism or Condominium', (2002) 96 *American Journal of International Law* 359 at p. 364.

Doctrine without recourse to the United Nations. However, the term, as well as the bleak consequences painted by Farer, are equally applicable to those advocating 'unilateral' interpretations of Security Council resolutions and the UN Charter. In effect, both are aspects of the unilateralist perspective that are the antithesis of Hilaire's work on multilateral legal regimes. McCoubrey and Morris' words in a different context have a particular resonance in the light of the increasing tendency of states to step outside multilateral frameworks when they are dissatisfied with those regimes:

> It is ... the case that the end of the Cold War has created a positive opportunity for the regeneration of a genuine collective security system in which the UN, manifestly, cannot be expected itself to be the unique source of peace support action, but will function rather as the mechanism through which a variety of resources will be deployed to that end in cases of need.[103]

While the Security Council may well survive the decision of the USA and United Kingdom of 20 March 2003 to use force against Iraq outside of the UN framework, the danger is that the unwillingness of powerful states to put their coercive power in the hands of the Council except on their terms, will contribute to a weaker collective security system, but more fundamentally to an erosion of the rules governing the use of force that are the foundation of such a system. Although the immediate result of this military action seems to be that a genuine collective security system is even further from our grasp, the critical reaction of state and public opinion to the decision to use force against Iraq is indicative that the majority of the world will not necessarily accept this weakening and erosion. There is clearly a pressing need to carry on Hilaire's work of building on the foundations of authority and legitimacy unique to the United Nations by advocating a collective security system that will more effectively regulate violent actions by states and non-state actors.

103 H. McCoubrey and J. Morris, *Regional Peacekeeping in the Post-Cold War Era* (Kluwer, 2000), p. 243.

13

International law and the suppression of maritime violence

SCOTT DAVIDSON

Introduction

Since time immemorial mariners have fallen prey to the violence of pirates and sea robbers.[1] In Ancient Greece, pirates were never far from the routes of maritime commerce, and the Cretans, Athenians and Rhodians engaged in periodic anti-piracy campaigns.[2] Even the might of Rome could not prevent pirates from exacting their toll on merchant vessels, and Julius Caesar was, perhaps, the first person of note whose capture and ransoming by pirates was chronicled.[3] Needless to say, Caesar's revenge upon these brigands was, inevitably, swift, decisive and bloody.[4] Piracy was not, however, restricted to the Mediterranean during this time. The Germanic and Frankish tribes were efficient and ruthless maritime predators, and the Dark Ages also saw the rise of the Vikings who might be described as having committed piracy on a grand scale.[5] Pirates were also much in evidence in South East Asia, especially in the Indian Ocean and South China Sea, during the fourteenth and fifteenth centuries. So great indeed was the pirate menace in the South

[1] H. A. Ormerod, *Piracy in the Ancient World: Essays in Mediterranean History* (Liverpool University Press, 1978), p. 13. For an overview of the development of piracy see J. A. Gottschalk and B. P. Flanagan, *Jolly Roger with an Uzi: The Rise and Threat of Modern Piracy* (Naval Institute Press, 2000), pp. 1–27.

[2] Ormerod, *Piracy in the Ancient World*, pp. 59–74. Ormerod notes the existence of treaties between the Greek city states to combat piracy, at pp. 73–4.

[3] Ormerod, *Piracy in the Ancient World*, pp. 20, 23; Captain C. Johnson, *A General History of the Robberies and Murders of the Most Notorious Pirates* (with an introduction and commentary by David Cordingly) (Conway, 1998), pp. 2–4.

[4] Apparently, after promising them safe passage he had them hunted down and crucified, Ormerod, *Piracy in the Ancient World*, p. 55.

[5] J. Haywood, *Dark Age Naval Power: a Reassessment of Frankish and Anglo-Saxon Seafaring Activity* (Anglo-Saxon, 1999), chs. 2 and 3.

China Sea that the Ming Emperor organized a fleet of over 3,000 warships to tackle the problem.[6] It is, however, the so-called 'Golden Age' of Caribbean piracy of the seventeenth and eighteenth centuries that most people have in mind when reference is made to pirates. Although the period has been invested with a certain romance, the sea robbers of this time were as ruthless and brutal as their predecessors. The names of Ned Teach or Blackbeard and Henry Morgan are synonymous with rapacity and cruelty.[7] During the early part of the nineteenth century the focus of piracy once again switched to the Mediterranean where the Royal Navy and the fledgling United States Navy were heavily engaged in suppressing the Corsairs of North Africa.[8]

Characteristics of contemporary maritime violence

During the twentieth and twenty-first centuries, the threat of piracy and armed robbery at sea has been supplemented by the additional peril of maritime terrorism. While armed robbery at sea remains the greatest menace to seafarers, and while true piracy or piracy *iure gentium* has diminished with the evolution of new maritime zones, terrorism at sea represents a hazard of considerable potential, not only to the safety of mariners and ships' passengers but also to the security of sea lines of communication (SLOC).[9] The range of targets available to terrorists is considerable. In 1985, Palestinian terrorists hijacked the Italian cruise ship *Achille Lauro*, a vessel of 24,000 tons and with a passenger complement of 800. By comparison, today's superliners often exceed 60,000 tons and have a passenger complement of 2,000 or more. Vessels of this kind represent a significant target for the maritime terrorist.[10] Furthermore, there are many straits around the world which, if blocked, could seriously disrupt the international

[6] Gottschalk and Flanagan, *Jolly Roger with an Uzi*, p. 2.

[7] See Johnson, *A General History*; D. Cordingly, *Life Among the Pirates: The Romance and the Reality* (Little Brown, 1995).

[8] G. Tucker, *Dawn Like Thunder: The Barbary Wars and the Birth of the US Navy* (Bobbs-Merrill, 1966).

[9] J. L. Batongbacal, 'Maritime Terrorism: Scenarios and Challenges', paper given at the Eleventh Meeting of CSCAP Maritime Cooperation Working Group, 18–19 February, Seoul.

[10] Following the *Achille Lauro* incident the IMO adopted MSC/Circ. 443 of 26 September 1986, *Measures to Prevent Unlawful Acts Against Passengers and Crews on Board Ships.* This circular provides a comprehensive checklist of practical measures designed to increase port and ship security. MSC/Circ. 443 was supplemented and extended to

economy.[11] Interference with freedom of navigation in the Straits of Hormuz, the Bosporus and the Straits of Malacca would have a profound effect on world trade. Eighty-five per cent of Middle Eastern oil to the Far East passes through the Straits of Malacca which could be blocked by the sinking of a 250,000 ton VLCC (very large crude carrier) in the narrowest and shallowest part of the Straits.[12] The environmental calamity to which such an act might lead is also apparent.[13] Similarly, terrorist operations against offshore installations provide an opportunity for economic and environmental mayhem. At present, the terrorist threat to shipping is evident primarily in the seas around Sri Lanka where the Tamil Tigers have attacked various vessels and in the maritime area to the South of Philippine archipelago where Abu Sayaf separatists, reportedly backed by Al Qaeda, have attacked shipping and taken hostages.[14] Al Qaeda itself signalled its terrorist intentions in 2000 with an attack upon the *USS Cole* in Yemen.[15] Furthermore, the Gerekan Aceh Merdeka (GAM) or Free Aceh Movement has indicated that it is prepared to disrupt maritime traffic in the Malacca Straits in pursuit of its secessionist ambitions.[16]

deal with passenger ferries in MSC/Circ. 754, 5 July 1996, *Passenger Ferry Security*. In November 2001, the International Chamber of Shipping issued Guidance for Shipowners, Ship Operators and Masters on the Protection of Ships from Terrorism and Sabotage, 21 November 2001, which is based on MSC/Circ. 443, see www.imo.org/includes/blastDataOnly.asp/data_id%3D3827/msccirc443measuresto-prevent.pdf, visited 26 March 2004 and MSC/Circ. 754, see www.imo.org/includes/blastDataOnly.asp/data_id%3D3829/msccirc754passengerferrysecurity.pdf visited 26 March 2004.

[11] Such straits are known as 'choke points': L. Paul, 'Strategic, Legal and Political Initiatives for Cooperative Maintenance of Law and Order at Sea', in S. Bateman (ed.), *Maritime Cooperation in the Asia-Pacific Region: Current Situation and Prospects* (Australian National University, 1999), pp. 121–43 at pp. 121–5.

[12] S. B. Weeks, *Sea Lines of Communication (SLOC) Security and Access* (Policy Paper 33, University of California Institute on Global Conflict and Cooperation, 1998).

[13] 'Asia Seen at High Risk for Oil Spills due to Piracy', *South China Morning Post*, 26 April 2001; 'Australia Warned on Terrorist Oil Risk', *Times of India*, 22 April 2002.

[14] Batongbacal, 'Maritime Terrorism'.

[15] For an account of the facts and American responses see IIP Archives, 'Attack on the USS Cole', http://usinfo.state.gov/topical/pol/terror/colearch.htm, visited 30 March 2002.

[16] 'Gam Says it Controls Ship Lanes', *Nation*, 4 September 2001. On 25 August 2001, the coal transporter *Ocean Silver* was hijacked by members of GAM who were armed with guns and grenade launchers. The hijackers released six crew members, but held another six hostage and demanded a ransom for their release: ICC International Maritime Bureau, *Piracy and Armed Robbery Against Ships: Annual Report, 1 January – 31 December 2001*, p. 36.

Despite the terrorist threat, most maritime violence continues to be perpetrated by those who are motivated by economic rather than political considerations. A glance at the reports collected by the International Maritime Organisation (IMO),[17] the Piracy Reporting Centre of the International Maritime Bureau (IMB)[18] and the Anti-Shipping Activity Messages (ASAMs) of the US National Imagery and Mapping Agency (NIMA)[19] demonstrates not only the extent of maritime violence, but also the *modus operandi* and objectives of modern pirates and maritime robbers. The major 'hot spot' for piracy and armed robbery at sea is undoubtedly South East Asia.[20] The reasons for this may be attributed to a variety of factors including the archipelagic nature of much of the region which provides a haven for would-be criminals; the diminution of major power warship presence in the region since the end of the Cold War; the lack of appropriate policing resources for such a large maritime area; and the opportunity cost of maritime robbery in a largely economically underdeveloped region. The last three of these factors also apply to other regions of the world where piracy and armed robbery against ships is high, such as the west coast of Africa, the Red Sea and the Indian Ocean.[21] Changes in the type of shipping in recent years has also made pirates and armed robbers bolder. Large, technically advanced vessels require smaller crews, and it is not uncommon, for example, for a watch on a large modern merchant ship to consist solely of an officer and an able seaman. Ships are also prey to robbers when in harbour, particularly where port security is poor.[22]

The methods used by maritime robbers and their objectives vary, but broad categories of both can be compiled from the various reports. Frequently robbers are armed, usually with knives and machetes but

[17] IMO, *Reports on Acts of Piracy and Armed Robbery Against Ships*, www.imo.org/HOME.html, visited 26 March 2004. This website is frequently updated.

[18] For weekly piracy reports to the IMB see www.iccwbo.org/ccs/imb_piracy/weekly_piracy_report.asp. The most recent annual report is IMB, *Annual Report 2001*.

[19] See http://pollux.nss.nima.mil/index/, visited 26 March 2004.

[20] The IMB reports that 166 attacks by armed robbers and pirates took place in 2001. Of these attacks, 91 occurred in Indonesian waters, 19 in Malaysian waters and 17 in the Malacca Straits: IMB, *Annual Report 2001*, pp. 6, 71.

[21] IMB, *Annual Report 2001*, pp. 50–8 (Africa) and pp. 41–9 (Indian sub-continent).

[22] A recent example of this was reported in ASAM Reference no. 2004–62 dated 6 March 2004 in Indonesian waters. The report states that 'an unidentified cargo ship was boarded 6 Mar at 0640 local time at a Tajung Priok berth in approximate position 06–06S 106–53E. Three persons armed with knives and battens beat up a duty officer injuring his stomach, back and legs, but escaped empty handed. This was reportedly the second attack on this ship in two days.'

sometimes with firearms, including automatic weapons.[23] There have been reports suggesting that both Indonesian and Chinese military personnel have been 'moonlighting' as armed robbers, but such reports remain essentially unconfirmed.[24] Sometimes a vessel's crew is attacked and crew members injured or killed; sometimes, the crew is simply robbed and then incarcerated while the robbers go about their business on board the vessel. The threat to navigation and the environment when a vessel is under way and not under command because the crew is imprisoned below deck is palpable. Robbers or pirates usually seek to steal cash in the ship's safe or the ship's equipment or cargo.

Occasionally, robbers or pirates may take both the ship and cargo. This sometimes leads to the phenomenon known as 'phantom ships'. Phantom ships work in the following way: after acquiring a vessel, and repainting, renaming and reregistering it, the robbers or pirates obtain a registration certificate, usually at a consulate office. This is often done by offering a bribe to the appropriate official or by using false or forged documents. The new certificate of registration provides the vessel with a new, seemingly official identity. The pirates or robbers then seek a trader or shipping agent with a letter of credit which has almost expired, a not infrequent situation since the demand for shipping capacity often exceeds supply. The ship is then loaded and the shipper receives his bill of lading. The pirates or robbers subsequently sail to a port other than that which is named as the destination on the bill of lading. There they unload the cargo either to a collaborator or an unsuspecting buyer. The vessel might then be disposed of, but more often than not the same

[23] IMB, *Annual Report 2001*, p. 10, Table 9, 'Types of arms used during attacks, January to December 1991–2001'. This table shows that armed attacks have more than tripled from 107 to 335 during the decade reviewed.

[24] The MSIC report on the *M/V Hye Mieko* states that on 23 June 1995 twelve men wearing Chinese army uniforms boarded this Panamanian registered general cargo ship and hijacked the vessel north of Redang Island off the east coast of Malaysia in international waters. The ship was carrying cigarettes and photographic equipment valued at US$2 million. On 25 June, the ship was reported to be under escort by a Chinese patrol boat 140nm southeast of Ho Chi Minh City. The hijackers sailed the vessel to the Chinese port of Shanwei. On 23 July, after removing the cargo, the ship and crew were released. It might be inferred from the facts that these were members of the Chinese provincial coastguard engaged in freelance activities. See also J. Vagg, 'Rough Seas? Contemporary Piracy in South East Asia', (1995) 35 *British Journal of Criminology* 63 (suggesting that given the sophistication of weapons and equipment involved in some attacks, it might be inferred that members of the Indonesian military have been involved in armed robbery and piracy).

process occurs again, reaping significant rewards for the criminals and an equally significant loss to the shipping industry.

While phantom vessels are at the sophisticated and lucrative end of the market in terms of maritime crime, and often underwritten by organized crime syndicates, pirates and robbers are also not averse to minor criminal activity such as preying upon fishermen by taking and selling their catch or, a trend noted by the IMB in its 2001 annual report, taking and ransoming hostages.[25] Previously this kind of activity had been restricted to the Red Sea, but in recent years it has extended to areas of South East Asia and the Indian Ocean.[26] The connection between this type of maritime crime and other criminal activity at sea should also be noted. Those who are engaged in people trafficking or smuggling and drug and small arms trafficking are also identifiable as begetters of maritime violence. Although there may be an intimate connection between these other types of maritime crime and piracy or robbery at sea, this chapter is restricted to a consideration of the latter.

Defining maritime crime

Maritime crime is not a term of art but an omnibus description bringing together those offences which are committed against ships and their crews either in port or at sea. As noted above, the crimes under consideration here are those of piracy, armed robbery against ships and terrorism, but crimes involving the trafficking of persons, narcotics or weapons, various kinds of shipping fraud and crimes associated with fisheries and the environment might also be brought under this heading.

Piracy

Piracy is defined by Article 101 of the United Nations Convention on the Law of the Sea (UNCLOS)[27] as any illegal act of violence, detention or depredation, committed on the high seas or in a place outside the jurisdiction of any state for private ends by the crew or the passengers

[25] IMB, *Annual Report 2001*, p. 17. [26] *Ibid.*

[27] UN doc. A/Conf.62/122; (1982) 21 *International Legal Materials* 1261. UNCLOS Article 101 replicates Article 15 of the Geneva Convention on the High Seas 1958. For an in-depth discussion of the evolution of these provisions, see B. H. Dubner, *The Law of International Sea Piracy* (Martinus Nijhoff, 1980).

of a private ship or aircraft against another ship or aircraft or against persons or property on board that ship or aircraft. Since piracy *iure gentium* can only be committed on the high seas or on *terra nullius*,[28] it is clear that most acts of so-called piracy today are simply crimes under the domestic law of states since they take place predominantly within waters over which states have sovereignty, that is the internal waters, territorial sea and archipelagic waters of states. Furthermore, the existence of the exclusive economic zone (EEZ) seems to add a further complicating factor, since the high seas are defined in Article 86 of the UNCLOS as excluding waters included within a state's EEZ. Article 58 of the UNCLOS, however, reserves the application of Articles 88 to 115, which includes the provisions on piracy, to the EEZ in so far as they are not incompatible with the EEZ regime. It seems unlikely that the repression of piracy in the EEZ by the warships of a third state would be incompatible, unless it was disproportionate and interfered with the coastal state's resource management and exploitation rights in the zone. Brown suggests that any other conclusion would 'be highly undesirable since it would mean that only the government ships of the coastal State would be able to arrest "pirates" in their exclusive economic zone'.[29] The concept of piracy in international law is also further restricted by the fact that the acts must be done for private ends and that they must be committed by one ship (or aircraft) against another ship (or aircraft). There is no guidance in UNCLOS as to the meaning of 'private ends'. Perhaps the robust approach adopted by Sir Charles Hedges in the seventeenth century might be of assistance. He stated that 'piracy is only a term for sea-robbery, piracy being committed within the jurisdiction of Admiralty'.[30]

Where, however, does the private act end and the public act begin? The incidents involving the *Santa Maria* and the *Achille Lauro* are instructive on this point. In the case of the *Santa Maria*, a Portuguese cruise ship was reported to have been captured by pirates in the

[28] Brown suggests that 'islands and areas of Antarctica over which no State has established sovereignty' appear to be the cases that were envisaged by the Law Commission when it drafted the original provision. He also suggests that drifting 'ice islands' might also fall within the definition: E. D. Brown, *The International Law of the Sea*, vol. I, *Introductory Manual* (Dartmouth, 1994), pp. 302–3. It may be questioned whether or not this formulation includes territory whose title is in dispute but over which the competing states claim jurisdiction e.g. the Spratly Islands in the South China Sea whose territorial sovereignty has not been conclusively resolved.

[29] Brown, *International Law of the Sea*, p. 303.

[30] *R* v. *Dawson*, 13 State Trials 451 at 454.

Caribbean.[31] The Portuguese government issued a request for assistance from the British, Dutch and American navies which began searching for the vessel. Following investigation by the US State Department, however, it was discovered that the *Santa Maria* had been boarded by a Captain Henrique Galvao and his men while the ship was in port and had been hijacked on the high seas by Galvao and his men to make a political point before the Portuguese elections. In consequence of this, it was clear that the hijacking was not piracy because it had not been undertaken for private ends, and the USA refused to intervene further.[32] Similarly, in the incident involving the *Achille Lauro*, the vessel, an Italian-registered cruise liner, had been hijacked in Egyptian territorial waters by Palestinian terrorists who held the passengers and crew hostage and murdered an American citizen on board.[33] The terrorists were eventually apprehended, tried by the Italian courts and convicted of murder. Although the USA issued warrants for their arrest on the grounds, *inter alia*, of piracy under American domestic law,[34] it seems reasonably clear that their actions did not constitute piracy under international law.[35]

The case of the *Castle John*[36] raises an interesting counterpoint to the positions adopted in the *Santa Maria* and *Achille Lauro* incidents. Here,

[31] Whiteman, *Digest* (1965), vol. 4, pp. 665–7; Dubner, *International Sea Piracy*, pp. 146–9; L. C. Green, 'The Santa Maria: Rebels or Pirates?', (1961) 37 *British Yearbook of International Law* 496.

[32] It can also be observed that this incident did not satisfy the 'two vessel' requirement of Article 15 of the Geneva Convention on the High Seas 1958, whose terms, as noted above, were incorporated without amendment as Article 101 of the UNCLOS. Galvao and his insurgents eventually put into the Brazilian port of Recife and were granted political asylum.

[33] N. Ronzitti (ed.), *Maritime Terrorism and International Law* (Martinus Nijhoff, 1990); D. Freestone, 'The Convention for the Suppression of Unlawful Acts Against the Safety of Navigation', (1988) 3 *International Journal of Esturine and Coastal Law* 305; M. Halberstam, 'Terrorism on the High Sea: The Achille Lauro, Piracy and the IMO Convention on Maritime Safety', (1988) 82 *American Journal of International Law* 269.

[34] 18 USC § 1651.

[35] T. Treves, 'The Rome Convention for the Suppression of Unlawful Acts Against the Safety of Maritime Navigation', in Ronzitti, *Maritime Terrorism and International Law*, pp. 69–90 at pp. 70–1. Menefee, however, suggests that an argument could be made that the PLO members were guilty of piracy despite the internal takeover of the vessel: Samuel Pyeatt Menefee, 'Piracy, Terrorism and the Insurgent Passenger: A Historical and Legal Perspective', in Ronzitti, *Maritime Terrorism and International Law*, pp. 43–61 at pp. 59–61. Halberstam argues that the actions of the *Achille Lauro* hijackers could be considered piracy under customary international law: Halberstam, 'Terrorism on the High Sea', pp. 272–91. This is not the generally accepted position.

[36] *Castle John and Nederlandse Stichting Sirius* v. *Nv Marjlo and Nv Parfin* (1986) 77 ILR 537.

the boarding, occupation and damage of two Dutch vessels by members of Greenpeace to prevent alleged environmental damage by the dumping of titanium dioxide in the North Sea was held by the Belgian Cour de Cassation to be piracy within the meaning of Article 15 of the Geneva Convention on the High Seas, since, despite the political colour of the acts in question, they were done for 'personal ends'. This decision is difficult to reconcile with the idea of piracy being committed for some kind of personal gain, whether monetary or otherwise. The actions of Greenpeace might well be offences against navigation attracting the penal jurisdiction of a state's criminal courts, but it seems inappropriate to classify them as piracy *iure gentium*. One might imagine that the directors of Greenpeace would not take kindly to their organization being classified as *hostis humanis generis* – an enemy of all mankind.[37] The *Castle John* does, however, demonstrate the satisfaction of the two vessel requirement in the law of piracy; a criterion which was satisfied neither in the *Santa Maria* nor the *Achille Lauro* incidents.[38]

Given the particularly restrictive and somewhat archaic definition of piracy in international law, it might be questioned whether or not piracy should be redefined to deal with the problems of contemporary maritime violence. Certainly, the *Achille Lauro* incident highlighted the difficulties associated with the two vessel requirement of Article 101 and its predecessor, and in direct consequence of this Italy initiated the drafting of the Convention for the Suppression of Unlawful Acts Against the Safety of Navigation 1988 (SUA) and the Protocol for the Suppression of Unlawful Acts Against the Safety of Fixed Platforms Located on the Continental Shelf 1988 (SUAPROT) under the auspices of the IMO.[39] These instruments have been described by the UN Secretary-General in his 1998 *Report on Oceans and the Law of the Sea* as a 'more useful vehicle for prosecution than the nineteenth century piracy statutes'.[40] They are still not perfect, however, and leave some unresolved issues in the legal coverage of unlawful acts at sea. It is arguable that in the light of these and other developments, however, there is little need to contemplate redefining piracy. Much of what is

[37] S.P. Menefee, 'The Case of the Castle John, or Greenbeard the Pirate?: Environmentalism, Piracy and the Development of International Law', (1993) 24 *California Western International Law Journal* 1.

[38] N. Ronzitti, 'The Law of the Sea and the Use of Force Against Terrorist Activities', in Ronzitti, *Maritime Terrorism and International Law*, pp. 1–14 at p. 2.

[39] Treves, 'Rome Convention for the Suppression of Unlawful Acts', p. 69.

[40] UN doc. A/53/456, para. 151.

referred to as 'piracy' in common parlance[41] is, in fact, simply criminal activity which takes place within the jurisdiction of states. Admittedly, the complexity of the jurisdictional matrix governing criminal activity at sea can make it difficult to deal with the perpetrators of maritime violence, but it is submitted that the essential legal framework is in place to deal with it effectively; all that is required is for certain states to exhibit the political will both to participate in the appropriate legal instruments and to cooperate fully with their neighbours in suppressing maritime crimes of violence.[42] Indeed, maritime crime exhibits many of the characteristics of other forms of transnational crime, and the solutions which present themselves are also similar.

Armed robbery against ships

A review of most acts of 'piracy' reported to the Piracy Reporting Centre of the IMB, the IMO or NIMA fall within the category of what is now termed armed robbery against ships. In its draft Code of Practice for the Investigation of Crimes of Piracy and Armed Robbery against Ships ('draft Code of Practice'), the IMO distinguishes clearly between piracy proper and armed robbery against ships.[43] Under the draft Code of Practice, 'piracy means unlawful acts as defined by Article 101 (UNCLOS)'[44] while 'armed robbery against ships' means:

> Any unlawful act of violence or detention or any act of depredation, or threat thereof, other than an act of 'piracy', directed against a ship or against persons or property on board such ship, *within a State's jurisdiction over such offences.*[45]

It will be noted that while this definition bears similarity to the definition of piracy in Article 101, it omits the two vessel requirement and says nothing about the private motive of such unlawful acts. The main requirement is that the acts be unlawful, presumably under the law

[41] Or in the IMB definition of 'piracy', on which, see below.

[42] For an analysis of the jurisdictional issues associated with maritime crime see D. Mackinnon, 'Transnational Dimensions of Maritime Crime', paper presented at the Transnational Crime Conference convened by the Australian Institute of Criminology in association with the Australian Federal Police and Australian Customs Service held in Canberra, 9–10 March 2000. See also Council for Security Cooperation in the Asia Pacific, *CSCAP Memorandum No 5: Cooperation for Law and Order at Sea* (February 2001).

[43] MSC/Circ. 984, 20 December 2000.

[44] *Ibid.*, para. 2.1.

[45] *Ibid.*, para. 2.2. Emphasis added.

of the coastal state. The IMB definition does not make a distinction between piracy and armed robbery, but since it is for statistical purposes alone, this has little significance from a legal point of view.[46] It is interesting, however, that the IMB definition of piracy and armed robbery includes inchoate offences, as well as those crimes which have been consummated. The definition provides that piracy and armed robbery is: 'An act of boarding or attempting to board any ship with the intent to commit theft or any other crime and with the intent or capability to use force in furtherance of that act.'[47]

It is also noticeable that the *locus* of the offence is irrelevant under the IMB definition, and this is confirmed by an examination of the many incidents contained in that organization's annual reports. Furthermore, the IMO and IMB definitions comprehend crimes which extend beyond the notions of theft or armed robbery, and thus acts of violence done for political purposes would still fall within these definitions.

Terrorism

There has been considerable and lengthy argument about the legal meaning of terrorism and whether there is need for a comprehensive instrument to deal with the issue.[48] As yet, however, there is no international legal instrument which provides such a definition nor a comprehensive instrument to tackle the problem. Indeed, the response has been piecemeal or, to use McWhinny's term, 'sectorial'.[49] There are a number of instruments which clearly deal with the phenomenon of terrorism or aspects of it,[50] but significantly, they fail to define it.[51]

46 IMB, *Annual Report 2001*, p. 3. 47 *Ibid.*

48 Laqueur states that between 1936 and 1981 no less than 109 different definitions of terrorism were advanced in a variety of forums. See W. Laqueur, 'Reflections on Terrorism', (1986) 65 *Foreign Affairs* 86.

49 E. McWhinney, *Aerial Piracy and International Terrorism* (2nd edn, Nijhoff, 1987), pp. 130–3.

50 Treves, 'Rome Convention for the Suppression of Unlawful Acts', pp. 70–1.

51 The following conventions deal with various aspects of terrorism: the Convention on Offences and Certain Other Acts Committed on Board Aircraft ('Tokyo Convention' 1963); Convention for the Suppression of Unlawful Seizure of Aircraft ('Hague Convention' 1970); Convention for the Suppression of Unlawful Acts Against the Safety of Civil Aviation ('Montreal Convention' 1971); Convention on the Prevention and Punishment of Crimes Against Internationally Protected Persons (1973); International Convention Against the Taking of Hostages (1979); Convention on the Physical Protection of Nuclear Material (1980); Protocol for the Suppression of Unlawful Acts of Violence at Airports Serving International Civil Aviation,

In General Assembly Resolution 51/210, entitled 'Measures to Eliminate International Terrorism', the General Assembly stated that it:[52]

> 1. Strongly condemns all acts, methods, and practices of terrorism as criminal and unjustifiable, wherever and by whomsoever committed;
> 2. Reiterates that criminal acts intended or calculated to provoke a state of terror in the general public, a group of persons or particular persons for political purposes are in any circumstance unjustifiable, whatever the considerations of a political, philosophical, ideological, racial, ethnic, religious or other nature that may be invoked to justify them.

In short, it might be said that terrorism, in a colloquial sense, is politically motivated violence perpetrated against both military and civilian targets by individuals or non-state entities. Whatever the motivation for terrorism, it is clear that the use of violence will constitute a crime under most states' criminal law. As demonstrated above, politically motivated crime will generally take it outside the ambit of the traditional definition of piracy, but it can also create difficulties when dealing with fugitive offenders. In extradition proceedings, especially in circumstances where politically motivated crime is concerned, a person whose extradition is requested might plead the political offence exception. The claim here is that the criminal offence in question was motivated by political factors, such as a desire to overthrow an incumbent government or to change a particular government's policy, and that as a consequence of this the fugitive offender should not be surrendered, but should, instead, be granted asylum.[53] Different states deal with the political offence exception in different ways, but most recognize this category of defence in extradition proceedings.[54] Certain treaties have tried to grapple with the relationship between politically motivated

supplementary to the Convention for the Suppression of Unlawful Acts Against the Safety of Civil Aviation (1988); Convention for the Suppression of Unlawful Acts Against the Safety of Maritime Navigation (1988); Protocol for the Suppression of Unlawful Acts Against the Safety of Fixed Platforms Located on the Continental Shelf (1988); Convention on the Marking of Plastic Explosives for the Purpose of Detection (1991); International Convention for the Suppression of Terrorist Bombing (1997 UN General Assembly Resolution); International Convention for the Suppression of the Financing of Terrorism (1999).

[52] UN GAOR 51/210, 17 December 1996.

[53] G. Gilbert, *Aspects of Extradition Law* (Martinus Nijhoff, 1991), pp. 113–82.

[54] *Ibid.*, pp. 120–31.

terrorism and the political offence exception, but it remains a largely intractable conundrum which has yet to be resolved satisfactorily.[55]

Jurisdictional barriers: problems and solutions

The major problem in dealing satisfactorily with maritime violence is the multiple, overlapping jurisdictional regimes which might apply to what appears at first sight to be a relatively simple criminal case. Take, for instance, a robbery committed on board a ship. Let us assume that the ship is Panamanian registered; that it is sailing through Singapore's territorial sea; that a Bulgarian officer is seriously injured in the robbery; that the robbers are of Indonesian nationality and that after the robbery they flee by unregistered craft into Malaysia's territorial sea where they are subsequently apprehended by the Malaysian navy. The states having a jurisdictional interest in this case would be Panama, as the state of registration of the vessel; Singapore, as the state in whose territory the offence was committed; Bulgaria, on the grounds of passive personality jurisdiction and Malaysia, as the state in whose territory the fugitive offenders were apprehended. It has been a criticism of open registry states such as Panama that they are not interested in exercising their penal jurisdiction in circumstances such as those described above, therefore it is unlikely that it would press its claim. Bulgaria might wish to seek extradition of the offenders, although conducting a criminal case several thousand miles away from the place where it occurred raises a number of practical problems involving evidence and, more particularly, the availability of witnesses. Singapore would have a strong case for securing the surrender of the offenders from Malaysia since Singapore's claim to jurisdiction is based on the territorial principle, and it would probably wish to send a signal to other maritime robbers that Singapore will make every effort to bring such offenders to account if they commit crimes in Singaporean waters. If the robbery had been committed on the high seas, it would be piracy within the meaning of international law and Malaysia would be able to take jurisdiction, but since the offence was committed within the maritime territory of Singapore, Malaysia would not have *prima facie* jurisdiction, other than that involved in the apprehension of fugitive offenders.

[55] See, e.g., the 1985 USA–United Kingdom agreement which excluded from the political offence exception persons who used certain weapons against certain targets.

From this scenario it will be apparent that maritime violence can only be countered effectively where states are willing to take and enforce criminal jurisdiction, and where they are prepared to cooperate to defeat transnational crime of this kind. The development of appropriate jurisdictional regimes thus requires the development of international instruments, but other forms of cooperation can also occur either on a formal or informal basis. At the multilateral level, the SUA represents a tailor-made solution to the problem of acquiring jurisdiction and enforcing criminal law in an appropriate way. As noted above, the SUA was adopted under the auspices of the IMO largely to deal with the threat of terrorism against ships. The SUA, however, has a much broader scope than this and it comprehends a broad range of criminal activity, including armed robbery and piracy, directed at ships and continental shelf platforms. SUA is modelled on similar conventions designed to deal with aircraft hijacking, but has been modified to deal with particular problems associated with maritime crime.[56]

Article 3 of the SUA specifies as offences a number of acts against shipping, including the seizure or destruction of ships and the endangering of safe navigation by the use of violence against any person on a ship or by damaging a ship, its cargo or equipment, including its navigational facilities. Article 5 requires states to make these offences punishable under their laws, while Article 6(1) requires that they establish jurisdiction over offences committed on or against their ships or in their territory or by their nationals. States may also assert jurisdiction over offences committed by stateless persons habitually resident within their territory, offences where their nationals are victims and offences aimed at compelling a state to do or abstain from doing some act.[57] The offences identified in the SUA are, in accordance with Article 11, to be included as extraditable offences in extradition treaties between states parties, and a state party in whose territory an alleged offender is found is either obliged to extradite him or her to a requesting state party or to prosecute him or her.[58] In order to ensure that this latter is possible, states parties are required, under Article 6(4), to ensure that the appropriate jurisdictional arrangements are in place to allow prosecution to

[56] Treves, 'Rome Convention for the Suppression of Unlawful Acts', pp. 71, 74.

[57] SUA Article 6(2). This was the case in the *Achille Lauro* incident where the objective of the terrorists was to secure the release of a number of their comrades from imprisonment in Israel.

[58] SUA Article 10. This represents an application of the *aut dedere aut judicare* principle.

take place. In terms of general cooperation to defeat unlawful acts against shipping, Article 12 of the SUA states that states parties must afford each other the greatest measure of assistance in connection with criminal proceedings brought in respect of the offences in Article 3, while Article 13 of the SUA further provides:

> 1. States Parties shall cooperate in the prevention of the offences set forth in Article 3, particularly by:
> (a) taking all practicable measures to prevent preparations in their respective territories for the commission of those offences within or outside their territories;
> (b) exchange information in accordance with their national law, and co-ordinating administrative and other measures taken as appropriate to prevent the commission of offences set forth in Article 3.

This provision implicitly recognizes that acts preparatory to the commission of maritime crime very often take place on land. Vessels must be crewed and provisioned and this will usually take place either at some remote port or other coastal facility. Sound policing practices on or close to shore will often be a major plank in defeating both pirates and maritime criminals.

Since the SUA is based on the aircraft hijacking conventions, its application *ratione territoriae* is similarly predicated upon a vessel being engaged or potentially engaged in an international voyage. This was designed to make the territorial scope of the SUA as broad as possible.[59] Article 4 provides:

> (1) This Convention applies if the ship is navigating or is scheduled to navigate into, through or from waters beyond the outer limit of the territorial sea of a single State, or the lateral limits of its territorial sea with adjacent States.
>
> (2) In cases where the Convention does not apply pursuant to paragraph 1, it nevertheless applies when the offender or the alleged offender is found in the territory of a State party other than the State referred to in paragraph 1.

On the basis of this provision, therefore, it is of no significance where an offence occurs, as long as the vessel against which it is directed is scheduled to navigate beyond the outer limit of the territorial sea. What constitutes 'beyond the outer limit of the territorial sea' might vary from state to state, depending on geographical location. It might be that the EEZ of the coastal state lies beyond the outer limit of its territorial sea, or it might be the

[59] Treves, 'Rome Convention for the Suppression of Unlawful Acts', p. 73.

territorial sea of another state. Similarly, the reference to the lateral limits of a state's territorial sea with an adjacent state means that vessels involved in the coastal trade are also covered by the SUA. The absence of an international element, however, prevents engagement of the SUA. Thus, a voyage which begins and ends in one state's territorial sea or internal waters will be a matter of concern for that state alone.

While the SUA has the potential to be an effective weapon against maritime violence, states have been slow to ratify it, despite calls upon them to do so from the United Nations and the shipping industry.[60] As noted above, the UN Secretary-General suggested in his 1998 *Report on Oceans and the Law of the Sea* that the SUA provided a useful means of combating piracy.[61] More recently, the UN General Assembly in Resolution 56/12,[62] urged states to become parties to the SUA and the SUAPROT and to ensure its effective implementation through the adoption of legislation aimed at ensuring that there is a proper framework for responses to incidents of armed robbery at sea.

The IMO has been active in attempting to facilitate cooperative measures to deal with maritime violence. In June 1999, the IMO's Maritime Safety Committee (MSC) issued Circular 622/Rev. 1 entitled *Recommendations to Governments for Preventing and Suppressing Piracy and Armed Robbery Against Ships.*[63] Here, the IMO suggested that states should develop action plans for dealing with piracy,[64] as well as establishing the necessary infrastructure and operational arrangements for the purposes of preventing and suppressing piracy and armed robbery against ships.[65] On the question of jurisdiction, the IMO recommended

[60] IMO, 'Summary of Status of Conventions as at 30 April 2001', www.imo.org/HOME.html. For details of ratifications see IMO, 'Status of Complete Listings of Conventions', *ibid.* It is noticeable that neither Indonesia nor Malaysia have ratified the SUA or SUAPROT.

[61] UN doc. A/53/456, para. 151.

[62] Oceans and Law of the Sea, A/RES/56/12, 13 December 2001.

[63] MSC/Circ. 622/Rev.1, 16 June 1999.

[64] At an international conference involving fifteen regional states which took place in Tokyo in March 2000, the IMO and a number of ship-owners and their associations issued the Tokyo Declaration and a Model Action Plan which closely follows the IMO Recommendations. These relate primarily to reporting structures and the development of effective communications between the various law enforcement agencies of regional states. The Conference communiqué noted, however, that anti-piracy activities 'including potential cooperation can only be done subject to relevant international treaties, each Participating Administration's domestic legislation as well as its availability of adequate resources to sustain these activities'. Copy on file with author.

[65] MSC/Circ. 622/Rev.1, para. 4.

that states should take such measures as may be necessary to establish their jurisdiction over the offences of piracy and armed robbery at sea, including adjustment of their legislation to enable them to apprehend and prosecute persons committing such offences.[66] Although the IMO did not refer to the SUA, many of the jurisdictional issues raised in its *Recommendations* would be remedied by the expedient of ratifying this particular instrument. As a further adjunct to the assumption of state jurisdiction over the offences of piracy and armed robbery against ships, however, the IMO stated that a person apprehended outside the territorial sea of any state for committing these crimes should be prosecuted under the laws of the investigating state by mutual agreement with other substantially interested states.[67] In this context, a 'substantially interested state' means a state:[68]

(1) which is the flag state of a ship that is the subject of an investigation; or
(2) in whose territorial sea the incident has occurred; or
(3) where the incident caused, or threatened, serious harm to the environment of that state, or within those areas over which the state is entitled to exercise jurisdiction under international law; or
(4) where the consequences of an incident caused, or threatened to cause serious harm to that state or to artificial islands, installations or structures over which it is entitled to exercise jurisdiction; or
(5) where, as a result of an incident, nationals of that state lost their lives or received serious injuries; or
(6) that has at its disposal important information that may be of use to the investigation; or
(7) that, for some other reason, establishes an interest that is considered significant by the lead investigating state;
(8) that was requested by another state to assist in the repression of violence against crews, passengers, ships, cargoes or the collection of evidence; or
(9) that intervened under UNCLOS Article 100, exercised its right of visit under UNCLOS Article 110, or effected the seizure of a pirate/armed robber, ship or aircraft under UNCLOS Article 105 in port or on land.

The broadening of the jurisdictional bases which the IMO recommends would undoubtedly assist in combating maritime violence, but given the failure of a number of interested states to grasp the opportunity presented by the SUA, these are unlikely to eventuate in the near future.

[66] *Ibid.*, para. 17. [67] *Ibid.*, para. 16. [68] *Ibid.*

A further initiative suggested by the IMO is the adoption of a Regional Agreement on Cooperation in Preventing and Suppressing Acts of Piracy and Armed Robbery against Ships.[69] The agreement, which at the time of writing has not been adopted, stresses the need for international cooperation in suppressing piracy and armed robbery at sea. While it reiterates both the right and obligation of a state to take measures to suppress piracy[70] and armed robbery in its own waters, it none the less also recognizes that jurisdictional boundaries inhibit effective action against fugitive offenders. The draft regional agreement thus establishes a process for cooperation which would permit the vessels of one state to pursue offenders into the national waters of another state. Such pursuit would, under UNCLOS Article 6, only be allowed where a law enforcement liaison officer is embarked on the law enforcement vessel of the other state and gives his or her consent for pursuit into national waters. This form of delegated state authorization which would allow a foreign state to engage in law enforcement activities in the territory of another state appears to be some way from becoming a reality, but it does not preclude other forms of bilateral cooperation in the interim.[71] Indeed, a number of bilateral initiatives have been introduced in recent times. In 1992, Singapore and Indonesia agreed to establish direct communications between their navies and agreed to coordinate anti-piracy patrols,[72] as well as provisions for coordinating the pursuit of pirates who fled from the waters of one state to the other. With prior authorization, the warships of one state were permitted to pursue pirates or armed robbers into the territorial waters of the other.[73] In December 1992, Malaysia and Indonesia, using their Joint Border

69 MSC/Circ. 622/Rev.1, App. 5.

70 This obligation is stated in UNCLOS Article 100. It provides: 'All states shall cooperate to the fullest possible extent in the repression of piracy on the high seas or in any other place outside the jurisdiction of any state.'

71 The authorization of vessels to pursue offenders into the coastal waters of a foreign state appears to be modelled upon similar agreements based on Article 17 of the UN Convention Against Illicit Traffic in Narcotic Drugs and Psychotropic Substances 1988. See W.C. Gilmore, 'Drug Trafficking by Sea: The 1998 United Nations Convention Against Illicit Traffic in Narcotic Drugs and Psychotropic Substances', (1991) 15 *Marine Policy* 183; W.C. Gilmore, 'Narcotics Interdiction at Sea: UK–US Cooperation', (1989) 13 *Marine Policy* 218; W.C. Gilmore, 'Narcotics Interdiction at Sea: the 1995 Council of Europe Agreement', (1996) 20 *Marine Policy* 3.

72 Referred to as Indo-Sin Coordinated Patrols (ISCP).

73 R. Beckman, 'Issues of Public International Law relating to Piracy and Armed Robbery Against Ships in the Malacca and Singapore Straits', available at www.sils.org/seminar/1999-piracy-03.htm (stating that operations conducted by the Indonesian Navy in 1992

Committee, established a mechanism to coordinate maritime cooperation in the Straits of Malacca. This mechanism led to coordinated patrols in the Straits. The result of this, together with unilateral measures against piracy by Singapore, Indonesia and Malaysia, is reported to have led to a noticeable decrease in piracy in this area during the period 1993 to 1999.

There have been other, more recent, forms of bilateral cooperation in the Asian region. In October 2000, Vietnam and Cambodia conducted joint anti-drug smuggling and anti-piracy patrols in each other's national waters, and in March 2001 the Japanese coastguard and the Singaporean navy engaged in joint anti-piracy exercises in the area of the Malacca Straits and Singapore Straits. The Japanese coastguard has also conducted anti-piracy exercises with the Indian navy in the Indian Ocean,[74] and trains regional personnel in anti-piracy measures at its coastguard College. Even more recently, the Filipino and Malaysian navies have agreed to cooperate in sharing information to combat piracy, robbery and kidnappings which have occurred within their contiguous territories.[75]

Concluding remarks

It is unlikely that maritime violence will ever be totally defeated. The reasons for this pessimistic assessment are not only based upon the practical difficulties of policing the maritime environment, but also upon the absence of appropriate and sufficient capacity in the form of maritime surveillance aircraft, vessels which can be used for enforcement and even the inability of states to buy sufficient satellite surveillance time.[76] Even in states with considerable material resources,

under this agreement resulted in the capture of thirty-eight sea robbers operating along the Singapore Strait and Phillips Channel).

[74] S. B. Weeks, 'Sea Lines of Communication (SLOC) Security and Access' (Policy Paper 33, University of California Institute on Global Conflict and Cooperation, 1998); 'Japanese Coast Guard Vessel to Visit India to Conduct Joint Exercise with Indian Coast Guard at Chennai', at www.japan-emb.org.in/PressReleases/Embassy_Of_Japan/press-embassy34.htm; M. Valencia, 'Joining Up With Japan to Patrol Asian Waters', *International Herald Tribune*, 28 April 2000; N. Chanda, 'Foot in the Water: A Japanese Plan to Send Armed Coastguard Vessels to Combat Pirate Attacks in Asia's Sea Lanes is Finding a Surprisingly Positive Response', *Far Eastern Economic Review*, 9 March 2000.

[75] 'Navies Agree to Anti-crime Move', *The Star*, 8 August 2001.

[76] J. Kidd, 'Indonesia's Overstretched Navy', *IISS Strategic Pointers*, at www.iiss.org/pub/sp/sp01004.asp, visited 30 April 2002. See also Office of Naval Intelligence, Civil Maritime Analysis Department, 'Worldwide Threat to Shipping Mariner Warning

maritime violence still occurs and the perpetrators often escape. Despite this, there is a perception that in some states there is an absence of either political capacity or political will to undertake the necessary legislative action in order to help ameliorate the situation.[77] It is also significant that in an area of the world where maritime violence is rife, South East Asia, the two states most obviously affected by piracy and armed robbery against ships, that is Indonesia and Malaysia, have so far failed to ratify the SUA.[78] While legal regimes do not, and cannot, of themselves prevent maritime violence, a rational and predictable legal framework is a prerequisite for taking appropriate action against the perpetrators of maritime violence. Although there is evidence of inter-state cooperation at both multilateral and bilateral levels, there is clearly a need for greater coordination in developing an appropriate legal framework for action in this area. This coordination is being pursued in a number of fora, of both a governmental and non-governmental nature,[79] but as the calls from the shipping industry and other maritime organizations suggest, not enough is being done, nor is it being done with sufficient haste.[80] In such circumstances, there can be little surprise that the shipping

Information', 27 February 2002, http://164.214.12.145/MISC/wwtts/, visited 30 April 2002 (reporting that the Indonesian navy requires 239 vessels and 115 aircraft to patrol its territory effectively). It currently has 115 vessels and 60 aircraft. Indonesia is receiving assistance in the provision of police vessels from Australia.

77 This perception is not always well founded. A report of 12 February 2002 states that Indonesia is setting up a third anti-piracy centre based out of Bangka, Sumatra Island. This centre will augment existing centres operating from Medan City and Batam Island: Office of Naval Intelligence, Civil Maritime Analysis Department, 'Worldwide Threat to Shipping Mariner Warning Information', 27 February 2002, at http://164.214.12.145/MISC/wwtts/, visited 26 March 2004. A recent report states that Malaysia has offered to host a new regional anti-piracy coordination centre. The new centre will coordinate among Asian nations in disseminating reports of maritime crime among participating governments and would also liaise with the IMB Piracy Reporting Centre. See http://164.214.12.145/MISC/wwtts/wwtts_20020417000000.txt, visited 30 April 2002.

78 IMO, 'Summary of Status of Conventions as at 30 April 2001', at www.imo.org/HOME.html. For details of ratifications see IMO, 'Status of Complete Listings of Conventions', *ibid.*

79 See, e.g., the work done by the Council for Security Cooperation in Asia Pacific (CSCAP) referred to above. CSCAP recommendations from its various working groups, including the Maritime Cooperation Working Group, are forwarded to the ASEAN Regional Forum for consideration. See M. J. Valencia, 'Prospects for Multilateral Maritime Regime Building in Asia', in Bateman, *Maritime Cooperation in the Asia-Pacific Region*, pp. 27–67.

80 See, e.g., Safe Navigation and Environment Committee (SNEC) of the Asian Shipowners Forum, Press Release, 2 November 2000; Office of Naval Intelligence, Civil Maritime Analysis Department, 'Worldwide Threat to Shipping Mariner Warning Information', 27 February 2002, http://164.214.12.145/MISC/wwtts/, visited

industry is taking matters into its own hands, with operators who can afford such things installing satellite tracking devices in their vessels.[81] And while some security firms advocate the carrying of arms, the IMO considers that such a development is more, rather than less, likely to endanger mariners' lives.[82]

30 April 2002, reported that the President of the Baltic and International Maritime Council (BIMCO) appealed on 16 October 2001 to the Secretary-General of the United Nations to take action to put the United Nations' weight behind increasing awareness of the needs to improve and standardize vessel, port and terminal security not only to fight crime such as piracy but also to mesh with concerns about international terrorism.

81 IMB advocates the fitting of the SHIPLOC device which allows shipping operators to monitor their vessels at sea. See S. Davidson, 'Piracy in SE Asia', [2001] *New Zealand Law Journal* 11. The IMO has also agreed to accelerate the implementation system for the mandatory fitting of Automatic Identification Systems (AIS) for all ships of 500 GWT and above on international voyages, www.imo.org/HOME.html, visited 26 March 2004.

82 MSC/Circ. 623/Rev.1, 16 June 1999, 'Piracy and Armed Robbery Against Ships: Guidance to Shipowners and Ship Operators, Shipmasters and Crews on Preventing and Suppressing Acts of Piracy and Armed Robbery Against Ships', paras. 44–5. The danger of resorting to firearms is graphically demonstrated by the death of round the world yachtsman and America's Cup winner Sir Peter Blake who was killed after discharging a rifle at robbers who had boarded his yacht in the Amazon: ICC International Movitime Bureau, *Piracy and Armed Robbery Against Ships: Annual Report, 1 January–31 December 2002*, p. 21.

14

Law, power and force in an unbalanced world

JUSTIN MORRIS

Introduction

Hilaire McCoubrey and I collaborated extensively during his time at Hull, producing a co-authored book and a number of journal articles. Though identified with different disciplines and working in different departments, our work together benefited immeasurably from our shared view of the way in which the world works, particularly the complex interplay between legal and political issues. A prodigious legal scholar, Hilaire was also acutely sensitive to the broader political context within which legal mechanisms operate. He understood international law to be a process through which states seek political objectives, while at the same time operating to shape the nature of such objectives and the means through which they might be pursued. I am indebted to Hilaire for the wisdom and knowledge he shared with me, and it is a matter of great sadness and regret that his untimely death deprived the field of international humanitarian law of one of its leading scholars and more personally the opportunity for the two of us to realize our plans for future joint ventures.

This chapter draws in part on the McCoubrey Memorial Lecture which I was honoured to deliver in May 2003,[1] though it has been significantly amended to account for changed context and intervening events. In the broadest sense it seeks to shed light on issues raised by

For much of the time during the writing of this chapter and preparation of this volume I was Visiting Fellow at the University of Wales, Aberystwyth. I would like to thank Prof. Nicholas Wheeler for his many helpful comments in the preparation of this chapter. I would also like to thank Prof. Ian Clark for the illuminating discussions of legitimacy which helped inform much of what follows. Of course, any errors are mine alone.

[1] 'The United Nations Security Council: Prospects for Reform', the second Hilaire McCoubrey Memorial Lecture, 28 May 2003, available at www.law.hull.ac.uk/research/intlaw_lectures.html#morris

many of the other contributors to this volume, particularly those discussed by Nigel White, though as befitting our respective disciplinary foci, it does so from a somewhat different perspective. Whereas the other contributors provide detailed legal analysis, in White's case of recent developments regarding the regulation of the use of force, my concern is with the associated political issues: to what extent can international society utilize international law to constrain the behaviour of states, especially the great powers and particularly with regard to the use of force? What role can the United Nations play in this? And would a reconstituted Security Council be better equipped to perform such a task, particularly in the face of American omnipotence?

The chapters collected in this volume provide positive answers to some of these questions, if at times with necessary caution. In many cases the chapters demonstrate the manner in which international legal mechanisms have come to constitute an increasingly important aspect of international society's attempts to deal with the security challenges of the late twentieth and early twenty-first centuries. This stance is one which Hilaire would no doubt have supported, and with increased vigour and tenacity given the threat posed to the international legal framework by events surrounding the terrorist attacks of 11 September 2001, the subsequent 'War on Terror', and the conflict in Iraq. His death deprives like-minded scholars of a formidable ally as they seek to confront the pervasive cynicism – apparently vindicated by recent American–UK action over Iraq – regarding the United Nations (or at least certain aspects of its functioning) and international law, a perception which finds support in the dominant discourse of international relations, namely realism.

Realism, the English School and international law

Realism, particularly in its 'neo' guise, provides an account of the international realm which is characterized, first and foremost, by 'anarchy', understood as the lack of a central, overriding authority operating above states. Anarchy (in contrast to the domestic ordering principle of 'hierarchy'), with its attendant logic of self-help and struggle for survival; state centrism, with states compelled by their anarchic environment to act in a 'functionally undifferentiated' manner; and power accumulation, because 'distinctions among [states] arise principally from their varied capabilities', form the basis of the realist reading of international politics.[2] This adds up to a most unforgiving environment in which norms, *stricto sensu*, have no role to play, for, as Kimberly Hutchings notes, according to the realist account:

> The international sphere [is one] in which structural constraints dictate the pattern of inter-state behaviour against the specific nature and ideology of particular political orders. In effect, neorealists reject the notion of international normative theory in principle since within the international there is no room for changing the system and no possibility of bringing together the realm of what is with what ought to be.[3]

It follows that international law, a key mechanism through which alternative accounts of international relations suggest the 'ought' can be pursued, is either marginalized to the point of irrelevance, or else maligned as an instrument of the powerful. This latter depiction derives in significant part from neorealism's 'classical' precursor, and in particular E. H. Carr's damning critique of the 1919 settlements. He maintained that the legitimizing codes (such as international law) to which states have recourse are representations of the views and interests of the dominant within the system.[4] Realism's aggregated impact has, therefore, been to provide the intellectual underpinning for the common view of international law whereby it is seen as either irrelevant, because 'structure' is the dominant factor, or as of relevance only as a weapon in states' armouries of *realpolitik*. Moreover, as Chris Brown notes, this is a view which has come to transcend academic debate. According to Brown:

> After 1945, realism became [and remains] the dominant theory of International Relations, offering a conception of the world which seemed to define the 'common sense' of the subject. Most practising diplomats had always held views on international relations which were more or less realist; they were now joined by academics ... and by opinion makers more generally, as the leader writers and columnists of influential newspapers and journals came increasingly to work from the same general perspective.[5]

2 See K. N. Waltz, *Theory of International Politics* (McGraw-Hill, 1979); J. J. Mearsheimer, *The Tragedy of Great Power Politics* (Norton & Co., 2001) and J. Donnelly, *Realism and International Relations* (Cambridge University Press, 2000).

3 K. Hutchins, *International Political Theory: Rethinking Ethics in a Global Era* (Sage, 1999), p. 21.

4 E. H. Carr, *The Twenty Years' Crisis 1919–1939: An Introduction to the Study of International Relations* (2nd edn, Macmillan, 1948); see also H. J. Morgenthau, *Politics Among Nations: The Struggle for Power and Peace* (McGraw-Hill, 1948).

5 C. Brown, *Understanding International Relations* (2nd edn, Palgrave, 2001), pp. 30–1.

Yet despite the powerful influence of this coalition of forces, realism's claims, particularly with regard to the role of norms, have not gone unchallenged, most notably by English School scholars.[6] Key to their critique of realism is the assertion that normative, rather than material, factors lie at the heart of international relations, and though the systemic determinants identified by realism are important in understanding the behaviour of states, they are not alone definitive. Hence, in his seminal text *The Anarchical Society*, Hedley Bull distinguishes between an international *system*, in which 'states have sufficient contact between them, and have sufficient impact on one another's decisions, to cause them to behave – at least in some measure – as parts of a whole'[7] and the more complex notion of an international *society*. The latter situation can be said to exist, according to Bull's classic formulation, when:

> A group of states, conscious of certain common interests and common values, form a society in the sense that they conceive themselves to be bound by a common set of rules in their relations with one another, and share in the working of common institutions.[8]

Bull presents a complex picture in which the element of international society competes with a 'Hobbesian' element characterized by interstate warfare, and a cosmopolitan element which perceives the essence of international politics as lying in a realizable community of all, premised on the transnational social bonds that link individual human beings.[9] The complexity of international politics is born of the manner in which these three elements compete with one another over time and place, as the nature of state interaction alters. Through this addition of alternative, competing notions of the nature and potentiality of international relations, English School scholars are able to conceive of a more comprehensive international model than that offered by realist accounts. While anarchy

[6] M. Wight, *International Theory: The Three Traditions* (University of Leicester Press, 1991); H. Bull, *The Anarchical Society: A Study of Order in World Politics* (Macmillan, 1977) and R. Jackson, *The Global Covenant: Human Conduct in a World of States* (Oxford University Press, 2000). See also A. Wendt, *Social Theory of International Politics* (Cambridge University Press, 1999). Wendt's 'constructivist' position shares much common ground with the English School, including the assertion that ideational factors play a markedly different role in international politics to that suggested by realism. See also T. Dunne, 'The Social Construction of International Society', (1995) 1 *European Journal of International Relations* 367.

[7] Bull, *Anarchical Society*, pp. 9–10. [8] *Ibid.*, p. 13.

[9] *Ibid.*, pp. 24–7. See also Wendt's discussion of 'cultures of anarchy' in *Social Theory*, pp. 246–312.

is an essential characteristic of the international realm, the manner in which states respond to this environment is not predetermined.

The subtle richness and persuasive nature of the English School's depiction of the international realm lies in its multidimensional nature. Crucially, in acknowledging the coexistence of the Hobbesian, societal and cosmopolitan elements, each vying for dominance, it is possible to conceive of a variable relationship between ideational and material power. Consequently, realism's understanding of norms as being of limited relevance and essentially self-serving, is replaced by the view that they *may*, in certain situations, also be employed by states in a non-instrumental fashion so as to facilitate the pursuit of the shared objectives of international society. Hence, Bull cites international law (along with the balance of power, the great powers, diplomacy and war) as one of the five 'common institutions' through which states act to preserve the society of states. This divergence regarding the role of norms is the quintessential distinction between the realist and English School accounts of international relations. English School scholars answer in the affirmative Bull's question as to 'whether the rules of international law are observed to a sufficient degree ... to justify our treating them as a substantial factor at work in international politics, and, in particular, as a means of preserving international order'.[10] 'Substantial' should not, of course, be read as meaning definitive; as Bull puts it, 'it is not necessary to establish an *identity* as between actual and prescribed behaviour',[11] but there must be, and it is argued in fact that there is, a degree of congruence between the two.

That this should be so is perhaps unsurprising in regard to states which enjoy a cooperative relationship, but it is also the case where relations are more strained, or, indeed, hostile. Where cooperation and the rule of law are supplanted by conflict and the 'law of the jungle', the politically feasible continues to be subject to legal framing; there are in fact legal rules to the game, even when ostensibly the only rule is that might is right. So it is that in such circumstances legal justifications are still given and aspects of the relationship are enshrined in legal instruments, if only to a limited extent. Moreover, it is an oversimplification to suggest that a given state adopts a particular approach to its international relations and to international law, for in reality, and by necessity, actions and attitudes will be dynamic, changing over time, and according to actor, issue and context. So it was, for example, that the

[10] Bull, *Anarchical Society*, p. 137. [11] *Ibid.*, p. 136 (original emphasis).

ideological differences of the Cold War combined with huge nuclear arsenals and the threat of mutually assured destruction to create a realist logic between its principal protagonists, while over the same period both, but most especially the USA, embroiled themselves in a myriad of legal relations. At the same time almost all states, through the workings of the United Nations, at least proclaimed adherence to a rule-based international order, and within the Euro-Atlantic community states were forging ever more intimate relations. In each of these arenas, international law performed an indispensable task: in the Cold War context it served to delimit the conflict through instruments such as the Nuclear Non-Proliferation Treaty, the Anti-Ballistic Missile Treaty and the various other arms limitation agreements; globally, through the UN Charter, the Universal Declaration on Human Rights and the Covenants on Civil and Political Rights and Economic, Social and Cultural Rights, it sought to prescribe behaviour and establish aspirational targets, and through a plethora of trade instruments it provided regulation and the necessary predictability; and in the West (and in Western Europe even more so) it provided the basis for ever closer cooperation between states seeking to redefine their sovereign relations.

These empirically demonstrable facts – that states regulate their relations through international law, and that there exists a correlation between prescribed and actual behaviour – in turn beg questions as to what motivates compliance with legal regulations. Attempting to fathom such matters is a central part of the English School intellectual endeavour. Belief that the content and/or institution of the law is legitimate and hence worthy of respect provides one possible explanation as to why states may comply with its edicts – though on this point Bull himself was notably sceptical[12] – but as scholars such as Alexander Wendt and Ian Hurd have argued, compliance may also result from other factors, such as fear of coercion or calculations of self-interest.[13] Helpful as such distinctions may be, it must be borne in mind that while analytically distinct, in practice such factors are most unlikely to be mutually exclusive, distinct, fixed over time, or, indeed, necessarily clear or consistent within a given state's leadership.[14] Moreover, claims

[12] *Ibid.*, p. 139.

[13] Wendt, *Social Theory*, pp. 246–312; I. Hurd, 'Legitimacy and Authority in International Relations', (1999) 53 *International Organisation* 379.

[14] For an excellent account of the differing attitudes toward international law and the UN system prevalent within the Bush Administration during the build up to the 2003 Iraq conflict see B. Burrough, 'The Path to War', *Vanity Fair*, May 2004, pp. 100–20.

as to whether, in any particular case, international law is being employed for instrumental or non-instrumental purposes will ultimately remain non-falsifiable. This should not, however, be understood to undermine the English School position, since as Ian Hurd argues:

> [i]t is unreasonable to use the difficulty of proving any one motivation to justify the retreat [as realism tends to] to the default position that privileges another, without requiring similar proof ... We have no better reason to assume coercion [or self-interest] than to assume legitimacy.[15]

As such, whilst it would be naïve, and, indeed, unnecessary, to suggest that states' recourse to legal discourse is always motivated by non-instrumental concerns, it is equally unsustainable to argue that they are always motivated purely by self-interest or fear of coercion.

Just as it is unnecessary for the English School to maintain a counsel of perfection regarding adherence to and respect for the law, so it is to suggest that all are equal before it. The principle of sovereign equality notwithstanding, international society recognizes the status of the great powers and ascribes to them special rights and duties. The great powers, along with the balance which exists between them, are central to the preservation of international order and society.[16] Crucially, it is to these states that responsibility for determining issues of international peace and security primarily falls, as does the duty to modify their behaviour so as to accord with their managerial responsibilities. Pursuant to this the great powers are required, the English School argues, to exploit their preponderant power so as to bestow upon international society a sense of central direction, and international law, as an institution of international society, is a key mechanism through which this helmsmanship can be undertaken.[17] This prescriptive claim is central to the English School's notion of an international society, and we will return to it in due course.[18] Before then, however, it is necessary to consider the complex descriptive claims which the English School makes regarding the relationship between the balance of power, the great powers and international law.

In practice, all states will seek to exploit and shape international society, as they attempt to secure promotion of, and congruence with, their own particular interests and values. Their relative abilities to

[15] Hurd, 'Legitimacy and Authority', p. 392.
[16] See Bull, *Anarchical Society*, pp. 101–26 and 200–29. [17] *Ibid.*, pp. 127–61.
[18] See 'Power and Responsibility' below.

succeed in this endeavour will, however, be determined to a significant degree by their material power. With like-minded counterparts, states will seek to enshrine their relationships through legally binding treaties or, where the requisite criteria are met, this may be achieved through the acceptance of the relevant behavioural norms as rules of customary international law.[19] The legal status of these instruments should not, however, be taken to suggest that they are other than the product of political negotiation, and hence their content and terms will reflect the relative strengths of the negotiating parties, framed within the legal context of the issue in hand. The ubiquitous nature of such activity demonstrates its centrality to international politics, but it is within the particular context of negotiations which lead to the establishment of society-wide norms that the role of the great powers becomes most pronounced, for in such circumstances it is the voices of the greatest powers which will be the most audible. It does not, however, follow that these are the only voices to be heard. Decolonization, human, social and politics rights, and anti-Apartheid, all stand as examples of normative agendas forced onto the international political stage in the face of powerful, if often disunited, opposition. Nevertheless, for such a case to succeed it remains for some within the ranks of the great powers to pick up the normative baton, for invariably only they are able to deploy the requisite material and diplomatic resources to ensure success in the diplomatic mêlée from which laws emerge.

To this extent, then, Carr was correct; international law does reflect the values and interests of the most powerful members of international society. Yet however important to our understanding of international law this observation is, it is a partial, and on its own misleading, reading of the manner in which international law operates, tending to exaggerate the degree to which legal structures can be established, redefined and subsequently employed so as to suit the interests of the powerful. As Finnemore and Sikkink note, '[n]ew norms never enter a normative vacuum but instead emerge in a highly contested normative space where they must compete with other norms and perceptions of interest',[20] but crucially this is not a contest the outcome of which can be wholly dictated, no matter how powerful the advocate. To the extent that

[19] For a brief discussion of sources on international law see I. Brownlie, *Principles of Public International Law* (Oxford University Press, 1998).

[20] M. Finnemore and K. Sikkink, 'International Norm Dynamics and Political Change', (1998) 52 *International Organization* 887 at p. 897.

laws are established and manipulated to satisfy particular interests, the ability to do this successfully is limited by the degree to which *others* come to accept the legitimacy of the rule in question. As Quentin Skinner explains, 'the nature and range of the evaluative concepts which any agent can hope to apply in order to legitimate [its] behaviour can in no case be set by the agent himself'.[21] Moreover, whilst in part the process of securing support for a rule may be dependent upon exogenous factors over which the 'norm innovator'[22] has little or no control, such as the ideological or religious stance of other states, it will in significant part also turn upon endogenous considerations. Hence, a state which is inconsistent in the manner it seeks to apply a given rule to like cases undermines its own position. Similarly, the more frequently a state seeks (in the absence of fundamentally changed circumstances) to amend or reinterpret a rule so as to provide justification for its own policy concerns, the less favourably will its proclaimed normative concerns be viewed. Inconsistent or contradictory invocation of the law impairs its persuasive power. It is also the case that the manner in which a state seeks to apply a rule must be plausible; it must be sufficiently accordant with the meaning of the rule concerned, which will in turn depend upon the clarity and specificity of the rule, or what Thomas Franck refers to as the 'determinacy' of a rule.[23] Hence, there are limits to the extent to which a rule can be stretched so as to cover a situation, and where this elasticity is exceeded, the argument becomes, as Franck puts it, 'laughable'.[24] As he demonstrates, the importance and pervasiveness of this plausibility test applies even to the most powerful of states, as illustrated by the decision of the USA in the *Nicaragua* case[25] not to depend on a reservation it had entered to the jurisdiction of the ICJ because to do so would have entailed arguing that the mining of Nicaraguan ports was a 'domestic' matter as determined by the USA. The USA was not prepared to advance such a palpably ludicrous

[21] Q. Skinner, 'Some Problems in the Analysis of Political Thought and Action', in J. Tully (ed.), *Meaning and Context: Quentin Skinner and his Critics* (Polity, 1988), pp. 97–118 at 117.

[22] See J. Morris, 'Normative Innovation and the Great Powers', in A. Bellamy, *International Society and Its Critics* (Oxford University Press, 2005).

[23] T. Franck, *The Power of Legitimacy Among Nations* (Oxford University Press, 1990).

[24] T. Franck, *Fairness in International Law and Institutions* (Oxford University Press, 1995), p. 32.

[25] *Military and Paramilitary Activities in and Against Nicaragua (Nicaragua* v. *United States)*, Merits, judgment, [1986] ICJ Reports 14.

plea, even though doing so would have halted litigation which ultimately it lost.[26]

To these tests of consistency and plausibility we should add Skinner's observation that:

> Even if the agent is not in fact motivated by any of the principles he professes, he will nevertheless be obliged to behave in such a way that his actions remain compatible with the claim that these principles genuinely motivated him.[27]

This demand for compatibility means, of course, that where states seek to justify their actions through legal discourse, they restrict available policy options and to a significant extent circumscribe the degree to which they can employ material means through which policies can be pursued. So it is that today's most powerful states, namely the developed liberal democracies of the West – and lead amongst them the USA – must behave in a manner commensurate with the ideals they profess (e.g. the rule of law, human rights etc.) and where they fail to do so they open themselves up to international and domestic criticism which carries with it very real political costs. This begs the question as to why states resort to normative, and particularly legal, argumentation, and it turns on its head the idea that international law is simply a tool of the powerful. For Christian Reus-Smit 'the answer lies in both the politics of legitimacy and pragmatism'.[28] Recourse to legal argument, where successful, enables states to portray their particular actions and interests as being commensurate with those of international society as a whole, since ends which are legally permissible fall within the behavioural parameters which international society has collectively established. And recourse to law, as a guide to action, also allows for a more efficient securing of ends through the employment of standardized, socially approved means.[29] The idea that law functions as a kind of political facilitator and lubricant also suggests a relationship which is more complex and dynamic than that suggested by realist thinkers – who see law (along with other normative codes) effectively as a mere function of politics – a symbiotic relationship in which each serves to shape and define the extent, content and import of the other. As Reus-Smit explains:

[26] Franck, *Fairness in International Law*, p. 32. [27] Skinner, 'Some problems', p. 116.

[28] C. Reus-Smit, 'The Politics of International Law', in C. Reus-Smit, *The Politics of International Law* (Cambridge University Press, 2004), p. 38.

[29] *Ibid.*

> Politics is a form of reason and action that generates multiple institutional imperatives, and because of this, institutional practices such as modern international law are deeply structured and permeated by politics. It is important to remember, however, that institutions [e.g. international law] are created by political actors as structuring or ordering devices, as mechanisms for framing politics in ways that enshrine the predominant notions of legitimate agency, stabilise individual and collective purposes, and facilitate the pursuit of instrumental goals.[30]

And so we are drawn ineluctably to the conclusion that, to recall Alexander Wendt's notable formulation,[31] anarchy (to a significant extent) is 'what states make of it', and that, as they seek to exploit the structural flexibility available to them to build their anarchy of choice, international law plays an essential role (just as municipal law is central to shaping and enshrining the nature of domestic society). The absence of an authority higher than the state may differentiate the international from the domestic, but states retain an ability to determine for themselves the nature of their relations with one another, and the extent to which these are to be subject to the rule of law. Of course, in neither the domestic nor the international setting are actors *totally* free to determine the nature of their relations, not least because they will inevitably be susceptible to the impact of external factors over which agents have no control. Moreover, in the anarchic environment in which states interact, prudence may demand that, in the absence of dependable security guarantees, states adopt a defensively cautious approach toward one another in initially building their relations. Third party interposition and the insecurities inherent in anarchy may, to some extent, be mitigated through the possession and exercise of power, but conversely, the standing of the powerful may well court such complications, especially where great power relations are tense, others covet high status, or where they harbour fears regarding the implications of particular policies or actions. Nevertheless, from bilateral arrangements to regional institutions such as the European Union, and beyond to the global aspirations of the United Nations, history is replete with evidence which suggests

[30] *Ibid.*, p. 36. See also V. Gowlland-Debbas, 'The Functions of the United Nations Security Council in the International Legal System', in M. Byers (ed.), *The Role of Law in International Politics: Essays in International Law and International Relations* (Oxford University Press, 2000), pp. 277–313.

[31] A. Wendt, 'Anarchy is What States Make of It: The Social Construction of Power Politics', (1992) 41 *International Organization* 335.

that this default setting is one which can successfully be varied so as to develop closer cooperative ties.

Such legal arrangements inevitably reflect the ideological outlooks and politico-strategic circumstances of the actors concerned. Once established, however, they come to shape these very same factors. Crucially, embodying relationships in legal arrangements entrenches them in such a way that the behaviour of the parties is thereafter interpreted and anticipated in light of the agreement. International law thus provides an enhanced level of stability and predictability, and serves as a key foundational element upon which states can develop their future relations and (possibly) work to achieve collective ends. Somewhat paradoxically, in this latter regard international law facilitates progress while simultaneously denying to states policy directions which contradict the general progression. As such it acts as a form of international ratchet, though its effectiveness in this regard is likely to vary significantly depending on the power of the actors concerned and the activity subject to regulation. Nevertheless, irrespective of the material means of the parties and the relative importance of the activity, where states seek to avoid or transgress the terms of agreements into which they have entered, they will incur costs (in terms of international and domestic reputation, future opportunity costs, cross-functional costs, etc.) which they would not otherwise have to pay but for having entered into the agreement. Moreover, such costs are likely to be markedly higher where the parties recognize their relations to be 'legal', rather than merely expedient or habitual.

As noted above, there is one further regard in which the realist account of the relationship between power and international law differs from that offered by the English School, namely that the latter makes important prescriptive claims regarding the manner in which those possessing preponderant power should behave. While realism views states as rational egoists which will inevitably and exclusively utilize international law to pursue their own national self-interest, the English School, while acknowledging this element, nevertheless recognizes states as being, at least potentially, social in nature. As such they bear rights and responsibilities to the other members of international society, and the great powers, by virtue of their status, should accept the managerial role which befalls them. Thus, for the English School, not only is it the case that the great powers will be the most influential parties in formulating and enforcing international law – a position which the School shares with realists – they additionally maintain that they *should* exercise this role, and in so doing should act to further the interests of international society as a whole. It is to a consideration of this claim, and of the extent to which the great powers have discharged their collective burden of responsibility that we now turn.

Power and responsibility

The relationship between the balance of power, the role of the great powers within it and the efficacy of international law is a complex one. A balance of power, in the sense of a sufficiently diffuse distribution of power such that no state can impose its will on the rest of international society, is a prerequisite for the effective functioning of international law. Hence, Bull cites as one of the functions of the balance of power the provision of the conditions within which the other institutions of international society, including international law, are able to operate,[32] and he approvingly cites Vattel's definition of the balance of power as meaning 'a state of affairs such that no one power is in a position where it is preponderant and can lay down the law to others'.[33] Laying down the law can here be taken both metaphorically and literally, for where unipolarity prevails, there is nothing other than self-restraint to ensure that, in exercising its predominance over the 'legislative' and enforcement processes, the hegemon will act for the good of society rather than for itself alone. While self-restraint may, under unipolarity just as under bi- or multipolarity, induce rule compliance, where the hegemon is invulnerable to coercion, the temptation to succumb to the benefits proffered by delinquent behaviour is intensified. Moreover, where power is so unevenly distributed that a state can achieve its objectives regardless of the reactions of others, reciprocity carries little weight, though it may be added that in today's highly interdependent world such a state of affairs would require a very high degree of imbalance indeed. This final point notwithstanding, a clear correlation can be seen to exist: the greater the imbalance in the distribution of power, the less efficacious international law is likely to be. The ability of a predominant power to dictate legal edicts, to breach the law secure in the knowledge

[32] Bull, *Anarchical Society*, pp. 106–7.

[33] *Ibid.*, p. 101. For further discussion of the various ways in which the term may be applied see M. Wight, 'The Balance of Power', in H. Butterfield and M. Wight (eds.), *Diplomatic Investigations: Essays in the Theory of International Politics* (Allen and Unwin, 1966), pp. 149–76.

that it will face no effective sanction, and to act to enforce the law only when and where its self-interest directs, undermines the potential of legal regulation.[34]

This captures, however, only one aspect of the relationship between power and international law, namely the objective nature of the distribution of power – for while a sufficiently diffuse distribution of power is conducive to the effective functioning of the law, it is not, by itself, sufficient to ensure this. For international law to operate successfully as an institution of international society it is necessary for those states which possess the greatest power to acknowledge and act commensurate to the responsibilities which flow from their status. Such standing within international society does not, therefore, accrue as a simple consequence of aggregated military, economic and political power, but flows from the fact that certain states are 'recognised by others to have, and [are] conceived by their own leaders and peoples to have, certain special rights and duties',[35] modifying their policies and exploiting their power so as to ensure order and impart a degree of central direction to the workings of international society as a whole.[36] The critical importance of this subjective element of the balance of power is captured well by Herbert Butterfield's classic exposition on the subject, in which he notes how, over time:

> the balance of power not only became a diplomatic objective but was exalted into being the very highest of such objectives. The element of egotism in state policy was clearly recognised all the time; but in so far as you were being egotistical, you were supposed now to aim at the preservation of the international order, the maintenance of the balance of power. The principle did in fact prescribe limits to egotism and ambition, and the check did actually operate. It operated because it involved a more enlightened view of your own interests – it was a case of limiting your short-term objectives for the sake of your long-term advantage.[37]

It is for this reason that the great powers are themselves also recognized as being amongst the institutions of international society. The balance

[34] Bull, *Anarchical Society*, pp. 131–2. [35] *Ibid.*, p. 202.

[36] *Ibid.*, pp. 206–7; see also H. Bull, 'The Great Irresponsibles? The United States, the Soviet Union, and World Order', in R. O. Matthews, A. G. Rubinoff and J. G. Stein (eds.), *International Conflict and Conflict Management: Readings in World Politics* (Prentice-Hall, 1984), pp. 386–92.

[37] H. Butterfield, 'The Balance of Power', in Butterfield and Wight, *Diplomatic Investigations*, p. 140.

of power is not simply a state of affairs, a mere pattern of power distribution, it is a contrived mechanism through which order within international society is maintained, and it is to the great powers that this feat of international engineering falls.

To be sure, question marks loom large over the extent to which the great powers have in practice sought and succeeded to discharge this burden of responsibility. It is certainly the case that, in the post-Second World War era, the great powers' credentials in this regard look decidedly weak. Inis Claude comments with characteristic perception and lucidity how, during the San Francisco Conference at which the UN Charter was finalized, the great powers 'were somewhat disingenuous' in discussing their role and position within the United Nations 'in terms of their willingness to assume special responsibility rather than their insistence upon being granted special privileges'.[38] It is true that in the rhetoric of at least one of the great powers, for a time this sentiment prevailed, for having secured the privileges of permanent Security Council membership and the power of the veto, the USA was notable in the early years of the United Nations' life for rebuking its fellow permanent members for failing to recognize that as such they were under a responsibility to represent the interests of the UN membership as a whole, rather than those of their national governments.[39] Yet however noble this view, one cannot but ponder its veracity given the evidence of later years and the USA's behaviour in the face of a less favourable membership balance and an agenda less conducive to its own interests. It was in light of their behaviour within and without the United Nations that Bull was moved to dub the USA and the USSR the 'great *ir*responsibles',[40] and for the duration of the Cold War it is difficult to identify them as having imparted central direction to a world in which international order – and indeed planetary survival – hung by the thread of mutually assured destruction.

These imperfections of practice notwithstanding, the UN system demonstrates well the interplay between power, great power status and international law, most particularly with regard to the regulation of the use of force. In both its *jus ad bellum* and *jus in bello* aspects,

38 I. L. Claude, Jr., *Swords into Plowshares: The Problems and Progress of International Organization* (4th edn, McGraw-Hill, 1984), p. 154.

39 See I. Clark, *Legitimacy in International Society* (Oxford University Press, forthcoming 2005).

40 Bull, 'The Great Irresponsibles?'.

international law seeks to play both an aspirational and a regulatory role, prescribing behavioural standards and seeking to provide mechanisms through which conformity with these can be ensured. It is important to distinguish between these two separate – though clearly related – aspects, in part because it helps dispel the more general notion that law is solely concerned with the issue of enforcement (a misperception which caused great frustration on Hilaire's part),[41] and also because, in the particular context of the UN Charter and the *jus ad bellum*, confusion over the issue of enforcement has caused particularly acute problems regarding evaluations of the efficacy of the UN system, especially in relation to its ability to constrain the behaviour of the great powers.

The UN Charter stipulates (in Articles 2(4) and 51) acceptable modes of behaviour with respect to the use of force, and provides (through Chapter VII) a mechanism through which these rules can be enforced and behaviour policed. In their application, these aspects of the Charter system are independent; all members of the United Nations are prohibited from using force (other than in self-defence), irrespective of whether the United Nations is willing and able to utilize its Chapter VII enforcement procedures.[42] Regardless of whether a Security Council response to a threat to international order is stymied by a general lack of motivation to act, or by the casting of a veto by one of the Council's permanent members, *all* member states, *including the five permanent members* and any clients or allies to whom they may extend their veto umbrella, remain bound by their Article 2(4) obligations. It follows that, while the veto 'protects' certain states against potential UN policing action – a potential in many cases more technical than real – where acting in breach of their Charter obligation, even these states remain subject to the political costs associated with normative deviancy. Lesser UN members that illegally resort to force face the threat of collective enforcement authorized by the Security Council, its permanent members and their allies do not. But even these states must calculate their adherence to the Charter in the knowledge that felonious behaviour is likely to lead to their international standing being damaged and, in extremis, they may have to face the retribution of their fellow great

[41] See H. McCoubrey, *International Humanitarian Law: Modern Developments in the Limitation of Warfare* (2nd edn, Dartmouth, 1998), p. 279.

[42] For the classic exposition of this debate see T. M. Franck, 'Who Killed Article 2(4)? Or: Changing Norms Governing the Use of Force By States', (1970) 64 *American Journal of International Law* 809 and L. Henkin, 'The Reports of the Death of Article 2(4) are Greatly Exaggerated', (1971) 65 *American Journal of International Law* 544.

powers. For the permanent members of the Security Council it is not collective restraint in accordance with the law, but rather self-restraint conceived as responsibility in regard of the law and the materiality of the balance of power, which are the central factors in determining policy. Herein lies the true rationale for the veto power accorded the great powers. Far from being a misconceived mechanism premised on the naive assumption that great power cooperation would continue after the war, it was in fact designed to ensure first that action could not be sanctioned by a majority but in the absence of great power backing, and secondly to provide that there could be no UN call to action against a great power, the effect of which would be to place lesser powers under a legal obligation to wage war against an infinitely more formidable foe. As such the veto was designed not to protect the great powers against collective action, for their protection against such a threat lay in their material strength, but rather to safeguard the organization and the weaker members of international society.[43]

In practice, of course, it was neither collective action through the United Nations, nor the responsible management of the great powers which maintained the uneasy order of the Cold War years. In an era of mutually assured destruction this role was almost exclusively the domain of the balance of power. However, the end of the Cold War heralded, for a brief time at least, an unparalleled level of post-1945 great power consensus, and in this profoundly different political and strategic context there lay the potential for the leading members of international society to realize their managerial responsibilities and in so doing to enlist international law to enshrine a new set of social objectives. Pursuit of these aims would, however, test the very fabric of international society which had, throughout the duration of its post-colonial phase, been premised upon the principles of non-use of force, sovereign equality and non-intervention. In accordance with such principles, and within the highly restrictive geo-strategic confines of the Cold War, the United Nations had all too often been an idle bystander as state elites abused their power to commit gross violations of human rights. Now such principles and practices, for five decades the bedrock of international society's compact of coexistence, were threatened by a reinvigorated and emboldened liberal democratic ideology which emerged victorious from the ideological struggle of the Cold War. Its adherents rejected the

[43] See I. Claude, *Power and International Relations* (Random House, 1962), pp. 155–72; and Claude, *Swords into Plowshares*, pp. 141–62.

pluralism of the past and sought instead to promote an agenda in which human rights and good governance would play a far more prominent role. Moreover, in cases such as Iraqi Kurdistan, Somalia, Rwanda and Haiti, they demonstrated an unprecedented willingness to use force to promote their cause.[44]

The permissive political context which accommodated such action was the product of a particularly fortuitous coincidence of factors: a strategic environment within which, absent the exigencies of the Cold War of the past (or, as it would come to pass, the 'War on Terror' of the future) there was political space for humanitarian concerns; the attendant 'peace dividend', which freed up resources for what were expected to be less costly and complex military operations; the 'victory' of liberal democracy, the ideals of which gave impetus for interventions designed to save lives rather than gain politico-strategic advantage; the euphoria which followed the successful prosecution of the 1990–1 Gulf Conflict; and an imbalance of power within which no state(s) could decisively oppose the might of the USA and its Western allies, at least at a viable cost. In this combination of inevitably ephemeral factors lay both the potential and limits of the humanitarian project. The strategic space eventually closed; resources were demanded for other (domestic) activities, as interventions in any case proved far from inexpensive and simple; ideals became sullied (or at least were seen to be); and past successes faded into the annals of history. In the absence of such supporting features, the humanitarian agenda began increasingly to resemble a political imposition by the powerful on the weak rather than responsible management, a state of affairs possible only because of the imbalance of power which characterized the international environment.

The debate around the legitimacy of humanitarian intervention thus presents in microcosm that regarding the role of international law in international society. To what extent had the institution of international law been hijacked so as to allow a small, unrepresentative, but overwhelmingly powerful group of states to create an international society exclusively of their making? Leaving aside the intricacies and implications of the humanitarian intervention debate itself, two conclusions may be drawn from this period in UN history: first, whatever the long-term implications of the various cases of intervention, it is clear that

[44] N. J. Wheeler, *Saving Strangers: Humanitarian Intervention in International Society* (Oxford University Press, 2000); and S. Chesterman, *Just War or Just Peace? Humanitarian Intervention and International Law* (Oxford University Press, 2001).

state leaders may no longer invoke the shield of sovereignty as a defence when they embark upon policies of gross domestic wrongdoing. Whether such action will result in a coercive military response from those within international society able to mount such an operation is one of the matters which remain undetermined, but the days of absolute, unfettered sovereignty are now in the past. Secondly, this normative development came at a price, namely the damage done to the process through which international society evolves, at the heart of which lies the United Nations and its Security Council. There is, of course, a perilously thin line between management and dictation, particularly in an environment such as the international one, devoid as it is of clear authority structures. It may also be added that some of those critical of the humanitarian agenda were motivated as much by fear of its implications for their own tyrannical regimes as by concerns over abuse of process. Nevertheless, the perception that the UN system was being abused was a damaging one, especially for an organization which deals primarily in the currency of legitimacy. The view that the great powers were once more failing to live up to their societal responsibilities was no less deleterious.

Long viewed as a body unrepresentative of the wider membership of international society, concerns over the legitimacy of the Council had, for much of its life, been tempered by its own ineffectiveness. But once it became a centrally active participant in international relations, long-standing concerns regarding its representative credentials were made more acute by the perception that within the chamber it was an even smaller clique of states calling the shots:

> The council, exult northerners, has been reborn to keep the peace in a manner that fits with modern times. No, grumble southerners, the council is becoming a flag of convenience for old-time neo-imperialists.[45]

What enabled this alleged legal flag of convenience to fly was the discretion granted to the Security Council in determining what constitutes a 'threat to international peace and security', the trigger mechanism for the utilization of its Charter powers under Chapter VII. It had been a conscious decision in 1945 to grant the Council a wide discretion in making such a determination, unfettered by restricting definitions or guidelines.[46] It was to be political debate, the balance of power entrenched

[45] 'Open the Club', *The Economist*, 29 August 1992, p. 14.

[46] L. Goodrich and E. Hambro, *Charter of the United Nations: Commentary and Documents* (2nd edn, Stevens and Sons, 1949), p. 156.

by permanent membership of the great powers, and ultimately the ability to veto which were to provide the brakes in determining when UN involvement was appropriate. But in a condition of profound imbalance, with resort to the veto stymied by broader diplomatic concerns (namely the need of China and Russia to maintain good relations with the Western powers for reasons of trade and foreign investment) for many political debate began to resemble political dictation. And yet from a legal perspective, the breadth of discretion granted the Council, the lack of determinacy associated with the concept of a 'threat to international peace and security', meant that the term was highly elastic, capable of being stretched a very long way before the breaking point of Franck's 'laughter' test was reached. Hence, through the mechanisms of the Security Council, the political agenda of a small number of Western, liberal democratic states became legally actionable against all members of international society, irrespective of consent. With no need to amend the UN Charter or associated legal devices (e.g. the Genocide Convention), processes which would have required broad based participation and consent, for many states the symbiotic relationship between law and politics broke down; unable to input their politics into the legal framing process, the disenfranchised nevertheless remained subject to the strictures of the law.

For the UN system (and international law more generally), the cases in which intervention was backed by the Security Council were a significant cause of tension, but this was further intensified by the willingness of the Western powers to act in the absence of Council authorization in situations in which it proved impossible to secure.[47] Lacking even the legitimacy which flows from the legalization process of Security Council sanction – however flawed that process itself might be – for critics of such action it amounted to the policing of internal state behaviour by a self-appointed constabulary of Western powers – the very kind of scenario which the centralized mechanism of the United Nations was intended to prevent. The first such case involved NATO intervention in Kosovo. However, Kosovo, arguably at least, did not

[47] See A. Bellamy, *Kosovo and International Society* (Palgrave Macmillan, 2002); S. Chesterman, 'Legality Versus Legitimacy: Humanitarian Intervention, the Security Council and the Rule of Law', (2002) 33 *Security Dialogue* 293; A. Roberts, 'The Laws of War After Kosovo', (2001) 31 *Israeli Yearbook of Human Rights* 79; and N. J. Wheeler, 'The Humanitarian Responsibilities of Sovereignty: Explaining the Development of a New Norm of Military Humanitarian Intervention in International Society', in J. Welsh (ed.), *Humanitarian Intervention and International Relations* (Oxford University Press, 2004).

constitute a total rejection of UN principles: NATO member states insisted that they were acting pursuant to previous Security Council resolutions and in accordance with human rights principles enshrined in the UN Charter; a draft Russian-sponsored resolution condemning NATO action was overwhelmingly defeated by twelve votes to three; there was widespread support for NATO action outside of the Council, though this was never tested in the General Assembly; and, following the cessation of hostilities, the United Nations assumed responsibility for maintaining security in the region. As with the cases of intervention which preceded it, the full implications of the Kosovo case remain a matter of heated debate. Indisputably it was a use of force undertaken in the absence of explicit Security Council authorization, but in the light of the above noted factors, some have concluded that the action, though technically illegal, was nevertheless legitimate.[48] Such an argument may lend credence to the actions of NATO, but it provides little comfort for the United Nations. Any such disjuncture between legality and legitimacy begs difficult questions of the prevailing legal order, not least regarding its longer term sustainability. This is a matter to which we will return in due course, but to complete the account of recent events regarding the use of force we must first briefly consider the recent conflict in Iraq.

As with action in Kosovo, force was employed against Iraq in the absence of explicit Security Council authorization. The participating states again claimed that the acts undertaken were pursuant to prior Security Council resolutions, and that they conformed to general principles of the UN Charter and international law.[49] Two distinct arguments were made in the latter regard: first, that in the twenty-first century world of global terrorism and proliferated weapons of mass destruction, the traditional interpretation of the right of self-defence, even if taken to include a limited right of anticipatory action, represented an unreasonable and ultimately unsustainable restriction on a state's right to defend itself. The seemingly boundless tactical lengths to which terrorist organizations such as Al Qaeda will go, coupled with the destructive potential of WMD, provide a compelling logic to this

[48] See, e.g., Independent International Commission on Kosovo, *Kosovo Report: Conflict, International Responses, Lessons Learned* (Oxford University Press, 2000), p. 4.

[49] See chapter 12 by Nigel White. See also C. Gray, 'From Unity to Polarization: International Law and the Use of Force Against Iraq', (2002) 15 *European Journal of International Law* 1; A. Roberts, 'Law and the Use of Force After Iraq', (2003) 45 *Survival* 31; and D. Kritsiotis, 'Arguments of Mass Confusion', (2004) 15 *European Journal of International Law* 233.

argument, but it was undermined by the inability of the USA and United Kingdom to convince others that *in practice* Iraq represented such a threat.[50] Subsequent events suggest that indeed it did not. Secondly, the USA and United Kingdom focused on the nature of the Iraqi regime itself, not just as a potential weapons proliferator, but as a non-democratic, human rights abusing, despotism. Once again, there is much to commend this argument; the Iraqi regime was undoubtedly abhorrent, but it failed to convince the doubters because the regime was perceived to be no worse than many others, and thus failed to reach the somewhat mercurial threshold required before intervention is by some deemed permissible.[51] Moreover, while each of these arguments has its merits, the manner in which the US and UK governments vacillated between them, and indeed other justifications, served to cloud and thus undermine, rather than reinforce, their position.

Given the paucity of support for action in Iraq the case presents an even greater challenge to the UN system and international society than that of Kosovo. The USA and United Kingdom were unable in the case of Iraq to gain explicit Council authorization not because of vetoes on the part of a minority of isolated permanent members, but because there was insufficient general support within the Council for their proposed action. A degree of caution is prudent in making such a statement because, but for the French declaration that they would veto an authorizing resolution, it is uncertain how the so-called 'swing six states' would have responded to American and UK diplomatic efforts to secure their support.[52] Nevertheless, it is safe to suggest that any additional support that may have been secured in the absence of the French statement would have been at a premium, reflecting the very widespread discontent among UN member states over the use of force in Iraq.[53] There are three factors which underpin this lack of support. First, the USA and

[50] For a robust defence of the American position on this matter see L. Feinstein and A.-M. Slaughter, 'A Duty to Prevent', (2004) 83 *Foreign Affairs* 136.

[51] See report of the International Commission on Intervention and State Sovereignty (ICISS), *The Responsibility to Protect* (International Development Research Centre, 2001); ICISS, *The Responsibility to Protect: Research, Bibliography, Background* (International Development Research Centre, 2001); T. G. Weiss, 'The Sunset of Humanitarian Intervention? The Responsibility to Protect in a Unipolar Era', (2004) 35 *Security Dialogue* 135.

[52] I am indebted to Dr David Malone, President of the International Peace Academy, for this point.

[53] See M. Byers, 'Agreeing to Disagree: Security Council Resolution 1441 and Intentional Ambiguity', (2004) 10 *Global Governance* 165.

United Kingdom were unable to convince others that the facts of the case warranted the proposed action. In the absence of such evidence, most UN members preferred to continue with the existing policy of containment, and the inspections regime already established by the United Nations. Secondly, the Bush Administration, through its bellicose, unilateralist rhetoric, alienated large swathes of international society.[54] Despite its belated and temporary conversion to multilateralism, and minority voices such as that of Secretary of State Powell asserting that '[p]artnership is the watchword of this administration' and '[b]eyond partnership come principle',[55] this was the self-inflicted image which most associated with the USA. Finally, the reinterpretation of international law at the very least implicit in the USA's pleadings prior to the conflict was simply too radical for states to accept, threatening, as it did, the whole normative structure relating to the regulation of the use of force. Not only would the suggested reinterpretation of the self-defence principle significantly undermine the Security Council's central position regarding the maintenance of international peace and security, even more worryingly, American rhetoric suggested limited entitlement to the new self-defence principle, extending in practice only as far as the USA and its allies.[56] This sense of exceptionalism is wholly inimical to the prevailing normative regime, and for many it threatened to undermine the very foundations of international society.[57]

International society in a unipolar world

It remains a matter of heated debate as to how best to interpret the events which followed the end of the Cold War. For some it was a resumption of great power responsibility, the utilization of power to

[54] See the National Security Strategy of the United States of America, September 2002, available at www.whitehouse.gov/nsc/nss.pdf See also E. Rhodes, 'The Imperial Logic of Bush's Liberal Agenda', (2003) 45 *Survival* 131.

[55] C. L. Powell, 'A Strategy of Partnership', *Foreign Affairs* (January/February 2004), 22, pp. 23, 24.

[56] See N. J. Wheeler, 'The Bush Doctrine: The Dangers of American Exceptionalism in a Revolutionary Age', (2003) 27 *Asian Perspective* 183.

[57] See T. Dunne, 'Society and Hierarchy in International Relations', (2003) 17 *International Relations* 303; T. G. Weiss, 'The Illusion of UN Security Council Reform', (2003) 26 *Washington Quarterly* 147; and M. J. Glennon, 'Why the Security Council Failed', (2003) 82 *Foreign Affairs* 16. For responses to Glennon see contributions from E. C. Luck, A.-M. Slaughter and I. Hurd in 'Staying Alive: The Rumours of the UN's Death Have Been Exaggerated', (2003) 82 *Foreign Affairs* 201.

impart central direction as international society adapted to new realities and developed so as to be able to deliver a better world for its ultimate members, namely individual human beings. For others it was no more than a cynical exploitation of power in the absence of meaningful opposition, resulting in the imposition of standards and beliefs alien to non-Western cultures. As such it was a violation of the foundational principles of international society. To be sure, the new agenda which the Western powers, led by the USA, sought to promote was one which created considerable tensions, but the common ground discovered and the progress made should not be allowed to pass here without comment. Most notably, while international society maintains as its primary constituent unit the territorially defined sovereign state, sovereignty no longer stands as a shield behind which heinous acts can be committed with impunity. The most appropriate means by which such behaviour can be prevented remains a matter of conjecture – a debate which includes within it the suitability of the use of force – but such uncertainty should not cloud the normative advance which this move represents. It is also worthy of note that while it was undoubtedly the prevailing imbalance of power which facilitated such developments, they were for the most part achieved within the legal order of the United Nations and without Franck's laughter limit ever being exceeded. Even Kosovo, where action was taken in the absence of explicit Council authorization, maintained plausible claims to legality and even stronger ones to a sense of international legitimacy. Has all this work been undone by events in Iraq, overshadowed by the actions of a US administration which refuses to play by or even acknowledge the rules of the international game?

At the time of writing,[58] the dust has settled on Iraq neither proverbially nor actually. However the action is judged by history, what is currently clear is that the conflict brought international society, and one of its most important organizations, the United Nations, to the brink of collapse. The USA and its allies may, of course, argue that they were indeed acting as responsible managers of international society, seizing the moment offered by an opportune coincidence of factors – among them the favourable distribution of power, the momentum created by previous interventions, and the coincidence of states' interests inherent in the 'War against Terror' – to force its members to confront the challenges of a new era. It is also the case that, however paradoxical it may seem, the USA's unassailable position at the head of

[58] July 2004.

international society makes it uniquely vulnerable to assaults by those, such as international terrorist networks and the rogue states willing to support them, who oppose the very idea of a society premised on the idea of sovereign, territorially defined states. Given this, the incentive to act becomes clearer and perhaps appears more reasonable. The problem with this argument is that, in acting as they did, these states exceeded the limits of normative elasticity and political accommodation which the majority of others deemed acceptable. In a world in which threats to international order emanate more from internal conflict and transnational acts of violence than traditional inter-state warfare, the normative basis and management of international society require careful reconsideration. Pluralist notions of coexistence no longer suffice in such circumstances, and in extreme cases it will be necessary to pierce the sovereign veil to ensure minimal levels of internal good governance and social responsibility. As Andrew Hurrell notes, this new reality does require a more intrusive international society, and where necessary a legal framework the applicability and enforceability of which is based on consensus rather than consent.[59] Such an approach opens up a zone of adaptability capable of responding to the evolving demands of international society. It does not, however, provide justifications for American–UK action against Iraq since this was unable to generate even this more limited consensus.

The UN Secretary-General, Kofi Annan, himself alluded to these problems in his address to the UN General Assembly in September 2003.[60] Annan warned member states that they had reached a 'fork in the road . . . a moment no less decisive than 1945 itself', insisting that they 'must not shy away from questions about the adequacy, and effectiveness, of the rules and instruments at [their] disposal'. And he counselled states on the need to consider beginning 'a discussion on the criteria for an early authorisation of coercive measures to address certain types of threats, for instance, terrorist groups armed with weapons of mass destruction'. The Secretary-General's call serves as a reminder that much of the discord over Iraq was about suitability of means, timing and process, rather than ends. The preservation of international society remains the goal for which states must strive, and this can only be achieved through a norm-governed system, collaborative means and with the active cooperation of

[59] A. Hurrell, 'International Law and the Changing Constitution of International Society', in Byers (ed.), *Role of Law in International Politics*, pp. 327–47 at p. 337.

[60] Available at www.un.org/webcast/ga/58/statements/sg2eng030923.htm, visited 9 July 2004.

the powerful acting as 'great responsibles'. This does not require that the USA act selflessly, abrogating its interests so as to protect and promote those of others, but rather that it recognizes that operating within the confines of a legally delineated system provides the best means by which to ensure a sustainable realization of its interests. As Hurrell notes:

> States need international law and institutions both to share the material and political costs of protecting their interests and to gain the authority and legitimacy that the possession of crude power can never on its own secure ... [S]trong states need law and institutions to share burdens and reduce the costs of promoting their interests by coercion. Even imperfectly legitimated power is likely to be much more effective than crude coercion.[61]

The wisdom of these words is aptly demonstrated by the vastly differing experiences of the USA in attempting to elicit international financial support for the 1990–1, as opposed to the current, conflict in Iraq. Reducing the notion of 'costs' in such a way may be rather crude, but as the bill facing the UN taxpayer heads into the hundreds of billions of dollars, it is a stark illustration and one the implications of which a President facing re-election may yet rue. Normative and human costs, it goes without saying, will prove far greater in the long term.

What all of this means in practice is that the United Nations, and the laws of war which its Charter both enshrines and seeks to operationalize, remain viable, indeed indispensable, elements of international society. They are not, however, without need of reform. In addition to Annan's call for a reconsideration of the rules themselves, few now question the need for reform of the Security Council, a body no longer sufficiently representative of the post-colonial world. While massive hurdles still stand in the way of the reform process, such is the centrality of the chamber to the workings of the United Nations that ensuring its legitimacy is an essential key to securing the international normative consensus to which Hurrell refers.[62] Further progress in this latter regard may also be generated by improving Council practices, with greater transparency and possibly reform to the voting procedures. Constraints on the

[61] Hurrell, 'International Law and the Changing Constitution of International Society', pp. 331 and 344.

[62] For further discussion of Security Council reform see J. Morris, 'UNSC Reform: A Counsel for the 21st Century', (2000) 31 *Security Dialogue* 265; and D. M. Malone (ed.), *The UN Security Council: From the Cold War to the 21st Century* (Rienner, 2004), Part 3.

exercise of the veto, both generally in terms of resort, and specifically through modifications requiring, for example, that two vetoes be required to block the passage of a resolution, may provide a fruitful area for negotiation, though the current P5 are notably reluctant to accept such restrictions. Where member states disagree over the facts of a case or the implications to be drawn from them (as, for example, was the case where Council members disagreed over whether Iraq had WMD and, if so, whether it represented a threat of proliferation), more explicit in-built fact-finding measures may also be helpful. Resolutions which effectively state that, if, after period 'A', situation 'B' is found by independent body 'C' to exist, then action 'D' will be taken, would have the advantage of compelling support – since no state would wish to be seen to be deliberately preventing necessary action – and would avoid the kind of prevarication witnessed over Iraq.[63] One final possibility worthy of note is that, faced with a Security Council unwilling or unable to act, greater use may be made of the General Assembly.[64] Representing all UN member states, such proposals have an obvious appeal, though the danger noted earlier remains, namely that the Assembly may pass resolutions which it lacks the wherewithal to enforce,[65] and the idea is further undermined by the reluctance of the current P5 to see control of the United Nations' security machinery being lost to a body over which they have no overriding control.[66] This is far from an exhaustive set of proposals as to how the UN system may be reformed so as to better meet the challenges of the twenty-first century, nor is it suggested that they are unproblematic in their realization. In brief, however, they point to avenues worthy of exploration in our attempts to adapt existing collective security mechanisms to better deal with the contemporary threats we face and the nature of the world in which we live. As such they may form part of the means by which states act to maintain an international society with an omnipotent USA amongst its members.

[63] I am indebted to Prof. Thomas Franck for raising this point.

[64] See N. D. White, 'The Legality of Bombing in the Name of Humanity', (2000) 5 *Journal of Conflict and Security Law* 27. On the relative importance of legal formalities compared to approval and consent see C. Brown, 'Self-Defence in an Imperfect World' available at www.cceia.org/printerfriendlymedia.php/prmID/851, visited 22 April 2004.

[65] See above n. 42 and associated text.

[66] See N. J. Wheeler, 'Legitimating Humanitarian Intervention: Principles and Procedures', (2001) 2 *Melbourne Journal of International Law* 550 at p. 566.

Conclusion

The relationship between power and international law is far more complex than realist readings of international politics would suggest. In his masterly English School text, Hedley Bull did much to illuminate this issue, and it is on this insight that this final chapter of this collection has attempted to draw in order to refute the notion that the relationship is one in which power determines all that law enshrines and imposes. In fact, it is too stark a conclusion to suggest that in a world characterized by an acute imbalance of power, international law is unable to function, but it is the case that, the greater the imbalance, the greater the temptation for the powerful to renege on their social and managerial responsibilities. In such circumstances those who should be at the forefront of legal innovation and enforcement instead serve as its Nemesis. Whatever the short-term benefits that may accrue from such an approach, they are transitory. In today's interdependent world, international law performs the indispensable task of facilitating international collaboration and allows for the achievement of objectives which cannot be secured in any sustainable fashion through the application of brute force alone. The cost of such facilitation is that international law also constrains, first, and most directly, in the sense that it prescribes behaviour, but more fundamentally in the sense that it provides a medium through which political views and interests are distilled and given substance. This process is one which cannot be dictated or imposed, even by the most powerful, for if states are to accept the limits of the politically feasible which law in part determines, they must be satisfied that they have contributed to the framing process and that their interests and needs are met by the social order in which it results. This conception of the interplay between law and politics is one which is well captured by Thomas Franck when he comments:

> The need to explain, to expatiate, is the deference which political power pays to the social potential of law. The adoption of norms seems to be the price which the individual actor – person or state – must pay to participate in an interactive community.[67]

This is a view with which the Reverend Professor Hilaire McCoubrey would, without doubt, have concurred.

[67] T. M. Franck, *Fairness in International Law and Institutions* (Oxford University Press, 1995), p. 477.

BIBLIOGRAPHY OF HILAIRE McCOUBREY'S WORK

Books

Regional Peacekeeping in the Post Cold-War Era (Kluwer, 2000) with J. Morris

A Text Book on Jurisprudence (3rd edn, Blackstone Press, 1999) with N. White

International Humanitarian Law: The Regulation of Armed Conflicts (1st edn, Dartmouth, 1990)

International Humanitarian Law: Modern Developments in the Limitation of Warfare (2nd edn, Dartmouth, 1998)

The Obligation to Obey in Legal Theory (Dartmouth, 1997)

The Blue Helmets: Legal Regulation of United Nations Military Operations (Dartmouth, 1996) with N. White

International Organisations and Civil Wars (Dartmouth, 1995) with N. White

International Law and Armed Conflict (Dartmouth, 1992) with N. White

Effective Planning Appeals (BSP Professional, 1988)

The Development of Naturalist Legal Theory (Croom Helm, 1987)

Edited collections

Reflections on Law and Armed Conflicts: The Selected Works on the Laws of War by the late Professor Colonel G. I. A. D. Draper (Kluwer, 1998) with M. Meyer

Articles

'From Nuremberg to Rome: Restoring the Defence of Superior Orders', (2001) 50 International and Comparative Law Quarterly 386

'The Protection of Creed and Opinion in the Laws of Armed Conflict', (2000) 5 Journal of Conflict and Security Law 135

'International Law, International Relations and the Development of European Collective Security', (1999) 4 Journal of Armed Conflict Law 195 with J. Morris

'International Security, the United Nations and the Post-Cold War Era', (1999) 26 Journal of Malaysian and Comparative Law 193 with J. C. Morris

'Kosovo, NATO and International Law', (1999) 14 International Relations 29

'Regional Peacekeeping in the Post Cold-War Era', (1999) 6 International Peacekeeping 129 with J. C. Morris

'Medical Ethics and the Laws of Armed Conflict', (1998) 3 Journal of Armed Conflict Law 133 with M. Gunn

'War Crimes Jurisdiction and a Permanent International Criminal Court: Advantages and Difficulties', (1998) 3 Journal of Armed Conflict Law 9

'Due Process and British Courts Martial: A Commentary upon the *Findlay* Case', (1997) 2 Journal of Armed Conflict Law 83

'The Concept and Treatment of War Crimes', (1996) 1 Journal of Armed Conflict Law 121

'Before "Geneva" Law: a British Surgeon in the Crimean War', (1995) 304 International Review of the Red Cross 69

'Medical Ethics, Negligence and the Battlefield', (1995) 34 La Revue de Droit Militaire et de Droit de la Guerre 103

'International Law and National Contingents in UN Forces', (1994) 12 International Relations 39

'Security, Planning Regulation and Defence Establishments', (1994) Journal of Planning and Environmental Law 1075

'The Armed Conflict in Bosnia and Proposed War Crimes Trials', (1993) 11 International Relations 411

'The Laws of Armed Conflict and United Nations Forces: Regulation Military Action for Peace', (1993) 20 Journal of Malaysian and Comparative Law 59

'War Crimes: the Criminal Jurisprudence of Armed Conflict', (1992) 31 Revue de Droit Militaire et de Droit de la Guerre 167

'Yugoslavia at War: International Laws of Armed Conflict and the Yugoslav Crisis', (1992) 136 Solicitors' Journal 914

'International Law and the Use of Force in the Gulf', (1991) 10 International Relations 347 with N. D. White

'The Nature of the Modern Doctrine of Military Necessity', (1991) 30 Revue de Droit Militaire et de Droit de la Guerre 217

'Rules of Engagement', (1990) New Law Journal 1527

'The English Model of Planning Legislation in Developing Countries', (1988) 10 Third World Planning Review 371

'Councillor's Rights of Access to Confidential Information', (1983) 127 Solicitors' Journal 6

'Councillor's Access to Confidential Information', (1983) 127 Solicitors' Journal 739

'Rights of Action to Seek Continuance of Local Authority Policies', (1982) New Law Journal 491

'Countryside Conservation and the Wildlife and Countryside Act 1981', (1982) New Law Journal 826

'The Reform of the Russian Legal System under Alexander II', (1980) 24 Renaissance and Modern Studies 115

Chapters

'Collective Regional Security and Evolving Methods of Dealing with Confrontations', in C. Harding and C. L. Lim, *Renegotiating Westphalia: Essays and Commentary on the European and Conceptual Foundations of Modern International Law* (Martinus Nijhoff, 1999), p. 97

'Natural Law, Religion and the Development of International Law', in M. Janis and C. Evans, *Religion and International Law* (Martinus Nijhoff, 1999), p. 177

'Giving Legal Evidence in Proliferation Cases', in J. Dahlitz, *Future Legal Restraints on Arms Proliferation: Arms Control and Disarmament Law* (United Nations Publishing, 1996), p. 125 with F. Hampson

'The Regulation of Biological and Chemical Weapons', in H. Fox and M. Meyer, *Armed Conflict and the New Law*, vol. 2, *Effecting Compliance* (BIICL, 1993), p. 123

'The Wounded and the Sick' and 'Civilians in Occupied Territories', in P. Rowe, *The Gulf War 1990–91 in International and English Law* (Routledge, 1993), pp. 171 and 205

Other papers

'International Laws of Armed Conflict: Practical Prescriptions of Dangerous Utopia?', University of Hull Inaugural Lecture, 5 March 1996 (University of Hull Press, 1996)

Protection of Creed and Opinion in the Laws of Armed Conflict (University of Nottingham Research Papers in Law No. 7, 1993)

The Idea of War Crimes and Crimes Against Peace Since 1945 (University of Nottingham Research Papers in Law No. 2, 1992)

Law Reform in Late Imperial Russia: A Legal History with Modern Implications? (University of Nottingham Department of Law, 1994)

INDEX